Building Data Science Applications with FastAPI

Develop, manage, and deploy efficient machine learning applications with Python

François Voron

BIRMINGHAM—MUMBAI

Building Data Science Applications with FastAPI

Copyright © 2023 Packt Publishing

Group Product Manager: Ali Abidi

Publishing Product Managers: Dhruv J. Kataria and Tejashwini

Content Development Editor: Shreya Moharir

Technical Editor: Devanshi Ayare

Copy Editor: Safis Editing

Project Coordinator: Farheen Fathima

Proofreader: Safis Editing

Indexer: Tejal Soni

Production Designer: Jyoti Chauhan

Marketing Coordinator: Vinishka Kalra

First published: October 2021

Second published: July 2023

Production reference: 1140723

Published by Packt Publishing Ltd.
Grosvenor House
11 St Paul's Square
Birmingham
B3 1RB

ISBN 978-1-83763-274-9

www.packtpub.com

This second edition has been in the making for almost a year. During that time, I was blessed with an extraordinary gift: the arrival of our baby boy, Arthur, who has brought immeasurable joy into our lives. I dedicate this book to him and my beloved wife, whose unwavering support has been a constant source of inspiration and encouragement throughout this journey.

Contributors

About the author

François Voron graduated from the University of Saint-Étienne (France) and the University of Alicante (Spain) with a master's degree in machine learning and data mining. A full stack web developer and a data scientist, François has a proven track record working in the SaaS industry, with a special focus on Python backends and REST APIs. He is also the creator and maintainer of FastAPI Users, the #1 authentication library for FastAPI, and is one of the top experts in the FastAPI community.

About the reviewers

Izabela dos Santos Guerreiro graduated in information technology management and systems analysis and development. A machine learning enthusiast, she is a postgraduate in artificial intelligence, machine learning, and data science. She is a software developer specialist and tech lead and has nine years of experience, always working with Python. She was introduced to FastAPI about three years ago and became an enthusiast of the framework, collaborating on the translation of the documentation into her native language, Portuguese. She has already organized PyLadies and Django Girls events.

Prajjwal Nijhara is an upcoming PhD computer scholar at IIT Jodhpur. With a passion for technology and research, Prajjwal has embarked on an academic journey to advance his expertise in computer science. Prior to this, Prajjwal gained industry experience as a software developer intern at Spiti and DeepSource, where he contributed to software development projects. Additionally, he served as a TGT guest faculty member at Pragyan Sthali School, imparting his knowledge and inspiring students in these subjects.

I am deeply grateful to my brother, Roopak, and his partner, Chandrapurima, for their unwavering support. My heartfelt thanks also go to my parents, Subhash and Versha, who have been my rock throughout. Their love and guidance made the book review process smooth. I am truly blessed to have such incredible family members who believe in me and inspire me to pursue my aspirations.

Akshat Gurnani is a highly qualified individual with a background in the field of computer science and machine learning. He has a master's degree in computer science and a deep understanding of various machine learning techniques and algorithms. He has experience working on various projects related to natural language processing, computer vision, and deep learning. He has also published several research papers in top-tier journals and conferences and has a proven track record in the field. He has a passion for keeping up to date with the latest developments in his fields and has a strong desire to continue learning and contributing to the field of artificial intelligence.

Table of Contents

Preface   xv

Part 1: Introduction to Python and FastAPI

1

Python Development Environment Setup   3

Technical requirements   3   Installing Python packages with pip   8
Installing a Python distribution   Installing the HTTPie command-line
using pyenv   4   utility   9
Creating a Python virtual environment   7   Summary   12

2

Python Programming Specificities   13

Technical requirements   13   Operating over sequences – list
Basics of Python programming   14   comprehensions and generators   30
Running Python scripts   14   List comprehensions   31
Indentation matters   15   Generators   33
Working with built-in types   16   Writing object-oriented programs   35
Working with data structures – lists, tuples,   Defining a class   35
dictionaries, and sets   17   Implementing magic methods   36
Performing Boolean logic and a few other   Reusing logic and avoiding repetition with
operators   21   inheritance   40
Controlling the flow of a program   23
Defining functions   26   Type hinting and type checking with
Writing and using packages and modules   28   mypy   43
                                                   Getting started   44

Type data structures   45
Type function signatures with Callable   48
Any and cast   49

Working with asynchronous I/O   51
Summary   54

3

Developing a RESTful API with FastAPI   55

Technical requirements   55
**Creating a first endpoint and
running it locally   56**
Handling request parameters   59
Path parameters   59
Query parameters   65
The request body   67
Form data and file uploads   71
Headers and cookies   76

The request object   78
Customizing the response   79
Path operation parameters   79
The response parameter   84
Raising HTTP errors   88
Building a custom response   90
**Structuring a bigger project with
multiple routers   95**
Summary   98

4

Managing Pydantic Data Models in FastAPI   99

Technical requirements   99
**Defining models and their field types
with Pydantic   99**
Standard field types   100
Optional fields and default values   105
Validating email addresses and URLs with
Pydantic types   108
**Creating model variations with class
inheritance   110**

**Adding custom data validation with
Pydantic   112**
Applying validation at the field level   112
Applying validation at the object level   113
Applying validation before Pydantic parsing   114
Working with Pydantic objects   115
Converting an object into a dictionary   115
Creating an instance from a sub-class object   117
Updating an instance partially   119
Summary   121

5

Dependency Injection in FastAPI   123

Technical requirements	123	Using class methods as dependencies	131
What is dependency injection?	124	**Using dependencies at the path, router, and global level**	**133**
Creating and using a function dependency	**125**	Using a dependency on a path decorator	133
Getting an object or raising a 404 error	128	Using a dependency on a whole router	134
		Using a dependency on a whole application	136
Creating and using a parameterized dependency with a class	**129**	**Summary**	**137**

Part 2: Building and Deploying a Complete Web Backend with FastAPI

6

Databases and Asynchronous ORMs   141

Technical requirements	141	Updating and deleting objects	155
An overview of relational and NoSQL databases	**142**	Adding relationships	157
		Setting up a database migration system with Alembic	161
Relational databases	142		
NoSQL databases	143	**Communicating with a MongoDB database using Motor**	**166**
Which one should you choose?	144		
Communicating with a SQL database with SQLAlchemy ORM	**145**	Creating models that are compatible with MongoDB ID	166
		Connecting to a database	167
Creating ORM models	146	Inserting documents	168
Defining Pydantic models	148	Getting documents	169
Connecting to a database	149	Updating and deleting documents	172
Creating objects	152	Nesting documents	173
Getting and filtering objects	153	**Summary**	**175**

7

Managing Authentication and Security in FastAPI   177

Technical requirements	177	Implementing a database access token	184
Security dependencies in FastAPI	178	Implementing a login endpoint	186
Storing a user and their password securely in a database	181	Securing endpoints with access tokens	189
Creating models	181	Configuring CORS and protecting against CSRF attacks	190
Hashing passwords	182	Understanding CORS and configuring it in	
Implementing registration routes	183	FastAPI	191
Retrieving a user and generating an access token	184	Implementing double-submit cookies to prevent CSRF attacks	196
		Summary	201

8

Defining WebSockets for Two-Way Interactive Communication in FastAPI   203

Technical requirements	203	Using dependencies	211
Understanding the principles of two-way communication with WebSockets	204	Handling multiple WebSocket connections and broadcasting messages	213
Creating a WebSocket with FastAPI	205	Summary	219
Handling concurrency	209		

9

Testing an API Asynchronously with pytest and HTTPX   221

Technical requirements	222	Reusing test logic by creating fixtures	226
An introduction to unit testing with pytest	222	Setting up testing tools for FastAPI with HTTPX	228
Generating tests with parametrize	224		

Writing tests for REST API endpoints 232

Writing tests for POST endpoints   233
Testing with a database   235

Writing tests for WebSocket
endpoints   241
Summary   243

10

Deploying a FastAPI Project   245

Technical requirements   245
Setting and using environment
variables   246
Using a .env file   249

Managing Python dependencies   250
Adding Gunicorn as a server process for
deployment   252

Deploying a FastAPI application on a
serverless platform   253
Adding database servers   256

Deploying a FastAPI application with
Docker   256
Writing a Dockerfile   257
Adding a prestart script   258
Building a Docker image   259
Running a Docker image locally   259
Deploying a Docker image   260

Deploying a FastAPI application on a
traditional server   261
Summary   263

Part 3: Building Resilient and Distributed Data Science Systems with FastAPI

11

Introduction to Data Science in Python   267

Technical requirements   267
What is machine learning?   267
Supervised versus unsupervised learning   268
Model validation   268

Manipulating arrays with NumPy
and pandas   270
Getting started with NumPy   271

Manipulating arrays with NumPy –
computation, aggregations, and comparisons 276
Getting started with pandas   280

Training models with scikit-learn   285
Training models and predicting   286
Chaining preprocessors and estimators with
pipelines   288
Validating the model with cross-validation 292

Summary   293

12

Creating an Efficient Prediction API Endpoint with FastAPI   295

Technical requirements	295	Implementing an efficient prediction endpoint	298
Persisting a trained model with Joblib	296		
Dumping a trained model	296	Caching results with Joblib	301
Loading a dumped model	297	Choosing between standard or async functions	303
		Summary	306

13

Implementing a Real-Time Object Detection System Using WebSockets with FastAPI   307

Technical requirements	307	Implementing a WebSocket to perform object detection on a stream of images	314
Using a computer vision model with Hugging Face	308		
Implementing a REST endpoint to perform object detection on a single image	312	Sending a stream of images from the browser in a WebSocket	317
		Showing the object detection results in the browser	320
		Summary	324

14

Creating a Distributed Text-to-Image AI System Using the Stable Diffusion Model   325

Technical requirements	326	Implementing a worker	333
Generating images from text prompts with Stable Diffusion	326	Implementing the REST API	336
Implementing the model in a Python script	327	Storing results in a database and object storage	337
Executing the Python script	329	Sharing data between the worker and the API	338
Creating a Dramatiq worker and defining an image-generation task	331	Storing and serving files in object storage	344
		Summary	352

15

Monitoring the Health and Performance of a Data Science System   353

Technical requirements	353	Understanding Prometheus and the different metrics	366
Configuring and using a logging facility with Loguru	354	Measuring and exposing metrics	368
Understanding log levels	355	Adding Prometheus metrics to FastAPI	369
Adding logs with Loguru	355	Adding Prometheus metrics to Dramatiq	373
Understanding and configuring sinks	357	**Monitoring metrics in Grafana**	**376**
Structuring logs and adding context	359	Configuring Grafana to collect metrics	376
Configuring Loguru as the central logger	362	Visualizing metrics in Grafana	380
Adding Prometheus metrics	**366**	**Summary**	**386**

Index   387

Other Books You May Enjoy   398

Preface

FastAPI is a web framework for building APIs with Python 3.6 and its later versions based on standard Python type hints. With this book, you'll be able to create fast and reliable data science API backends using practical examples.

This book starts with the basics of the FastAPI framework and associated modern Python programming concepts. You'll then be taken through all the aspects of the framework, including its powerful dependency injection system and how you can use it to communicate with databases, implement authentication, and integrate machine learning models. Later, you will cover the best practices relating to testing and deployment to run a high-quality, robust application. You'll also be introduced to the extensive ecosystem of Python data science packages. As you progress, you'll learn how to build data science applications in Python using FastAPI. The book also demonstrates how to develop fast and efficient machine learning prediction backends. For this, you'll be taken through two projects covering typical use cases of AI: real-time object detection and text-to-image generation.

By the end of this FastAPI book, you'll have not only learned how to implement Python in data science projects but also how to maintain and design them to meet high programming standards with the help of FastAPI.

Who this book is for

This book is for data scientists and software developers interested in gaining knowledge of FastAPI and its ecosystem to build data science applications. Basic knowledge of data science and machine learning concepts and how to apply them in Python is recommended.

What this book covers

Chapter 1, *Python Development Environment Setup*, is aimed at setting up the development environment so that you can start working with Python and FastAPI. We'll introduce the various tools that are commonly used in the Python community to ease development.

Chapter 2, *Python Programming Specificities*, introduces you to the specificities of programming in Python, specifically block indentation, control flow statements, exception handling, and the object-oriented paradigm. We'll also cover features such as list comprehensions and generators. Finally, we'll see how type hinting and asynchronous I/O work.

Chapter 3, Developing a RESTful API with FastAPI, covers the basics of the creation of a RESTful API with FastAPI: routing, parameters, request body validation, and response. We'll also show how to properly structure a FastAPI project with dedicated modules and separate routers.

Chapter 4, Managing Pydantic Data Models in FastAPI, covers in more detail the definition of data models with Pydantic, the underlying data validation library used by FastAPI. We'll explain how to implement variations of the same model without repeating ourselves, thanks to class inheritance. Finally, we'll show how to implement custom data validation logic on those models.

Chapter 5, Dependency Injection in FastAPI, explains how dependency injection works and how we can define our own dependencies to reuse logic across different routers and endpoints.

Chapter 6, Databases and Asynchronous ORMs, demonstrates how we can set up a connection with a database to read and write data. We'll cover how to use SQLAlchemy to work asynchronously with SQL databases and how they interact with the Pydantic model. Finally, we'll also show you how to work with MongoDB, a NoSQL database.

Chapter 7, Managing Authentication and Security in FastAPI, shows us how to implement a basic authentication system to protect our API endpoints and return the relevant data for the authenticated user. We'll also talk about the best practices around CORS and how to be safe from CSRF attacks.

Chapter 8, Defining WebSockets for Two-Way Interactive Communication in FastAPI, is aimed at understanding WebSockets and how to create them and handle the messages received with FastAPI.

Chapter 9, Testing an API Asynchronously with pytest and HTTPX, shows us how to write tests for our REST API endpoints.

Chapter 10, Deploying a FastAPI Project, covers the common configuration for running FastAPI applications smoothly in production. We'll also explore several deployment options: PaaS platforms, Docker, and the traditional server setup.

Chapter 11, Introduction to Data Science in Python, gives a quick introduction to machine learning before moving on to two core libraries for data science in Python: NumPy and pandas. We'll also show the basics of the scikit-learn library, a set of ready-to-use tools to perform machine learning tasks in Python.

Chapter 12, Creating an Efficient Prediction API Endpoint with FastAPI, shows how we can efficiently store a trained machine learning model using Joblib. Then, we'll integrate it into a FastAPI backend, considering some technical details of FastAPI internals to achieve maximum performance. Finally, we'll show a way to cache results using Joblib.

Chapter 13, Implementing a Real-Time Object Detection System Using WebSockets with FastAPI, implements a simple application to perform object detection in the browser, backed by a FastAPI WebSocket and a pre-trained computer vision model from the Hugging Face library.

Chapter 14, Creating a Distributed Text-to-Image AI System Using the Stable Diffusion Model, implements a system able to generate images from text prompts using the popular Stable Diffusion model. Since this task is a resource-intensive, slow process, we'll see how to create a distributed system using worker queues that'll stand behind our FastAPI backend and will perform the computations in the background.

Chapter 15, Monitoring the Health and Performance of a Data Science System, covers the extra mile so you are able to build robust, production-ready systems. One of the most important aspects to achieve this is to have all the data we need to ensure the system is operating correctly and detect as soon as possible when something goes wrong so we can take corrective actions. In this chapter, we'll see how to set up a proper logging facility and how we can monitor the performance and health of our software in real time.

To get the most out of this book

In this book, we'll mainly work with the Python programming language. The first chapter will explain how to set up a proper Python environment on your operating system. Some examples also involve running web pages with JavaScript, so you'll need a modern browser such as Google Chrome or Mozilla Firefox.

In *Chapter 14*, we'll run the Stable Diffusion model, which requires a powerful machine. We recommend a computer with 16 GB of RAM and a modern NVIDIA GPU to be able to generate good-looking images.

Software/hardware covered in the book	Operating system requirements
Python 3.10+	Windows, macOS, or Linux
Javascript	

Download the example code files

You can download the example code files for this book from GitHub at `https://github.com/PacktPublishing/Building-Data-Science-Applications-with-FastAPI-Second-Edition`. If there's an update to the code, it will be updated in the GitHub repository.

We also have other code bundles from our rich catalog of books and videos available at `https://github.com/PacktPublishing/`. Check them out!

Conventions used

There are a number of text conventions used throughout this book.

`Code in text`: Indicates code words in text, database table names, folder names, filenames, file extensions, pathnames, dummy URLs, user input, and Twitter handles. Here is an example: "Obviously, if everything is okay, we get a `Person` instance and have access to the properly parsed fields."

A block of code is set as follows:

```
from fastapi import FastAPI

app = FastAPI()

@app.get("/users/{type}/{id}")
async def get_user(type: str, id: int):
    return {"type": type, "id": id}
```

When we wish to draw your attention to a particular part of a code block, the relevant lines or items are set in bold:

```
class PostBase(BaseModel):
    title: str
    content: str
    def excerpt(self) -> str:
        return f"{self.content[:140]}..."
```

Any command-line input or output is written as follows:

```
$ http http://localhost:8000/users/abc
HTTP/1.1 422 Unprocessable Entity
content-length: 99
content-type: application/json
date: Thu, 10 Nov 2022 08:22:35 GMT
server: uvicorn
```

> **Tips or important notes**
> Appear like this.

Get in touch

Feedback from our readers is always welcome.

General feedback: If you have questions about any aspect of this book, email us at customercare@packtpub.com and mention the book title in the subject of your message.

Errata: Although we have taken every care to ensure the accuracy of our content, mistakes do happen. If you have found a mistake in this book, we would be grateful if you would report this to us. Please visit www.packtpub.com/support/errata and fill in the form.

Piracy: If you come across any illegal copies of our works in any form on the internet, we would be grateful if you would provide us with the location address or website name. Please contact us at copyright@packtpub.com with a link to the material.

If you are interested in becoming an author: If there is a topic that you have expertise in and you are interested in either writing or contributing to a book, please visit authors.packtpub.com.

Share Your Thoughts

Once you've read *Building Data Science Applications with FastAPI, Second Edition*, we'd love to hear your thoughts! Scan the QR code below to go straight to the Amazon review page for this book and share your feedback.

https://packt.link/r/1-837-63274-X

Your review is important to us and the tech community and will help us make sure we're delivering excellent quality content.

Download a free PDF copy of this book

Thanks for purchasing this book!

Do you like to read on the go but are unable to carry your print books everywhere?

Is your eBook purchase not compatible with the device of your choice?

Don't worry, now with every Packt book you get a DRM-free PDF version of that book at no cost.

Read anywhere, any place, on any device. Search, copy, and paste code from your favorite technical books directly into your application.

The perks don't stop there, you can get exclusive access to discounts, newsletters, and great free content in your inbox daily

Follow these simple steps to get the benefits:

1. Scan the QR code or visit the link below

https://packt.link/free-ebook/9781837632749

2. Submit your proof of purchase
3. That's it! We'll send your free PDF and other benefits to your email directly

Part 1: Introduction to Python and FastAPI

After setting up the development environment, we'll introduce the specificities of Python before starting to explore the basic features of FastAPI and running our first REST API.

This section comprises the following chapters:

- *Chapter 1, Python Development Environment Setup*
- *Chapter 2, Python Programming Specificities*
- *Chapter 3, Developing a RESTful API with FastAPI*
- *Chapter 4, Managing Pydantic Data Models in FastAPI*
- *Chapter 5, Dependency Injection in FastAPI*

1

Python Development Environment Setup

Before we can go through our FastAPI journey, we need to configure a Python environment following the best practices and conventions Python developers use daily to run their projects. By the end of this chapter, you'll be able to run Python projects and install third-party dependencies in a contained environment that won't raise conflicts if you happen to work on another project that uses different versions of the Python language or dependencies.

In this chapter, we will cover the following main topics:

- Installing a Python distribution using `pyenv`
- Creating a Python virtual environment
- Installing Python packages with `pip`
- Installing the HTTPie command-line utility

Technical requirements

Throughout this book, we'll assume you have access to a Unix-based environment, such as a Linux distribution or macOS.

If you haven't done so already, macOS users should install the *Homebrew* package (`https://brew.sh`), which helps a lot in installing command-line tools.

If you are a Windows user, you should enable **Windows Subsystem for Linux** (**WSL**) (`https://docs.microsoft.com/windows/wsl/install-win10`) and install a Linux distribution (such as Ubuntu) that will run alongside the Windows environment, which should give you access to all the required tools. There are currently two versions of WSL: WSL and WSL2. Depending on your Windows version, you might not be able to install the newest version. However, we do recommend using WSL2 if your Windows installation supports it.

Installing a Python distribution using pyenv

Python is already bundled with most Unix environments. To ensure this is the case, you can run this command in a command line to show the Python version currently installed:

```
$ python3 --version
```

The output version displayed will vary depending on your system. You may think that this is enough to get started, but it poses an important issue: *you can't choose the Python version for your project*. Each Python version introduces new features and breaking changes. Thus, it's important to be able to switch to a recent version for new projects to take advantage of the new features but still be able to run older projects that may not be compatible. This is why we need pyenv.

The **pyenv** tool (https://github.com/pyenv/pyenv) helps you manage and switch between multiple Python versions on your system. It allows you to set a default Python version for your whole system but also per project.

Beforehand, you need to install several build dependencies on your system to allow pyenv to compile Python on your system. The official documentation provides clear guidance on this (https://github.com/pyenv/pyenv/wiki#suggested- build-environment), but here are the commands you should run:

1. Install the build dependencies:

    *   For macOS users, use the following:

        ```
        $ brew install openssl readline sqlite3 xz zlib tcl-tk
        ```

    *   For Ubuntu users, use the following:

        ```
        $ sudo apt update; sudo apt install make build-essential libssl-
        dev zlib1g-dev \
        libbz2-dev libreadline-dev libsqlite3-dev wget curl llvm \
        libncursesw5-dev xz-utils tk-dev libxml2-dev libxmlsec1-dev
        libffi-dev liblzma-dev
        ```

> **Package managers**
>
> brew and apt are what are commonly known as package managers. Their role is to automate the installation and management of software on your system. Thus, you don't have to worry about where to download them from and how to install and uninstall them. Those commands just tell the package manager to update its internal package index and then install the list of required packages.

2. Install pyenv:

```
$ curl https://pyenv.run | bash
```

> **Tip for macOS users**
>
> If you are a macOS user, you can also install it with Homebrew: `brew install pyenv`.

3. This will download and execute an installation script that will handle everything for you. At the end, it'll prompt you with some instructions to add some lines to your shell scripts so that pyenv is discovered properly by your shell:

   - If your shell is `bash` (the default for most Linux distributions and older versions of macOS), run the following commands:

   ```
   echo 'export PYENV_ROOT="$HOME/.pyenv"' >> ~/.bashrc
   echo 'command -v pyenv >/dev/null || export PATH="$PYENV_ROOT/
   bin:$PATH"' >> ~/.bashrc
   echo 'eval "$(pyenv init -)"' >> ~/.bashrc
   ```

   - If your shell is `zsh` (the default in the latest version of macOS), run the following commands:

   ```
   echo 'export PYENV_ROOT="$HOME/.pyenv"' >> ~/.zshrc
   echo 'command -v pyenv >/dev/null || export PATH="$PYENV_ROOT/
   bin:$PATH"' >> ~/.zshrc
   echo 'eval "$(pyenv init -)"' >> ~/.zshrc
   ```

> **What is a shell and how do I know the one I'm using?**
>
> The shell is the underlying program running when you start a command line. It's responsible for interpreting and running your commands. Several variants of those programs have been developed over time, such as `bash` and `zsh`. Even though they have their differences, in particular the names of their configuration files, they are mostly inter-compatible. To find out which shell you're using, you can run the `echo $SHELL` command.

4. Reload your shell configuration to apply those changes:

```
$ exec "$SHELL"
```

5. If everything went well, you should now be able to invoke the pyenv tool:

```
$ pyenv
>>> pyenv 2.3.6
>>> Usage: pyenv <command> [<args>]
```

6. We can now install the Python distribution of our choice. Even though FastAPI is compatible with Python 3.7 and later, we'll use Python 3.10 throughout this book, which has a more mature handling of the asynchronous paradigm and type hinting. All the examples in the book were tested with this version but should work flawlessly with newer versions. Let's install Python 3.10:

    ```
    $ pyenv install 3.10
    ```

    This may take a few minutes since your system will have to compile Python from the source.

    > **What about Python 3.11?**
    >
    > You might wonder why we use Python 3.10 here while Python 3.11 is already released and is available. At the time of writing, not every library we'll use throughout this book officially supports this newest version. That's why we prefer to stick with a more mature version. Don't worry, though: what you'll learn here will still be relevant to future versions of Python.

7. Finally, you can set the default Python version with the following command:

    ```
    $ pyenv global 3.10
    ```

    This will tell your system to always use Python 3.10 by default unless specified otherwise in a specific project.

8. To make sure everything is in order, run the following command to check the Python version that is invoked by default:

    ```
    $ python --version
    Python 3.10.8
    ```

Congratulations! You can now handle any version of Python on your system and switch it whenever you like!

> **Why does it show 3.10.8 instead of just 3.10?**
>
> The 3.10 version corresponds to a major version of Python. The Python core team regularly publishes major versions with new features, depreciations, and sometimes breaking changes. However, when a new major version is published, previous versions are not forgotten: they continue to receive bug and security fixes. It's the purpose of the third part of the version.
>
> It's very possible by the time you're reading this book that you've installed a more recent version of Python 3.10, such as 3.10.9. It just means that fixes have been published. You can find more information about how the Python life cycle works and how long the Python core team plans to support previous versions in this official document: https://devguide.python.org/versions/.

Creating a Python virtual environment

As for many programming languages of today, the power of Python comes from the vast ecosystem of third-party libraries, including FastAPI, of course, that help you build complex and high-quality software very quickly. The **Python Package Index (PyPi)** (`https://pypi.org`) is the public repository that hosts all those packages. This is the default repository that will be used by the built-in Python package manager, `pip`.

By default, when you install a third-party package with `pip`, it will install it for the *whole system*. This is different from some other languages, such as Node.js' npm, which by default creates a local directory for the current project to install those dependencies. Obviously, this may cause issues when you work on several Python projects with dependencies having conflicting versions. It also makes it difficult to retrieve only the dependencies necessary to deploy a project properly on a server.

This is why Python developers generally use **virtual environments**. Basically, a virtual environment is just a directory in your project containing a copy of your Python installation and the dependencies of your project. This pattern is so common that the tool to create them is bundled with Python:

1. Create a directory that will contain your project:

    ```
    $ mkdir fastapi-data-science
    $ cd fastapi-data-science
    ```

    > **Tip for Windows with WSL users**
    >
    > If you are on Windows with WSL, we recommend that you create your working folder on the Windows drive rather than the virtual filesystem of the Linux distribution. It'll allow you to edit your source code files in Windows with your favorite text editor or **integrated development environment** (**IDE**) while running them in Linux.
    >
    > To do this, you can access your `C:` drive in the Linux command line through `/mnt/c`. You can thus access your personal documents using the usual Windows path, for example, `cd /mnt/c/Users/YourUsername/Documents`.

2. You can now create a virtual environment:

    ```
    $ python -m venv venv
    ```

    Basically, this command tells Python to run the `venv` package of the standard library to create a virtual environment in the `venv` directory. The name of this directory is a convention, but you can choose another name if you wish.

3. Once this is done, you have to activate this virtual environment. It'll tell your shell session to use the Python interpreter and the dependencies in the local directory instead of the global ones. Run the following command:

    ```
    $ source venv/bin/activatee
    ```

After doing this, you may notice the prompt adds the name of the virtual environment:

```
(venv) $
```

Remember that the activation of this virtual environment is only available for the *current session*. If you close it or open other command prompts, you'll have to activate it again. This is quite easy to forget, but it will become natural after some practice with Python.

You are now ready to install Python packages safely in your project!

Installing Python packages with pip

As we said earlier, `pip` is the built-in Python package manager that will help us install third-party libraries.

> **A word on alternate package managers such as Poetry, Pipenv, and Conda**
>
> While exploring the Python community, you may hear about alternate package managers such as Poetry, Pipenv, and Conda. These managers were created to solve some issues posed by `pip`, especially around sub-dependencies management. While they are very good tools, we'll see in *Chapter 10, Deploying a FastAPI Project*, that most cloud hosting platforms expect dependencies to be managed with the standard `pip` command. Therefore, they may not be the best choice for a FastAPI application.

To get started, let's install FastAPI and Uvicorn:

```
(venv) $ pip install fastapi "uvicorn[standard]"
```

We'll talk about it in later chapters, but Uvicorn is required to run a FastAPI project.

> **What does "standard" stand for after "uvicorn"?**
>
> You probably noticed the `standard` word inside square brackets just after `uvicorn`. Sometimes, some libraries have sub-dependencies that are not required to make the library work. Usually, they are needed for optional features or specific project requirements. The square brackets are here to indicate that we want to install the standard sub-dependencies of `uvicorn`.

To make sure the installation worked, we can open a Python interactive shell and try to import the `fastapi` package:

```
(venv) $ python
>>> from fastapi import FastAPI
```

If it passes without any errors, congratulations, FastAPI is installed and ready to use!

Installing the HTTPie command-line utility

Before getting to the heart of the topic, there is one last tool that we'll install. FastAPI is, as you probably know, mainly about building **REST APIs**. Thus, we need a tool to make HTTP requests to our API. To do so, we have several options:

- **FastAPI automatic documentation**

- **Postman**: A GUI tool to perform HTTP requests

- **cURL**: The well-known and widely used command-line tool to perform network requests

Even if visual tools such as FastAPI automatic documentation and Postman are nice and easy to use, they sometimes lack some flexibility and may not be as productive as command-line tools. On the other hand, cURL is a very powerful tool with thousands of options, but it can be complex and verbose for testing simple REST APIs.

This is why we'll introduce **HTTPie**, a command-line tool aimed at making HTTP requests. Compared to cURL, its syntax is much more approachable and easier to remember, so you can run complex requests off the top of your head. Besides, it comes with built-in JSON support and syntax highlighting. Since it's a **command-line interface** (CLI) tool, we keep all the benefits of the command line: for example, we can directly pipe a JSON file and send it as the body of an HTTP request. It's available to install from most package managers:

- macOS users can use this:

  ```
  $ brew install httpie
  ```

- Ubuntu users can use this:

  ```
  $ sudo apt-get update && sudo apt-get install httpie
  ```

Let's see how to perform simple requests on a dummy API:

1. First, let's retrieve the data:

   ```
   $ http GET https://603cca51f4333a0017b68509.mockapi.io/todos
   >>>
   HTTP/1.1 200 OK
   Access-Control-Allow-Headers: X-Requested-With,Content-
   Type,Cache-Control,access_token
   Access-Control-Allow-Methods: GET,PUT,POST,DELETE,OPTIONS
   Access-Control-Allow-Origin: *
   Connection: keep-alive
   Content-Length: 58
   Content-Type: application/json
   Date: Tue, 08 Nov 2022 08:28:30 GMT
   Etag: "1631421347"
   ```

```
Server: Cowboy
Vary: Accept-Encoding
Via: 1.1 vegur
X-Powered-By: Express

[
    {
        "id": "1",
        "text": "Write the second edition of the book"
    }
]
```

As you can see, you can invoke HTTPie with the `http` command and simply type the HTTP method and the URL. It outputs both the HTTP headers and the JSON body in a clean and formatted way.

2.   HTTPie also supports sending JSON data in a request body very quickly without having to format the JSON yourself:

```
$ http -v POST https://603cca51f4333a0017b68509.mockapi.io/todos
text="My new task"
POST /todos HTTP/1.1
Accept: application/json, */*;q=0.5
Accept-Encoding: gzip, deflate
Connection: keep-alive
Content-Length: 23
Content-Type: application/json
Host: 603cca51f4333a0017b68509.mockapi.io
User-Agent: HTTPie/3.2.1

{
    "text": "My new task"
}


HTTP/1.1 201 Created
Access-Control-Allow-Headers: X-Requested-With,Content-
Type,Cache-Control,access_token
Access-Control-Allow-Methods: GET,PUT,POST,DELETE,OPTIONS
Access-Control-Allow-Origin: *
Connection: keep-alive
Content-Length: 31
Content-Type: application/json
Date: Tue, 08 Nov 2022 08:30:10 GMT
Server: Cowboy
Vary: Accept-Encoding
Via: 1.1 vegur
```

```
X-Powered-By: Express

{
    "id": "2",
    "text": "My new task"
}
```

By simply typing the property name and its value separated by =, HTTPie will understand that it's part of the request body in JSON. Notice here that we specified the -v option, which tells HTTPie to *output the request* before the response, which is very useful to check that we properly specified the request.

3.   Finally, let's see how we can specify *request headers*:

```
$ http -v GET https://603cca51f4333a0017b68509.mockapi.io/todos
"My-Header: My-Header-Value"
GET /todos HTTP/1.1
Accept: */*
Accept-Encoding: gzip, deflate
Connection: keep-alive
Host: 603cca51f4333a0017b68509.mockapi.io
My-Header: My-Header-Value
User-Agent: HTTPie/3.2.1


HTTP/1.1 200 OK
Access-Control-Allow-Headers: X-Requested-With,Content-
Type,Cache-Control,access_token
Access-Control-Allow-Methods: GET,PUT,POST,DELETE,OPTIONS
Access-Control-Allow-Origin: *
Connection: keep-alive
Content-Length: 90
Content-Type: application/json
Date: Tue, 08 Nov 2022 08:32:12 GMT
Etag: "1849016139"
Server: Cowboy
Vary: Accept-Encoding
Via: 1.1 vegur
X-Powered-By: Express

[
    {
        "id": "1",
        "text": "Write the second edition of the book"
    },
    {
```

```
        "id": "2",
        "text": "My new task"
    }
]
```

That's it! Just type your header name and value separated by a colon to tell HTTPie it's a header.

Summary

You now have all the tools and setup required to confidently run the examples of this book and all your future Python projects. Understanding how to work with pyenv and virtual environments is a key skill to ensure everything goes smoothly when you switch to another project or when you have to work on somebody else's code. You also learned how to install third-party Python libraries using pip. Finally, you saw how to use HTTPie, a simple and efficient way to run HTTP queries that will make you more productive while testing your REST APIs.

In the next chapter, we'll highlight some of Python's peculiarities as a programming language and grasp what it means *to be Pythonic*.

2

Python Programming Specificities

The Python language was designed to emphasize code readability. As such, it provides syntaxes and constructs that allow developers to quickly express complex concepts in a few readable lines. This makes it quite different from other programming languages.

The goal of this chapter is thus to get you acquainted with its specificities, but we expect you already have some experience with programming. We'll first get started with the basics of the language, the standard types, and the flow control syntaxes. You'll also be introduced to the list comprehension and generator concepts, which are very powerful ways to go through and transform sequences of data. You'll also see that Python can be used as an object-oriented language, still through a very lightweight yet powerful syntax. Before moving on, we'll also review the concepts of type hinting and asynchronous I/O, which are quite new in Python but are at the core of the **FastAPI** framework.

In this chapter, we're going to cover the following main topics:

- Basics of Python programming
- List comprehensions and generators
- Classes and objects
- Type hinting and type checking with mypy
- Asynchronous I/O

Technical requirements

You'll need a Python virtual environment, as we set up in *Chapter 1, Python Development Environment Setup*.

You'll find all the code examples of this chapter in the book's dedicated GitHub repository: `https://github.com/PacktPublishing/Building-Data-Science-Applications-with-FastAPI-Second-Edition/tree/main/chapter02`.

Basics of Python programming

First of all, let's review some of the key aspects of Python:

- It's an **interpreted language**. Contrary to languages such as C or Java, it doesn't need to be compiled, which allows us to run Python code interactively.

- It's **dynamically typed**. The type of values is determined at runtime.

- It supports several **programming paradigms**: procedural, object-oriented, and functional programming.

This makes Python quite a versatile language, from simple automation scripts to complex data science projects.

Let's now write and run some Python!

Running Python scripts

As we said, Python is an interpreted language. Hence, the simplest and quickest way to run some Python code is to launch an interactive shell. Just run the following command to start a session:

```
$ python
Python 3.10.8 (main, Nov   8 2022, 08:55:03) [Clang 14.0.0 (clang-
1400.0.29.202)] on darwin
Type "help", "copyright", "credits" or "license" for more information.
>>>
```

This shell makes it very easy to run some simple statements and do some experiments:

```
>>> 1 + 1
2
>>> x = 100
>>> x * 2
200
```

To exit the shell, use the *Ctrl + D* keyboard shortcut.

Obviously, this can become tedious when you start to have more statements or if you just wish to keep your work to reuse it later. Python scripts are saved in files with the `.py` extension. Let's create a file named `chapter2_basics_01.py` in our project directory and add this code:

---

chapter02_basics_01.py

```
print("Hello world!")
x = 100
print(f"Double of {x} is {x * 2}")
```

```
https://github.com/PacktPublishing/Building-Data-Science-Applica-
tions-with-FastAPI-Second-Edition/blob/main/chapter02/chapter02_
basics_01.py
```

Quite simply, this script prints Hello world on the console, assigns the value 100 to a variable named x, and prints a string with the value of x and its double. To run it, simply add the path of your script as a parameter of the Python command:

```
$ python chapter2_basics_01.py
Hello world!
Double of 100 is 200
```

> **f-strings**
>
> You have probably noticed the string starting with f. This syntax, called *f-strings*, is a very convenient and neat way to perform string interpolation. Within, you can simply insert variables between curly braces; they will automatically be converted into strings to build the resulting string. We'll use it quite often in our examples.

That's it! You are now able to write and run simple Python scripts. Let's now dive deeper into the Python syntax.

Indentation matters

One of the most iconic aspects of Python is that code blocks are not defined using curly braces like many other programming languages, but rather with **whitespace indentation**. This may sound a bit strange, but it's at the heart of the readability philosophy of Python. Let's see how you can write a script that finds the even numbers in a list:

chapter02_basics_02.py

```python
numbers = [1, 2, 3, 4, 5, 6, 7, 8, 9, 10]
even = []

for number in numbers:
        if number % 2 == 0:
                even.append(number)

print(even)     # [2, 4, 6, 8, 10]
```

```
https://github.com/PacktPublishing/Building-Data-Science-Applica-
tions-with-FastAPI-Second-Edition/blob/main/chapter02/chapter02_
basics_02.py
```

In this script, we define `numbers`, a list of numbers from 1 to 10, and `even`, an empty list that will contain the even numbers.

Then, we define a `for` loop statement to go through each element of `numbers`. As you see, we open a block with a colon, `:`, break a line, and start writing the next statement with an indentation.

The next line is a conditional statement to check the parity of the current number. Once again, we open a block with a colon, `:`, and write the next statement with an additional indentation level. This statement adds the even number to the even list.

After that, the next statements are not intended. This means that we are out of the `for` loop block; they should be executed after the iteration is finished.

Let's run it:

```
$ python chapter02_basics_02.py
[2, 4, 6, 8, 10]
```

> **Indentation style and size**
>
> You can choose the indentation style (tabs or spaces) and size (2, 4, 6…) you prefer; the only constraint is that you should be consistent *within* a block. However, by convention, Python developers usually go for a *four-space indentation*.

This aspect of Python may sound weird but with some practice, you'll find that it enforces clear formatting and greatly improves the readability of your scripts.

We'll now review the built-in types and data structures.

Working with built-in types

Python is quite conventional regarding scalar types. There are six of them:

- `int`, to store **integer** values, such as `x = 1`

- `float`, for **floating-point numbers**, such as `x = 1.5`

- `complex`, for **complex numbers**, such as `x = 1 + 2j`

- `bool`, for **Boolean** values, either `True` or `False`

- `str`, for **string** values, such as `x = "abc"`

- `NoneType`, to indicate **null** values, such as `x = None`

It's worth noting that Python is **strongly typed**, meaning that the interpreter will limit implicit type conversions. For example, trying to add an `int` value and a `str` value will raise an error, as you can see in the following example:

```
>>> 1 + "abc"
Traceback (most recent call last):
    File "<stdin>", line 1, in <module>
TypeError: unsupported operand type(s) for +: 'int' and 'str'
```

Still, adding an `int` value and a `float` value will automatically upcast the result to `float`:

```
>>> 1 + 1.5
2.5
```

As you may have noticed, Python is quite traditional regarding those standard types. Let's see now how basic data structures are handled.

Working with data structures – lists, tuples, dictionaries, and sets

Besides the scalar types, Python also provides handy data structures: an array structure, of course, called a *list* in Python, but also *tuples*, *dictionaries*, and *sets*, which are very convenient in lots of cases. Let's start with lists.

Lists

Lists are the equivalent in Python of the classic array structure. Defining a list is quite straightforward:

```
>>> l = [1, 2, 3, 4, 5]
```

As you see, wrapping a suite of elements in **square brackets** denotes a list. You can, of course, access single elements by index:

```
>>> l[0]
1
>>> l[2]
3
```

It also supports **negative indexing**, which allows you to retrieve elements from the end of the list: the -1 index is the last element, -2 is the second last element, and so on:

```
>>> l[-1]
5
>>> l[-4]
2
```

Another useful syntax is slicing, which quickly allows you to retrieve a sub-list:

```
>>> l[1:3]
[2, 3]
```

The first number is the start index (inclusive) and the second one is the end index (exclusive), separated by a colon. You can omit the first one; in this case, 0 is assumed:

```
>>> l[:3]
[1, 2, 3]
```

You can also omit the second one; in this case, the length of the list is assumed:

```
>>> l[1:]
[2, 3, 4, 5]
```

Finally, this syntax also supports a third argument to specify the step size. It can be useful to select every second element of the list:

```
>>> l[::2]
[1, 3, 5]
```

A useful trick with this syntax is to use -1 to reverse the list:

```
>>> l[::-1]
[5, 4, 3, 2, 1]
```

Lists are **mutable**. This means that you can reassign elements or add new ones:

```
>>> l[1] = 10
>>> l
[1, 10, 3, 4, 5]
>>> l.append(6)
[1, 10, 3, 4, 5, 6]
```

This is different from their cousins, the tuples, which are **immutable**.

Tuples

Tuples are very similar to lists. Instead of square brackets, they are defined using parentheses:

```
>>> t = (1, 2, 3, 4, 5)
```

They support the same syntax as lists to access elements or slicing:

```
>>> t[2]
3
>>> t[1:3]
```

```
(2, 3)
>>> t[::-1]
(5, 4, 3, 2, 1)
```

However, tuples are immutable. You can't reassign elements or add new ones. Trying to do so will raise an error:

```
>>> t[1] = 10
Traceback (most recent call last):
    File "<stdin>", line 1, in <module>
TypeError: 'tuple' object does not support item assignment
>>> t.append(6)
Traceback (most recent call last):
    File "<stdin>", line 1, in <module>
AttributeError: 'tuple' object has no attribute 'append'
```

A common way to use them is for functions that have multiple return values. In the following example, we define a function to compute and return both the quotient and remainder of the Euclidean division:

chapter02_basics_03.py

```
def euclidean_division(dividend, divisor):
        quotient = dividend // divisor
        remainder = dividend % divisor
        return (quotient, remainder)
```

https://github.com/PacktPublishing/Building-Data-Science-Applications-with-FastAPI-Second-Edition/blob/main/chapter02/chapter02_basics_03.py

This function simply returns the quotient and remainder wrapped in a tuple. Let's now compute the Euclidean division of 3 and 2:

chapter02_basics_03.py

```
t = euclidean_division(3, 2)
print(t[0])     # 1
print(t[1])     # 1
```

https://github.com/PacktPublishing/Building-Data-Science-Applications-with-FastAPI-Second-Edition/blob/main/chapter02/chapter02_basics_03.py

In this case, we assign the result to a tuple named t and simply retrieve the quotient and remainder *by index*. However, we can do something better than that. Let's compute the Euclidean division of 42 and 4:

chapter02_basics_03.py

```
q, r = euclidean_division(42, 4)
print(q)     # 10
print(r)     # 2
```

```
https://github.com/PacktPublishing/Building-Data-Science-Applica-
tions-with-FastAPI-Second-Edition/blob/main/chapter02/chapter02_
basics_03.py
```

You can see here that we directly assign the quotient and remainder to the q and r variables, respectively. This syntax is called **unpacking** and is very convenient for assigning variables from lists or tuple elements. It's worth noting that since t is a tuple, it's immutable, so you can't reassign the values. On the other hand, q and r are new variables and therefore are mutable.

Dictionaries

A dictionary is also a widely used data structure in Python, used to map keys to values. One is defined using curly braces, with a list of keys and values separated by a colon:

```
>>> d = {"a": 1, "b": 2, "c": 3}
```

Elements can be accessed by key:

```
>>> d["a"]
1
```

Dictionaries are mutable, so you can reassign or add elements in the mapping:

```
>>> d["a"] = 10
>>> d
{'a': 10, 'b': 2, 'c': 3}
>>> d["d"] = 4
>>> d
{'a': 10, 'b': 2, 'c': 3, 'd': 4}
```

Sets

A set is a convenient data structure for storing a collection of unique items. It is defined using curly braces:

```
>>> s = {1, 2, 3, 4, 5}
```

Elements can be added to the set, but the structure ensures elements appear only once:

```
>>> s.add(1)
>>> s
{1, 2, 3, 4, 5}
>>> s.add(6)
{1, 2, 3, 4, 5, 6}
```

Convenient methods are also provided to perform operations such as unions or intersections on two sets:

```
>>> s.union({4, 5, 6})
{1, 2, 3, 4, 5, 6}
>>> s.intersection({4, 5, 6})
{4, 5}
```

That's all for this overview of the Python data structures. You'll probably use them quite often in your programs, so take some time to get acquainted with them. Obviously, we didn't cover all of their methods and specificities, but you can have a look at the official Python documentation for exhaustive information: https://docs.python.org/3/library/stdtypes.html.

Let's now talk about the different types of operators available in Python that will allow us to perform some logic on this data.

Performing Boolean logic and a few other operators

Predictably, Python provides operators to perform Boolean logic. However, we'll also see that there are other operators that are less common but make Python a very efficient language to work with.

Performing Boolean logic

Boolean logic is performed with the and, or, and not keywords. Let's review some simple examples:

```
>>> x = 10
>>> x > 0 and x < 100
True
>>> x > 0 or (x % 2 == 0)
True
>>> not (x > 0)
False
```

You'll probably use them quite often in your programs, especially with conditional blocks. Let's now review the identity operators.

Checking whether two variables are the same

The `is` and `is not` identity operators check whether two variables *refer* to the same object. This is different from the comparison operators, `==` and `!=`, which check whether two variables have the same *value*.

Internally, Python stores variables in pointers. The goal of the identity operators is thus to check whether two variables actually point to the same object in memory. Let's review some examples:

```
>>> a = [1, 2, 3]
>>> b = [1, 2, 3]
>>> a is b
False
```

Even though the a and b lists are identical, they're not the same object in memory, so `a is b` is false. However, `a == b` is true. Let's see what happens if we assign a to b:

```
>>> a = [1, 2, 3]
>>> b = a
>>> a is b
True
```

In this case, the b variable will now refer to the same object as a, that is, the same list in memory. Thus, the identity operator is true.

"is None" or "== None"?

To check whether a variable is null, you could write `a == None`. While it will work most of the time, it's generally advised to write `a is None`.

Why? In Python, classes can implement custom comparison operators, so the result of `a == None` may be unpredictable in some cases, since a class can choose to attach a special meaning to the `None` value.

We'll now review the membership operators.

Checking whether a value is present in a data structure

The membership operators, `in` and `not in`, are very useful for checking whether an element is present in data structures such as lists or dictionaries. They are idiomatic in Python and make this operation very efficient and easy to write. Let's review some examples:

```
>>> l = [1, 2, 3]
>>> 2 in l
True
>>> 5 not in l
True
```

With the membership operators, we can check in one statement whether an element is present or not in a list. It also works with tuples and sets:

```
>>> t = (1, 2, 3)
>>> 2 in t
True
>>> s = {1, 2, 3}
>>> 2 in s
True
```

Finally, it also works with dictionaries. In this case, the membership operators check whether the *key* is present, not the value:

```
>>> d = {"a": 1, "b": 2, "c": 3}
>>> "b" in d
True
>>> 3 in d
False
```

We are now clear about those common operations. We'll now put them to use with conditional statements.

Controlling the flow of a program

A programming language would not be a programming language without its control flow statements. Once again, you'll see that Python is a bit different from other languages. Let's start with conditional statements.

Executing operations conditionally – if, elif, and else

Classically, these statements are here for performing some logic based on some Boolean conditions. In the following example, we'll consider a situation where we have a dictionary containing information about an e-commerce website order. We'll write a function that will change the order status to the next step given the current status:

chapter02_basics_04.py

```
def forward_order_status(order):
        if order["status"] == "NEW":
                order["status"] = "IN_PROGRESS"
        elif order["status"] == "IN_PROGRESS":
                order["status"] = "SHIPPED"
        else:
                order["status"] = "DONE"
        return order
```

https://github.com/PacktPublishing/Building-Data-Science-Applications-with-FastAPI-Second-Edition/blob/main/chapter02/chapter02_basics_04.py

The first condition is noted as if, followed by a Boolean condition. We then open an indented block, as we explained in the *Indentation matters* section of this chapter.

The alternate conditions are noted as elif (not else if) and the fallback block is noted as else. Of course, those are *optional* if you don't need alternate or fallback conditions.

It's also worth noting that, contrary to many other languages, Python does not provide a switch statement.

Repeating operations over an iterator – the for loop statement

We'll now move on to another classic control flow statement: the for loop. You can repeat operations over a sequence using the for loop statement.

We already saw an example of the for loop in action in the *Indentation matters* section of this chapter. As you probably understood, this statement is useful for repeating the execution of a code block.

You also may have noticed that it works a bit differently from other languages. Usually, programming languages define for loops like this: for (i = 0; i <= 10; i++). They give you the responsibility to define and control the variable used for the iteration.

Python doesn't work this way. Instead, it expects you to feed the loop with an **iterator**. An iterator can be seen as a sequence of elements that you can retrieve one by one. Lists, tuples, dictionaries, and sets can behave like an iterator and be used in a for loop. Let's see some examples:

```
>>> for i in [1,2,3]:
...         print(i)
...
1
2
3
>>> for k in {"a": 1, "b": 2, "c": 3}:
...         print(k)
...
a
b
c
```

But what if you just wish to iterate a certain number of times? Thankfully, Python has built-in functions that generate some useful iterators. The most well known is range, which precisely creates a sequence of numbers. Let's see how it works:

```
>>> for i in range(3):
...         print(i)
...
0
1
2
```

`range` will generate a sequence of the size you provided in the first argument, starting with zero.

You could also be more precise by specifying two arguments: the start index (inclusive) and the last index (exclusive):

```
>>> for i in range(1, 3):
...         print(i)
...
1
2
```

Finally, you may even provide a step as a third argument:

```
>>> for i in range(0, 5, 2):
...         print(i)
...
0
2
4
```

Note that this syntax is quite similar to the slicing syntax we saw earlier in this chapter in the sections dedicated to *lists* and *tuples*.

> **range output is not a list**
>
> A common misconception is to think `range` returns a *list*. It's actually a `Sequence` object that only stores the *start*, *end*, and *step* arguments. That's why you could write `range(1000000000)` without blowing up your system's memory: the billions of elements are not assigned to memory all at once.

As you see, the `for` loop syntax in Python is quite straightforward to understand and emphasizes readability. We'll now have a word about its cousin, the `while` loop.

Repeating operations until a condition is met – the while loop statement

The classical `while` loop is also available in Python. At the risk of disappointing you, there is nothing truly special about this one. Classically, this statement allows you to repeat instructions until a condition is met. We'll review an example in which we use a `while` loop to retrieve paginated elements until we reach the end:

chapter02_basics_05.py

```
def retrieve_page(page):
        if page > 3:
                return {"next_page": None, "items": []}
        return {"next_page": page + 1, "items": ["A", "B", "C"]}
```

```
items = []
page = 1
while page is not None:
        page_result = retrieve_page(page)
        items += page_result["items"]
        page = page_result["next_page"]


print(items)    # ["A", "B", "C", "A", "B", "C", "A", "B", "C"]
```

https://github.com/PacktPublishing/Building-Data-Science-Applica-
tions-with-FastAPI-Second-Edition/blob/main/chapter02/chapter02_
basics_05.py

The `retrieve_page` function is a dummy function that returns a dictionary with the items for the page passed in an argument and the next page number or None if we reached the last page. *A priori*, we don't know how many pages there are. Thus, we repeatedly call `retrieve_page` until the page is None. At each iteration, we save the current page items in an accumulator, `items`.

This kind of use case is quite common when you are dealing with third-party REST APIs and you wish to retrieve all items available, and `while` loops perfectly help with this.

Finally, there are cases where you wish to prematurely end the loop or skip an iteration. To solve this, Python implements the classic `break` and `continue` statements.

Defining functions

Now that we know how to use the common operators and control the flow of our program, let's put it in reusable logic. As you may have guessed, we'll look at **functions** and how to define them. We already saw them in some of our previous examples, but let's introduce them more formally.

In Python, functions are defined using the `def` keyword followed by the name of the function. Then, you have the list of supported arguments in parentheses, before a colon that indicates the start of the function body. Let's see a simple example:

```
>>> def f(a):
...         return a
...
>>> f(2)
2
```

That's it! Python also supports default values on arguments:

```
>>> def f(a, b = 1):
...         return a, b
...
>>> f(2)
(2, 1)
>>> f(2, 3)
(2, 3)
```

When calling a function, you can specify the value of arguments using their name:

```
>>> f(a=2, b=3)
(2, 3)
```

Those arguments are called *keyword arguments*. They are especially useful if you have several default arguments but only wish to set one of them:

```
>>> def f(a = 1, b = 2, c = 3):
...         return a, b, c
...
>>> f(c=1)
(1, 2, 1)
```

> **Function naming**
>
> By convention, functions should be named using **snake case**: my_wonderful_function but not MyWonderfulFunction.

But there is more! You can actually define functions accepting a dynamic number of arguments.

Accepting arguments dynamically with *args and **kwargs

Sometimes, you may need a function that supports a dynamic number of arguments. Those arguments are then handled in your function logic at runtime. To do this, you have to use the *args and **kwargs syntax. Let's define a function that uses this syntax and prints the value of those arguments:

```
>>> def f(*args, **kwargs):
...         print("args", args)
...         print("kwargs", kwargs)
...
>>> f(1, 2, 3, a=4, b=5)
args (1, 2, 3)
kwargs {'a': 4, 'b': 5}
```

As you can see, standard arguments are placed in a *tuple*, in the same order as they were called. Keyword arguments, on the other hand, have been placed in a *dictionary*, with the key being the name of the argument. It's up to you then to use this data to perform your logic!

Interestingly, you can mix both approaches so that you have hardcoded arguments and dynamic ones:

```
>>> def f(a, *args):
...         print("a", a)
...         print("arg", args)
...
>>> f(1, 2, 3)
a 1
arg (2, 3)
```

Well done! You have learned how to write functions in Python to organize the logic of your program. The next step now is to organize those functions into modules and import them into other modules to take advantage of them!

Writing and using packages and modules

You probably already know that, apart from small scripts, your source code shouldn't live in one big file with thousands of lines. Instead, you should split it into logical blocks of reasonable size that are easy to maintain. That's exactly what packages and modules are for! We'll see how they work and how you can define your own.

First of all, Python comes with its own set of modules, the standard library, which are directly importable in a program:

```
>>> import datetime
>>> datetime.date.today()
datetime.date(2022, 12, 1)
```

With just the import keyword, you can use the datetime module and access all its content by referring to its namespace, datetime.date, which is the built-in class to work with dates. However, you may sometimes wish to explicitly import a part of this module:

```
>>> from datetime import date
>>> date.today()
datetime.date(2022, 12, 1)
```

Here, we explicitly import the date class to use it directly. The same principles apply to third-party packages installed with pip, such as FastAPI.

Using existing packages and modules is nice but writing your own is even better. In Python, a **module** is a single file containing declarations but can also contain instructions that will be executed when the module is first imported. You'll find the definition of a very simple module in the following example:

chapter02_basics_module.py

```
def module_function():
        return "Hello world"


print("Module is loaded")
```

https://github.com/PacktPublishing/Building-Data-Science-Applica-tions-with-FastAPI-Second-Edition/blob/main/chapter02/chapter02_basics_module.py

This module only contains a function, `module_function`, and a `print` statement. Create a file containing this code at the root of your project directory and name it `module.py`. Then, open a Python interpreter and run this command:

```
>>> import module
Module is loaded
```

Notice that the `print` statement was executed when you imported it. You can now use the function:

```
>>> module.module_function()
'Hello world'
```

Congratulations! You've just written your first Python module!

Now, let's see how to structure a **package**. A package is a way to organize modules in a hierarchy, which you can then import using their namespace.

At the root of your project, create a directory named `package`. Inside, create another directory named `subpackage` and move `module.py` into it. Your project structure should look like the one shown in *Figure 2.1*:

```
└ 📁 your-project
    └ 📁 package
        └ 📁 subpackage
            └ </> module.py
```

Figure 2.1 – Python package sample hierarchy

You can then import your module using the full namespace:

```
>>> import package.subpackage.module
Module is loaded
```

It works! However, to define a proper Python package, it's *strongly recommended* to create an empty __init__.py file at the root of each package and sub-package. In older Python versions, it was compulsory to make a package recognizable by the interpreter. This became optional in more recent versions, but there are actually some subtle differences between a package with an __init__.py file (a package) and one without (a **namespace package**). We won't explain it further in this book, but you could check the documentation about namespace packages here if you wish to learn more details: https://packaging.python.org/en/latest/guides/packaging-namespace-packages/.

Therefore, you generally always should create __init__.py files. In our example, our project structure would finally look like this:

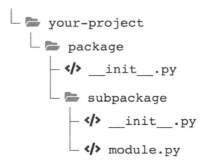

Figure 2.2 – Python package hierarchy with __init__.py files

It's worth noting that even if empty __init__.py files are perfectly fine, you can actually write some code in them. In this case, it is executed the first time you import the package or one of its sub-modules. It's useful to perform some initialization logic for your package. You now have a good overview of how to write some Python code. Feel free to write some small scripts to get acquainted with its peculiar syntax. We'll now explore more advanced topics about the language that will prove useful during our journey with FastAPI.

Operating over sequences – list comprehensions and generators

In this section, we'll cover what are probably the most idiomatic constructions in Python: list comprehensions and generators. You'll see that they are very useful for reading and transforming sequences of data with minimal syntax.

List comprehensions

In programming, a very common task is to transform a sequence (let's say, a *list*) into another, for example, to filter out or transform elements. Usually, you would write such an operation as we did in one of the previous examples of this chapter:

chapter02_basics_02.py

```
numbers = [1, 2, 3, 4, 5, 6, 7, 8, 9, 10]
even = []

for number in numbers:
        if number % 2 == 0:
                even.append(number)

print(even)     # [2, 4, 6, 8, 10]
```

https://github.com/PacktPublishing/Building-Data-Science-Applications-with-FastAPI-Second-Edition/blob/main/chapter02/chapter02_basics_02.py

With this approach, we simply iterate over each element, check a condition, and add the element in an accumulator if it passes this condition.

To go further in its readability philosophy, Python supports a neat syntax to perform this operation in only one statement: **list comprehensions**. Let's see what our previous example looks like with this syntax:

chapter02_list_comprehensions_01.py

```
numbers = [1, 2, 3, 4, 5, 6, 7, 8, 9, 10]
even = [number for number in numbers if number % 2 == 0]
print(even)     # [2, 4, 6, 8, 10]
```

https://github.com/PacktPublishing/Building-Data-Science-Applications-with-FastAPI-Second-Edition/blob/main/chapter02/chapter02_list_comprehensions_01.py

That's it! Basically, a list comprehension works by *packing* a for loop and wrapping it with square brackets. The element to add to the result list appears first, followed by the iteration. Optionally, we can add a condition, as we did here, to filter some elements of the list input.

Actually, the result element can be any valid Python expression. In the following example, we use the `randint` function of the `random` standard module to generate a list of random integers:

chapter02_list_comprehensions_02.py

```
from random import randint, seed

seed(10)     # Set random seed to make examples reproducible
random_elements = [randint(1, 10) for I in range(5)]
print(random_elements)     # [10, 1, 7, 8, 10]
```

https://github.com/PacktPublishing/Building-Data-Science-Applications-with-FastAPI-Second-Edition/blob/main/chapter02/chapter02_list_comprehensions_02.py

This syntax is widely used by Python programmers and you'll probably grow quite fond of it. The nice thing about this syntax is that it also works for *sets* and *dictionaries*. Quite simply, just replace the square brackets with curly braces to generate a set:

chapter02_list_comprehensions_03.py

```
from random import randint, seed

seed(10)     # Set random seed to make examples reproducible
random_unique_elements = {randint(1, 10) for i in range(5)}
print(random_unique_elements)     # {8, 1, 10, 7}
```

https://github.com/PacktPublishing/Building-Data-Science-Applications-with-FastAPI-Second-Edition/blob/main/chapter02/chapter02_list_comprehensions_03.py

To create a dictionary, specify both the key and the value separated by a colon:

chapter02_list_comprehensions_04.py

```
from random import randint, seed

seed(10)     # Set random seed to make examples reproducible
random_dictionary = {i: randint(1, 10) for i in range(5)}
print(random_dictionary)     # {0: 10, 1: 1, 2: 7, 3: 8, 4: 10}
```

https://github.com/PacktPublishing/Building-Data-Science-Applications-with-FastAPI-Second-Edition/blob/main/chapter02/chapter02_list_comprehensions_04.pyeee

Generators

You might think that if you replace the square brackets with parentheses, you could obtain a tuple. Actually, you get a **generator** object. The main difference between generators and list comprehensions is that elements are generated *on demand* and not computed and stored all at once in memory. You could see a generator as a recipe to generate values.

As we said, a generator can be defined simply by using the same syntax as list comprehensions, with parentheses:

---

chapter02_list_comprehensions_05.py

```
numbers = [1, 2, 3, 4, 5, 6, 7, 8, 9, 10]
even_generator = (number for number in numbers if number % 2 == 0)
even = list(even_generator)
even_bis = list(even_generator)

print(even)       # [2, 4, 6, 8, 10]
print(even_bis)     # []
```

https://github.com/PacktPublishing/Building-Data-Science-Applications-with-FastAPI-Second-Edition/blob/main/chapter02/chapter02_list_comprehensions_05.py

---

In this example, we define `even_generator` to output the even number of the `numbers` list. Then, we call the `list` constructor with this generator and assign it to the variable named `even`. This constructor will exhaust the iterator passed in the argument and build a proper list. We do it a second time and assign it to `even_bis`.

As you can see, `even` is a list with all the even numbers. However, `even_bis` is an *empty* list. This simple example is here to show you that a generator can be used *only once*. Once all the values have been produced, it's over.

This can be useful because you can start to iterate on the generator, stop to do something else, and resume iterating.

Another way to create generators is to define **generator functions**. In the following example, we'll define a generator function that outputs even numbers from 2 to the limit passed in an argument:

---

chapter02_list_comprehensions_06.py

```
def even_numbers(max):
        for i in range(2, max + 1):
                if i % 2 == 0:
                        yield i
```

```
even = list(even_numbers(10))
print(even)      # [2, 4, 6, 8, 10]
```

https://github.com/PacktPublishing/Building-Data-Science-Applica-
tions-with-FastAPI-Second-Edition/blob/main/chapter02/chapter02_
list_comprehensions_06.py

As you can see in this function, we use the `yield` keyword instead of `return`. When the interpreter reaches this statement, it *pauses* the function execution and *yields* the value to the generator consumer. When the main program asks for another value, the function is resumed in order to yield again.

This allows us to implement complex generators, even ones that will output different types of values over their course. Another interesting property of generator functions is that they allow us to execute some instructions when they have finished generating values. Let's add a `print` statement at the end of the function we just reviewed:

chapter02_list_comprehensions_07.py

```
def even_numbers(max):
        for i in range(2, max + 1):
                if i % 2 == 0:
                        yield i
        print("Generator exhausted")


even = list(even_numbers(10))
print(even)
```

https://github.com/PacktPublishing/Building-Data-Science-Applica-
tions-with-FastAPI-Second-Edition/blob/main/chapter02/chapter02_
list_comprehensions_07.py

If you execute it in a Python interpreter, you'll get this output:

```
$ python chapter02_list_comprehensions_07.py
Generator exhausted
[2, 4, 6, 8, 10]
```

We get `Generator exhausted` in the output, which means that our code *after* the last `yield` statement is well executed.

This is especially useful when you want to perform some *cleanup operations* after your generator has been exhausted: close a connection, remove temporary files, and so on.

Writing object-oriented programs

As we said in the first section of this chapter, Python is a multi-paradigm language, and one of those paradigms is **object-oriented programming**. In this section, we'll review how you can define classes and how you can instantiate and use objects. You'll see that Python syntax is once again very lightweight.

Defining a class

Defining a class in Python is straightforward: use the `class` keyword, type the name of your class, and begin a new block. You can then define methods under it just like you would for regular functions. Let's review an example:

chapter02_classes_objects_01.py

```python
class Greetings:
    def greet(self, name):
        return f"Hello, {name}"


c = Greetings()
print(c.greet("John"))    # "Hello, John"
```

https://github.com/PacktPublishing/Building-Data-Science-Applications-with-FastAPI-Second-Edition/blob/main/chapter02/chapter02_classes_objects_01.py

Notice that the first argument of each method must be `self`, which is a reference to the current object instance (the equivalent of `this` in other languages).

To instantiate a class, simply call the class as you would for a function and assign it to a variable. You can then access the methods using dot notation.

> **Class and method naming**
>
> By convention, classes should be named using **camel case**: `MyWonderfulClass` but not `my_wonderful_class`. Methods should use snake case, like regular functions.

Obviously, you can also set **class properties**. To do this, we'll implement the `__init__` method, whose goal is to initialize values:

chapter02_classes_objects_02.py

```python
class Greetings:
    def __init__(self, default_name):
```

```
                self.default_name = default_name

        def greet(self, name=None):
                return f"Hello, {name if name else self.default_name}"


c = Greetings("Alan")
print(c.default_name)     # "Alan"
print(c.greet())     # "Hello, Alan"
print(c.greet("John"))     # "Hello, John"
```

https://github.com/PacktPublishing/Building-Data-Science-Applica-
tions-with-FastAPI-Second-Edition/blob/main/chapter02/chapter02_
classes_objects_02.py

In this example, __init__ allows us to set a default_name property, which will be used by the greet method if no name is provided in the argument. As you can see, you can simply access this property through dot notation.

Be careful though: __init__ is not a constructor. In typical object-oriented languages, a constructor is a method to actually create the object in memory. In Python, when __init__ is called, the object is already created in memory (notice we have access to the self instance). Actually, there is a method to define the constructor, __new__, but it's rarely used in common Python programs.

> **Private methods and properties**
>
> In Python, there is no such thing as *private* methods or properties. Everything will always be accessible from the outside. However, by convention, you can prefix your private methods and properties with an underscore to *suggest* that they should be considered private: _private_method.

You now have the basics of object-oriented programming in Python! We'll now focus on magic methods, which will allow us to do clever things with objects.

Implementing magic methods

Magic methods are a set of predefined methods that bear a special meaning in the language. They are easy to recognize as they start and end with two underscores. Actually, we already saw one of those magic methods: __init__! Those methods are not called directly but are used by the interpreter when using other constructs such as standard functions or operators.

To understand how they are useful, we'll review the most used ones. Let's start with __repr__ and __str__.

Object representations – __repr__ and __str__

When you define a class, it's generally useful to be able to get a readable and clear string representation of an instance. For this purpose, Python provides two magic methods: __repr__ and __str__. Let's see how they work on a class representing a temperature in either degrees Celsius or degrees Fahrenheit:

chapter02_classes_objects_03.py

```python
class Temperature:
        def __init__(self, value, scale):
                self.value = value
                self.scale = scale

        def __repr__(self):
                return f"Temperature({self.value}, {self.scale!r})"

        def __str__(self):
                return f"Temperature is {self.value} °{self.scale}"


t = Temperature(25, "C")
print(repr(t))    # "Temperature(25, 'C')"
print(str(t))     # "Temperature is 25 °C"
print(t)
```

https://github.com/PacktPublishing/Building-Data-Science-Applica-tions-with-FastAPI-Second-Edition/blob/main/chapter02/chapter02_classes_objects_03.py

If you run this example, you'll notice that print(t) prints the same thing as print(str(t)). Through print, the interpreter called the __str__ method to get the string representation of our object. This is what __str__ is for: giving a *nice string representation* of an object for the end user.

On the other hand, you saw that even though they're very similar, we implemented __repr__ in a different way. The purpose of this method is to give an *internal representation* of the object that is unambiguous. By convention, this should give the exact statement that would allow us to recreate the very same object.

Now that we can represent temperatures with our class, what would happen if we tried to compare them?

Comparison methods – __eq__, __gt__, __lt__, and so on

Of course, comparing two temperatures with different units would lead to unexpected results. Fortunately, magic methods allow us to overload the default operators to perform meaningful comparisons. Let's expand on our previous example:

chapter02_classes_objects_04.py

```python
class Temperature:
        def __init__(self, value, scale):
                self.value = value
                self.scale = scale
                if scale == "C":
                        self.value_kelvin = value + 273.15
                elif scale == "F":
                        self.value_kelvin = (value-- 32) * 5 / 9 +
273.15
```

https://github.com/PacktPublishing/Building-Data-Science-Applications-with-FastAPI-Second-Edition/blob/main/chapter02/chapter02_classes_objects_04.py

In the __init__ method, we convert the temperature value into Kelvin given the current scale. This will help us to make comparisons. Then, let's define __eq__ and __lt__:

chapter02_classes_objects_04.py

```python
        def __eq__(self, other):
                return self.value_kelvin == other.value_kelvin

        def __lt__(self, other):
                return self.value_kelvin < other.value_kelvin
```

https://github.com/PacktPublishing/Building-Data-Science-Applications-with-FastAPI-Second-Edition/blob/main/chapter02/chapter02_classes_objects_04.py

As you can see, those methods simply accept another argument, which is the other object instance to compare with. We then just have to perform our comparison logic. By doing this, we can perform comparison just as we would for any variable:

chapter02_classes_objects_04.py

```
tc = Temperature(25, "C")
tf = Temperature(77, "F")
tf2 = Temperature(100, "F")
print(tc == tf)    # True
print(tc < tf2)    # True
```

https://github.com/PacktPublishing/Building-Data-Science-Applica-tions-with-FastAPI-Second-Edition/blob/main/chapter02/chapter02_classes_objects_04.py

That's it! If you wish to have all the comparison operators available, you should also implement all the other comparison magic methods: __le__, __gt__, and __ge__.

> **The type of the other instance is not guaranteed**
>
> In this example, we assumed the other variable was also a Temperature object. In the real world, however, this is not guaranteed and developers could try to compare Temperature with another object, which would likely lead to errors or weird behaviors. To prevent this, you should check the type of the other variable using isinstance to ensure we handle Temperature, or raise a proper exception otherwise.

Operators – __add__, __sub__, __mul__, and so on

Similarly, you could also define what would happen when trying to add or multiply two Temperature objects. We won't go into much detail here as it works exactly like the comparison operators.

Callable object – __call__

The last magic method we'll review is __call__. This one is a bit special because it enables you to call your object instance like a *regular function*. Let's take an example:

chapter02_classes_objects_05.py

```
class Counter:
        def __init__(self):
                self.counter = 0

        def __call__(self, inc=1):
```

```
                    self.counter += inc


c = Counter()
print(c.counter)    # 0
c()
print(c.counter)    # 1
c(10)
print(c.counter)    # 11
```

https://github.com/PacktPublishing/Building-Data-Science-Applica-
tions-with-FastAPI-Second-Edition/blob/main/chapter02/chapter02_
classes_objects_05.py

The __call__ method can be defined like any other method, with any argument you wish. The only difference is how you call it: you just pass the argument directly on the object instance variable as you would do for a regular function.

This pattern can be useful if you want to define a function that maintains some kind of local state, as we did here in our example, or in cases where you need to provide a **callable** object but have to set some parameters. Actually, this is the use case we'll encounter when defining class dependencies for FastAPI.

As we saw, magic methods are an excellent way to implement operations for our custom classes and make them easy to use in a purely object-oriented way. We haven't covered every magic method available but you can find the complete list in the official documentation: https://docs.python.org/3/reference/datamodel.html#special-method-names.

We'll now focus on another essential characteristic of object-oriented programming: inheritance.

Reusing logic and avoiding repetition with inheritance

Inheritance is one of the core concepts of object-oriented programming: it allows you to derive a new class from existing ones, enabling you to reuse some logic and overload the parts that are specific to this new class. Of course, this is supported in Python. We'll take very simple examples to understand the mechanism underneath.

First of all, let's take an example of very simple inheritance:

chapter02_classes_objects_06.py

```
class A:
        def f(self):
                return "A"
```

```
class Child(A):
        pass
```

The Child class inherits from the A class. The syntax is simple: the class we want to inherit from is specified between parentheses after the child class name.

> **The pass statement**
>
> pass is a statement that *does nothing*. Since Python relies only on indentation to denote blocks, it's a useful statement to create an *empty block*, as you would do with curly braces in other programming languages.
>
> In this example, we don't want to add some logic to the Child class, so we just write pass.
>
> Another way to do it is to add a docstring just below the class definition.

If you wish to overload a method but still want to get the result of the parent method, you can call the super function:

chapter02_classes_objects_07.py

```
class A:
        def f(self):
                return "A"

class Child(A):
        def f(self):
                parent_result = super().f()
                return f"Child {parent_result}"
```

You now know how to use basic inheritance in Python. But there is more: we can also have multiple inheritance!

Multiple inheritance

As its name suggests, multiple inheritance allows you to derive a child class from multiple classes. This way, you can combine the logic of several classes into one. Let's take an example:

chapter02_classes_objects_08.py

```
class A:
        def f(self):
                return "A"

class B:
        def g(self):
                return "B"

class Child(A, B):
        pass
```

https://github.com/PacktPublishing/Building-Data-Science-Applica-
tions-with-FastAPI-Second-Edition/blob/main/chapter02/chapter02_
classes_objects_08.py

Once again, the syntax is quite straightforward: just list all the parent classes with a comma. Now, the Child class can call both methods, f and g.

> **Mixins**
>
> Mixins are common patterns in Python that take advantage of the multiple inheritance feature. Basically, mixins are short classes containing a single feature that you often want to reuse. You can then compose concrete classes by combining mixins.

However, what would happen if both A and B classes implemented a method named f? Let's try it out:

chapter02_classes_objects_09.py

```
class A:
        def f(self):
                return "A"

class B:
        def f(self):
                return "B"
```

```
class Child(A, B):
        pass
```

https://github.com/PacktPublishing/Building-Data-Science-Applica-
tions-with-FastAPI-Second-Edition/blob/main/chapter02/chapter02_
classes_objects_09.py

If you call the f method of Child, you'll get the value "A". In this simple case, Python will consider the first matching method following the order of the parent classes. However, for more complex hierarchies, the resolution may not be so obvious: this is the purpose of the **Method Resolution Order (MRO)** algorithm. We won't go into much detail here but you can have a look at the official document explaining the algorithm implemented by Python: https://www.python.org/download/releases/2.3/mro/.

If you are confused about the MRO of your class, you can call the mro method on your class to get a list of considered classes in order:

```
>>> Child.mro()
[<class 'chapter2_classes_objects_09.Child'>, <class 'chapter2_
classes_objects_09.A'>, <class 'chapter2_classes_objects_09.B'>,
<class 'object'>]
```

Well done! You now have a good overview of object-oriented programming in Python. Those concepts will be helpful when defining dependencies in FastAPI.

We'll now review some of the most recent and trending features in Python, upon which FastAPI relies heavily. We'll start with **type hinting**.

Type hinting and type checking with mypy

In the first section of this chapter, we said that Python was a dynamically typed language: the interpreter doesn't check types at compile time but rather at runtime. This makes the language a bit more flexible and the developer a bit more efficient. However, if you are experienced with that kind of language, you probably know that it's easy to produce errors and bugs in this context: forgetting arguments, type mismatches, and so on.

This is why Python introduced type hinting starting in *version 3.5*. The goal is to provide a syntax to annotate the source code with **type annotations**: each variable, function, and class can be annotated to give indications about the types they expect. This *doesn't mean* that Python becomes a statically typed language. Those annotations remain completely *optional* and are *ignored* by the interpreter. However, those annotations can be used by **static type checkers**, which will check whether your code is valid and consistent following the annotations. Hence, it greatly helps you to reduce errors and write self-explanatory code. One of those tools, mypy, is widely used by the community in this context.

Getting started

To understand how type annotations work, we'll review a simple annotated function:

---

chapter02_type_hints_01.py

```
def greeting(name: str) -> str:
        return f"Hello, {name}"
```

https://github.com/PacktPublishing/Building-Data-Science-Applica-
tions-with-FastAPI-Second-Edition/blob/main/chapter02/chapter02_
type_hints_01.py

As you can see here, we simply added the type of the name argument after a colon. We also specified the **return type** after an arrow. For built-in types, such as str or int, we can simply use them as type annotations. We'll see a little later in this section how to annotate more complex types such as lists or dictionaries.

We'll now install mypy to perform a type check on this file. This can be done like any other Python package:

```
$ pip install mypy
```

Then, you can run a type check on your source file:

```
$ mypy chapter02_type_hints_01.py
Success: no issues found in 1 source file
```

As you can see, mypy tells us that everything is good with our typing. Let's try to modify our code a bit to provoke a type error:

```
def greeting(name: str) -> int:
        return f"Hello, {name}"
```

Quite simply, we just said that the return type of our function is now int, but we are still returning a string. If you run this code, it'll execute perfectly well: as we said, the interpreter ignores type annotations. However, let's see what mypy tells us about it:

```
$ mypy chapter02_type_hints_01.py
chapter02_type_hints_01.py:2: error: Incompatible return value type
(got "str", expected "int")    [return-value]
Found 1 error in 1 file (checked 1 source file)
```

This time, it complains. It clearly tells us what is wrong here: the return value is a string, while an integer was expected!

Code editors and IDE integration

Having type checking is good, but it may be a bit tedious to run mypy manually on the command line. Fortunately, it integrates well with the most popular code editors and IDEs. Once configured, it'll perform type checking while you type and show you errors directly on faulty lines. Type annotations also help the IDE to perform clever things such as *auto-completion*.

You can check in the official documentation of mypy how to set it up for your favorite editor: https://github.com/python/mypy#integrations.

You understand the basics of type hinting in Python. We'll now review more advanced examples, especially with non-scalar types.

Type data structures

So far, we've seen how to annotate variables for scalar types such as str or int. But we've seen that there are data structures such as lists and dictionaries that are widely used in Python. In the following example, we'll show how to type-hint the basic data structures in Python:

---

chapter02_type_hints_02.py

```
l: list[int] = [1, 2, 3, 4, 5]
t: tuple[int, str, float] = (1, "hello", 3.14)
s: set[int] = {1, 2, 3, 4, 5}
d: dict[str, int] = {"a": 1, "b": 2, "c": 3}
```

https://github.com/PacktPublishing/Building-Data-Science-Applications-with-FastAPI-Second-Edition/blob/main/chapter02/chapter02_type_hints_02.py

---

You can see here that we can use the list, tuple, set, and dict standard classes as type hints. However, they expect you to provide the type of the values composing your structure. It's the well-known concept of **generics** in object-oriented programming. In Python, they are defined using square brackets.

Of course, there are more complex use cases. For example, having a list with elements of different types is perfectly valid in Python. To make this work with type checkers, we can simply use the | notation to specify several allowed types:

chapter02_type_hints_03.py

```
l: list[int | float] = [1, 2.5, 3.14, 5]
```

https://github.com/PacktPublishing/Building-Data-Science-Applica-tions-with-FastAPI-Second-Edition/blob/main/chapter02/chapter02_type_hints_03.py

In this case, our list will accept either integers or floating-point numbers. Of course, mypy will complain if you try to add an element in this list that is neither an int nor a float type.

There is also another case where this is useful: quite often, you'll have function arguments or return types that either return a value or None. Thus, you could write something like this:

chapter02_type_hints_04.py

```
def greeting(name: str | None = None) -> str:
        return f"Hello, {name if name else 'Anonymous'}"
```

https://github.com/PacktPublishing/Building-Data-Science-Applica-tions-with-FastAPI-Second-Edition/blob/main/chapter02/chapter02_type_hints_04.py

The allowed value is either a string or None.

> **Type annotations were different before Python 3.9**
>
> Before Python 3.9, it wasn't possible to annotate lists, tuples, sets, and dictionaries using the standard class. We needed to import special classes from the typing module: l: List[int] = [1, 2, 3, 4, 5].
>
> The | notation wasn't available either. We needed to use a special Union class from typing: l: List[Union[int, float]] = [1, 2.5, 3.14, 5]
>
> This way of annotating is now deprecated, but you may still find it in older code bases.

When dealing with complex types, it may be useful to *alias* and reuse them at will without the need to rewrite them each time. To do this, you can simply assign them as you would do for any variable:

chapter02_type_hints_05.py

```
IntStringFloatTuple = tuple[int, str, float]

t: IntStringFloatTuple = (1, "hello", 3.14)
```

https://github.com/PacktPublishing/Building-Data-Science-Applications-with-FastAPI-Second-Edition/blob/main/chapter02/chapter02_type_hints_05.py

By convention, types should be named using camel case, like classes. Talking about classes, let's see how type hinting works with them:

chapter02_type_hints_06.py

```
class Post:
        def __init__(self, title: str) -> None:
                self.title = title

        def __str__(self) -> str:
                return self.title

posts: list[Post] = [Post("Post A"), Post("Post B")]
```

https://github.com/PacktPublishing/Building-Data-Science-Applications-with-FastAPI-Second-Edition/blob/main/chapter02/chapter02_type_hints_06.py

Actually, there is nothing special about classes' type hinting. You just annotate the methods as you would for a regular function. If you need to use your class in an annotation, like here for a list of posts, you just have to use the class name.

Sometimes, you'll have to write a function or method that accepts another function in an argument. In this case, you'll need to give the **type signature** of this function.

Type function signatures with Callable

A more advanced use case is to be able to have types for function signatures. For example, it can be useful when you need to pass functions as arguments of other functions. For this task, we can use the `Callable` class, available in the `collections.abc` module. In the following example, we'll implement a function called `filter_list` expecting as arguments a list of integers and a function returning a Boolean given an integer:

chapter02_type_hints_07.py

```
from collections.abc import Callable

ConditionFunction = Callable[[int], bool]

def filter_list(l: list[int], condition: ConditionFunction) ->
list[int]:
        return [i for i in l if condition(i)]
```

https://github.com/PacktPublishing/Building-Data-Science-Applica-
tions-with-FastAPI-Second-Edition/blob/main/chapter02/chapter02_
type_hints_07.py

> **What is the collections.abc module?**
>
> `collections.abc` is a module from the standard Python library providing abstract base classes for the common objects we use daily in Python: iterators, generators, callables, sets, mappings, and so on. They are mainly useful in advanced use cases where we need to implement new custom objects that should behave *like* an iterator, generator, and so on. Here, we only use them as type hints.

You can see here that we define a type alias, `ConditionFunction`, thanks to `Callable`. Once again, this is a generic class that expects two things: first, the list of argument types and then the return type. Here, we expect a single integer argument and the return type is a Boolean.

We can then use this type in the annotation of the `filter_list` function. `mypy` will then ensure that the condition function passed in the argument conforms to this signature. For example, we could write a simple function to check the parity of an integer, as shown in the next sample:

chapter02_type_hints_07.py

```
def is_even(i: int) -> bool:
        return i % 2 == 0

filter_list([1, 2, 3, 4, 5], is_even)
```

https://github.com/PacktPublishing/Building-Data-Science-Applica-tions-with-FastAPI-Second-Edition/blob/main/chapter02/chapter02_type_hints_07.py

It's worth noting, however, that there is no syntax to indicate optional or keyword arguments. In this case, you can write `Callable[..., bool]`, the ellipsis (`...`) here meaning *any number of arguments*.

Any and cast

In some situations, the code is so dynamic or complicated that it won't be possible to annotate it correctly or the type checker may not correctly infer the type. For this, we can use `Any` and `cast`. They are available in the `typing` module, which was introduced by Python to help with more specific use cases and constructs regarding type hints.

`Any` is a type annotation telling the type checker the variable or argument can be anything. In this case, any type of value will be valid for the type checker:

chapter02_type_hints_08.py

```
from typing import Any

def f(x: Any) -> Any:
        return x

f("a")
f(10)
f([1, 2, 3])
```

https://github.com/PacktPublishing/Building-Data-Science-Applica-tions-with-FastAPI-Second-Edition/blob/main/chapter02/chapter02_type_hints_08.py

The second one, `cast`, is a function that lets you override the type inferred by the type checker. It'll force the type checker to consider the type you specify:

chapter02_type_hints_09.py

```
from typing import Any, cast


def f(x: Any) -> Any:
        return x


a = f("a")      # inferred type is "Any"
a = cast(str, f("a"))      # forced type to be "str"
```

https://github.com/PacktPublishing/Building-Data-Science-Applications-with-FastAPI-Second-Edition/blob/main/chapter02/chapter02_type_hints_09.py

Be careful though: the `cast` function is only meaningful for type checkers. As for every other type of annotation, the interpreter completely ignores it and *doesn't* perform a real cast.

While convenient, try to refrain from using those utilities too often. If everything is Any or cast to a different type, you completely miss the benefits of static type checking.

As we have seen, type hinting and type checking are really helpful in reducing errors while developing and maintaining high-quality code. But that's not all. Actually, Python allows you to retrieve type annotations at runtime and perform some logic based on them. This enables you to do clever things such as **dependency injection**: just by type hinting an argument in a function, a library can automatically interpret it and inject the corresponding value at runtime. This concept is at the heart of FastAPI.

Another key approach in FastAPI is **asynchronous I/O**. This will be the last subject we'll cover in this chapter.

Working with asynchronous I/O

If you have already worked with JavaScript and Node.js, you have probably come across the concepts of *promises* and `async`/`await` keywords, which are characteristic of the asynchronous I/O paradigm. Basically, this is a way to make I/O operations non-blocking and allow the program to perform other tasks while the read or write operation is ongoing. The main motivation behind this is that I/O operations are *slow*: reading from disk, network requests are *million* times slower than reading from RAM or processing instructions. In the following example, we have a simple script that reads a file on disk:

chapter02_asyncio_01.py

```
with open(__file__) as f:
        data = f.read()
# The program will block here until the data has been read
print(data)
```

```
https://github.com/PacktPublishing/Building-Data-Science-Applica-
tions-with-FastAPI-Second-Edition/blob/main/chapter02/chapter02_
asyncio_01.py
```

We see that the script will block until we have retrieved the data from the disk and, as we said, this can be a long time. 99% percent of the execution time of the program is spent on waiting for the disk. Usually, it's not an issue for simple scripts like this because you probably won't have to perform other operations in the meantime.

However, in other situations, it could be an opportunity to perform other tasks. The typical case that is of great interest in this book is web servers. Imagine we have a first user making a request that performs a 10-second-long database query before sending the response. If a second user makes another request in the meantime, they'll have to wait for the first response to finish before getting their answer.

To solve this, traditional Python web servers based on the **Web Server Gateway Interface** (**WSGI**), such as Flask or Django, spawn several **workers**. Those are sub-processes of the web server that are all able to answer requests. If one is busy processing a long request, others can answer new requests.

With asynchronous I/O, a single process won't block when processing a request with a long I/O operation. While it waits for this operation to finish, it can answer other requests. When the I/O operation is done, it resumes the request logic and can finally answer the request.

Technically, this is achieved through the concept of an **event loop**. Think of it as a conductor that will manage all the asynchronous tasks you send to it. When data is available or when the write operation is done for one of those tasks, it'll ping the main program so that it can perform the next operations. Underneath, it relies upon the operating system `select` and `poll` calls, which are precisely there to ask for events about I/O operations at the operating system level. You can read very interesting details about this in the article *Async IO on Linux: select, poll, and epoll* by Julia Evans: `https://jvns.ca/blog/2017/06/03/async-io-on-linux--select--poll--and-epoll.`

Python first implemented asynchronous I/O in version 3.4 and it has since greatly evolved, notably with the introduction of the `async`/`await` keywords in version 3.6. All the utilities to manage this paradigm are available through the standard `asyncio` module. Not long after, the spiritual successor of WSGI for asynchronous-enabled web servers, **Asynchronous Server Gateway Interface** (**ASGI**), was introduced. FastAPI relies on this, and this is one of the reasons why it shows such *great performance*.

We'll now review the basics of asynchronous programming in Python. The following example is a simple *Hello world* script using `asyncio`:

chapter02_asyncio_02.py

```
import asyncio

async def main():
        print("Hello ...")
        await asyncio.sleep(1)
        print("... World!")

asyncio.run(main())
```

https://github.com/PacktPublishing/Building-Data-Science-Applications-with-FastAPI-Second-Edition/blob/main/chapter02/chapter02_asyncio_02.py

When you wish to define an asynchronous function, you just have to add the `async` keyword before `def`. This allows you to use the `await` keyword inside it. Such async functions are called **coroutines**.

Inside it, we first call the `print` function and then call the `asyncio.sleep` coroutine. This is the `async` equivalent of `time.sleep`, which blocks the program for a given number of seconds. Notice that we prefixed the call with the `await` keyword. This means that we want to wait for this coroutine to finish before proceeding. This is the main benefit of `async`/`await` keywords: writing code that *looks like* synchronous code. If we omitted `await`, the coroutine object would have been created but never executed.

Finally, notice that we use the `asyncio.run` function. This is the machinery that will create a new event loop, execute your coroutine, and return its result. It should be the main entry point of your `async` program.

This example is nice but not very interesting from an asynchronous point of view: since we are waiting for only one operation, this is not very impressive. Let's see an example where we execute two coroutines concurrently:

chapter02_asyncio_03.py

```python
import asyncio

async def printer(name: str, times: int) -> None:
        for i in range(times):
                print(name)
                await asyncio.sleep(1)

async def main():
        await asyncio.gather(
                printer("A", 3),
                printer("B", 3),
        )

asyncio.run(main())
```

https://github.com/PacktPublishing/Building-Data-Science-Applications-with-FastAPI-Second-Edition/blob/main/chapter02/chapter02_asyncio_03.py

Here, we have a `printer` coroutine that prints its name a given number of times. Between each print, it sleeps for 1 second.

Then, our main coroutine uses the `asyncio.gather` utility, which schedules several coroutines for concurrent execution. If you run this script, you'll get the following result:

```
$ python chapter02_asyncio_03.py
A
B
A
B
A
B
```

We get a succession of A and B. It means our coroutines were executed concurrently and that we didn't wait for the first one to finish before starting the second one.

You might wonder why we added the `asyncio.sleep` call in this example. Actually, if we removed it, we would have obtained this result:

```
A
A
A
B
B
B
```

That doesn't look very concurrent, and indeed, it's not. This is one of the main pitfalls of `asyncio`: writing code in a coroutine *doesn't necessarily mean* that it won't block. Regular operations such as computations *are* blocking and *will* block the event loop. Usually, this is not a problem since those operations are fast. The only operations that won't block are proper I/O operations that are *designed* to work asynchronously. This is different from **multiprocessing** where operations are executed on child processes, which, by nature, doesn't block the main one.

Because of this, you'll have to be careful when choosing a third-party library for interacting with databases, APIs, and so on. Some have been adapted to work asynchronously and some alternatives have been developed in parallel with the standard ones. We'll see some of them in the following chapters, especially when working with databases.

We'll end this quick introduction to asynchronous I/O here. There are some other subtleties underneath but, generally, the basics we've seen here will allow you to leverage the power of `asyncio` with FastAPI.

Summary

Congratulations! In this chapter, you discovered the basics of the Python language, a very clean and efficient language to work with. You were introduced to the more advanced concepts of list comprehensions and generators, which are idiomatic ways of handling sequences of data. Python is also a multi-paradigm language and you saw how to leverage the object-oriented syntax.

Finally, you discovered some of the most recent features of the language: type hinting, which allows static type checking to reduce errors and speed up development, and asynchronous I/O, a set of new tools and syntax to maximize performance and allow concurrency while doing I/O-bound operations.

You're now ready to begin your journey with FastAPI! You'll see that the framework takes advantage of all those Python features to propose a fast and enjoyable development experience. In the next chapter, you'll learn how to write your very first REST API with FastAPI.

3

Developing a RESTful API with FastAPI

Now it's time to begin learning about **FastAPI**! In this chapter, we'll cover the basics of FastAPI. We'll go through very simple and focused examples that will demonstrate the different features of FastAPI. Each example will lead to a working API endpoint that you'll be able to test yourself using HTTPie. In the final section of this chapter, we'll show you a more complex FastAPI project, with routes split across several files. It will give you an overview of how you can structure your own application.

By the end of this chapter, you'll know how to start a FastAPI application and how to write an API endpoint. You'll also be able to handle request data and build a response according to your own logic. Finally, you'll learn a way to structure a FastAPI project into several modules that will be easier to maintain and work with in the long term.

In this chapter, we'll cover the following main topics:

- Creating the first endpoint and running it locally
- Handling request parameters
- Customizing the response
- Structuring a bigger project with multiple routers

Technical requirements

You'll need a Python virtual environment, as we set up in *Chapter 1, Python Development Environment Setup*.

You'll find all the code examples of this chapter in the dedicated GitHub repository: `https://github.com/PacktPublishing/Building-Data-Science-Applications-with-FastAPI-Second-Edition/tree/main/chapter03`.

Creating a first endpoint and running it locally

FastAPI is a framework that is easy to use and quick to write. In the following example, you'll realize that this is not just a promise. In fact, creating an API endpoint involves just a few lines:

chapter03_first_endpoint_01.py

```python
from fastapi import FastAPI

app = FastAPI()

@app.get("/")
async def hello_world():
    return {"hello": "world"}
```

https://github.com/PacktPublishing/Building-Data-Science-Applica-tions-with-FastAPI-Second-Edition/tree/main/chapter03/chapter03_first_endpoint_01.py

In this example, we define a GET endpoint at the root path, which always returns the { "hello" : "world" } JSON response. To do this, we first instantiate a FastAPI object, app. It will be the main application object that will wire all the API routes.

Then, we simply define a coroutine that contains our route logic, the **path operation function**. Its return value is automatically handled by FastAPI to produce a proper HTTP response with a JSON payload.

Here, the most important part of this code is probably the line starting with @, which can be found above the coroutine definition, the **decorator**. In Python, a decorator is a syntactic sugar that allows you to wrap a function or class with common logic without compromising readability. It's roughly equivalent to app.get("/")(hello_world).

FastAPI exposes *one decorator per HTTP method* to add new routes to the application. The one shown here adds a GET endpoint with the **path** as the first argument.

Now, let's run this API. Copy the example to the root of your project and run the following command:

```
$ uvicorn chapter03_first_endpoint_01:app
INFO:       Started server process [21654]
INFO:       Waiting for application startup.
INFO:       Application startup complete.
INFO:       Uvicorn running on http://127.0.0.1:8000 (Press CTRL+C to
quit)
```

As we mentioned in *Chapter 2, Python Programming Specificities*, in the *Asynchronous I/O* section, FastAPI exposes an **Asynchronous Server Gateway Interface** (**ASGI**)-compatible application. To run it, we require a web server compatible with this protocol. Uvicorn is a good option to use. It gives a command to quickly start a web server. In the first argument, it expects the *dotted namespace* of the Python module, which contains your app instance, followed by a colon, `:`, and, finally, the variable name of your ASGI app instance (in our example, this is `app`). Afterward, it takes care of instantiating the application and exposing it on your local machine.

Let's try our endpoint with HTTPie. Open another terminal and run the following command:

```
$ http http://localhost:8000
HTTP/1.1 200 OK
content-length: 17
content-type: application/json
date: Thu, 10 Nov 2022 07:52:36 GMT
server: uvicorn

{
    "hello": "world"
}
```

It works! As you can see, we did get a JSON response with the payload we wanted, using just a few lines of Python and a command!

One of the most beloved features of FastAPI is the *automatic interactive documentation*. If you open the `http://localhost:8000/docs` URL in your browser, you should get a web interface that looks similar to the following screenshot:

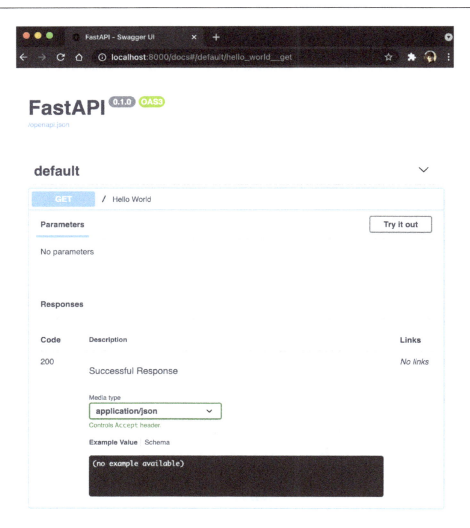

Figure 3.1 – The FastAPI automatic interactive documentation

FastAPI will automatically list all your defined endpoints and provide documentation about the expected inputs and outputs. You can even try each endpoint directly in this web interface. Under the hood, it relies on the OpenAPI specification and the associated tools from Swagger. You can read more about this on its official website at `https://swagger.io/`.

That's it! You've created your very first API with FastAPI. Of course, this is just a very simple example, but next, you'll learn how to handle input data and start making meaningful things!

> **On the shoulder of giants**
>
> It's worth noting that FastAPI is built upon two main Python libraries: Starlette, a low-level ASGI web framework (`https://www.starlette.io/`), and Pydantic, a data validation library based on type hints (`https://pydantic-docs.helpmanual.io/`).

Handling request parameters

The main goal of a **representational state transfer** (**REST**) API is to provide a structured way to interact with data. As such, it's crucial for the end user to send some information to tailor the response they need, such as path parameters, query parameters, body payloads, headers, and so on.

Web frameworks usually ask you to manipulate a request object to retrieve the parts you are interested in and manually apply validation to handle them. However, that's not necessary with FastAPI! Indeed, it allows you to define all of your parameters declaratively. Then, it'll automatically retrieve them in the request and apply validation based on the type hints. This is why we introduced type hinting in *Chapter 2, Python Programming Specificities*: it's used by FastAPI to perform data validation!

Next, we'll explore how you can use this feature to retrieve and validate this input data from different parts of the request.

Path parameters

The API path is the main thing that the end user will interact with. Therefore, it's a good spot for dynamic parameters. A typical example is to put the unique identifier of an object we want to retrieve, such as `/users/123`. Let's examine how to define this with FastAPI:

chapter03_path_parameters_01.py

```python
from fastapi import FastAPI

app = FastAPI()

@app.get("/users/{id}")
async def get_user(id: int):
    return {"id": id}
```

`https://github.com/PacktPublishing/Building-Data-Science-Applications-with-FastAPI-Second-Edition/tree/main/chapter03/chapter03_path_parameters_01.py`

In this example, we defined an API that expects an integer in the last part of its path. We did this by putting the parameter name in the path around curly braces. Then, we defined this same parameter as an argument for our path operation function. Notice that we add a type hint to specify that the parameter is an integer.

Let's run this example. You can refer to the previous *Creating a first endpoint and running it locally* section, to learn how to run a FastAPI app with Uvicorn.

First, we'll try to make a request that omits our path parameter:

```
$ http http://localhost:8000/users
HTTP/1.1 404 Not Found
content-length: 22
content-type: application/json
date: Thu, 10 Nov 2022 08:20:51 GMT
server: uvicorn


{
    "detail": "Not Found"
}
```

We get a response with a 404 status. That's expected: our route awaits a parameter after /users, so if we omit it, it simply doesn't match any pattern.

Let's now try with a proper integer parameter:

```
http http://localhost:8000/users/123
HTTP/1.1 200 OK
content-length: 10
content-type: application/json
date: Thu, 10 Nov 2022 08:21:27 GMT
server: uvicorn


{
    "id": 123
}
```

It works! We get a 200 status, and the response does contain the integer we passed in the parameter. Notice that it has been properly *cast* as an integer.

So, what happens if we pass a value that's not a valid integer? Let's find out:

```
$ http http://localhost:8000/users/abc
HTTP/1.1 422 Unprocessable Entity
content-length: 99
content-type: application/json
date: Thu, 10 Nov 2022 08:22:35 GMT
```

```
server: uvicorn

{
    "detail": [
        {
            "loc": [
                "path",
                "id"
            ],
            "msg": "value is not a valid integer",
            "type": "type_error.integer"
        }
    ]
}
```

We get a response with a 422 status! Since abc is not a valid integer, the validation fails and outputs an error. Notice that we have a very detailed and structured error response telling us exactly which element caused the error and why. All we need to do to trigger this validation is to *type hint* our parameter!

Of course, you are not limited to just one path parameter. You can have as many as you want, with different types. In the following example, we've added a type parameter of the string type:

chapter03_path_parameters_02.py

```python
from fastapi import FastAPI

app = FastAPI()

@app.get("/users/{type}/{id}")
async def get_user(type: str, id: int):
    return {"type": type, "id": id}
```

https://github.com/PacktPublishing/Building-Data-Science-Applications-with-FastAPI-Second-Edition/tree/main/chapter03/chapter03_path_parameters_02.py

This works well, but the endpoint will accept any string as the type parameter.

Limiting allowed values

So, what if we just want to accept a limited set of values? Once again, we'll lean on type hinting. Python has a very useful class for this: Enum. An enumeration is a way to list all the valid values for a specific kind of data. Let's define an Enum class that will list the different types of users:

chapter03_path_parameters_03.py

```
class UserType(str, Enum):
    STANDARD = "standard"
    ADMIN = "admin"
```

https://github.com/PacktPublishing/Building-Data-Science-Applications-with-FastAPI-Second-Edition/tree/main/chapter03/chapter03_path_parameters_03.py

To define a string enumeration, we inherit from both the str type and the Enum class. Then, we simply list the allowed values as class properties: the property name and its actual string value. Finally, we only have to type hint the type argument with this class:

chapter03_path_parameters_03.py

```
@app.get("/users/{type}/{id}")
async def get_user(type: UserType, id: int):
    return {"type": type, "id": id}
```

https://github.com/PacktPublishing/Building-Data-Science-Applications-with-FastAPI-Second-Edition/tree/main/chapter03/chapter03_path_parameters_03.py

If you run this example and call the endpoint with a type that is not in the enumeration, you'll get the following response:

```
$ http http://localhost:8000/users/hello/123
HTTP/1.1 422 Unprocessable Entity
content-length: 184
content-type: application/json
date: Thu, 10 Nov 2022 08:33:36 GMT
server: uvicorn

{
    "detail": [
        {
            "ctx": {
                "enum_values": [
```

```
                        "standard",
                        "admin"
                    ]
                },
                "loc": [
                    "path",
                    "type"
                ],
                "msg": "value is not a valid enumeration member;
    permitted: 'standard', 'admin'",
                "type": "type_error.enum"
            }
        ]
    }
```

As you can see, you get a nice validation error with the allowed values for this parameter!

Advanced validation

We can take one step further by defining more advanced validation rules, particularly for numbers and strings. In this case, the type of hint is no longer enough. We'll rely on the functions provided by FastAPI, allowing us to set some options on each of our parameters. For path parameters, the function is named `Path`. In the following example, we'll only allow an `id` argument that is greater than or equal to `1`:

---

chapter03_path_parameters_04.py

```python
from fastapi import FastAPI, Path

app = FastAPI()

@app.get("/users/{id}")
async def get_user(id: int = Path(..., ge=1)):
    return {"id": id}
```

https://github.com/PacktPublishing/Building-Data-Science-Applications-with-FastAPI-Second-Edition/tree/main/chapter03/chapter03_path_parameters_04.py

---

There are several things to pay attention to here: the result of `Path` is used as a *default value* for the `id` argument in the path operation function.

Additionally, you can see that we use the **ellipsis** syntax as the first parameter of `Path`. Indeed, it expects the default value for the parameter as the first argument. In this scenario, we don't want a default value: the parameter is required. Therefore, ellipses are here to tell FastAPI that we don't want a default value.

> **Ellipsis doesn't always mean this in Python**
>
> Using the ellipsis symbol to specify that a parameter is required, as we show here, is specific to FastAPI: it's the choice of FastAPI creators to use it like this. In other Python programs, this symbol could be used for another means.

Then, we can add the keyword arguments we are interested in. In our example, we use ge, greater than or equal to, and its associated value. Here is the list of available keywords to validate numbers:

- gt: Greater than
- ge: Greater than or equal to
- lt: Less than
- le: Less than or equal to

There are also validation options for string values, which are based on *length* and *regular expression*. In the following example, we want to define a path parameter that accepts license plates in the form of AB-123-CD (French license plates). A first approach would be to force the string to be a length of 9 (that is, two letters, a dash, three digits, a dash, and two letters):

chapter03_path_parameters_05.py

```python
@app.get("/license-plates/{license}")
async def get_license_plate(license: str = Path(..., min_length=9,
max_length=9)):
    return {"license": license}
```

https://github.com/PacktPublishing/Building-Data-Science-Applications-with-FastAPI-Second-Edition/tree/main/chapter03/chapter03_path_parameters_05.py

Now we just have to define the min_length and max_length keyword arguments, just as we did for the number of validations. Of course, a better solution for this use case is to use a regular expression to validate the license plate number:

chapter03_path_parameters_06.py

```python
@app.get("/license-plates/{license}")
async def get_license_plate(license: str = Path(..., regex=r"^\w{2}-
\d{3}-\w{2}$")):
    return {"license": license}
```

https://github.com/PacktPublishing/Building-Data-Science-Applications-with-FastAPI-Second-Edition/tree/main/chapter03/chapter03_path_parameters_06.py

Thanks to this regular expression, we only accept strings that exactly match the license plate format. Notice that the regular expression is prefixed with `r`. Just like `f-strings`, this is a Python syntax that is used to indicate that the following string should be considered a regular expression.

Parameter metadata

Data validation is not the only option accepted by the parameter function. You can also set options that will add information about the parameter in the automatic documentation, such as `title`, `description`, and `deprecated`.

Now you should be able to define path parameters and apply some validation to them. Other useful parameters to put inside the URL are **query parameters**. We'll discuss them next.

Query parameters

Query parameters are a common way to add some dynamic parameters to a URL. You can find them at the end of the URL in the following form: `?param1=foo&param2=bar`. In a REST API, they are commonly used on read endpoints to apply pagination, a filter, a sorting order, or selecting fields.

You'll discover that they are quite straightforward to define with FastAPI. In fact, they use the exact same syntax as path parameters:

---

chapter03_query_parameters_01.py

```
@app.get("/users")
async def get_user(page: int = 1, size: int = 10):
    return {"page": page, "size": size}
```

https://github.com/PacktPublishing/Building-Data-Science-Applications-with-FastAPI-Second-Edition/tree/main/chapter03/chapter03_query_parameters_01.py

---

You simply have to declare them as arguments of your path operation function. If they don't appear in the path pattern, as they do for path parameters, FastAPI automatically considers them to be query parameters. Let's try it:

```
$ http "http://localhost:8000/users?page=5&size=50"
HTTP/1.1 200 OK
content-length: 20
content-type: application/json
date: Thu, 10 Nov 2022 09:35:05 GMT
server: uvicorn

{
```

```
      "page": 5,
      "size": 50
}
```

Here, you can see that we have defined a default value for those arguments, which means they are *optional* when calling the API. Of course, if you wish to define a *required* query parameter, simply leave out the default value:

chapter03_query_parameters_02.py

```
from enum import Enum

from fastapi import FastAPI

class UsersFormat(str, Enum):
    SHORT = "short"
    FULL = "full"

app = FastAPI()

@app.get("/users")
async def get_user(format: UsersFormat):
    return {"format": format}
```

https://github.com/PacktPublishing/Building-Data-Science-Applica-
tions-with-FastAPI-Second-Edition/tree/main/chapter03/chapter03_
query_parameters_02.py

Now, if you omit the `format` parameter in the URL, you'll get a 422 error response. Additionally, notice that, in this example, we defined a `UsersFormat` enumeration to limit the number of allowed values for this parameter; this is exactly what we did in the previous section for path parameters.

We also have access to more advanced validations through the `Query` function. It works in the same way that we demonstrated in the *Path parameters* section:

chapter03_query_parameters_03.py

```
from fastapi import FastAPI, Query

app = FastAPI()

@app.get("/users")
async def get_user(page: int = Query(1, gt=0), size: int = Query(10,
```

```
le=100)):
    return {"page": page, "size": size}
```

Here, we force the page to be *greater than 0* and the size to be *less than or equal to 100*. Notice how the default parameter value is the first argument of the Query function.

Naturally, when it comes to sending request data, the most obvious way is to use the request body. Let's examine how it works.

The request body

The body is the part of the HTTP request that contains raw data representing documents, files, or form submissions. In a REST API, it's usually encoded in JSON and used to create structured objects in a database.

For the simplest cases, retrieving data from the body works exactly like query parameters. The only difference is that you always have to use the Body function; otherwise, FastAPI will look for it inside the query parameters by default. Let's explore a simple example where we want to post some user data:

chapter03_request_body_01.py

```
@app.post("/users")
async def create_user(name: str = Body(...), age: int = Body(...)):
    return {"name": name, "age": age}
```

In the same way as query parameters, we define each argument with a type hint along with the Body function with no default value to make them required. Let's try the following endpoint:

```
$ http -v POST http://localhost:8000/users name="John" age=30
POST /users HTTP/1.1
Accept: application/json, */*;q=0.5
Accept-Encoding: gzip, deflate
Connection: keep-alive
Content-Length: 29
Content-Type: application/json
Host: localhost:8000
User-Agent: HTTPie/3.2.1
```

```
{
    "age": "30",
    "name": "John"
}

HTTP/1.1 200 OK
content-length: 24
content-type: application/json
date: Thu, 10 Nov 2022 09:42:24 GMT
server: uvicorn

{
    "age": 30,
    "name": "John"
}
```

Here, we used the -v option of HTTPie so that you can clearly see the JSON payload we sent. FastAPI successfully retrieves the data for each field from the payload. If you send a request with a missing or invalid field, you'll get a 422 status error response.

You also have access to more advanced validation through the Body function. It works in the same way as we demonstrated in the *Path parameters* section.

However, defining payload validations such as this has some major drawbacks. First, it's quite verbose and makes the path operation function prototype huge, especially for bigger models. Second, usually, you'll need to reuse the data structure on other endpoints or in other parts of your application.

This is why FastAPI uses **Pydantic models** for data validation. Pydantic is a Python library for *data validation* and is based on classes and type hints. In fact, the Path, Query, and Body functions that we've learned about so far use Pydantic under the hood!

By defining your own Pydantic models and using them as type hints in your path arguments, FastAPI will automatically instantiate a model instance and validate the data. Let's rewrite our previous example using this method:

chapter03_request_body_02.py

```
from fastapi import FastAPI
from pydantic import BaseModel

class User(BaseModel):
    name: str
    age: int

app = FastAPI()
```

```
@app.post("/users")
async def create_user(user: User):
    return user
```

https://github.com/PacktPublishing/Building-Data-Science-Applications-with-FastAPI-Second-Edition/tree/main/chapter03/chapter03_request_body_02.py

First, we import `BaseModel` from `pydantic`. This is the base class that *every* model should inherit from. Then, we define our `User` class and list all of the properties as *class properties*. Each one of them should have a proper type hint: this is how Pydantic will be able to validate the type of the field.

Finally, we just declare `user` as an argument for our path operation function with the `User` class as a type hint. FastAPI automatically understands that the user data can be found in the request payload. Inside the function, you have access to a proper `user` object instance, where you can access individual properties by simply using the dot notation, such as `user.name`.

Notice that if you just return the object, FastAPI is smart enough to convert it automatically into JSON to produce the HTTP response.

In the following chapter, *Chapter 4*, *Managing Pydantic Data Models in FastAPI*, we'll explore, in more detail, the possibilities of Pydantic, particularly in terms of validation.

Multiple objects

Sometimes, you might have several objects that you wish to send in the same payload all at once. For example, both `user` and `company`. In this scenario, you can simply add several arguments that have been type hinted by a Pydantic model, and FastAPI will automatically understand that there are several objects. In this configuration, it will expect a body containing each object *indexed by its argument name*:

chapter03_request_body_03.py

```
@app.post("/users")
async def create_user(user: User, company: Company):
    return {"user": user, "company": company}
```

https://github.com/PacktPublishing/Building-Data-Science-Applications-with-FastAPI-Second-Edition/tree/main/chapter03/chapter03_request_body_03.py

Here, Company is a simple Pydantic model with a single string name property. In this configuration, FastAPI expects a payload that looks similar to the following:

```
{
    "user": {
        "name": "John",
        "age": 30
    },
    "company": {
        "name": "ACME"
    }
}
```

For more complex JSON structures, it's advised that you *pipe* a formatted JSON into HTTPie rather than use parameters. Let's try this as follows:

```
$ echo '{"user": {"name": "John", "age": 30}, "company": {"name":
"ACME"}}' | http POST http://localhost:8000/users
HTTP/1.1 200 OK
content-length: 59
content-type: application/json
date: Thu, 10 Nov 2022 09:52:12 GMT
server: uvicorn

{
    "company": {
        "name": "ACME"
    },
    "user": {
        "age": 30,
        "name": "John"
    }
}
```

And that's it!

You can even add **singular body values** with the Body function, just as we saw at the beginning of this section. This is useful if you wish to have a single property that's not part of any model:

chapter03_request_body_04.py

```
@app.post("/users")
async def create_user(user: User, priority: int = Body(..., ge=1,
le=3)):
    return {"user": user, "priority": priority}
```

```
https://github.com/PacktPublishing/Building-Data-Science-Applica-
tions-with-FastAPI-Second-Edition/tree/main/chapter03/chapter03_
request_body_04.py
```

The `priority` property is an integer between 1 and 3, which is expected *beside* the `user` object:

```
$ echo '{"user": {"name": "John", "age": 30}, "priority": 1}' | http
POST http://localhost:8000/users
HTTP/1.1 200 OK
content-length: 46
content-type: application/json
date: Thu, 10 Nov 2022 09:53:51 GMT
server: uvicorn

{
    "priority": 1,
    "user": {
        "age": 30,
        "name": "John"
    }
}
```

You now have a good overview of how to handle JSON payload data. However, sometimes, you'll find that you need to accept more traditional-form data or even file uploads. Let's find out how to do this next!

Form data and file uploads

Even if REST APIs work most of the time with JSON, sometimes, you might have to handle form-encoded data or file uploads, which have been encoded either as `application/x-www-form-urlencoded` or `multipart/form-data`.

Once again, FastAPI allows you to implement this case very easily. However, you'll need an additional Python dependency, `python-multipart`, to handle this kind of data. As usual, you can install it with `pip`:

```
$ pip install python-multipart
```

Then, you can use the FastAPI features that are dedicated to form data. First, let's take a look at how you can handle simple form data.

Form data

The method to retrieve form data fields is similar to the one we discussed in the *The request body* section to retrieve singular JSON properties. The following example is roughly the same as the one you explored there. However, this example expects form-encoded data instead of JSON:

chapter03_form_data_01.py

```
@app.post("/users")
async def create_user(name: str = Form(...), age: int = Form(...)):
    return {"name": name, "age": age}
```

https://github.com/PacktPublishing/Building-Data-Science-Applica-tions-with-FastAPI-Second-Edition/tree/main/chapter03/chapter03_form_data_01.py

The only difference here is that we use the Form function instead of Body. You can try this endpoint with HTTPie and the --form option to force the data to be form-encoded:

```
$ http -v --form POST http://localhost:8000/users name=John age=30
POST /users HTTP/1.1
Accept: */*
Accept-Encoding: gzip, deflate
Connection: keep-alive
Content-Length: 16
Content-Type: application/x-www-form-urlencoded; charset=utf-8
Host: localhost:8000
User-Agent: HTTPie/3.2.1

name=John&age=30

HTTP/1.1 200 OK
content-length: 24
content-type: application/json
date: Thu, 10 Nov 2022 09:56:28 GMT
server: uvicorn

{
    "age": 30,
    "name": "John"
}
```

Pay attention to how the Content-Type header and the body data representation have changed in the request. You can also see that the response is still provided in JSON. Unless specified otherwise, FastAPI will always output a JSON response by default, no matter the form of the input data.

Of course, the validation options we saw for Path, Query, and Body are still available. You can find a description for each of them in the *Path parameters* section.

It's worth noting that, contrary to JSON payloads, FastAPI doesn't allow you to define Pydantic models to validate form data. Instead, you have to manually define each field as an argument for the path operation function.

Now, let's go on to discuss how to handle file uploads.

File uploads

Uploading files is a common requirement for web applications, whether this is images or documents. FastAPI provides a parameter function, File, that enables this.

Let's take a look at a simple example where you can directly retrieve a file as a bytes object:

chapter03_file_uploads_01.py

```
from fastapi import FastAPI, File

app = FastAPI()

@app.post("/files")
async def upload_file(file: bytes = File(...)):
    return {"file_size": len(file)}
```

https://github.com/PacktPublishing/Building-Data-Science-Applications-with-FastAPI-Second-Edition/tree/main/chapter03/chapter03_file_uploads_01.py

Once again, you can see that the approach is still the same: we define an argument for the path operation function, file, add a type hint, bytes, and then we use the File function as a default value for this argument. By doing this, FastAPI understands that it will have to retrieve raw data in a part of the body named file and return it as bytes.

We simply return the size of this file by calling the len function on this bytes object.

In the code example repository, you should be able to find a picture of a cat: https://github.com/PacktPublishing/ Building-Data-Science-Applications-with-FastAPI-Second-Edition/blob/main/assets/cat.jpg.

Let's upload it on our endpoint using HTTPie. To upload a file, type in the name of the file upload field (here, it is `file`), followed by @ and the path of the file you want to upload. Don't forget to set the `--form` option:

```
$ http --form POST http://localhost:8000/files file@./assets/cat.jpg
HTTP/1.1 200 OK
content-length: 19
content-type: application/json
date: Thu, 10 Nov 2022 10:00:38 GMT
server: uvicorn

{
    "file_size": 71457
}
```

It works! We have correctly got the size of the file in bytes.

One drawback to this approach is that the uploaded file is entirely stored *in memory*. So, while it'll work for small files, it is likely that you'll run into issues for larger files. Besides, manipulating a `bytes` object is not always convenient for file handling.

To fix this problem, FastAPI provides an `UploadFile` class. This class will store the data in memory up to a certain threshold and, after this, will automatically store it *on disk* in a temporary location. This allows you to accept much larger files without running out of memory. Furthermore, the exposed object instance exposes useful metadata, such as the content type, and a **file-like** interface. This means that you can manipulate it as a regular file in Python and feed it to any function that expects a file.

To use it, you simply have to specify it as a type hint instead of `bytes`:

chapter03_file_uploads_02.py

```python
from fastapi import FastAPI, File, UploadFile

app = FastAPI()

@app.post("/files")
async def upload_file(file: UploadFile = File(...)):
    return {"file_name": file.filename, "content_type": file.content_
type}
```

```
https://github.com/PacktPublishing/Building-Data-Science-Applica-
tions-with-FastAPI-Second-Edition/tree/main/chapter03/chapter03_
file_uploads_02.py
```

Notice that, here, we return the `filename` and `content_type` properties. The content type is especially useful for *checking the type* of the uploaded file and possibly rejecting it if it's not one of the types you expect.

Here is the result with HTTPie:

```
$ http --form POST http://localhost:8000/files file@./assets/cat.jpg
HTTP/1.1 200 OK
content-length: 51
content-type: application/json
date: Thu, 10 Nov 2022 10:04:22 GMT
server: uvicorn

{
    "content_type": "image/jpeg",
    "file_name": "cat.jpg"
}
```

You can even accept multiple files by type hinting the argument as a list of `UploadFile`:

chapter03_file_uploads_03.py

```
@app.post("/files")
async def upload_multiple_files(files: list[UploadFile] = File(...)):
    return [
        {"file_name": file.filename, "content_type": file.content_
type}
        for file in files
    ]
```

https://github.com/PacktPublishing/Building-Data-Science-Applica-
tions-with-FastAPI-Second-Edition/tree/main/chapter03/chapter03_
file_uploads_03.py

To upload several files with HTTPie, simply repeat the argument. It should appear as follows:

```
$ http --form POST http://localhost:8000/files files@./assets/cat.jpg
files@./assets/cat.jpg
HTTP/1.1 200 OK
content-length: 105
content-type: application/json
date: Thu, 10 Nov 2022 10:06:09 GMT
server: uvicorn

[
    {
```

```
            "content_type": "image/jpeg",
            "file_name": "cat.jpg"
        },
        {
            "content_type": "image/jpeg",
            "file_name": "cat.jpg"
        }
    ]
```

Now, you should be able to handle form data and file uploads in a FastAPI application. So far, you've learned how to manage user-facing data. However, there are also very interesting pieces of information that are less visible: **headers**. We'll explore them next.

Headers and cookies

Besides the URL and the body, another major part of the HTTP request are the headers. They contain all sorts of metadata that can be useful when handling requests. A common usage is to use them for authentication, for example, via the famous **cookies**.

Once again, retrieving them in FastAPI only involves a type hint and a parameter function. Let's take a look at a simple example where we want to retrieve a header named `Hello`:

chapter03_headers_cookies_01.py

```
@app.get("/")
async def get_header(hello: str = Header(...)):
    return {"hello": hello}
```

https://github.com/PacktPublishing/Building-Data-Science-Applica-
tions-with-FastAPI-Second-Edition/tree/main/chapter03/chapter03_
headers_cookies_01.py

Here, you can see that we simply have to use the `Header` function as a default value for the `hello` argument. The name of the argument determines the *key of the header* that we want to retrieve. Let's see this in action:

```
$ http GET http://localhost:8000 'Hello: World'
HTTP/1.1 200 OK
content-length: 17
content-type: application/json
date: Thu, 10 Nov 2022 10:10:12 GMT
server: uvicorn

{
```

```
        "hello": "World"
}
```

FastAPI was able to retrieve the header value. Since there was no default value specified (we put in an ellipsis), the header is required. If it's missing, once again, you'll get a 422 status error response.

Additionally, notice that FastAPI automatically converts the header name into *lowercase*. Besides that, since header names are usually separated by a hyphen, -, it also automatically converts it into snake case. Therefore, it works out of the box with any valid Python variable name. The following example shows this behavior by retrieving the User-Agent header:

chapter03_headers_cookies_02.py

```
@app.get("/")
async def get_header(user_agent: str = Header(...)):
    return {"user_agent": user_agent}
```

```
https://github.com/PacktPublishing/Building-Data-Science-Applica-
tions-with-FastAPI-Second-Edition/tree/main/chapter03/chapter03_
headers_cookies_02.py
```

Now, let's make a very simple request. We'll keep the default user agent of HTTPie to see what happens:

```
$ http -v GET http://localhost:8000
GET / HTTP/1.1
Accept: */*
Accept-Encoding: gzip, deflate
Connection: keep-alive
Host: localhost:8000
User-Agent: HTTPie/3.2.1

HTTP/1.1 200 OK
content-length: 29
content-type: application/json
date: Thu, 10 Nov 2022 10:12:17 GMT
server: uvicorn

{
    "user_agent": "HTTPie/3.2.1"
}
```

> **What is a user agent?**
>
> The user agent is an HTTP header added automatically by most HTTP clients, such as HTTPie or cURL and web browsers. It's a way for web servers to identify which kind of application made the request. In some cases, web servers can use this information to adapt the response.

One very special case of the header is cookies. You could retrieve them by parsing the `Cookie` header yourself, but that would be a bit tedious. FastAPI provides another parameter function that automatically does it for you.

The following example simply retrieves a cookie named `hello`:

chapter03_headers_cookies_03.py

```
@app.get("/")
async def get_cookie(hello: str | None = Cookie(None)):
    return {"hello": hello}
```

https://github.com/PacktPublishing/Building-Data-Science-Applica-
tions-with-FastAPI-Second-Edition/tree/main/chapter03/chapter03_
headers_cookies_03.py

Notice that we type hinted the argument as `str | None`, and we set a default value of `None` to the `Cookie` function. This way, even if the cookie is not set in the request, FastAPI will proceed and not generate a `422` status error response.

Headers and cookies can be very useful tools for implementing authentication features. In *Chapter 7, Managing Authentication and Security in FastAPI*, you'll learn that there are built-in security functions that can help you to implement common authentication schemes.

The request object

Sometimes, you might find that you need to access a raw request object with all of the data associated with it. That's possible. Simply declare an argument on your path operation function type hinted with the `Request` class:

chapter03_request_object_01.py

```
from fastapi import FastAPI, Request

app = FastAPI()

@app.get("/")
```

```
async def get_request_object(request: Request):
    return {"path": request.url.path}
```

https://github.com/PacktPublishing/Building-Data-Science-Applications-with-FastAPI-Second-Edition/tree/main/chapter03/chapter03_request_object_01.py

Under the hood, this is the `Request` object from Starlette, which is a library that provides all the core server logic for FastAPI. You can view a complete description of the methods and properties of this object in the official documentation of Starlette (`https://www.starlette.io/requests/`).

Congratulations! You have now learned all of the basics regarding how to handle request data in FastAPI. As you learned, the logic is the same no matter what part of the HTTP request you want to look at. Simply name the argument you want to retrieve, add a type hint, and use a parameter function to tell FastAPI where it should look. You can even add some validation logic!

In the next section, we'll explore the other side of a REST API job: returning a response.

Customizing the response

In the previous sections, you learned that directly returning a dictionary or a Pydantic object in your path operation function was enough for FastAPI to return a JSON response.

Most of the time, you'll want to customize this response a bit further; for instance, by changing the status code, raising validation errors, and setting cookies. FastAPI offers different ways to do this, from the simplest case to the most advanced one. First, we'll learn how to customize the response declaratively by using path operation parameters.

Path operation parameters

In the *Creating a first endpoint and running it locally* section, you learned that in order to create a new endpoint, you had to put a decorator on top of the path operation function. This decorator accepts a lot of options, including ones to customize the response.

The status code

The most obvious thing to customize in an HTTP response is the **status code**. By default, FastAPI will always set a 200 status when everything goes well during your path operation function execution.

Sometimes, it might be useful to change this status. For example, it's good practice in a REST API to return a 201 Created status when the execution of the endpoint ends up in the creation of a new object.

To set this, simply specify the status_code argument on the path decorator:

chapter03_response_path_parameters_01.py

```
from fastapi import FastAPI, status
from pydantic import BaseModel

class Post(BaseModel):
    title: str

app = FastAPI()

@app.post("/posts", status_code=status.HTTP_201_CREATED)
async def create_post(post: Post):
    return post
```

https://github.com/PacktPublishing/Building-Data-Science-Applications-with-FastAPI-Second-Edition/tree/main/chapter03/chapter03_response_path_parameters_01.py

The decorator arguments come right after the path as keyword arguments. The status_code option simply expects an integer representing the status code. We could have written status_code=201, but FastAPI provides a useful list in the status sub-module that improves code comprehensiveness, as you can see here.

We can try this endpoint to obtain the resulting status code:

```
$ http POST http://localhost:8000/posts title="Hello"
HTTP/1.1 201 Created
content-length: 17
content-type: application/json
date: Thu, 10 Nov 2022 10:24:24 GMT
server: uvicorn

{
    "title": "Hello"
}
```

We got our 201 status code.

It's important to understand that this option to override the status code is only useful *when everything goes well*. If your input data was invalid, you would still get a 422 status error response.

Another interesting scenario for this option is when you have nothing to return, such as when you delete an object. In this case, the 204 No content status code is a good fit. In the following example, we implement a simple delete endpoint that sets this response status code:

chapter03_response_path_parameters_02.py

```
# Dummy database
posts = {
    1: Post(title="Hello", nb_views=100),
}


@app.delete("/posts/{id}", status_code=status.HTTP_204_NO_CONTENT)
async def delete_post(id: int):
    posts.pop(id, None)
    return None
```

https://github.com/PacktPublishing/Building-Data-Science-Applica-
tions-with-FastAPI-Second-Edition/tree/main/chapter03/chapter03_
response_path_parameters_02.py

Notice that you can very well return None in your path operation function. FastAPI will take care of it and return a response with an empty body.

In the *Setting the status code dynamically* section, you'll learn how to customize the status code dynamically inside the path operation logic.

The response model

With FastAPI, the main use case is to directly return a Pydantic model that automatically gets turned into properly formatted JSON. However, quite often, you'll find that there are some differences between the input data, the data you store in your database, and the data you want to show to the end user. For instance, perhaps some fields are private or only for internal use, or perhaps some fields are only useful during the creation process and then discarded afterward.

Now, let's consider a simple example. Assume you have a database containing blog posts. Those blog posts have several properties, such as a title, content, or creation date. Additionally, you store the number of views of each one, but you don't want the end user to see it.

You could take the standard approach as follows:

chapter03_response_path_parameters_03.py

```
from fastapi import FastAPI
from pydantic import BaseModel
```

```python
class Post(BaseModel):
    title: str
    nb_views: int

app = FastAPI()

# Dummy database
posts = {
    1: Post(title="Hello", nb_views=100),
}

@app.get("/posts/{id}")
async def get_post(id: int):
    return posts[id]
```

https://github.com/PacktPublishing/Building-Data-Science-Applica-tions-with-FastAPI-Second-Edition/tree/main/chapter03/chapter03_response_path_parameters_03.py

And then call this endpoint:

```
$ http GET http://localhost:8000/posts/1
HTTP/1.1 200 OK
content-length: 32
content-type: application/json
date: Thu, 10 Nov 2022 10:29:33 GMT
server: uvicorn

{
    "nb_views": 100,
    "title": "Hello"
}
```

The nb_views property is in the output. However, we don't want this. This is exactly what the response_model option is for, to specify another model that only outputs the properties we want. First, let's define another Pydantic model with only the title property:

chapter03_response_path_parameters_04.py

```python
class PublicPost(BaseModel):
    title: str
```

https://github.com/PacktPublishing/Building-Data-Science-Applica-tions-with-FastAPI-Second-Edition/tree/main/chapter03/chapter03_response_path_parameters_04.py

Then, the only change is to add the `response_model` option as a keyword argument for the path decorator:

chapter03_response_path_parameters_04.py

```
@app.get("/posts/{id}", response_model=PublicPost)
async def get_post(id: int):
    return posts[id]
```

https://github.com/PacktPublishing/Building-Data-Science-Applications-with-FastAPI-Second-Edition/tree/main/chapter03/chapter03_response_path_parameters_04.py

Now, let's try to call this endpoint:

```
$ http GET http://localhost:8000/posts/1
HTTP/1.1 200 OK
content-length: 17
content-type: application/json
date: Thu, 10 Nov 2022 10:31:43 GMT
server: uvicorn

{
    "title": "Hello"
}
```

The `nb_views` property is no longer there! Thanks to the `response_model` option, FastAPI automatically converted our `Post` instance into a `PublicPost` instance before serializing it. Now our private data is safe!

The good thing is that this option is also considered by the interactive documentation, which will show the correct output schema to the end user, as you can see in *Figure 3.2*:

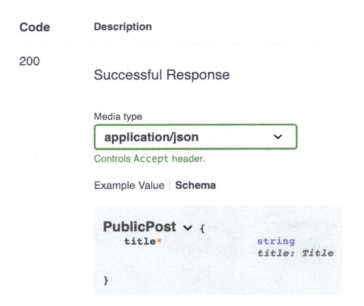

Figure 3.2 – The response model schema in the interactive documentation

So far, you've looked at options that can help you quickly customize the response generated by FastAPI. Now, we'll introduce another approach that will open up more possibilities.

The response parameter

The body and status code are not the only interesting parts of an HTTP response. Sometimes, it might be useful to return some custom headers or set cookies. This can be done dynamically using FastAPI directly within the path operation logic. How so? By injecting the `Response` object as an argument of the path operation function.

Setting headers

As usual, this only involves setting the proper type hinting to the argument. The following example shows you how to set a custom header:

chapter03_response_parameter_01.py

```python
from fastapi import FastAPI, Response

app = FastAPI()

@app.get("/")
```

```
async def custom_header(response: Response):
    response.headers["Custom-Header"] = "Custom-Header-Value"
    return {"hello": "world"}
```

https://github.com/PacktPublishing/Building-Data-Science-Applications-with-FastAPI-Second-Edition/tree/main/chapter03/chapter03_response_parameter_01.py

The `Response` object gives you access to a set of properties, including `headers`. It's a simple dictionary where the key is the name of the header, and the value is its associated value. Therefore, it's relatively straightforward to set your own custom header.

Also, notice that you *don't have to return* the `Response` object. You can still return JSON-encodable data, and FastAPI will take care of forming a proper response, including the headers you've set. Therefore, the `response_model` and `status_code` options we discussed in the *Path operation parameters* section are still honored.

Let's view the result:

```
$ http GET http://localhost:8000
HTTP/1.1 200 OK
content-length: 17
content-type: application/json
custom-header: Custom-Header-Value
date: Thu, 10 Nov 2022 10:35:11 GMT
server: uvicorn

{
    "hello": "world"
}
```

Our custom header is part of the response.

As we mentioned earlier, the good thing about this approach is that it's within your path operation logic. That means you can dynamically set headers depending on what's happening in your business logic.

Setting cookies

Cookies can also be particularly useful when you want to maintain the user's state within the browser between each of their visits.

To prompt the browser to save some cookies in your response, you could, of course, build your own Set-Cookie header and set it in the headers dictionary, just as we saw in the preceding command block. However, since this can be quite tricky to do, the Response object exposes a convenient set_cookie method:

chapter03_response_parameter_02.py

```
@app.get("/")
async def custom_cookie(response: Response):
    response.set_cookie("cookie-name", "cookie-value", max_age=86400)
    return {"hello": "world"}
```

https://github.com/PacktPublishing/Building-Data-Science-Applications-with-FastAPI-Second-Edition/tree/main/chapter03/chapter03_response_parameter_02.py

Here, we simply set a cookie, named cookie-name, with the value of cookie-value. It'll be valid for 86,400 seconds before the browser removes it.

Let's try it:

```
$ http GET http://localhost:8000
HTTP/1.1 200 OK
content-length: 17
content-type: application/json
date: Thu, 10 Nov 2022 10:37:47 GMT
server: uvicorn
Set-Cookie: cookie-name=cookie-value; Max-Age=86400; Path=/;
SameSite=lax

{
    "hello": "world"
}
```

Here, you can see that we have a nice Set-Cookie header with all of the properties of our cookie.

As you may know, cookies have a lot more options than the ones we have shown here; for instance, path, domain, and HTTP-only. The set_cookie method supports all of them. You can read about the full list of options in the official Starlette documentation (since Response is also borrowed from Starlette) at https://www.starlette.io/responses/#set-cookie.

If you're not familiar with the Set-Cookie header, we also recommend that you refer to *MDN Web Docs*, which can be accessed at https://developer.mozilla.org/en-US/docs/Web/HTTP/Headers/Set-Cookie.

Of course, if you need to set several cookies, you can call this method several times.

Setting the status code dynamically

In the *Path operation parameters* section, we discussed a way to declaratively set the status code of the response. The drawback to this approach is that it'll always be the same no matter what's happening inside.

Let's assume that we have an endpoint that updates an object in the database or creates it if it doesn't exist. A good approach would be to return a 200 OK status when the object already exists or a 201 Created status when the object has to be created.

To do this, you can simply set the status_code property on the Response object:

chapter03_response_parameter_03.py

```python
# Dummy database
posts = {
    1: Post(title="Hello"),
}


@app.put("/posts/{id}")
async def update_or_create_post(id: int, post: Post, response:
Response):
    if id not in posts:
        response.status_code = status.HTTP_201_CREATED
    posts[id] = post
    return posts[id]
```

https://github.com/PacktPublishing/Building-Data-Science-Applica-tions-with-FastAPI-Second-Edition/tree/main/chapter03/chapter03_response_parameter_03.py

First, we check whether the ID in the path exists in the database. If not, we change the status code to 201. Then, we simply assign the post to this ID in the database.

Let's try with an existing post first:

```
$ http PUT http://localhost:8000/posts/1 title="Updated title"
HTTP/1.1 200 OK
content-length: 25
content-type: application/json
date: Thu, 10 Nov 2022 10:41:47 GMT
server: uvicorn

{
    "title": "Updated title"
}
```

The post with an ID of 1 already exists, so we get a 200 status. Now, let's try with a non-existing ID:

```
$ http PUT http://localhost:8000/posts/2 title="New title"
HTTP/1.1 201 Created
content-length: 21
content-type: application/json
date: Thu, 10 Nov 2022 10:42:20 GMT
server: uvicorn


{
    "title": "New title"
}
```

We get a 201 status!

Now you have a way to dynamically set the status code in your logic. Bear in mind, though, that they *won't be detected by the automatic documentation.* Therefore, they won't appear as a possible response status code in it.

You might be tempted to use this approach to set *error status codes*, such as 400 Bad Request or 404 Not Found. In fact, you *shouldn't do that.* FastAPI provides a dedicated way to do this: HTTPException.

Raising HTTP errors

When calling a REST API, quite frequently, you might find that things don't go very well; you might come across the wrong parameters, invalid payloads, or objects that don't exist anymore. Errors can happen for a lot of reasons.

That's why it's critical to detect them and raise a clear and unambiguous error message to the end user so that they can correct their mistake. In a REST API, there are two very important things that you can use to return an informative message: the status code and the payload.

The status code can give you a precious hint about the nature of the error. Since HTTP protocols provide a wide range of error status codes, your end user might not even need to read the payload to understand what's wrong.

Of course, it's always better to provide a clear error message at the same time in order to give further details and add some useful information regarding how the end user can solve the issue.

> **Error status codes are crucial**
>
> Some APIs choose to always return a 200 status code with the payload containing a property stating whether the request was successful or not, such as { "success": false }. Don't do that. The RESTful philosophy encourages you to use the HTTP semantics to give meaning to the data. Having to parse the output and look for a property to determine whether the call was successful is a bad design.

To raise an HTTP error in FastAPI, you'll have to raise a Python exception, `HTTPException`. This exception class will allow us to set a status code and an error message. It is caught by FastAPI error handlers that take care of forming a proper HTTP response.

In the following example, we'll raise a `400 Bad Request` error if the `password` and `password_confirm` payload properties don't match:

chapter03_raise_errors_01.py

```python
@app.post("/password")
async def check_password(password: str = Body(...), password_confirm:
str = Body(...)):
    if password != password_confirm:
        raise HTTPException(
            status.HTTP_400_BAD_REQUEST,
            detail="Passwords don't match.",
        )
    return {"message": "Passwords match."}
```

https://github.com/PacktPublishing/Building-Data-Science-Applications-with-FastAPI-Second-Edition/tree/main/chapter03/chapter03_raise_errors_01.py

As you can see here, if the passwords are not equal, we directly raise `HTTPException`. The first argument is the status code, and the `detail` keyword argument lets us write an error message.

Let's examine how it works:

```
$ http POST http://localhost:8000/password password="aa" password_
confirm="bb"
HTTP/1.1 400 Bad Request
content-length: 35
content-type: application/json
date: Thu, 10 Nov 2022 10:46:36 GMT
server: uvicorn

{
    "detail": "Passwords don't match."
}
```

Here, we do get a `400` status code, and our error message has been wrapped nicely in a JSON object with the `detail` key. This is how FastAPI handles errors by default.

In fact, you are not limited to a simple string for the error message: you can return a dictionary or a list in order to get structured information about the error. For example, take a look at the following code snippet:

chapter03_raise_errors_02.py

```
        raise HTTPException(
            status.HTTP_400_BAD_REQUEST,
            detail={
                "message": "Passwords don't match.",
                "hints": [
                    "Check the caps lock on your keyboard",
                    "Try to make the password visible by clicking on
 the eye icon to check your typing",
                ],
            },
        )
```

https://github.com/PacktPublishing/Building-Data-Science-Applica-tions-with-FastAPI-Second-Edition/tree/main/chapter03/chapter03_raise_errors_02.py

And that's it! You now have the power to raise errors and give meaningful information about them to the end user.

So far, the methods you have seen should cover the majority of cases you'll encounter during the development of an API. Sometimes, however, you'll have scenarios where you'll need to build a complete HTTP response yourself. This is the subject of the next section.

Building a custom response

Most of the time, you'll let FastAPI take care of building an HTTP response by simply providing it with some data to serialize. Under the hood, FastAPI uses a subclass of Response called JSONResponse. Quite predictably, this response class takes care of serializing some data to JSON and adding the correct Content-Type header.

However, there are other response classes that cover common cases:

*   HTMLResponse: This can be used to return an HTML response

*   PlainTextResponse: This can be used to return raw text

*   RedirectResponse: This can be used to make a redirection

- `StreamingResponse`: This can be used to stream a flow of bytes

- `FileResponse`: This can be used to automatically build a proper file response given the path of a file on the local disk

You have two ways of using them: either setting the `response_class` argument on the path decorator or directly returning a response instance.

Using the response_class argument

This is the simplest and most straightforward way to return a custom response. Indeed, by doing this, you won't even have to create a class instance: you'll just have to return the data as you usually do for standard JSON responses.

This is well suited for `HTMLResponse` and `PlainTextResponse`:

chapter03_custom_response_01.py

```python
from fastapi import FastAPI
from fastapi.responses import HTMLResponse, PlainTextResponse

app = FastAPI()

@app.get("/html", response_class=HTMLResponse)
async def get_html():
    return """
        <html>
            <head>
                <title>Hello world!</title>
            </head>
            <body>
                <h1>Hello world!</h1>
            </body>
        </html>
    """

@app.get("/text", response_class=PlainTextResponse)
async def text():
    return "Hello world!"
```

https://github.com/PacktPublishing/Building-Data-Science-Applications-with-FastAPI-Second-Edition/tree/main/chapter03/chapter03_custom_response_01.py

By setting the `response_class` argument on the decorator, you can change the class that will be used by FastAPI to build the response. Then, you can simply return valid data for this kind of response. Notice that the response classes are imported through the `fastapi.responses` module.

The nice thing about this is that you can combine this option with the ones we saw in the *Path operation parameters* section. Using the `Response` parameter that we described in *The response parameter* section also works perfectly!

For the other response classes, however, you'll have to build the instance yourself and then return it.

Making a redirection

As mentioned earlier, `RedirectResponse` is a class that helps you build an HTTP redirection, which simply is an HTTP response with a `Location` header pointing to the new URL and a status code in the *3xx range*. It simply expects the URL you wish to redirect to as the first argument:

chapter03_custom_response_02.py

```
@app.get("/redirect")
async def redirect():
    return RedirectResponse("/new-url")
```

https://github.com/PacktPublishing/Building-Data-Science-Applications-with-FastAPI-Second-Edition/tree/main/chapter03/chapter03_custom_response_02.py

By default, it'll use the `307 Temporary Redirect` status code, but you can change this through the `status_code` argument:

chapter03_custom_response_03.py

```
@app.get("/redirect")
async def redirect():
    return RedirectResponse("/new-url", status_code=status.HTTP_301_
MOVED_PERMANENTLY)
```

https://github.com/PacktPublishing/Building-Data-Science-Applications-with-FastAPI-Second-Edition/tree/main/chapter03/chapter03_custom_response_03.py

erving a file

Now, let's examine how `FileResponse` works. This is useful if you wish to propose some files to download. This response class will automatically take care of opening the file on disk and streaming the bytes along with the proper HTTP headers.

Let's take a look at how we can use an endpoint to download a picture of a cat. You'll find this in the code examples repository at `https://github.com/PacktPublishing/ Building-Data-Science-Applications-with-FastAPI-Second-Edition/blob/main/ assets/cat.jpg`.

We just need to return an instance of `FileResponse` with the path of the file we want to serve as the first argument:

chapter03_custom_response_04.py

```python
@app.get("/cat")
async def get_cat():
    root_directory = Path(__file__).parent.parent
    picture_path = root_directory / "assets" / "cat.jpg"
    return FileResponse(picture_path)
```

`https://github.com/PacktPublishing/Building-Data-Science-Applications-with-FastAPI-Second-Edition/tree/main/chapter03/chapter03_ custom_response_04.py`

> **The pathlib module**
>
> Python provides a module to help you work with file paths, `pathlib`. It's the recommended way to manipulate paths, as it takes care of handling them correctly, depending on the operating system you are running. You can read about the functions of this module in the official documentation at `https://docs.python.org/3/library/pathlib.html`.

Let's examine what the HTTP response looks like:

```
$ http GET http://localhost:8000/cat
HTTP/1.1 200 OK
content-length: 71457
content-type: image/jpeg
date: Thu, 10 Nov 2022 11:00:10 GMT
etag: c69cf2514977e3f18251f1bcf1433d0a
last-modified: Fri, 16 Jul 2021 07:08:42 GMT
server: uvicorn
```

```
+------------------------------------------+
| NOTE: binary data not shown in terminal  |
+------------------------------------------+
```

As you can see, we have the right `Content-Length` and `Content-Type` headers for our image. The response even sets the `Etag` and `Last-Modified` headers so that the browser can properly cache the resource. HTTPie doesn't show the binary data in the body; however, if you open the endpoint in your browser, you'll see the cat appear!

Custom responses

Finally, if you really have a case that's not covered by the provided classes, you always have the option to use the `Response` class to build exactly what you need. With this class, you can set everything, including the body content and the headers.

The following example shows you how to return an XML response:

chapter03_custom_response_05.py

```python
@app.get("/xml")
async def get_xml():
    content = """<?xml version="1.0" encoding="UTF-8"?>
        <Hello>World</Hello>
    """
    return Response(content=content, media_type="application/xml")
```

https://github.com/PacktPublishing/Building-Data-Science-Applications-with-FastAPI-Second-Edition/tree/main/chapter03/chapter03_custom_response_05.py

You can view the complete list of arguments in the Starlette documentation at https://www.starlette.io/responses/#response.

> **Path operation parameters and response parameters won't have any effect**
>
> Bear in mind that when you directly return a `Response` class (or one of its subclasses), the parameters you set on the decorator or the operations you make on the injected `Response` object won't have any effect. They are completely overridden by the `Response` object you return. If you need to customize the status code or the headers, then use the `status_code` and `headers` arguments when instantiating your class.

Well done! Now you have all the knowledge required to create the response you need for your REST API. You've learned that FastAPI comes with sensible defaults that can help you create proper JSON responses in no time. At the same time, it also gives you access to more advanced objects and options to allow you to make custom responses.

So far, all of the examples we've looked at have been quite short and simple. However, when you're developing a real application, you'll probably have dozens of endpoints and models. In the final section of this chapter, we'll examine how to organize such projects to make them modular and easier to maintain.

Structuring a bigger project with multiple routers

When building a real-world web application, you're likely to have a lot of code and logic: data models, API endpoints, and services. Of course, all of those can't live in a single file; we have to structure the project so that it's easy to maintain and evolve.

FastAPI supports the concept of **routers**. They are "sub-parts" of your API and are usually dedicated to a single type of object, such as users or posts, which are defined in their own files. You can then include them in your main FastAPI app so that it can route it accordingly.

In this section, we'll explore how to use routers and how you can structure a FastAPI project. While this structure is one way to do it and works quite well, it's not a golden rule and can be adapted to your own needs.

In the code examples repository, there is a folder named chapter03_project, which contains a sample project with this structure: https://github.com/PacktPublishing/Building-Data-Science-Applications-with-FastAPI-Second-Edition/tree/main/chapter03_project

Here is the project structure:

```
.
└── chapter03_project/
    ├── schemas/
    │   ├── __init__.py
    │   ├── post.py
    │   └── user.py
    ├── routers/
    │   ├── __init__.py
    │   ├── posts.py
    │   └── users.py
    ├── __init__.py
    ├── app.py
    └── db.py
```

Here, you can see that we chose to have packages that contain Pydantic models on one side and routers on the other side. At the root of the project, we have a file named `app.py`, which will expose the main FastAPI application. The `db.py` file defines a dummy database for the sake of the example.

The `__init__.py` files are there to properly define our directories as Python packages. You can read more details about this in *Chapter 2, Python Programming Specificities*, in the *Packages, modules, and imports* section.

First, let's examine what a FastAPI router looks like:

users.py

```
from fastapi import APIRouter, HTTPException, status

from chapter03_project.db import db
from chapter03_project.schemas.user import User, UserCreate

router = APIRouter()

@router.get("/")
async def all() -> list[User]:
    return list(db.users.values())
```

https://github.com/PacktPublishing/Building-Data-Science-Appli-
cations-with-FastAPI-Second-Edition/tree/main/chapter03_project/
routers/users.py

As you can see here, instead of instantiating the `FastAPI` class, you instantiate the `APIRouter` class. Then, you can use it exactly the same way to decorate your path operation functions.

Also, notice that we import the Pydantic models from the relevant module in the `schemas` package.

We won't go into detail about the logic of the endpoints, but we invite you to read about it. It uses all the FastAPI features that we've explored so far.

Now, let's take a look at how to import this router and include it within a FastAPI application:

app.py

```python
from fastapi import FastAPI

from chapter03_project.routers.posts import router as posts_router
from chapter03_project.routers.users import router as users_router

app = FastAPI()

app.include_router(posts_router, prefix="/posts", tags=["posts"])
app.include_router(users_router, prefix="/users", tags=["users"])
```

https://github.com/PacktPublishing/Building-Data-Science-Appli-
cations-with-FastAPI-Second-Edition/tree/main/chapter03_project/
routers/app.py

As usual, we instantiate the `FastAPI` class. Then, we use the `include_router` method to add our sub-router. You can see that we simply imported the router from its relevant module and used it as the first argument of `include_router`. Notice that we used the `as` syntax while importing. Since both `users` and `posts` routers are named the same inside their module, this syntax allows us to alias their name and, thus, avoid **name collision**.

Additionally, you can see that we set the `prefix` keyword argument. This allows us to prefix the path of all the endpoints of this router. This way, you don't have to hardcode it into the router logic and can easily change it for the whole router. It can also be used to provide versioned paths of your API, such as `/v1`.

Finally, the `tags` argument helps you to group endpoints in the interactive documentation for better readability. By doing this, the `posts` and `users` endpoints will be clearly separated in the documentation.

And that's all you need to do! You can run this whole application, as usual, with Uvicorn:

```
$ uvicorn chapter03_project.app:app
```

If you open the interactive documentation at `http://localhost:8000/docs`, you'll see that all the routes are there, grouped by the tags we specified when including the router:

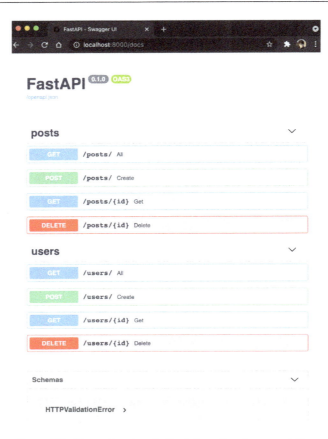

Figure 3.3 – Tagged routers in the interactive documentation

Once again, you can see that FastAPI is both powerful and very lightweight to use. The good thing about routers is that you can even nest them and include sub-routers in routers that include other routers themselves. Therefore, you can have a quite complex routing hierarchy with very low effort.

Summary

Well done! You're now acquainted with all the basic features of FastAPI. Throughout this chapter, you learned how to create and run API endpoints where you can validate and retrieve data from all parts of an HTTP request: the path, the query, the parameters, the headers, and, of course, the body. You also learned how to tailor the HTTP response to your needs, whether it is a simple JSON response, an error, or a file to download. Finally, you looked at how to define separate API routers and include them in your main application to keep a clean and maintainable project structure.

You have enough knowledge now to start building your own API with FastAPI. In the next chapter, we'll focus on Pydantic models. You now know that they are at the core of the data validation features of FastAPI, so it's crucial to fully understand how they work and how to manipulate them efficiently.

4

Managing Pydantic Data Models in FastAPI

This chapter will cover in detail the definition of a data model with Pydantic, the underlying data validation library used by FastAPI. We'll explain how to implement variations of the same model without repeating the same code again and again, thanks to class inheritance. Finally, we'll show how to implement custom data validation logic into Pydantic models.

In this chapter, we're going to cover the following main topics:

- Defining models and their field types with Pydantic
- Creating model variations with class inheritance
- Adding custom data validation with Pydantic
- Working with Pydantic objects

Technical requirements

To run the code examples, you'll need a Python virtual environment, which we set up in *Chapter 1, Python Development Environment Setup*.

You'll find all the code examples for this chapter in the dedicated GitHub repository at `https://github.com/PacktPublishing/Building-Data-Science-Applications-with-FastAPI-Second-Edition/tree/main/chapter04`.

Defining models and their field types with Pydantic

Pydantic is a powerful library for defining data models using Python classes and type hints. This approach makes those classes completely compatible with static type checking. Besides, since there are regular Python classes, we can use inheritance and also define our very own methods to add custom logic.

In *Chapter 3, Developing a RESTful API with FastAPI*, you learned the basics of defining a data model with Pydantic: you have to define a class inheriting from `BaseModel` and list all the fields as class properties, each one with a type hint to enforce their type.

In this section, we'll focus on model definition and see all the possibilities we have for defining the fields.

Standard field types

We'll begin by defining fields with standard types, which only involve simple type hints. Let's review a simple model representing information about a person. You can see this in the following code snippet:

chapter04_standard_field_types_01.py

```
from pydantic import BaseModel


class Person(BaseModel):
    first_name: str
    last_name: str
    age: int
```

https://github.com/PacktPublishing/Building-Data-Science-Applications-with-FastAPI-Second-Edition/tree/main/chapter04/chapter04_standard_field_types_01.py

As we said, you just have to write the names of the fields and type-hint them with the intended type. Of course, we are not limited to scalar types: we can use compound types, such as lists and tuples, or classes such as datetime and enum. In the following example, you can see a model using those more complex types:

chapter04_standard_field_types_02.py

```
from datetime import date
from enum import Enum

from pydantic import BaseModel, ValidationError


class Gender(str, Enum):
    MALE = "MALE"
    FEMALE = "FEMALE"
    NON_BINARY = "NON_BINARY"


class Person(BaseModel):
    first_name: str
    last_name: str
```

```
        gender: Gender
        birthdate: date
        interests: list[str]
```

https://github.com/PacktPublishing/Building-Data-Science-Applica-tions-with-FastAPI-Second-Edition/tree/main/chapter04/chapter04_standard_field_types_02.py

There are three things to notice in this example.

First, we used the standard Python Enum class as a type for the gender field. This allows us to specify a set of valid values. If we input a value that's not in this enumeration, Pydantic will raise an error, as illustrated in the following example:

chapter04_standard_field_types_02.py

```
# Invalid gender
try:
    Person(
        first_name="John",
        last_name="Doe",
        gender="INVALID_VALUE",
        birthdate="1991-01-01",
        interests=["travel", "sports"],
    )
except ValidationError as e:
    print(str(e))
```

https://github.com/PacktPublishing/Building-Data-Science-Applica-tions-with-FastAPI-Second-Edition/tree/main/chapter04/chapter04_standard_field_types_02.py

If you run the preceding example, you'll get this output:

```
1 validation error for Person
gender
  value is not a valid enumeration member; permitted: 'MALE',
'FEMALE', 'NON_BINARY' (type=type_error.enum; enum_values=[<Gender.
MALE: 'MALE'>, <Gender.FEMALE: 'FEMALE'>, <Gender.NON_BINARY: 'NON_
BINARY'>])
```

Actually, this is exactly what we did in *Chapter 3, Developing a RESTful API with FastAPI*, to limit the allowed values of the path parameter.

Then, we used the `date` Python class as a type for the `birthdate` field. Pydantic is able to automatically parse dates and times given as ISO format strings or timestamp integers and instantiate a proper `date` or `datetime` object. Of course, if the parsing fails, you'll also get an error. You can experiment with this in the following example:

chapter04_standard_field_types_02.py

```python
# Invalid birthdate
try:
    Person(
        first_name="John",
        last_name="Doe",
        gender=Gender.MALE,
        birthdate="1991-13-42",
        interests=["travel", "sports"],
    )
except ValidationError as e:
    print(str(e))
```

https://github.com/PacktPublishing/Building-Data-Science-Applications-with-FastAPI-Second-Edition/tree/main/chapter04/chapter04_standard_field_types_02.py

And here is the output:

```
1 validation error for Person
birthdate
   invalid date format (type=value_error.date)
```

Finally, we defined `interests` as a list of strings. Once again, Pydantic will check whether the field is a valid list of strings.

Obviously, if everything is okay, we get a `Person` instance and have access to the properly parsed fields. This is what we show in the following code snippet:

chapter04_standard_field_types_02.py

```python
# Valid
person = Person(
    first_name="John",
    last_name="Doe",
    gender=Gender.MALE,
    birthdate="1991-01-01",
    interests=["travel", "sports"],
)
```

```
# first_name='John' last_name='Doe' gender=<Gender.MALE: 'MALE'>
birthdate=datetime.date(1991, 1, 1) interests=['travel', 'sports']
print(person)
```

As you can see, this is quite powerful, and we can have quite complex field types. But that's not all: *fields can be Pydantic models themselves*, allowing you to have sub-objects! In the following code example, we expand the previous snippet to add an `address` field:

chapter04_standard_field_types_03.py

```
class Address(BaseModel):
    street_address: str
    postal_code: str
    city: str
    country: str


class Person(BaseModel):
    first_name: str
    last_name: str
    gender: Gender
    birthdate: date
    interests: list[str]
    address: Address
```

We just have to define another Pydantic model and use it as a type hint. Now, you can either instantiate a `Person` instance with an already valid `Address` instance or, even better, with a dictionary. In this case, Pydantic will automatically parse it and validate it against the address model.

In the following code snippet, we try to input an invalid address:

chapter04_standard_field_types_03.py

```
# Invalid address
try:
    Person(
        first_name="John",
        last_name="Doe",
```

```
        gender=Gender.MALE,
        birthdate="1991-01-01",
        interests=["travel", "sports"],
        address={
            "street_address": "12 Squirell Street",
            "postal_code": "424242",
            "city": "Woodtown",
            # Missing country
        },
    )
except ValidationError as e:
    print(str(e))
```

https://github.com/PacktPublishing/Building-Data-Science-Applica-tions-with-FastAPI-Second-Edition/tree/main/chapter04/chapter04_standard_field_types_03.py

This will generate the following validation error:

```
1 validation error for Person
address -> country
   field required (type=value_error.missing)
```

Pydantic clearly shows the missing field in the sub-object. Once again, if everything goes well, we get a Person instance and its associated Address, as you can see in the following extract:

chapter04_standard_field_types_03.py

```
# Valid
person = Person(
    first_name="John",
    last_name="Doe",
    gender=Gender.MALE,
    birthdate="1991-01-01",
    interests=["travel", "sports"],
    address={
        "street_address": "12 Squirell Street",
        "postal_code": "424242",
        "city": "Woodtown",
        "country": "US",
    },
)
print(person)
```

Optional fields and default values

Up to now, we've assumed that each field had to be provided when instantiating the model. Quite often, however, there are values that we want to be optional because they may not be relevant to each object instance. Sometimes, we also wish to set a default value for a field when it's not specified.

As you may have guessed, this is done quite simply, with the | None typing annotation, as illustrated in the following code snippet:

chapter04_optional_fields_default_values_01.py

```
from pydantic import BaseModel

class UserProfile(BaseModel):
    nickname: str
    location: str | None = None
    subscribed_newsletter: bool = True
```

When defining a field with the | None type hint, it accepts a None value. As you can see in the preceding code, the default value can be simply assigned by putting the value after an equals sign.

Be careful, though: *don't assign default values such as this for dynamic types* such as datetimes. If you do, the datetime instantiation will be evaluated only once when the model is imported. The effect of this is that all the objects you instantiate will then share the same value instead of having a fresh value. You can observe this behavior in the following example:

chapter04_optional_fields_default_values_02.py

```
class Model(BaseModel):
    # Don't do this.
    # This example shows you why it doesn't work.
    d: datetime = datetime.now()

o1 = Model()
print(o1.d)
```

```
time.sleep(1)   # Wait for a second

o2 = Model()
print(o2.d)

print(o1.d < o2.d)   # False
```

https://github.com/PacktPublishing/Building-Data-Science-Applica-tions-with-FastAPI-Second-Edition/tree/main/chapter04/chapter04_optional_fields_default_values_02.py

Even though we waited for 1 second between the instantiation of o1 and o2, the d datetime is the same! This means that the datetime is evaluated only once when the class is imported.

You can have the same kind of problem if you want to have a default list, such as l: list[str] = ["a", "b", "c"]. Notice that this is true for every Python object, not only Pydantic models, so you should bear this in mind.

So, how do we assign dynamic default values? Fortunately, Pydantic provides a Field function that allows us to set some advanced options on our fields, including one to set a factory for creating dynamic values. Before showing you this, we'll first introduce the Field function.

In *Chapter 3, Developing a RESTful API with FastAPI*, we showed how to apply some validation to the request parameters to check whether a number was in a certain range or whether a string matched a regular expression. Actually, these options directly come from Pydantic! We can use the same techniques to apply validation to the fields of a model.

To do this, we'll use the Field function from Pydantic and use its result as the default value of the field. In the following example, we define a Person model with the first_name and last_name required properties, which should be at least three characters long, and an optional age property, which should be an integer between 0 and 120. We show the implementation of this model in the following code snippet:

chapter04_fields_validation_01.py

```
from pydantic import BaseModel, Field, ValidationError

class Person(BaseModel):
    first_name: str = Field(..., min_length=3)
    last_name: str = Field(..., min_length=3)
    age: int | None = Field(None, ge=0, le=120)
```

https://github.com/PacktPublishing/Building-Data-Science-Applica-tions-with-FastAPI-Second-Edition/tree/main/chapter04/chapter04_fields_validation_01.py

As you can see, the syntax is very similar to the one we saw for Path, Query, and Body. The first positional argument defines the *default value* for the field. If the field is required, we use an ellipsis, ... Then, the keyword arguments are there to set options for the field, including some basic validation.

You can view a complete list of the arguments accepted by Field in the official Pydantic documentation, at https://pydantic-docs.helpmanual.io/usage/schema/#field-customization.

Dynamic default values

In the previous section, we warned you about setting dynamic values as defaults. Fortunately, Pydantic provides the default_factory argument on the Field function to cover this use case. This argument expects you to pass a function that will be called during model instantiation. Thus, the resulting object will be evaluated at runtime each time you create a new object. You can see how to use it in the following example:

chapter04_fields_validation_02.py

```python
from datetime import datetime

from pydantic import BaseModel, Field

def list_factory():
    return ["a", "b", "c"]

class Model(BaseModel):
    l: list[str] = Field(default_factory=list_factory)
    d: datetime = Field(default_factory=datetime.now)
    l2: list[str] = Field(default_factory=list)
```

https://github.com/PacktPublishing/Building-Data-Science-Applications-with-FastAPI-Second-Edition/tree/main/chapter04/chapter04_fields_validation_02.py

You simply have to pass a function to this argument. Don't put arguments on it: it'll be Pydantic that will automatically call the function for you when instantiating a new object. If you need to call a function with specific arguments, you'll have to wrap it into your own function, as we did for list_factory.

Notice also that the first positional argument used for the default value (such as None or . . .) is completely omitted here. This makes sense: it's not consistent to have both a default value and a factory. Pydantic will raise an error if you set those two arguments together.

Validating email addresses and URLs with Pydantic types

For convenience, Pydantic provides some classes to use as field types to validate some common patterns, such as email addresses or URLs.

In the following example, we'll use `EmailStr` and `HttpUrl` to validate an email address and an HTTP URL.

For `EmailStr` to work, you'll need an optional dependency, `email-validator`, which you can install with the following command:

```
(venv)$ pip install email-validator
```

Those classes work like any other type or class: just use them as a type hint for your field. You can see this in the following extract:

chapter04_pydantic_types_01.py

```
from pydantic import BaseModel, EmailStr, HttpUrl, ValidationError

class User(BaseModel):
    email: EmailStr
    website: HttpUrl
```

https://github.com/PacktPublishing/Building-Data-Science-Applica-
tions-with-FastAPI-Second-Edition/tree/main/chapter04/chapter04_
pydantic_types_01.py

In the following example, we check that the email address is correctly validated:

chapter04_pydantic_types_01.py

```
# Invalid email
try:
    User(email="jdoe", website="https://www.example.com")
except ValidationError as e:
    print(str(e))
```

https://github.com/PacktPublishing/Building-Data-Science-Applica-
tions-with-FastAPI-Second-Edition/tree/main/chapter04/chapter04_
pydantic_types_01.py

You will see the following output:

```
1 validation error for User
email
  value is not a valid email address (type=value_error.email)
```

We also check that the URL is correctly parsed, as follows:

chapter04_pydantic_types_01.py

```
# Invalid URL
try:
    User(email="jdoe@example.com", website="jdoe")
except ValidationError as e:
    print(str(e))
```

https://github.com/PacktPublishing/Building-Data-Science-Applica-
tions-with-FastAPI-Second-Edition/tree/main/chapter04/chapter04_
pydantic_types_01.py

You will see the following output:

```
1 validation error for User
website
  invalid or missing URL scheme (type=value_error.url.scheme)
```

If you have a look at a valid example, shown next, you'll see that the URL is parsed into an object, giving you access to the different parts of it, such as the scheme or hostname:

chapter04_pydantic_types_01.py

```
# Valid
user = User(email="jdoe@example.com", website="https://www.example.
com")
# email='jdoe@example.com' website=HttpUrl('https://www.example.com',
scheme='https', host='www.example.com', tld='com', host_type='domain')
print(user)
```

https://github.com/PacktPublishing/Building-Data-Science-Applica-
tions-with-FastAPI-Second-Edition/tree/main/chapter04/chapter04_
pydantic_types_01.py

Pydantic provides quite a big set of types that can help you in various situations. We invite you to review the full list of them in the official documentation at https://pydantic-docs.helpmanual.
io/usage/types/#pydantic-types.

You now have a better idea of how to define your Pydantic models finely by using more advanced types or leveraging the validation features. As we said, those models are at the heart of FastAPI, and you'll probably have to define several variations for the same entity to account for several situations. In the next section, we'll show how to do that with minimum repetition.

Creating model variations with class inheritance

In *Chapter 3, Developing a RESTful API with FastAPI*, we saw a case where we needed to define two variations of a Pydantic model in order to split the data we want to store in the backend and the data we want to show to the user. This is a common pattern in FastAPI: you define one model for creation, one for the response, and one for the data to store in the database.

We show this basic approach in the following example:

chapter04_model_inheritance_01.py

```python
from pydantic import BaseModel

class PostCreate(BaseModel):
    title: str
    content: str

class PostRead(BaseModel):
    id: int
    title: str
    content: str

class Post(BaseModel):
    id: int
    title: str
    content: str
    nb_views: int = 0
```

https://github.com/PacktPublishing/Building-Data-Science-Applica-tions-with-FastAPI-Second-Edition/tree/main/chapter04/chapter04_model_inheritance_01.py

We have three models here, covering three situations:

- `PostCreate` will be used for a `POST` endpoint to create a new post. We expect the user to give the title and the content; however, the **identifier (ID)** will be automatically determined by the database.

- `PostRead` will be used when we retrieve the data of a post. We want its title and content, of course, but also its associated ID in the database.

- `Post` will carry all the data we wish to store in the database. Here, we also want to store the number of views, but we want to keep this secret to make our own statistics internally.

You can see here that we are repeating ourselves quite a lot, especially with the `title` and `content` fields. In bigger examples with lots of fields and lots of validation options, this could quickly become unmanageable.

The way to avoid this is to leverage model inheritance. The approach is simple: identify the fields that are common to every variation and put them in a model, which will be used as a base for every other. Then, you only have to inherit from that model to create your variations and add the specific fields. In the following example, we see what our previous example looks like with this method:

chapter04_model_inheritance_02.py

```python
from pydantic import BaseModel

class PostBase(BaseModel):
    title: str
    content: str

class PostCreate(PostBase):
    pass

class PostRead(PostBase):
    id: int

class Post(PostBase):
    id: int
    nb_views: int = 0
```

https://github.com/PacktPublishing/Building-Data-Science-Applications-with-FastAPI-Second-Edition/tree/main/chapter04/chapter04_model_inheritance_02.py

Now, whenever you need to add a field for the whole entity, all you have to do is to add it to the `PostBase` model as shown in the following code snippet.

It's also very convenient if you wish to define methods on your model. Remember that Pydantic models are regular Python classes, so you can implement as many methods as you wish!

chapter04_model_inheritance_03.py

```
class PostBase(BaseModel):
    title: str
    content: str

    def excerpt(self) -> str:
        return f"{self.content[:140]}..."
```

https://github.com/PacktPublishing/Building-Data-Science-Applications-with-FastAPI-Second-Edition/tree/main/chapter04/chapter04_model_inheritance_03.py

Defining the excerpt method on PostBase means it'll be available in every model variation.

While it's not strictly required, this inheritance approach greatly helps to prevent code duplication and, ultimately, bugs. We'll see in the next section that it'll make even more sense with custom validation methods.

Adding custom data validation with Pydantic

Up to now, we've seen how to apply basic validation to our models through Field arguments or the custom types provided by Pydantic. In a real-world project, though, you'll probably need to add your own custom validation logic for your specific case. Pydantic allows this by defining **validators**, which are methods on the model that can be applied at the field level or the object level.

Applying validation at the field level

This is the most common case: having a validation rule for a single field. To define a validation rule in Pydantic, we just have to write a static method on our model and decorate it with the validator decorator. As a reminder, decorators are syntactic sugar, allowing the wrapping of a function or a class with common logic without compromising readability.

The following example checks a birth date by verifying that the person is not more than 120 years old:

chapter04_custom_validation_01.py

```
from datetime import date

from pydantic import BaseModel, ValidationError, validator
```

```
class Person(BaseModel):
    first_name: str
    last_name: str
    birthdate: date

    @validator("birthdate")
    def valid_birthdate(cls, v: date):
        delta = date.today() - v
        age = delta.days / 365
        if age > 120:
            raise ValueError("You seem a bit too old!")
        return v
```

https://github.com/PacktPublishing/Building-Data-Science-Applica-
tions-with-FastAPI-Second-Edition/tree/main/chapter04/chapter04_
custom_validation_01.py

As you can see, `validator` is a static class method (the first argument, `cls`, is the class itself), with the `v` argument being the value to validate. It's decorated by the `validator` decorator, which expects the name of the argument to validate to be its first argument.

Pydantic expects two things for this method, as follows:

- If the value is not valid according to your logic, you should raise a `ValueError` error with an explicit error message.

- Otherwise, you should return the value that will be assigned to the model. Notice that it doesn't need to be the same as the input value: you can easily change it to fit your needs. That's actually what we'll do in an upcoming section, *Applying validation before Pydantic parsing*.

Applying validation at the object level

Quite often, the validation of one field is dependent on another—for example, when checking whether a password confirmation matches the password or enforcing a field to be required in certain circumstances. To allow this kind of validation, we need to access the whole object data. To do this, Pydantic provides the `root_validator` decorator, which is illustrated in the following code example:

chapter04_custom_validation_02.py

```
from pydantic import BaseModel, EmailStr, ValidationError, root_
validator

class UserRegistration(BaseModel):
    email: EmailStr
    password: str
```

```
    password_confirmation: str

    @root_validator()
    def passwords_match(cls, values):
        password = values.get("password")
        password_confirmation = values.get("password_confirmation")
        if password != password_confirmation:
            raise ValueError("Passwords don't match")
        return values
```

https://github.com/PacktPublishing/Building-Data-Science-Applica-tions-with-FastAPI-Second-Edition/tree/main/chapter04/chapter04_custom_validation_02.py

The usage of this decorator is similar to the validator decorator. The static class method is called along with the values argument, which is a *dictionary* containing all the fields. Thus, you can retrieve each of them and implement your logic.

Once again, Pydantic expects two things for this method, as follows:

- If the values are not valid according to your logic, you should raise a ValueError error with an explicit error message.

- Otherwise, you should return a values dictionary that will be assigned to the model. Notice that you can change some values in this dictionary to fit your needs.

Applying validation before Pydantic parsing

By default, your validators are run after Pydantic has done its parsing work. This means that the value you get already conforms to the type of field you specified. If the type is incorrect, Pydantic raises an error without calling your validator.

However, you may sometimes wish to provide some custom parsing logic that allows you to transform input values that would have been incorrect for the type you set. In that case, you would need to run your validator before the Pydantic parser: this is the purpose of the pre argument on validator.

In the following example, we show how to transform a string with values separated by commas into a list:

chapter04_custom_validation_03.py

```
from pydantic import BaseModel, validator

class Model(BaseModel):
    values: list[int]

    @validator("values", pre=True)
```

```
    def split_string_values(cls, v):
        if isinstance(v, str):
            return v.split(",")
        return v

m = Model(values="1,2,3")
print(m.values)  # [1, 2, 3]
```

https://github.com/PacktPublishing/Building-Data-Science-Applica-
tions-with-FastAPI-Second-Edition/tree/main/chapter04/chapter04_
custom_validation_03.py

You can see here that our validator first checks whether we have a string. If we do, we split the comma-separated string and return the resulting list; otherwise, we directly return the value. Pydantic will run its parsing logic afterward, so you can still be sure that an error will be raised if v is an invalid value.

Working with Pydantic objects

When developing API endpoints with FastAPI, you'll probably get a lot of Pydantic model instances to handle. It's then up to you to implement the logic to make a link between those objects and your services, such as your database or your machine learning model. Fortunately, Pydantic provides methods that make this very easy. We'll review common use cases that will be useful for you during development.

Converting an object into a dictionary

This is probably the action you'll perform the most on a Pydantic object: convert it into a raw dictionary that'll be easy to send to another API or use in a database, for example. You just have to call the dict method on the object instance.

The following example reuses the Person and Address models we saw in the *Standard field types* section of this chapter:

chapter04_working_pydantic_objects_01.py

```
person = Person(
    first_name="John",
    last_name="Doe",
    gender=Gender.MALE,
    birthdate="1991-01-01",
    interests=["travel", "sports"],
    address={
        "street_address": "12 Squirell Street",
        "postal_code": "424242",
        "city": "Woodtown",
```

```
            "country": "US",
        },
    )

    person_dict = person.dict()
    print(person_dict["first_name"])  # "John"
    print(person_dict["address"]["street_address"])  # "12 Squirell
    Street"
```

https://github.com/PacktPublishing/Building-Data-Science-Applica-
tions-with-FastAPI-Second-Edition/tree/main/chapter04/chapter04_
working_pydantic_objects_01.py

As you can see, calling `dict` is enough to transform the whole data into a dictionary. Sub-objects
are also recursively converted: the `address` key points to a dictionary with the address properties.

Interestingly, the `dict` method supports some arguments, allowing you to select a subset of properties
to be converted. You can either state the ones you want to be included or the ones you want to exclude,
as you can see in the following snippet:

chapter04_working_pydantic_objects_02.py

```
    person_include = person.dict(include={"first_name", "last_name"})
    print(person_include)  # {"first_name": "John", "last_name": "Doe"}

    person_exclude = person.dict(exclude={"birthdate", "interests"})
    print(person_exclude)
```

https://github.com/PacktPublishing/Building-Data-Science-Applica-
tions-with-FastAPI-Second-Edition/tree/main/chapter04/chapter04_
working_pydantic_objects_02.py

The `include` and `exclude` arguments expect a set with the keys of the fields you want to include
or exclude.

For nested structures such as `address`, you can also use a dictionary to specify which sub-field you
want to include or exclude, as illustrated in the following example:

chapter04_working_pydantic_objects_02.py

```
    person_nested_include = person.dict(
        include={
            "first_name": ...,
            "last_name": ...,
            "address": {"city", "country"},
```

```
    }
)
# {"first_name": "John", "last_name": "Doe", "address": {"city":
"Woodtown", "country": "US"}}
print(person_nested_include)
```

The resulting `address` dictionary only contains the city and the country. Notice that when using this syntax, scalar fields such as `first_name` and `last_name` have to be associated with the ellipsis, `. . . .`

If you use a conversion quite often, it can be useful to put it in a method so that you can reuse it at will, as illustrated in the following example:

chapter04_working_pydantic_objects_03.py

```
class Person(BaseModel):
    first_name: str
    last_name: str
    gender: Gender
    birthdate: date
    interests: list[str]
    address: Address

    def name_dict(self):
        return self.dict(include={"first_name", "last_name"})
```

Creating an instance from a sub-class object

In the *Creating model variations with class inheritance* section, we studied the common pattern of having specific model classes, depending on the situation. In particular, you'll have a model dedicated to the creation endpoint, with only the required fields for creation, and a database model with all the fields we want to store.

Let's look at the Post example again:

chapter04_working_pydantic_objects_04.py

```python
class PostBase(BaseModel):
    title: str
    content: str

class PostCreate(PostBase):
    pass

class PostRead(PostBase):
    id: int

class Post(PostBase):
    id: int
    nb_views: int = 0
```

https://github.com/PacktPublishing/Building-Data-Science-Applica-tions-with-FastAPI-Second-Edition/tree/main/chapter04/chapter04_working_pydantic_objects_04.py

Suppose we have an API that creates endpoints. In this context, we would get a PostCreate instance with only title and content. However, we need to build a proper Post instance before storing it in the database.

A convenient way to do this is to jointly use the dict method and the unpacking syntax. In the following example, we implemented a creation endpoint using this approach:

chapter04_working_pydantic_objects_04.py

```python
@app.post("/posts", status_code=status.HTTP_201_CREATED, response_
model=PostRead)
async def create(post_create: PostCreate):
    new_id = max(db.posts.keys() or (0,)) + 1

    post = Post(id=new_id, **post_create.dict())

    db.posts[new_id] = post
    return post
```

https://github.com/PacktPublishing/Building-Data-Science-Applica-tions-with-FastAPI-Second-Edition/tree/main/chapter04/chapter04_working_pydantic_objects_04.py

As you can see, the path operation function gives us a valid `PostCreate` object. Then, we want to transform it into a `Post` object.

We first determine the missing `id` property, which is given to us by the database. Here, we use a dummy database based on a dictionary, so we simply take the highest key that's already present in the database and increment it. In a real-world situation, this would have been automatically determined by the database.

The most interesting line here is the `Post` instantiation. You can see that we first assign the missing fields using keyword arguments and then unpack the dictionary representation of `post_create`. As a reminder, the effect of `**` in a function call is to transform a dictionary such as `{"title": "Foo", "content": "Bar"}` into keyword arguments such as this: `title="Foo", content="Bar"`. It's a very convenient and dynamic approach to set all the fields we already have into our new model.

Notice that we also set the `response_model` argument on the path operation decorator. We explained this in *Chapter 3, Developing a RESTful API with FastAPI*, but basically, it prompts FastAPI to build a JSON response with only the fields of `PostRead`, even though we return a `Post` instance at the end of the function.

Updating an instance partially

In some situations, you'll want to allow partial updates. In other words, you'll allow the end user to only send the fields they want to change to your API and omit the ones that shouldn't change. This is the usual way of implementing a PATCH endpoint.

To do this, you would first need a special Pydantic model with all the fields marked as optional so that no error is raised when a field is missing. Let's see what this looks like with our `Post` example, as follows:

chapter04_working_pydantic_objects_05.py

```
class PostBase(BaseModel):
    title: str
    content: str


class PostPartialUpdate(BaseModel):
    title: str | None = None
    content: str | None = None
```

https://github.com/PacktPublishing/Building-Data-Science-Applications-with-FastAPI-Second-Edition/tree/main/chapter04/chapter04_working_pydantic_objects_05.py

We are now able to implement an endpoint that will accept a subset of our Post fields. Since it's an update, we'll retrieve an existing post in the database thanks to its ID. Then, we'll have to find a way to only update the fields in the payload and keep the others untouched. Fortunately, Pydantic once again has this covered, with handy methods and options.

Let's see how the implementation of such an endpoint could look in the following example:

chapter04_working_pydantic_objects_05.py

```python
@app.patch("/posts/{id}", response_model=PostRead)
async def partial_update(id: int, post_update: PostPartialUpdate):
    try:
        post_db = db.posts[id]

        updated_fields = post_update.dict(exclude_unset=True)
        updated_post = post_db.copy(update=updated_fields)

        db.posts[id] = updated_post
        return updated_post
    except KeyError:
        raise HTTPException(status.HTTP_404_NOT_FOUND)
```

https://github.com/PacktPublishing/Building-Data-Science-Applications-with-FastAPI-Second-Edition/tree/main/chapter04/chapter04_working_pydantic_objects_05.py

Our path operation function takes two arguments: the id property (from the path) and a PostPartialUpdate instance (from the body).

The first thing to do is to check whether this id property exists in the database. Since we use a dictionary for our dummy database, accessing a key that doesn't exist will raise a KeyError. If this happens, we simply raise an HTTPException with the 404 status code.

Now for the interesting part: updating an existing object. You can see that the first thing to do is transform PostPartialUpdate into a dictionary with the dict method. This time, however, we set the exclude_unset argument to True. The effect of this is that *Pydantic won't output the fields that were not provided* in the resulting dictionary: we only get the fields that the user sent in the payload.

Then, on our existing post_db database instance, we call the copy method. This is a useful method for cloning a Pydantic object into another instance. The nice thing about this method is that it even accepts an update argument. This argument expects a dictionary with all the fields that should be updated during the copy: that's exactly what we want to do with our updated_fields dictionary!

And that's it! We now have an updated `post` instance with only the changes required in the payload. You'll probably use the `exclude_unset` argument and the `copy` method quite often while developing with FastAPI, so be sure to keep them in mind — they'll make your life easier!

Summary

Congratulations! You've learned about another important aspect of FastAPI: designing and managing data models with Pydantic. You should now be confident about creating models and applying validation at the field level, with built-in options and types, and also by implementing your own validation methods. You also know how to apply validation at the object level to check consistency between several fields. You also learned how to leverage model inheritance to prevent code duplication and repetition while defining your model variations. Finally, you learned how to correctly work with Pydantic model instances in order to transform and update them in an efficient and readable way.

You know almost all the features of FastAPI by now. There is one last very powerful feature for you to learn about: **dependency injection**. This allows you to define your own logic and values and directly inject them into your path operation functions, as you do for path parameters and payload objects, which you'll be able to reuse everywhere in your project. That's the subject of the next chapter.

5

Dependency Injection in FastAPI

In this chapter, we'll focus on one of the most interesting parts of FastAPI: **dependency injection**. You'll see that it is a powerful and readable approach to reusing logic across your project. Indeed, it will allow you to create complex building blocks for your project, which you'll be able to use everywhere in your logic. An authentication system, a query parameter validator, or a rate limiter are typical use cases for dependencies. In FastAPI, a dependency injection can even call another one recursively, allowing you to build high-level blocks from basic features. By the end of this chapter, you'll be able to create your own dependencies for FastAPI and use them at several levels of your project.

In this chapter, we're going to cover the following main topics:

- What is dependency injection?
- Creating and using a function dependency
- Creating and using a parameterized dependency with a class
- Using dependencies at the path, router, and global level

Technical requirements

To run the code examples, you'll need a Python virtual environment, which we set up in *Chapter 1, Python Development Environment Setup*.

You'll find all the code examples for this chapter in the dedicated GitHub repository at https:// github.com/PacktPublishing/Building-Data-Science-Applications-with-FastAPI-Second-Edition/tree/main/chapter05.

What is dependency injection?

Generally speaking, **dependency injection** is a system to automatically instantiate objects and the ones they depend on. The responsibility of developers is then to only provide a declaration of how an object should be created, and let the system resolve all the dependency chains and create the actual objects at runtime.

FastAPI allows you to declare only the objects and variables you wish to have at hand by declaring them in the path operation function arguments. Actually, we already used dependency injection in the previous chapters. In the following example, we use the Header function to retrieve the user-agent header:

chapter05_what_is_dependency_injection_01.py

```
from fastapi import FastAPI, Header

app = FastAPI()


@app.get("/")
async def header(user_agent: str = Header(...)):
    return {"user_agent": user_agent}
```

https://github.com/PacktPublishing/Building-Data-Science-Applications-with-FastAPI-Second-Edition/tree/main/chapter05/chapter05_what_is_dependency_injection_01.py

Internally, the Header function has some logic to automatically get the request object, check for the required header, return its value, or raise an error if it's not present. From the developer's perspective, however, we don't know how it handled the required objects for this operation: we just ask for the value we need. *That's dependency injection.*

Admittedly, you could reproduce this example quite easily in the function body by picking the user-agent property in the headers dictionary of the request object. However, the dependency injection approach has numerous advantages over this:

- The *intent is clear*: you know what the endpoint expects in the request data without reading the function's code.

- You have a *clear separation of concerns between the logic of the endpoint and the more generic logic*: the header retrieval and the associated error-handling doesn't pollute the rest of the logic; it's self-contained in the dependency function. Besides, it can be reused easily in other endpoints.

- In the case of FastAPI, it's used to *generate the OpenAPI schema* so that the automatic documentation can clearly show which parameters are expected for this endpoint.

Put another way, whenever you need utility logic to retrieve or validate data, make security checks, or call external logic that you'll need several times across your application, a dependency is an ideal choice.

FastAPI relies heavily on this dependency injection system and encourages developers to use it to implement their building blocks. It may be a bit puzzling if you come from other web frameworks such as Flask or Express, but you'll surely be quickly convinced by its power and relevance.

To convince you, we'll now see how you can create and use your very own dependency, in the form of a function to begin with.

Creating and using a function dependency

In FastAPI, a dependency can be defined either as a function or as a callable class. In this section, we'll focus on the functions, which are the ones you'll probably work with most of the time.

As we said, a dependency is a way to wrap some logic that will retrieve some sub-values or sub-objects, make something with them, and finally, return a value that will be injected into the endpoint calling it.

Let's look at the first example where we define a function dependency to retrieve pagination query parameters, `skip` and `limit`:

chapter05_function_dependency_01.py

```
async def pagination(skip: int = 0, limit: int = 10) -> tuple[int,
int]:
    return (skip, limit)


@app.get("/items")
async def list_items(p: tuple[int, int] = Depends(pagination)):
    skip, limit = p
    return {"skip": skip, "limit": limit}
```

```
https://github.com/PacktPublishing/Building-Data-Science-Applica-
tions-with-FastAPI-Second-Edition/tree/main/chapter05/chapter05_
function_dependency_01.py
```

There are two parts to this example:

- First, we have the dependency definition, with the `pagination` function. You see that we define two arguments, `skip` and `limit`, which are integers with default values. Those will be the query parameters on our endpoint. We define them exactly like we would have done on a path operation function. That's the beauty of this approach: FastAPI will recursively handle the arguments on the dependency and match them with the request data, such as query parameters or headers if needed.

  We simply return those values as a tuple.

- Second, we have the path operation function, `list_items`, which uses the `pagination` dependency. You see here that the usage is quite similar to what we have done for header or body values: we define the name of our resulting argument and we use a function result as a default value. In the case of a dependency, we use the `Depends` function. Its role is to take a function in the argument and execute it when the endpoint is called. The sub-dependencies are automatically discovered and executed.

In the endpoint, we have the pagination directly in the form of a tuple.

Let's run this example with the following command:

```
$ uvicorn chapter05_function_dependency_01:app
```

Now, we'll try to call the `/items` endpoint and see whether it's able to retrieve the query parameters. You can try this with the following HTTPie command:

```
$ http "http://localhost:8000/items?limit=5&skip=10"
HTTP/1.1 200 OK
content-length: 21
content-type: application/json
date: Tue, 15 Nov 2022 08:33:46 GMT
server: uvicorn

{
    "limit": 5,
    "skip": 10
}
```

The `limit` and `skip` query parameters have correctly been retrieved thanks to our function dependency. You can also try to call the endpoint without the query parameter and notice that it will return the default values.

Type hint of a dependency return value

You may have noticed that we had to type hint the result of our dependency in the path operation arguments, even though we already type hinted the dependency function itself. Unfortunately, this is a limitation of FastAPI and its `Depends` function, which isn't able to forward the type of the dependency function. Therefore, we have to type hint the result by hand, as we did here.

And that's it! As you see, it's very simple and straightforward to create and use a dependency in FastAPI. Of course, you can now reuse it at will in several endpoints, as you can see in the rest of the example:

chapter05_function_dependency_01.py

```
@app.get("/things")
async def list_things(p: tuple[int, int] = Depends(pagination)):
    skip, limit = p
    return {"skip": skip, "limit": limit}
```

https://github.com/PacktPublishing/Building-Data-Science-Applications-with-FastAPI-Second-Edition/tree/main/chapter05/chapter05_function_dependency_01.py

We can do more complex things in those dependencies, just like we would in a regular path operation function. In the following example, we add some validation to those pagination parameters and cap the limit at 100:

chapter05_function_dependency_02.py

```
async def pagination(
    skip: int = Query(0, ge=0),
    limit: int = Query(10, ge=0),
) -> tuple[int, int]:
    capped_limit = min(100, limit)
    return (skip, capped_limit)
```

https://github.com/PacktPublishing/Building-Data-Science-Applications-with-FastAPI-Second-Edition/tree/main/chapter05/chapter05_function_dependency_02.py

As you can see, our dependency starts to become more complex:

- We added the Query function to our arguments to add a validation constraint; now, a 422 error will be raised if skip or limit are negative integers.
- We ensure that the limit is, at most, 100.

The code on our path operation functions doesn't have to change; we have a clear separation of concerns between the logic of the endpoint and the more generic logic for the pagination parameters.

Let's see another typical use of dependencies: get an object or raise a 404 error.

Getting an object or raising a 404 error

In a REST API, you'll typically have endpoints to get, update, and delete a single object given its identifier in the path. On each one, you'll likely have the same logic: try to retrieve this object in the database or raise a 404 error if it doesn't exist. That's a perfect use case for a dependency! In the following example, you'll see how to implement it:

chapter05_function_dependency_03.py

```python
async def get_post_or_404(id: int) -> Post:
    try:
        return db.posts[id]
    except KeyError:
        raise HTTPException(status_code=status.HTTP_404_NOT_FOUND)
```

https://github.com/PacktPublishing/Building-Data-Science-Applications-with-FastAPI-Second-Edition/tree/main/chapter05/chapter05_function_dependency_03.py

The dependency definition is simple: it takes, in an argument, the ID of the post we want to retrieve. It will be pulled from the corresponding path parameter. Then, we check whether it exists in our dummy dictionary database: if it does, we return it; otherwise, we raise an HTTP exception with a 404 status code.

That's the key takeaway of this example: *you can raise errors in your dependencies*. It's extremely useful to check for some pre-conditions before your endpoint logic is executed. Another typical example of this is authentication: if the endpoint requires a user to be authenticated, we can raise a 401 error in the dependency by checking for the token or the cookie.

Now, we can use this dependency in each of our API endpoints, as you can see in the following example:

chapter05_function_dependency_03.py

```python
@app.get("/posts/{id}")
async def get(post: Post = Depends(get_post_or_404)):
    return post


@app.patch("/posts/{id}")
async def update(post_update: PostUpdate, post: Post = Depends(get_post_or_404)):
    updated_post = post.copy(update=post_update.dict())
    db.posts[post.id] = updated_post
    return updated_post
```

```
@app.delete("/posts/{id}", status_code=status.HTTP_204_NO_CONTENT)
async def delete(post: Post = Depends(get_post_or_404)):
    db.posts.pop(post.id)
```

`https://github.com/PacktPublishing/Building-Data-Science-Applica-tions-with-FastAPI-Second-Edition/tree/main/chapter05/chapter05_function_dependency_03.py`

As you can see, we just had to define the `post` argument and use the `Depends` function on our `get_post_or_404` dependency. Then, within the path operation logic, we are guaranteed to have our `post` object at hand and we can focus on our core logic, which is now very concise. The `get` endpoint, for example, just has to return the object.

In this case, the only point of attention is to not forget the ID parameter in the path of those endpoints. According to the rules of FastAPI, if you don't set this parameter in the path, it will automatically be regarded as a query parameter, which is not what we want here. You can find more details about this in the *Path parameters* section of *Chapter 3, Developing a RESTful API with FastAPI*.

That's all for the function dependencies. As we said, those are the main building blocks of a FastAPI project. In some cases, however, you'll need to have some parameters on those dependencies – for example, with values coming from environment variables. For this, we can define class dependencies.

Creating and using a parameterized dependency with a class

In the previous section, we defined dependencies as regular functions, which work well in most cases. Still, you may need to set some parameters on a dependency to finely tune its behavior. Since the arguments of the function are set by the dependency injection system, we can't add an argument to the function.

In the pagination example, we added some logic to cap the limit value at `100`. If we wanted to set this maximum limit dynamically, how would we do that?

The solution is to create a class that will be used as a dependency. This way, we can set class properties – with the `__init__` method, for example – and use them in the logic of the dependency itself. This logic will be defined in the `__call__` method of the class. If you remember what we learned in the *Callable object* section of *Chapter 2, Python Programming Specificities*, you know that it makes the object callable, meaning it can be called like a regular function. Actually, that is all that `Depends` requires for a dependency: being callable. We'll use this property to create a parameterized dependency thanks to a class.

In the following example, we reimplemented the pagination example with a class, allowing us to set the maximum limit dynamically:

chapter05_class_dependency_01.py

```python
class Pagination:
    def __init__(self, maximum_limit: int = 100):
        self.maximum_limit = maximum_limit

    async def __call__(
        self,
        skip: int = Query(0, ge=0),
        limit: int = Query(10, ge=0),
    ) -> tuple[int, int]:
        capped_limit = min(self.maximum_limit, limit)
        return (skip, capped_limit)
```

https://github.com/PacktPublishing/Building-Data-Science-Applications-with-FastAPI-Second-Edition/tree/main/chapter05/chapter05_class_dependency_01.py

As you can see, the logic in the __call__ method is the same as in the function we defined in the previous example. The only difference here is that we can pull our maximum limit from our class properties, which we can set at the object initialization.

Then, you can simply create an instance of this class and use it as a dependency with Depends on your path operation function, as you can see in the following code block:

chapter05_class_dependency_01.py

```python
pagination = Pagination(maximum_limit=50)


@app.get("/items")
async def list_items(p: tuple[int, int] = Depends(pagination)):
    skip, limit = p
    return {"skip": skip, "limit": limit}
```

https://github.com/PacktPublishing/Building-Data-Science-Applications-with-FastAPI-Second-Edition/tree/main/chapter05/chapter05_class_dependency_01.py

Here, we hardcoded the 50 value, but we could very well pull it from a configuration file or an environment variable.

The other advantage of a class dependency is that it can maintain local values in memory. This property can be very useful if we have to make some heavy initialization logic, such as loading a machine learning model, for example, which we want to do only once at startup. Then, the callable part just has to call the loaded model to make the prediction, which should be quite fast.

Using class methods as dependencies

Even if the __call__ method is the most straightforward way to make a class dependency, you can directly pass a method to Depends. Indeed, as we said, it simply expects a callable as an argument, and a class method is a perfectly valid callable!

This approach can be very useful if you have common parameters or logic that you need to reuse in slightly different cases. For example, you could have one pre-trained machine learning model made with scikit-learn. Before applying the decision function, you may want to apply different preprocessing steps, depending on the input data.

To do this, simply write your logic in a class method and pass it to the Depends function through the dot notation.

You can see this in the following example, where we implement another style for our pagination dependency, with page and size parameters instead of skip and limit:

chapter05_class_dependency_02.py

```python
class Pagination:
    def __init__(self, maximum_limit: int = 100):
        self.maximum_limit = maximum_limit

    async def skip_limit(
        self,
        skip: int = Query(0, ge=0),
        limit: int = Query(10, ge=0),
    ) -> tuple[int, int]:
        capped_limit = min(self.maximum_limit, limit)
        return (skip, capped_limit)

    async def page_size(
        self,
        page: int = Query(1, ge=1),
        size: int = Query(10, ge=0),
    ) -> tuple[int, int]:
        capped_size = min(self.maximum_limit, size)
        return (page, capped_size)
```

```
https://github.com/PacktPublishing/Building-Data-Science-Applica-
tions-with-FastAPI-Second-Edition/tree/main/chapter05/chapter05_
class_dependency_02.py
```

The logic of the two methods is quite similar. We just look at different query parameters. Then, on our path operation functions, we set the /items endpoint to work with the skip/limit style, while the /things endpoint will work with the page/size style:

chapter05_class_dependency_02.py

```python
pagination = Pagination(maximum_limit=50)

@app.get("/items")
async def list_items(p: tuple[int, int] = Depends(pagination.skip_
limit)):
    skip, limit = p
    return {"skip": skip, "limit": limit}

@app.get("/things")
async def list_things(p: tuple[int, int] = Depends(pagination.page_
size)):
    page, size = p
    return {"page": page, "size": size}
```

```
https://github.com/PacktPublishing/Building-Data-Science-Applica-
tions-with-FastAPI-Second-Edition/tree/main/chapter05/chapter05_
class_dependency_02.py
```

As you can see, we only have to pass the method we want through the dot notation on the pagination object.

To sum up, the class dependency approach is more advanced than the function approach but can be very useful for cases when you need to set parameters dynamically, perform heavy initialization logic, or reuse common logic on several dependencies.

Until now, we've assumed that we care about the return value of the dependency. While this will probably be the case most of the time, you may occasionally need to call a dependency to check for some conditions but don't really need the returned value. FastAPI allows such use cases, and that's what we'll see now.

Using dependencies at the path, router, and global level

As we said, dependencies are the recommended way to create building blocks in a FastAPI project, allowing you to reuse logic across endpoints while maintaining maximum code readability. Until now, we've applied them to a single endpoint, but couldn't we expand this approach to a whole router? Or even a whole FastAPI application? Actually, we can!

The main motivation for this is to be able to apply some global request validation or perform side logic on several routes without the need to add a dependency on each endpoint. Typically, an authentication method or a rate limiter could be very good candidates for this use case.

To show you how it works, we'll implement a simple dependency that we will use across all the following examples. You can see it in the following example:

chapter05_path_dependency_01.py

```python
def secret_header(secret_header: str | None = Header(None)) -> None:
    if not secret_header or secret_header != "SECRET_VALUE":
        raise HTTPException(status.HTTP_403_FORBIDDEN)
```

https://github.com/PacktPublishing/Building-Data-Science-Applications-with-FastAPI-Second-Edition/tree/main/chapter05/chapter05_path_dependency_01.py

This dependency will simply look for a header in the request named Secret-Header. If it's missing or not equal to SECRET_VALUE, it will raise a 403 error. Please note that this approach is only for the sake of the example; there are better ways to secure your API, which we'll cover in *Chapter 7, Managing Authentication and Security in FastAPI*.

Using a dependency on a path decorator

Until now, we've assumed that we were always interested in the return value of the dependency. As our secret_header dependency clearly shows here, this is not always the case. This is why you can add a dependency on a path operation decorator instead of the arguments. You can see how in the following example:

chapter05_path_dependency_01.py

```python
@app.get("/protected-route", dependencies=[Depends(secret_header)])
async def protected_route():
    return {"hello": "world"}
```

https://github.com/PacktPublishing/Building-Data-Science-Applications-with-FastAPI-Second-Edition/tree/main/chapter05/chapter05_path_dependency_01.py

The path operation decorator accepts an argument, `dependencies`, which expects a list of dependencies. You see that, just like for dependencies you pass in arguments, you need to wrap your function (or callable) with the `Depends` function.

Now, whenever the `/protected-route` route is called, the dependency will be called and will check for the required header.

As you may have guessed, since `dependencies` is a list, you can add as many dependencies as you need.

That's interesting, but what if we want to protect a whole set of endpoints? It would be a bit cumbersome and error-prone to add it manually to each one. Fortunately, FastAPI provides a way to do that.

Using a dependency on a whole router

If you recall the *Structuring a bigger project with multiple routers* section in *Chapter 3, Developing a RESTful API with FastAPI*, you know that you can create several routers in your project to clearly split the different parts of your API and "wire" them to your main FastAPI application. This is done with the `APIRouter` class and the `include_router` method of the `FastAPI` class.

With this approach, it can be interesting to inject a dependency into the whole router, so that it's called for every route of this router. You have two ways of doing this:

- Set the `dependencies` argument on the `APIRouter` class, as you can see in the following example:

chapter05_router_dependency_01.py

```python
router = APIRouter(dependencies=[Depends(secret_header)])


@router.get("/route1")
async def router_route1():
    return {"route": "route1"}


@router.get("/route2")
async def router_route2():
    return {"route": "route2"}


app = FastAPI()
app.include_router(router, prefix="/router")
```

https://github.com/PacktPublishing/Building-Data-Science-Applications-with-FastAPI-Second-Edition/tree/main/chapter05/chapter05_router_dependency_01.py

- Set the `dependencies` argument on the `include_router` method, as you can see in the following example:

chapter05_router_dependency_02.py

```
router = APIRouter()

@router.get("/route1")
async def router_route1():
    return {"route": "route1"}

@router.get("/route2")
async def router_route2():
    return {"route": "route2"}

app = FastAPI()
app.include_router(router, prefix="/router",
dependencies=[Depends(secret_header)])
```

https://github.com/PacktPublishing/Building-Data-Science-Applications-with-FastAPI-Second-Edition/tree/main/chapter05/chapter05_router_dependency_02.py

In both cases, the `dependencies` argument expects a list of dependencies. You can see that, just like for dependencies you pass in arguments, you need to wrap your function (or callable) with the `Depends` function. Of course, since it's a list, you can add several dependencies if you need.

Now, how to choose between the two approaches? In both cases, the effect will be exactly the same, so we could say it doesn't really matter. Philosophically, we could say that we should declare a dependency on the `APIRouter` class if it's needed in the context of this router. Put another way, we could ask ourselves the question, *Does this router work without this dependency if we run it independently?* If the answer to this question is *no*, then you should probably set the dependency on the `APIRouter` class. Otherwise, declaring it in the `include_router` method may make more sense. But again, this is an intellectual choice that won't change the functionality of your API, so feel free to choose the one you're more comfortable with.

We are now able to set dependencies for a whole router. In some cases, it could also be interesting to declare them for a whole application!

Using a dependency on a whole application

If you have a dependency that implements some logging or rate-limiting functionality, for example, it could be interesting to execute it for every endpoint of your API. Fortunately, FastAPI allows this, as you can see in the following example:

chapter05_global_dependency_01.py

```python
app = FastAPI(dependencies=[Depends(secret_header)])

@app.get("/route1")
async def route1():
    return {"route": "route1"}

@app.get("/route2")
async def route2():
    return {"route": "route2"}
```

https://github.com/PacktPublishing/Building-Data-Science-Applications-with-FastAPI-Second-Edition/tree/main/chapter05/chapter05_global_dependency_01.py

Once again, you only have to set the `dependencies` argument directly on the main `FastAPI` class. Now, the dependency is applied to every endpoint in your API!

In *Figure 5.1*, we propose a simple decision tree to determine at which level you should inject your dependency:

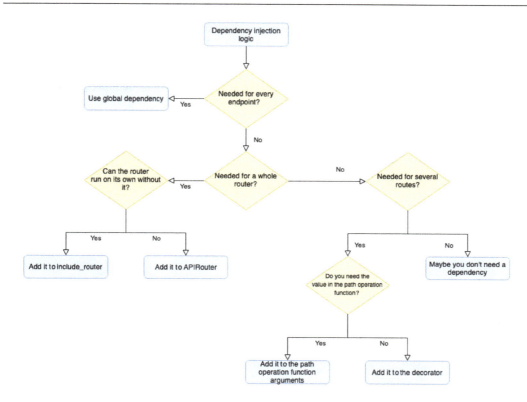

Figure 5.1 – At which level should I inject my dependency?

Summary

Well done! You should now be comfortable with one of the most iconic features of FastAPI: dependency injection. By implementing your own dependencies, you'll be able to keep common logic that you wish to reuse across your API separate from the endpoints' logic. This will make your project clean and maintainable while retaining maximum readability; dependencies just need to be declared as arguments of the path operation functions, which will help you to understand the intent without having to read the body of the function.

Those dependencies can be both simple wrappers to retrieve and validate request parameters, or complex services performing machine learning tasks. Thanks to the class-based approach, you can indeed set dynamic parameters or keep a local state for your most advanced tasks.

Finally, those dependencies can also be used at a router or global level, allowing you to perform common logic or checks for a set of routes or a whole application.

That's the end of the first part of this book! You're now acquainted with the main features of FastAPI and should now be able to write clean and performant REST APIs with the framework.

In the next part, we'll take your knowledge to the next level and show you how you can implement and deploy a robust, secure, and tested web backend. The first chapter will be dedicated to databases, a must-have for most APIs to be able to read and write data.

Part 2:
Building and Deploying
a Complete Web Backend
with FastAPI

The goal of this section is to show you how to build a real-world backend with FastAPI that can read and write data and authenticate users, and that is properly tested and correctly configured for a production environment.

This section comprises the following chapters:

- *Chapter 6, Databases and Asynchronous ORMs*
- *Chapter 7, Managing Authentication and Security in FastAPI*
- *Chapter 8, Defining WebSockets for Two-Way Interactive Communication in FastAPI*
- *Chapter 9, Testing an API Asynchronously with pytest and HTTPX*
- *Chapter 10, Deploying a FastAPI Project*

6

Databases and Asynchronous ORMs

The main goal of a REST API is, of course, to read and write data. So far, we've solely worked with the tools given by Python and FastAPI, allowing us to build reliable endpoints to process and answer requests. However, we haven't been able to effectively retrieve and persist that information: we don't have a **database**.

The goal of this chapter is to show you how you can interact with different types of databases and related libraries inside FastAPI. It's worth noting that FastAPI is completely agnostic regarding databases: you can use any system you want and it's your responsibility to integrate it. This is why we'll review two different approaches to integrating a database: using an **object-relational mapping** (**ORM**) system for SQL databases and using a NoSQL database.

In this chapter, we're going to cover the following main topics:

- An overview of relational and NoSQL databases

- Communicating with a SQL database with SQLAlchemy ORM

- Communicating with a MongoDB database using Motor

Technical requirements

For this chapter, you'll require a Python virtual environment, just as we set up in *Chapter 1, Python Development Environment Setup*.

For the *Communicating with a MongoDB database using Motor* section, you'll need a running MongoDB server on your local computer. The easiest way to do this is to run it as a Docker container. If you've never used Docker before, we recommend that you refer to the *Getting started* tutorial in the official documentation at https://docs.docker.com/get-started/. Once you have done this, you'll be able to run a MongoDB server using this simple command:

```
$ docker run -d --name fastapi-mongo -p 27017:27017 mongo:6.0
```

The MongoDB server instance will then be available on your local computer at port `27017`.

You can find all the code examples for this chapter in this book's dedicated GitHub repository at `https://github.com/PacktPublishing/Building-Data-Science-Applications-with-FastAPI-Second-Edition/tree/main/chapter06`.

An overview of relational and NoSQL databases

The role of a database is to store data in a structured way, preserve the integrity of the data, and offer a query language that enables you to retrieve this data when an application needs it.

Nowadays, when it comes to choosing a database for your web project, you have two main choices: **relational databases**, with their associated SQL query language, and **NoSQL databases**, named in opposition to the first category.

Selecting the right technology for your project is left up to you as it greatly depends on your needs and requirements. In this section, we'll outline the main characteristics and features of those two database families and try to give you some insights into choosing the right one for your project.

Relational databases

Relational databases have existed since the 1970s, and they have proved to be very performant and reliable over time. They are almost inseparable from SQL, which has become the de facto standard for querying such databases. Even if there are a few differences between one database engine and another, most of the syntax is common, simple to understand, and flexible enough to express complex queries.

Relational databases implement the relational model: each entity, or object, of the application is stored in **tables**. For example, if we consider a blog application, we could have tables that represent *users*, *posts*, and *comments*.

Each of those tables will have several **columns** representing the attributes of the entity. If we consider posts, we could have a *title*, a *publication date*, and *content*. In those tables, there will be several rows, each one representing a single entity of this type; each post will have its own row.

One of the key points of relational databases is, as their name suggests, *relationships*. Each table can be in a relationship with others, with rows referring to other rows in other tables. In our example, a post could be related to the user who wrote it. In the same way, a comment could be linked to the post that it relates to.

The main motivation behind this is to *avoid duplication*. Indeed, it wouldn't be very efficient to repeat the user's name or email on each post. If it needs to be modified at some point, we would have to go through each post, which is error-prone and puts data consistency at risk. This is why we prefer to *reference* the user in the posts. So, how can we do this?

Usually, each row in a relational database has an identifier, called a **primary key**. This is unique in the table and allows you to uniquely identify this row. Therefore, it's possible to use this key in another table to reference it. We call this a **foreign key**: the key is foreign in the sense that it refers to another table.

Figure 6.1 shows a representation of such a database schema using an entity-relationship diagram. Note that each table has its own primary key, named id. The Post table refers to a user, through the user_id foreign key. Similarly, the Comment table refers to both a post and a user through the user_id and post_id foreign keys:

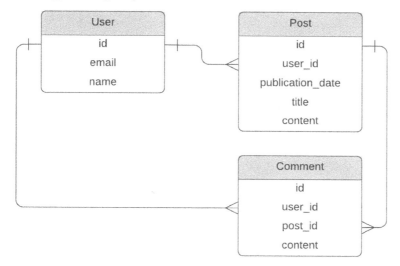

Figure 6.1 – A relational database schema example for a blog application

In an application, you'll likely want to retrieve a post, along with the comments and the users associated with them. To do so, we can perform a **join query**, which will return all the relevant records based on the foreign keys. Relational databases are designed to perform such tasks efficiently; however, those operations can become expensive if the schema is more complex. This is why it's important to carefully design a relational schema and its queries.

NoSQL databases

All database engines that are not relational fall back into the NoSQL category. This is a quite vague denomination that regroups different families of databases: key-value stores, such as Redis; graph databases, such as Neo4j; and document-oriented databases, such as MongoDB. That said, most of the time, when we talk about "NoSQL databases," we are implicitly referring to document-oriented databases. They are the ones we're interested in.

Document-oriented databases move away from the relational architecture and try to store all the information of a given object inside a single **document**. As such, performing a join query is much rarer and usually more difficult.

Those documents are stored in **collections**. Contrary to relational databases, documents in a collection might not have all of the same attributes: while tables in relational databases have a defined schema, collections accept any kind of document.

Figure 6.2 shows a representation of our previous blog example, which has been adapted into a document-oriented database structure. In this configuration, we have chosen to have a collection for users and another one for posts. However, notice that the comments are now part of a post, directly included as a list:

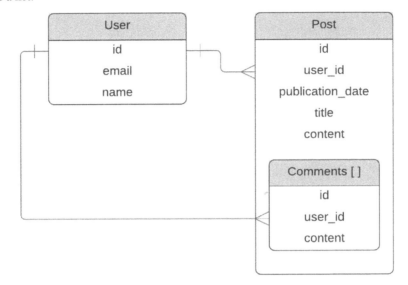

Figure 6.2 — A document-oriented schema example for a blog application

To retrieve a post and all of its comments, you don't need to perform a join query: all the data comes in one query. This was the main motivation behind the development of document-oriented databases: increase query performance by limiting the need to look at several collections. In particular, they proved to be useful for applications with huge data scales and less structured data, such as social networks.

Which one should you choose?

As we mentioned in the introduction to this section, your choice of database engine greatly depends on your application and needs. A detailed comparison between relational and document-oriented databases is beyond the scope of this book, but let's look at some elements for you to think about.

Relational databases are very good for storing structured data with a lot of relationships between entities. Besides, they maintain data consistency at all costs, even in the event of errors or hardware failures. However, you'll have to precisely define your schema and consider a migration system to update your schema if your needs evolve.

On the other hand, document-oriented databases don't require you to define a schema: they accept any document structure, so they can be convenient if your data is highly variable or if your project is not mature enough. The downside of this is that they are far less picky in terms of data consistency, which could result in data loss or inconsistencies.

For small and medium-sized applications, the choice doesn't matter too much: both relational databases and document-oriented databases are very optimized and will deliver awesome performance at such scales.

Next, we'll show you how to work with these different kinds of databases using FastAPI. When we introduced asynchronous I/O in *Chapter 2*, *Python Programming Specificities*, we mentioned that it was important to carefully select the libraries you use to perform I/O operations. Of course, databases are particularly important in this context!

While working with classic non-async libraries is perfectly possible in FastAPI, you could miss out on one of the key aspects of the framework and might not reach the best performance it can offer. That's why, in this chapter, we'll only focus on async libraries.

Communicating with a SQL database with SQLAlchemy ORM

To begin, we'll discuss how to work with a relational database using the SQLAlchemy library. SQLAlchemy has been around for years and is the most popular library in Python when you wish to work with SQL databases. Since version 1.4, it also natively supports async.

The key thing to understand about this library is that it's composed of two parts:

- **SQLAlchemy Core**, which provides all the fundamental features to read and write data to SQL databases
- **SQLAlchemy ORM**, which provides a powerful abstraction over SQL concepts

While you can choose to only use SQLAlchemy Core, it's generally more convenient to use ORM. The goal of ORM is to abstract away the SQL concepts of tables and columns so that you only have to deal with Python objects. The role of ORM is to *map* those objects to the tables and columns they belong to and generate the corresponding SQL queries automatically.

The first step is to install this library:

```
(venv) $ pip install "sqlalchemy[asyncio,mypy]"
```

Notice that we added two optional dependencies: `asyncio` and `mypy`. The first one ensures the tools for async support are installed.

The second one is a special plugin for mypy that provides special support for SQLAlchemy. ORM does a lot of magic things under the hood, which are hard for type checkers to understand. With this plugin, mypy learns to recognize those constructs.

As we said in the introduction, numerous SQL engines exist. You have probably heard of PostgreSQL and MySQL, which are among the most popular. Another interesting choice is SQLite, a tiny engine that stores all the data inside a single file on your computer, without the need for complex server software. It's ideal for testing and experimenting. To allow SQLAlchemy to talk to those engines, you'll need to install the corresponding **driver**. Here are the async drivers you'll need to install, depending on your engine:

- PostgreSQL:

  ```
  (venv) $ pip install asyncpg
  ```

- MySQL:

  ```
  (venv) $ pip install aiomysql
  ```

- SQLite:

  ```
  (venv) $ pip install aiosqlite
  ```

For the rest of this section, we'll work with SQLite databases. We'll show you, step by step, how to set up a complete database interaction. *Figure 6.4* shows the structure of the project:

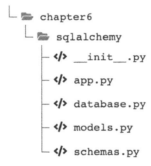

Figure 6.3 – The FastAPI and SQLAlchemy project structure

Creating ORM models

First, you need to define your ORM models. Each one is a Python class whose attributes represent the columns of your table. The actual entities of your database will be instances of this class, giving you access to its data, just like any other object. Under the hood, the role of SQLAlchemy ORM is to link this Python object and the row in the database. Let's take a look at the definition of our blog post model:

models.py

```python
from datetime import datetime

from sqlalchemy import DateTime, Integer, String, Text
```

```
from sqlalchemy.orm import DeclarativeBase, Mapped, mapped_column

class Base(DeclarativeBase):
    pass

class Post(Base):
    __tablename__ = "posts"

    id: Mapped[int] = mapped_column(Integer, primary_key=True,
autoincrement=True)
    publication_date: Mapped[datetime] = mapped_column(
        DateTime, nullable=False, default=datetime.now
    )
    title: Mapped[str] = mapped_column(String(255), nullable=False)
    content: Mapped[str] = mapped_column(Text, nullable=False)
```

https://github.com/PacktPublishing/Building-Data-Science-Applica-
tions-with-FastAPI-Second-Edition/tree/main/chapter06/sqlalchemy/
models.py

The first step is to create a `Base` class that inherits from `DeclarativeBase`. *All our models will inherit from this class.* Internally, SQLAlchemy uses it to keep all the information about your database schema together. This is why you should create it only once in your whole project and always use the same one throughout.

Next, we must define our `Post` class. Once again, notice how it inherits from `Base`. Inside this class, we can define each of our columns in the form of class properties. They are assigned thanks to the `mapped_column` function, which helps us define the type of the column and its related properties. For example, we define our `id` column as an integer primary key with auto-increment, which is quite common in a SQL database.

Note that we won't go through all the types and options provided by SQLAlchemy. Just know that they closely follow the ones that are usually provided by SQL databases. You can check the complete list in the official documentation, as follows:

- You can find the list of types at `https://docs.sqlalchemy.org/en/20/core/type_basics.html#generic-camelcase-types`

- You can find the list of `mapped_column` arguments at `https://docs.sqlalchemy.org/en/20/orm/mapping_api.html#sqlalchemy.orm.mapped_column`

Another interesting thing to notice here is that we added type hints to each property, which correspond to the Python type of our columns. This will greatly help us during development: for example, if we try to get the `title` property of a post object, the type checker will know it's a string. For this to work, notice that we wrap each type with the `Mapped` class. This is a special class provided by SQLAlchemy so that the type checker can understand the underlying type of the data when we assign it a `MappedColumn` object.

This is how you declare models in SQLAlchemy 2.0

The way we'll show you to declare models in this section is the newest way to do so, as introduced in SQLAlchemy 2.0.

If you look at older tutorials or documentation on the web, you'll probably come across a slightly different way where we assign properties to a `Column` object. While this older style still works in SQLAlchemy 2.0, it should be considered deprecated.

We now have a model that will help us read and write post data to our database. However, as you're now aware, with FastAPI, we'll also need Pydantic models so that we can validate input data and output the right representation in our API. If you need a refresher about this, you can check *Chapter 3, Developing a RESTful API with FastAPI*.

Defining Pydantic models

As we said, if we want to correctly validate the data coming in and out of our FastAPI application, we'll need Pydantic models. In an ORM context, they will help us *go back and forth with the ORM model*. That's the key takeaway of this section: we'll use Pydantic models to validate and serialize the data, but the database communication will be done with the ORM model.

To avoid confusion, we'll now refer to Pydantic models as **schemas**. When we talk about models, we'll be referring to the ORM model.

That's why the definitions of those schemas are placed in the `schemas.py` module, which can be seen here:

schemas.py

```
from datetime import datetime

from pydantic import BaseModel, Field

class PostBase(BaseModel):
    title: str
    content: str
    publication_date: datetime = Field(default_factory=datetime.now)
```

```
    class Config:
        orm_mode = True

class PostPartialUpdate(BaseModel):
    title: str | None = None
    content: str | None = None

class PostCreate(PostBase):
    pass

class PostRead(PostBase):
    id: int
```

https://github.com/PacktPublishing/Building-Data-Science-Applications-with-FastAPI-Second-Edition/tree/main/chapter06/sqlalchemy/schemas.py

The preceding code corresponds to the pattern we explained in *Chapter 4, Managing Pydantic Data Models in FastAPI*.

There is a new thing, though: you probably noticed the `Config` subclass, which is defined in `PostBase`. It's a way to add some configuration options to Pydantic schemas. Here, we set the `orm_mode` option to `True`. As its name suggests, it's an option to make Pydantic work better with ORM. In a standard setting, Pydantic is designed to parse data from dictionaries: if it wants to parse the `title` property, it'll use `d["title"]`. With ORM, however, we access the properties like an object – that is, by using dot notation (`o.title`). Enabling ORM mode allows Pydantic to use this style.

Connecting to a database

Now that our model and schemas are ready, we have to set up the connection between our FastAPI app and the database engine. For this, we'll create a `database.py` module where we'll put the objects we need for this task:

database.py

```
from collections.abc import AsyncGenerator

from sqlalchemy.ext.asyncio import AsyncSession, async_sessionmaker,
create_async_engine

from chapter06.sqlalchemy.models import Base

DATABASE_URL = "sqlite+aiosqlite:///chapter06_sqlalchemy.db"
```

```
engine = create_async_engine(DATABASE_URL)
async_session_maker = async_sessionmaker(engine, expire_on_
commit=False)
```

https://github.com/PacktPublishing/Building-Data-Science-Applica-
tions-with-FastAPI-Second-Edition/tree/main/chapter06/sqlalchemy/
database.py

Here, you can see that we have set our connection string inside the DATABASE_URL variable. Generally, it consists of the following:

- The database engine. Here, we use sqlite.

- Optionally, the driver, after a plus sign. Here, we set aiosqlite. In an async context, it's necessary to specify the async driver we want to use. Otherwise, SQLAlchemy will fall back to a standard, synchronous driver.

- Optionally, the authentication information.

- The hostname of the database server. In the case of SQLite, we simply have to specify the path of the file that will store all the data.

You can find an overview of this format in the official SQLAlchemy documentation at https://docs.sqlalchemy.org/en/20/core/engines.html#database-urls.

Then, we create an engine using the create_async_engine function and this URL. An engine is an object where SQLAlchemy will manage the connection with your database. At this point, it's important to understand that no connection is being made: we are just declaring things.

We then have a more cryptic line to define the async_session_maker variable. We won't go too much into the details of the async_sessionmaker function. Just know that it returns a function so that we can generate **sessions** tied to our database engine.

What is a session? It's a concept defined by ORM. A session will establish an actual connection with the database and represent a *zone* where it'll store all the objects you've read from the database and all the ones you've defined that'll be written to the database. It's the proxy between the ORM concepts and the fundamental SQL queries.

When building HTTP servers, we usually *open a fresh session when the request starts* and *close it when we answered the request*. Therefore, each HTTP request represents a unit of work with the database. That's why we must define a FastAPI dependency whose role is to yield us a fresh session:

---

database.py

```
async def get_async_session() -> AsyncGenerator[AsyncSession, None]:
    async with async_session_maker() as session:
        yield session
```

https://github.com/PacktPublishing/Building-Data-Science-Applications-with-FastAPI-Second-Edition/tree/main/chapter06/sqlalchemy/database.py

---

Having it as a dependency will greatly help us when implementing our path operation functions.

So far, we haven't had the opportunity to talk about the `with` syntax. In Python, this is what's called a **context manager**. Simply put, it's a convenient syntax for objects that need to execute *setup logic* when they are used and *teardown logic* when they are not needed anymore. When you *enter* the `with` block, the object automatically executes the setup logic. When you *exit* the block, it executes its teardown logic. You can read more about context managers in the Python documentation: `https://docs.python.org/3/reference/datamodel.html#with-statement-context-managers`.

In our case, `async_session_maker` works as a context manager. Among other things, it takes care of opening a connection to the database.

Notice that we define a generator here by using `yield`. This is important because it ensures that the *session remains open until the end of the request*. If we were to use a simple `return` statement, the context manager would close immediately. With `yield`, we make sure we only get out of the context manager when the request and our endpoint logic have been fully handled by FastAPI.

Using a dependency to retrieve a database instance

You might be wondering why we don't just call `async_session_maker` directly in our path operation functions rather than using a dependency. This would work, but it would make our life very hard when we try to implement unit tests. Indeed, it would be very difficult to replace this instance with a mock or test database. With a dependency, FastAPI makes it very easy to swap it with another function. We'll see this in more detail in *Chapter 9, Testing an API Asynchronously with pytest and HTTPX*.

The last thing we must define in this module is the `create_all_tables` function. Its goal is to create the table's schema inside our database. If we don't do that, our database will be empty and we wouldn't be able to save or retrieve data. Creating a schema like this is a simple approach that's only suitable for simple examples and experiments. In a real-world application, you should have a proper migration system whose role is to make sure your database schema is in sync. We'll learn how to set one up for SQLAlchemy later in this chapter.

To make sure our schema is created when our application starts, we must call this function the **lifespan handler** of FastAPI. This is useful to execute some logic when the application is started and stopped. That's what we'll do in our `app.py` module:

app.py

```python
@contextlib.asynccontextmanager
async def lifespan(app: FastAPI):
    await create_all_tables()
    yield
```

https://github.com/PacktPublishing/Building-Data-Science-Applications-with-FastAPI-Second-Edition/tree/main/chapter06/sqlalchemy/app.py

Creating objects

Let's start by inserting new objects inside our database. The main challenge is to take a Pydantic schema as input, transform it into a SQLAlchemy model, and save it in the database. Let's review this process, which is shown in the following example:

app.py

```python
@app.post(
    "/posts", response_model=schemas.PostRead, status_code=status.HTTP_201_CREATED
)
async def create_post(
    post_create: schemas.PostCreate, session: AsyncSession = Depends(get_async_session)
) -> Post:
    post = Post(**post_create.dict())
    session.add(post)
    await session.commit()

    return post
```

```
https://github.com/PacktPublishing/Building-Data-Science-Applica-
tions-with-FastAPI-Second-Edition/tree/main/chapter06/sqlalchemy/
app.py
```

Here, we have our POST endpoint, which accepts our PostCreate schema. Notice that we inject a fresh SQLAlchemy session using our get_async_session dependency. The core logic consists of two operations.

First, we transform post_create into a full Post model object. For this, we can simply call the dict method of Pydantic and *unpack* it with ** to directly assign the properties. At this point, the post is not in the database yet: we need to tell the session about it.

The first step is to *add it in the session*, through the add method. Now, the post is in the session memory, but not in the database yet. By calling the commit method, we tell the session to generate the appropriate SQL queries and execute them on the database. As we might expect, we see that we need to *await* this method: we perform an I/O operation on the database, so it's an async operation.

Finally, we can just return the post object. You may be surprised that we directly return a SQLAlchemy ORM object rather than a Pydantic schema. How could FastAPI correctly serialize it with the properties we specified? If you pay attention, you'll see that we set the response_model property in the path operation decorator. As you may recall from the *Response model* section of *Chapter 3, Developing a RESTful API with FastAPI*, you'll understand what is going on: FastAPI will automatically take care of transforming the ORM object into the specified schema. And that's exactly why we need to enable orm_mode of Pydantic, as shown in the previous section!

From this, you can see that the implementation is quite straightforward. Now, let's retrieve this data!

Getting and filtering objects

Usually, a REST API provides two types of endpoints to read data: one to list objects and one to get a specific object. This is exactly what we'll review next!

In the following example, you can see how we implemented the endpoint to list objects:

app.py

```
@app.get("/posts", response_model=list[schemas.PostRead])
async def list_posts(
    pagination: tuple[int, int] = Depends(pagination),
    session: AsyncSession = Depends(get_async_session),
) -> Sequence[Post]:
    skip, limit = pagination
    select_query = select(Post).offset(skip).limit(limit)
    result = await session.execute(select_query)
```

```
        return result.scalars().all()
```

The operation is performed in two steps. First, we build a query. The `select` function of SQLAlchemy allows us to begin defining a query. Conveniently, we can directly pass it the `model` class: it'll automatically understand which table we are talking about. From there, we can apply various methods and filters, which are a mirror of what we could expect in pure SQL. Here, we're able to apply our pagination parameters through `offset` and `limit`.

Then, we execute this query using the `execute` method of a fresh session object (which was, once again, injected by our dependency). Since we read data from the database, it's an async operation.

From this, we get a `result` object. This object is an instance of the `Result` class of SQLAlchemy. It's not directly our list of posts, but rather a set representing the results of the SQL query. That's why we need to call `scalars` and `all`. The first one will make sure we get actual `Post` objects, while the second will return them as a sequence.

Once again, we can directly return those SQLAlchemy ORM objects: FastAPI will transform them into the correct schema thanks to the `response_model` setting.

Now, let's see how we can retrieve a single post by ID:

app.py

```
@app.get("/posts/{id}", response_model=schemas.PostRead)
async def get_post(post: Post = Depends(get_post_or_404)) -> Post:
    return post
```

This is a simple GET endpoint that expects the ID of the post in the path parameter. The implementation is very light: we just return the post. Most of the logic is in the `get_post_or_404` dependency, which we'll reuse often in our application. Here is its implementation:

app.py

```
async def get_post_or_404(
    id: int, session: AsyncSession = Depends(get_async_session)
) -> Post:
```

```
select_query = select(Post).where(Post.id == id)
result = await session.execute(select_query)
post = result.scalar_one_or_none()

if post is None:
    raise HTTPException(status_code=status.HTTP_404_NOT_FOUND)

return post
```

https://github.com/PacktPublishing/Building-Data-Science-Applications-with-FastAPI-Second-Edition/tree/main/chapter06/sqlalchemy/app.py

As you can see, it's quite similar to what we've seen for the list endpoint. We also start by building a select query, but this time, we add a `where` clause so that we can retrieve only the post matching the desired ID. The clause itself might look strange.

First, we must set the actual column we want to compare. Indeed, when you access the properties of the `model` class directly, such as `Post.id`, SQLAlchemy automatically understands that you are referring to the column.

Then, we use the equality operator to compare the column with our actual `id` variable. It looks like a standard comparison that would result in a Boolean, not a SQL statement! In a general Python context, it would. However, SQLAlchemy developers have done something clever here: they overloaded the standard operators so that they produce SQL expressions instead of comparing objects. This is exactly what we saw in the *Magic methods* section of *Chapter 2, Python Programming Specificities*.

Now, we can simply execute the query and call `scalar_one_or_none` on the result set. It's a convenient shortcut that tells SQLAlchemy to return a single object if it exists, or `None` otherwise.

If the result is `None`, we can raise a `404` error: no post is matching this ID. Otherwise, we can simply return the post.

Updating and deleting objects

We'll finish by showing you how to update and delete existing objects. You'll see it's just a matter of manipulating the ORM object and calling the right method on `session`.

Check out the following code and review the implementation of the `update` endpoint:

app.py

```
@app.patch("/posts/{id}", response_model=schemas.PostRead)
async def update_post(
    post_update: schemas.PostPartialUpdate,
```

```
        post: Post = Depends(get_post_or_404),
        session: AsyncSession = Depends(get_async_session),
    ) -> Post:
        post_update_dict = post_update.dict(exclude_unset=True)
        for key, value in post_update_dict.items():
            setattr(post, key, value)

        session.add(post)
        await session.commit()

        return post
```

https://github.com/PacktPublishing/Building-Data-Science-Applica-tions-with-FastAPI-Second-Edition/tree/main/chapter06/sqlalchemy/app.py

Here, the main point of attention is that we'll operate directly on the post we want to modify. This is one of the key aspects when working with ORM: entities are objects that can be modified as you wish. When you are happy with the data, you can persist it in the database. This is exactly what we are doing here: we get a fresh representation of our post thanks to get_post_or_404. Then, we transform the post_update schema into a dictionary, and we iterate over the properties to set them on our ORM object. Finally, we can save it in the session and commit it to the database, as we did for creation.

The same concept is applied when you wish to delete an object: when you have an instance, you can pass it to the delete method of session so that it can schedule it for removal. You can view this in action in the following example:

app.py

```
@app.delete("/posts/{id}", status_code=status.HTTP_204_NO_CONTENT)
async def delete_post(
    post: Post = Depends(get_post_or_404),
    session: AsyncSession = Depends(get_async_session),
):
    await session.delete(post)
    await session.commit()
```

https://github.com/PacktPublishing/Building-Data-Science-Applica-tions-with-FastAPI-Second-Edition/tree/main/chapter06/sqlalchemy/app.py

Throughout these examples, you've seen that we always call commit after a write operation: your changes must be written in the database. Otherwise, they'll just stay in the session memory and be lost.

Adding relationships

As we mentioned at the beginning of this chapter, relational databases are all about data and its relationships. Quite often, you'll need to create entities that are linked to others. For example, in a blog application, comments are linked to the post they relate to. In this section, we'll examine how you can set up such relationships with SQLAlchemy ORM.

First, we need to define a new model for comments. This new model must be placed above Post in the code. We'll explain why this matters later. You can view its definition in the following example:

models.py

```python
class Comment(Base):
    __tablename__ = "comments"

    id: Mapped[int] = mapped_column(Integer, primary_key=True,
autoincrement=True)
    post_id: Mapped[int] = mapped_column(ForeignKey("posts.id"),
nullable=False)
    publication_date: Mapped[datetime] = mapped_column(
        DateTime, nullable=False, default=datetime.now
    )
    content: Mapped[str] = mapped_column(Text, nullable=False)

    post: Mapped["Post"] = relationship("Post", back_
populates="comments")
```

https://github.com/PacktPublishing/Building-Data-Science-Applications-with-FastAPI-Second-Edition/tree/main/chapter06/sqlalchemy_relationship/models.py

The important point here is the post_id column, which is of the ForeignKey type. This is a special type that tells SQLAlchemy to automatically handle the type of the column and the associated constraint. We simply have to give the table and column names it refers to.

But that's only the SQL part of the definition. We now need to tell ORM that our Comment object has a relationship with a Post object. This is the purpose of the post property, which is assigned to the relationship function. It's a special function exposed by SQLAlchemy ORM to *define how models relate to each other*. It won't create a new column in the SQL definition – that's the role of the ForeignKey column – but it'll allow us to directly get the Post object linked to a comment by using comment.post. You can also see that we define the back_populates argument. It allows us to do the opposite operation – that is, get the list of comments from a post. The name of this option determines the name of the property we'll use to access the comment. Here, this is post.comments.

> **Forward reference type hint**
>
> If you look at the type hint of the post property, you will see that we correctly set it to the Post class. However, we put it inside quotes: post: "Post" = ...
>
> This is what is called a **forward reference**. In some cases, the type hint we want is not yet defined. That's our case here since Post is defined after Comment. If we forget the quotes, Python will complain because we are trying to access something that doesn't exist yet. To solve this, we can put it inside quotes. Type checkers are smart enough to understand what you are referring to.

Now, if you look at the Post model, as follows, you'll see that we added one thing:

models.py

```python
class Post(Base):
    __tablename__ = "posts"

    id: Mapped[int] = mapped_column(Integer, primary_key=True,
autoincrement=True)
    publication_date: Mapped[datetime] = mapped_column(
        DateTime, nullable=False, default=datetime.now
    )
    title: Mapped[str] = mapped_column(String(255), nullable=False)
    content: Mapped[str] = mapped_column(Text, nullable=False)

    comments: Mapped[list[Comment]] = relationship("Comment",
cascade="all, delete")
```

https://github.com/PacktPublishing/Building-Data-Science-Applications-with-FastAPI-Second-Edition/tree/main/chapter06/sqlalchemy_relationship/models.py

We also defined the mirror relationship, taking care of *naming with the same name we chose for* back_populates. This time, we also set the cascade argument, which allows us to define the behavior of ORM when we delete a post: should we implicitly delete the comments as well? Or should we keep them as orphans? In this case, we chose to delete them. Note that it's *not the same thing* as the CASCADE DELETE construct of SQL: it has the same effect, but it will be handled by ORM in the Python code, not by the SQL database.

There are a lot of options regarding relationships, all of which you can find in the official documentation: https://docs.sqlalchemy.org/en/20/orm/relationship_api.html#sqlalchemy.orm.relationship.

Once again, adding this comments property doesn't change the SQL definition: it's just a way to wire things for ORM, on the Python side.

Now, we can define the Pydantic schemas for our comment entity. They are quite straightforward, so we won't go into the details. However, notice how we added the `comments` property to the `PostRead` schema:

schemas.py

```
class PostRead(PostBase):
    id: int
    comments: list[CommentRead]
```

https://github.com/PacktPublishing/Building-Data-Science-Applications-with-FastAPI-Second-Edition/tree/main/chapter06/sqlalchemy_relationship/schemas.py

Indeed, in a REST API, there are some cases where it makes sense to automatically retrieve the associated objects of an entity. Here, it'll be convenient to get the comments of a post in a single request. This schema will allow us to *serialize the comments, along with the post data.*

Now, we'll implement an endpoint to create a new comment. This is shown in the following example:

app.py

```
@app.post(
    "/posts/{id}/comments",
    response_model=schemas.CommentRead,
    status_code=status.HTTP_201_CREATED,
)
async def create_comment(
    comment_create: schemas.CommentCreate,
    post: Post = Depends(get_post_or_404),
    session: AsyncSession = Depends(get_async_session),
) -> Comment:
    comment = Comment(**comment_create.dict(), post=post)
    session.add(comment)
    await session.commit()

    return comment
```

https://github.com/PacktPublishing/Building-Data-Science-Applications-with-FastAPI-Second-Edition/tree/main/chapter06/sqlalchemy_relationship/app.py

This endpoint is defined, so we need to set the post ID directly in the path. It allows us to reuse the get_post_or_404 dependency and automatically have a 404 error occur if we try to add a comment to a non-existing post.

Other than that, it's very similar to what we saw in the *Creating objects* section of this chapter. The only point of attention here is that we manually set the post property on this new comment object. Thanks to the relationship definition, we can directly assign the post object, and ORM will automatically set the right value in the post_id column.

Earlier, we mentioned that we wanted to retrieve a post and its comments at the same time. To do this, we'll have to tweak our queries a bit when getting posts. The following sample shows what we did for the get_post_or_404 function, but the same goes for the list endpoint:

app.py

```python
async def get_post_or_404(
    id: int, session: AsyncSession = Depends(get_async_session)
) -> Post:
    select_query = (
        select(Post).options(selectinload(Post.comments)).where(Post.
id == id)
    )
    result = await session.execute(select_query)
    post = result.scalar_one_or_none()

    if post is None:
        raise HTTPException(status_code=status.HTTP_404_NOT_FOUND)

    return post
```

https://github.com/PacktPublishing/Building-Data-Science-Applica-tions-with-FastAPI-Second-Edition/tree/main/chapter06/sqlalche-my_relationship/app.py

As you can see, we added a call to options with a selectinload construct. This is a way to tell ORM to automatically retrieve the associated comments of the post when performing the query. If we don't do this, we'll get an error. Why? Because of the async nature of our queries. But let's start from the beginning.

In a classic synchronous ORM context, you can do this:

```python
comments = post.comments
```

If `comments` was not loaded in the first request, synchronous ORM will implicitly perform a new query on the SQL database. It's invisible to the user, but an I/O operation is performed. This is called **lazy loading**, and it's the default behavior for relationships in SQLAlchemy.

However, in an async context, I/O operations can't be done implicitly: we have to *await* them. This is why you will get an error if you forget to explicitly load the relationship into the first query. When Pydantic tries to serialize the `PostRead` schema, it'll try to reach `post.comments`, but SQLAlchemy can't perform this implicit query.

So, when working with async, you need to perform **eager loading** on the relationships you want to access directly from the ORM object. Admittedly, this is way less convenient than its sync counterpart. However, it has a massive advantage: you *finely control which queries are made*. Indeed, with a synchronous ORM, it's quite usual to have bad performance on an endpoint because the code performs dozens of implicit queries. With an asynchronous ORM, you can make sure you load everything in a single or few queries. It's a trade-off that can pay in the long run.

> **Eager loading can be configured on the relationship**
>
> If you're sure that you'll always need to load the related objects of an entity, regardless of the context, you can define the eager loading strategy directly on the `relationship` function. This way, you won't need to set it on each query. You can read more about this in the official documentation: `https://docs.sqlalchemy.org/en/20/orm/relationship_api.html#sqlalchemy.orm.relationship.params.lazy`.

Essentially, that's it for working with relationships with SQLAlchemy ORM. You've seen that the key thing is to correctly define the relationship so that ORM can understand how objects are linked together.

Setting up a database migration system with Alembic

When developing an application, you'll likely make changes to your database schema to add new tables, add new columns, or modify existing ones. Of course, if your application is already in production, you don't want to erase all your data to recreate the schema from scratch: you want it to be migrated to the new schema. Tools for this task have been developed, and in this section, we'll learn how to set up *Alembic*, from the creators of SQLAlchemy. Let's install this library:

```
(venv) $ pip install alembic
```

Once you've done this, you'll have access to the `alembic` command to manage this migration system. When starting a new project, the first thing you must do is initialize the migration environment, which includes a set of files and directories where Alembic will store its configuration and migration files. At the root of your project, run the following command:

```
(venv) $ alembic init alembic
```

This will create a directory, named `alembic`, at the root of your project. You can view the result of this command in the example repository shown in *Figure 6.4*:

Figure 6.4 – The Alembic migration environment structure

This folder will contain all the configurations for your migrations and your migration scripts themselves. It should be committed along with your code so that you have a record of the versions of those files.

Additionally, note that it created an `alembic.ini` file, which contains all the configuration options of Alembic. We'll review one important setting in this file: `sqlalchemy.url`. This can be seen in the following code:

alembic.ini

```
sqlalchemy.url = sqlite:///chapter06_sqlalchemy_relationship.db
```

https://github.com/PacktPublishing/Building-Data-Science-Applications-with-FastAPI-Second-Edition/tree/main/chapter06/sqlalchemy_relationship/alembic.ini

Predictably, this is the connection string of your database that will receive the migration queries. It follows the same convention that we saw earlier. Here, we set our SQLite database. However, note that we don't set the `aiosqlite` driver: Alembic will only work with synchronous drivers. It's not a big deal since it'll only run in dedicated scripts to perform migrations.

Next, we'll focus on the env.py file. This is a Python script that contains all the logic executed by Alembic to initialize the migration engine and execute the migrations. Being a Python script, it allows us to finely customize the execution of Alembic. For the time being, we'll keep the default one, except for one thing: we'll import our Base object. You can view this in the following example:

env.py

```
from chapter06.sqlalchemy_relationship.models import Base

# this is the Alembic Config object, which provides
# access to the values within the .ini file in use.
config = context.config

# Interpret the config file for Python logging.
# This line sets up loggers basically.
if config.config_file_name is not None:
    fileConfig(config.config_file_name)

# add your model's MetaData object here
# for 'autogenerate' support
# from myapp import mymodel
# target_metadata = mymodel.Base.metadata
target_metadata = Base.metadata
```

https://github.com/PacktPublishing/Building-Data-Science-Applications-with-FastAPI-Second-Edition/tree/main/chapter06/sqlalchemy_relationship/alembic/env.py

By default, the file defines a variable named target_metadata, which is set to None. Here, we changed it so that it refers to the Base.metadata object we imported from our models module. But why do we do that? Well, recall that Base is a SQLAlchemy object that contains all the information about your database schema. By providing it to Alembic, the migration system will be able to *automatically generate the migration scripts* just by looking at your schema! This way, you won't have to write them from scratch.

Once you have made changes to your database schema, you can run the following command to generate a new migration script:

```
(venv) $ alembic revision --autogenerate -m "Initial migration"
```

This will create a new script in the `versions` directory with the commands reflecting your schema changes. This file defines two functions: `upgrade` and `downgrade`. You can view `upgrade` in the following snippet:

eabd3f9c5b64_initial_migration.py

```python
def upgrade() -> None:
    # ### commands auto generated by Alembic - please adjust! ###
    op.create_table(
        "posts",
        sa.Column("id", sa.Integer(), autoincrement=True,
nullable=False),
        sa.Column("publication_date", sa.DateTime(), nullable=False),
        sa.Column("title", sa.String(length=255), nullable=False),
        sa.Column("content", sa.Text(), nullable=False),
        sa.PrimaryKeyConstraint("id"),
    )
    op.create_table(
        "comments",
        sa.Column("id", sa.Integer(), autoincrement=True,
nullable=False),
        sa.Column("post_id", sa.Integer(), nullable=False),
        sa.Column("publication_date", sa.DateTime(), nullable=False),
        sa.Column("content", sa.Text(), nullable=False),
        sa.ForeignKeyConstraint(
            ["post_id"],
            ["posts.id"],
        ),
        sa.PrimaryKeyConstraint("id"),
    )
    # ### end Alembic commands ###
```

https://github.com/PacktPublishing/Building-Data-Science-Applications-with-FastAPI-Second-Edition/tree/main/chapter06/sqlalchemy_relationship/alembic/versions/eabd3f9c5b64_initial_migration.py

This function is executed when we *apply the migration*. It describes the required operations to create our `posts` and `comments` table, with all of their columns and constraints.

Now, let's examine the other function in this file, `downgrade`:

eabd3f9c5b64_initial_migration.py

```
def downgrade() -> None:
    # ### commands auto generated by Alembic - please adjust! ###
    op.drop_table("comments")
    op.drop_table("posts")
    # ### end Alembic commands ###
```

https://github.com/PacktPublishing/Building-Data-Science-Applications-with-FastAPI-Second-Edition/tree/main/chapter06/sqlalchemy_relationship/alembic/versions/eabd3f9c5b64_initial_migration.py

This function describes the operations to *roll back the migration* so that the databases go back to their previous states. This is very important because if something goes wrong during the migration, or if you need to revert to an older version of your application, you'll be able to do so without breaking your data.

> **Autogeneration doesn't detect everything**
>
> Bear in mind that, even though autogeneration is very helpful, it's not always accurate, and sometimes, it's not able to detect ambiguous changes. For example, if you rename a column, it will delete the old one and create another. As a result, the data for this column will be lost! This is why you should always carefully review the migration scripts and make the required changes for edge cases like this.

Finally, you can apply the migrations to your database using the following command:

```
(venv) $ alembic upgrade head
```

This will run all the migrations that have not yet been applied to your database until the latest. It's interesting to know that, in the process, Alembic creates a table in your database so that it can remember all the migrations it has applied: this is how it detects which scripts to run.

Generally speaking, you should be *extremely careful* when you run such commands on your database, especially on a production one. Very bad things can happen if you make a mistake, and you can lose precious data. You should always test your migrations in a test environment and have fresh and working backups before running them on your production database.

This was a very quick introduction to Alembic and its powerful migration system. We strongly encourage you to go through its documentation to understand all of its mechanisms, especially regarding migration script operations. Please refer to https://alembic.sqlalchemy.org/en/latest/index.html.

That's it for the SQLAlchemy part of this chapter! It's a complex but powerful library for working with SQL databases. We'll now leave the world of relational databases to explore how we can work with a document-oriented database, MongoDB.

Communicating with a MongoDB database using Motor

As we mentioned at the beginning of this chapter, working with a document-oriented database, such as MongoDB, is quite different from a relational database. First and foremost, you don't need to configure a schema upfront: it follows the structure of the data that you insert into it. In the case of FastAPI, it makes our life slightly easier since we only have to work with Pydantic models. However, there are some subtleties around the document identifiers that we need to take into account. We'll review this next.

To begin, we'll install Motor, which is a library that is used to communicate asynchronously with MongoDB and is officially supported by the MongoDB organization. Run the following command:

```
(venv) $ pip install motor
```

Once you've done this, we can start working!

Creating models that are compatible with MongoDB ID

As we mentioned in the introduction to this section, there are some difficulties with the identifiers that MongoDB uses to store documents. Indeed, by default, MongoDB assigns every document an `_id` property that acts as a unique identifier in a collection. This causes two issues:

- In a Pydantic model, if a property starts with an underscore, it's considered to be private and thus, is not used as a data field for our model.

- `_id` is encoded as a binary object, called `ObjectId`, instead of a simple integer or string. It's usually represented in the form of a string such as `608d1ee317c3f035100873dc`. This type of object is not supported out of the box by Pydantic or FastAPI.

This is why we'll need some boilerplate code to ensure those identifiers work with Pydantic and FastAPI. To begin, in the following example, we have created a `MongoBaseModel` base class that takes care of defining the `id` field:

models.py

```python
class MongoBaseModel(BaseModel):
    id: PyObjectId = Field(default_factory=PyObjectId, alias="_id")

    class Config:
        json_encoders = {ObjectId: str}
```

https://github.com/PacktPublishing/Building-Data-Science-Appli-
cations-with-FastAPI-Second-Edition/tree/main/chapter06/mongodb/
models.py

First, we need to define an id field, which is of the PyObjectId type. This is a custom type that was defined in the preceding code. We won't go into the details of its implementation but just know that it's a class that makes ObjectId a compatible type for Pydantic. We define this same class as a default factory for this field. Interestingly, this kind of identifier allows us to generate them on the client side, contrary to traditional auto-incremented integers of relational databases, which could be useful in some cases.

The most interesting argument is alias. It's a Pydantic option that allows us to *change the name of the field during serialization*. In this example, when we call the dict method on an instance of MongoBaseModel, the identifier will be set on the _id key, which is the name expected by MongoDB. That solves the first issue.

Then, we add the Config subclass and set the json_encoders option. By default, Pydantic is completely unaware of our PyObjectId type, so it won't be able to correctly serialize it to JSON. This option allows us to *map custom types with a function that will be called to serialize them*. Here, we simply transform it into a string (this works because ObjectId implements the __str__ magic method). That solves the second issue for Pydantic.

Our base model for Pydantic is complete! We can now use it as a base class instead of BaseModel for our actual data models. Notice, however, that the PostPartialUpdate doesn't inherit from it. Indeed, we don't want the id field in this model; otherwise, a PATCH request might be able to replace the ID of the document, which could lead to weird issues.

Connecting to a database

Now that our models are ready, we can set up the connection with a MongoDB server. This is quite easy and only involves a class instantiation, as shown in the database.py module:

database.py

```
from motor.motor_asyncio import AsyncIOMotorClient,
AsyncIOMotorDatabase

# Connection to the whole server
motor_client = AsyncIOMotorClient("mongodb://localhost:27017")
# Single database instance
database = motor_client["chapter06_mongo"]

def get_database() -> AsyncIOMotorDatabase:
    return database
```

```
https://github.com/PacktPublishing/Building-Data-Science-Appli-
cations-with-FastAPI-Second-Edition/tree/main/chapter06/mongodb/
database.py
```

Here, you can see that `AsyncIOMotorClient` simply expects a connection string to your database. Generally, it consists of the scheme, followed by authentication information, and the hostname of the database server. You can find an overview of this format in the official MongoDB documentation at `https://docs.mongodb.com/manual/reference/connection-string/`.

However, be careful. Contrary to the libraries we've discussed so far, the client that's instantiated here is not bound to any database – that is, it's only a connection to a whole server. That's why we need the second line: by accessing the `chapter06_mongo` key, we get a database instance. It's worth noting that MongoDB doesn't require you to create the database upfront: it'll create it automatically if it doesn't exist.

Then, we create a simple function to return this database instance. We'll use this function as a dependency to retrieve this instance in our path operation functions. We explained the benefits of this pattern in the *Communicating with a SQL database with SQLAlchemy ORM* section.

That's it! We can now make queries to our database!

Inserting documents

We'll start by demonstrating how to implement an endpoint to create posts. Essentially, we just have to insert our transformed Pydantic model into a dictionary:

app.py

```python
@app.post("/posts", response_model=Post, status_code=status.HTTP_201_
CREATED)
async def create_post(
    post_create: PostCreate, database: AsyncIOMotorDatabase =
Depends(get_database)
) -> Post:
    post = Post(**post_create.dict())
    await database["posts"].insert_one(post.dict(by_alias=True))

    post = await get_post_or_404(post.id, database)

    return post
```

```
https://github.com/PacktPublishing/Building-Data-Science-Appli-
cations-with-FastAPI-Second-Edition/tree/main/chapter06/mongodb/
app.py
```

Classically, this is a `POST` endpoint that accepts a payload in the form of a `PostCreate` model. Additionally, we inject the database instance with the dependency we wrote earlier.

In the path operation itself, you can see that we start by instantiating a `Post` from the `PostCreate` data. This is usually a good practice if you have fields that only appear in `Post` that need to be initialized.

Then, we have the query. To retrieve a collection in our MongoDB database, we simply have to get it by name, like a dictionary. Once again, MongoDB will take care of creating it if it doesn't exist. As you can see, document-oriented databases are much more lightweight regarding schema than relational databases! In this collection, we can call the `insert_one` method to insert a single document. It expects a dictionary to map fields to their values. Therefore, the `dict` method of Pydantic objects is once again our friend. However, here, we can see something new: we call it with the `by_alias` argument set to `True`. By default, Pydantic will serialize the object with the real field name, not the alias name. However, we do need the `_id` identifier in our MongoDB database. Using this option, Pydantic will use the alias as a key in the dictionary.

To ensure we have a true and fresh representation of our document in the dictionary, we can retrieve one from the database thanks to our `get_post_or_404` function. We'll examine how this works in the next section.

> **Dependencies are like functions**
>
> In this section, we used `get_post_or_404` as a regular function to retrieve our newly created blog post. This is perfectly okay: dependencies don't have hidden or magic logic inside them, so you can reuse them at will. The only thing to remember is that you have to provide every argument manually since you are outside of the dependency injection context.

Getting documents

Of course, retrieving the data from the database is an important part of the job of a REST API. In this section, we'll demonstrate how to implement two classic endpoints – that is, to list posts and get a single post. Let's start with the first one and take a look at its implementation:

app.py

```python
@app.get("/posts", response_model=list[Post])
async def list_posts(
    pagination: tuple[int, int] = Depends(pagination),
    database: AsyncIOMotorDatabase = Depends(get_database),
) -> list[Post]:
    skip, limit = pagination
    query = database["posts"].find({}, skip=skip, limit=limit)
```

```
    results = [Post(**raw_post) async for raw_post in query]

    return results
```

https://github.com/PacktPublishing/Building-Data-Science-Appli-
cations-with-FastAPI-Second-Edition/tree/main/chapter06/mongodb/
app.py

The most interesting part is the second line, which is where we define the query. After retrieving the `posts` collection, we call the `find` method. The first argument should be the filtering query, following the MongoDB syntax. Since we want every document, we leave it empty. Then, we have keyword arguments that allow us to apply our pagination parameters.

MongoDB returns a result in the form of a list of dictionaries, which maps fields to their values. This is why we added a list comprehension construct to transform them back into `Post` instances – so that FastAPI can serialize them properly.

You might have noticed something quite surprising here: contrary to what we do usually, we didn't wait for the query directly. Instead, we added the `async` keyword to our list comprehension. Indeed, in this case, Motor returns **an asynchronous generator**. It's the asynchronous counterpart of the classic generator. It works in the same way, aside from the `async` keyword, which we have to add when iterating over it.

Now, let's take a look at the endpoint that retrieves a single post. The following example shows its implementation:

app.py

```
@app.get("/posts/{id}", response_model=Post)
async def get_post(post: Post = Depends(get_post_or_404)) -> Post:
    return post
```

https://github.com/PacktPublishing/Building-Data-Science-Appli-
cations-with-FastAPI-Second-Edition/tree/main/chapter06/mongodb/
app.py

As you can see, it's a simple GET endpoint that accepts the `id` post as a path parameter. Most of the logic's implementation is in the reusable `get_post_or_404` dependency. You can view what it looks like here:

app.py

```
async def get_post_or_404(
    id: ObjectId = Depends(get_object_id),
    database: AsyncIOMotorDatabase = Depends(get_database),
```

```
) -> Post:
    raw_post = await database["posts"].find_one({"_id": id})

    if raw_post is None:
        raise HTTPException(status_code=status.HTTP_404_NOT_FOUND)

    return Post(**raw_post)
```

https://github.com/PacktPublishing/Building-Data-Science-Appli-
cations-with-FastAPI-Second-Edition/tree/main/chapter06/mongodb/
app.py

The logic is quite similar to what we saw for the list endpoint. This time, however, we call the `find_one` method with a query to match the post identifier: the key is the name of the document attribute we want to filter on, and the value is the one we are looking for.

This method returns the document in the form of a dictionary or `None` if it doesn't exist. In this case, we raise a proper `404` error.

Finally, we transform it back into a `Post` model before returning it.

You might have noticed that we got `id` through a dependency, `get_object_id`. Indeed, FastAPI will return a string from the path parameter. If we try to make a query with `id` in the form of a string, MongoDB will not match with the actual binary IDs. That's why we use another dependency that transforms the identifier, represented as a string (such as `608d1ee317c3f035100873dc`), into a proper `ObjectId`.

As a side note, here's a very nice example of *nested dependencies*: endpoints use the `get_post_or_404` dependency, which itself gets a value from `get_object_id`. You can view the implementation of this dependency in the following example:

app.py

```
async def get_object_id(id: str) -> ObjectId:
    try:
        return ObjectId(id)
    except (errors.InvalidId, TypeError):
        raise HTTPException(status_code=status.HTTP_404_NOT_FOUND)
```

https://github.com/PacktPublishing/Building-Data-Science-Appli-
cations-with-FastAPI-Second-Edition/tree/main/chapter06/mongodb/
app.py

Here, we simply retrieve the `id` string from the path parameters and try to instantiate it back into an `ObjectId`. If it's not a valid value, we catch the corresponding errors and consider it a `404` error.

With this, we have solved every challenge posed by the MongoDB identifiers format. Now, let's discuss how to update and delete documents.

Updating and deleting documents

We'll now review the endpoints for updating and deleting documents. The logic is still the same and only involves building the proper query from the request payload.

Let's start with the `PATCH` endpoint, which you can view in the following example:

app.py

```
@app.patch("/posts/{id}", response_model=Post)
async def update_post(
    post_update: PostPartialUpdate,
    post: Post = Depends(get_post_or_404),
    database: AsyncIOMotorDatabase = Depends(get_database),
) -> Post:
    await database["posts"].update_one(
        {"_id": post.id}, {"$set": post_update.dict(exclude_
unset=True)}
    )

    post = await get_post_or_404(post.id, database)

    return post
```

https://github.com/PacktPublishing/Building-Data-Science-Applications-with-FastAPI-Second-Edition/tree/main/chapter06/mongodb/app.py

Here, we used the `update_one` method to update one document. The first argument is the filtering query, while the second one is the actual operation to apply to the document. Once again, it follows the MongoDB syntax: the `$set` operation allows us to only modify the fields we want to change by passing the `update` dictionary.

The DELETE endpoint is even simpler; it's just a single query, as you can see in the following example:

app.py

```
@app.delete("/posts/{id}", status_code=status.HTTP_204_NO_CONTENT)
async def delete_post(
    post: Post = Depends(get_post_or_404),
    database: AsyncIOMotorDatabase = Depends(get_database),
):
    await database["posts"].delete_one({"_id": post.id})
```

```
https://github.com/PacktPublishing/Building-Data-Science-Appli-
cations-with-FastAPI-Second-Edition/tree/main/chapter06/mongodb/
app.py
```

The `delete_one` method expects the filtering query as the first argument.

That's it! Of course, here, we've only demonstrated the simplest type of query, but MongoDB has a very powerful query language that allows you to do more complex things. If you're not familiar with this, we recommend that you read the nice introduction from the official documentation: `https://docs.mongodb.com/manual/crud`.

Nesting documents

At the beginning of this chapter, we mentioned that document-based databases, contrary to relational databases, aim to store all the data related to an entity in a single document. In our current example, if we wish to store the comments along with the post, we simply have to add a list where each item is the comment data.

In this section, we'll implement this behavior. You'll see that the functioning of MongoDB makes this straightforward.

We'll start by adding a new `comments` attribute to our `Post` model. You can view this in the following example:

models.py

```
class Post(PostBase):
    comments: list[Comment] = Field(default_factory=list)
```

```
https://github.com/PacktPublishing/Building-Data-Science-Applica-
tions-with-FastAPI-Second-Edition/tree/main/chapter06/mongodb_re-
lationship/models.py
```

This field is simply a list of Comment. We won't go into the details of the comment models since they are quite straightforward. Notice that we use the list function as the default factory for this attribute. This instantiates an empty list by default when we create a Post without setting any comments.

Now that we have our models, we can implement an endpoint to create a new comment. You can view it in the following example:

app.py

```
@app.post(
    "/posts/{id}/comments", response_model=Post, status_code=status.
HTTP_201_CREATED
)
async def create_comment(
    comment: CommentCreate,
    post: Post = Depends(get_post_or_404),
    database: AsyncIOMotorDatabase = Depends(get_database),
) -> Post:
    await database["posts"].update_one(
        {"_id": post.id}, {"$push": {"comments": comment.dict()}}
    )

    post = await get_post_or_404(post.id, database)

    return post
```

https://github.com/PacktPublishing/Building-Data-Science-Applica-tions-with-FastAPI-Second-Edition/tree/main/chapter06/mongodb_re-lationship/app.py

As we did before, we nest the endpoints under the path of a single post. Thus, we can reuse get_post_or_404 to retrieve the post we want to add a comment to if it exists.

Then, we trigger an update_one query: this time, using the $push operation. This is a useful operator for adding elements to a list attribute. Operators that remove elements from a list are also available. You can find a description of every update operator in the official documentation at https://docs.mongodb.com/manual/reference/operator/update/.

And that's it! We don't even have to modify the rest of our code. Because the comments are included in the whole document, we'll always retrieve them when querying for a post in the database. Besides, our Post model now expects a comments attribute, so Pydantic will take care of serializing them automatically.

That concludes this part regarding MongoDB. You've seen that it can be integrated into a FastAPI application very quickly, especially because of its very flexible schema.

Summary

Congratulations! You've reached another big milestone in mastering how to build a REST API with FastAPI. As you know, databases are an essential part of every system; they allow you to save data in a structured way and retrieve it precisely and reliably thanks to powerful query languages. You are now able to leverage their power in FastAPI, whether they are relational databases or document-oriented databases.

Serious things can now happen; users can send and retrieve data to and from your system. However, this poses a new challenge to tackle: this data needs to be protected so that it can remain private and secure. This is exactly what we'll discuss in the next chapter: how to authenticate users and set up FastAPI for maximum security.

7

Managing Authentication and Security in FastAPI

Most of the time, you don't want everyone on the internet to have access to your API, without any restrictions on the data they can create or read. That's why you'll need to at least protect your application with a private token or have a proper authentication system to manage the rights given to each user. In this chapter, we'll see how FastAPI provides security dependencies to help us retrieve credentials by following different standards that are directly integrated into the automatic documentation. We'll also build a basic user registration and authentication system to secure our API endpoints.

Finally, we'll cover the security challenges you must tackle when you want to call your API from a web application in a browser – in particular, the risks of CORS and CSRF attacks.

In this chapter, we're going to cover the following main topics:

- Security dependencies in FastAPI
- Retrieving a user and generating an access token
- Securing API endpoints for authenticated users
- Securing endpoints with access tokens
- Configuring CORS and protecting against CSRF attacks

Technical requirements

For this chapter, you'll require a Python virtual environment, just as we set up in *Chapter 1, Python Development Environment Setup*.

You'll find all the code examples of this chapter in the dedicated GitHub repository at https://github.com/PacktPublishing/Building-Data-Science-Applications-with-FastAPI-Second-Edition/tree/main/chapter07.

Security dependencies in FastAPI

To protect REST APIs, and HTTP endpoints more generally, lots of standards have been proposed. Here is a non-exhaustive list of the most common ones:

- **Basic HTTP authentication**: In this scheme, user credentials (usually, an identifier such as an email address and password) are put into an HTTP header called Authorization. The value consists of the Basic keyword, followed by the user credentials encoded in Base64. This is a very simple scheme to implement but not very secure since the password appears in every request.

- **Cookies**: Cookies are a useful way to store static data on the client side, usually on web browsers, that is sent in each request to the server. Typically, a cookie contains a session token that can be verified by the server and linked to a specific user.

- **Tokens** in the Authorization header: Probably the most used header in a REST API context, this simply consists of sending a token in an HTTP Authorization header. The token is often prefixed by a method keyword, such as Bearer. On the server side, this token can be verified and linked to a specific user.

Each standard has its pros and cons and is suitable for a specific use case.

As you already know, FastAPI is mainly about dependency injection and callables that are automatically detected and called at runtime. Authentication methods are no exception: FastAPI provides most of them out of the box as security dependencies.

First, let's learn how to retrieve an access token in an arbitrary header. For this, we can use the ApiKeyHeader dependency, as shown in the following example:

chapter07_api_key_header.py

```
from fastapi import Depends, FastAPI, HTTPException, status
from fastapi.security import APIKeyHeader

API_TOKEN = "SECRET_API_TOKEN"

app = FastAPI()
api_key_header = APIKeyHeader(name="Token")

@app.get("/protected-route")
async def protected_route(token: str = Depends(api_key_header)):
    if token != API_TOKEN:
        raise HTTPException(status_code=status.HTTP_403_FORBIDDEN)
    return {"hello": "world"}
```

https://github.com/PacktPublishing/Building-Data-Science-Applications-with-FastAPI-Second-Edition/tree/main/chapter07/chapter07_api_key_header.py

In this simple example, we hardcoded a token, API_TOKEN, and checked whether the token passed in the header was equal to this token, before authorizing the endpoint to be called. To do this, we used the APIKeyHeader security dependency, which is designed to retrieve a value from a header. It's a class dependency that can be instantiated with arguments. In particular, it accepts the name argument, which holds the name of the header it'll look for.

Then, in our endpoint, we injected this dependency to get the token's value. If it's equal to our token constant, we proceed with the endpoint logic. Otherwise, we raise a 403 error.

Our example from the *Path, router, and global dependencies* section of *Chapter 5, Dependency Injection in FastAPI*, is not very different from this one. We are simply retrieving a value from an arbitrary header and making an equality check. So, why bother with a dedicated dependency? There are two reasons:

- First, the logic to check whether the header exists and retrieve its value is included in APIKeyHeader. When you reach the endpoint, you are sure that a token value was retrieved; otherwise, a 403 error will be thrown.

- The second, and probably most important, thing is that it's detected by the OpenAPI schema and included in its interactive documentation. This means that endpoints using this dependency will display a lock icon, showing that it's a protected endpoint. Furthermore, you'll have access to an interface to input your token, as shown in the following screenshot. The token will then be automatically included in the requests you are making from the documentation:

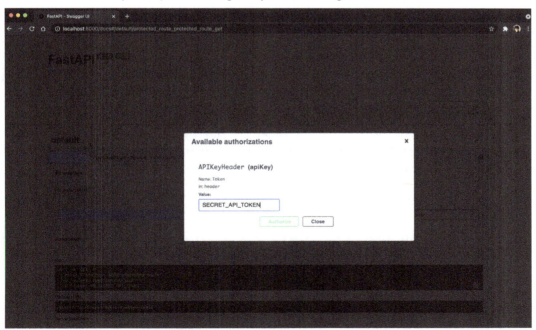

Figure 7.1 – Token authorization in interactive documentation

Of course, you can wrap the logic that checks the token value in its own dependency to reuse it across your endpoints, as shown in the following example:

chapter07_api_key_header_dependency.py

```
async def api_token(token: str = Depends(APIKeyHeader(name="Token"))):
    if token != API_TOKEN:
        raise HTTPException(status_code=status.HTTP_403_FORBIDDEN)


@app.get("/protected-route", dependencies=[Depends(api_token)])
async def protected_route():
    return {"hello": "world"}
```

https://github.com/PacktPublishing/Building-Data-Science-Applications-with-FastAPI-Second-Edition/tree/main/chapter07/chapter07_api_key_header.py

These kinds of dependencies are very good candidates to be used as routers or global dependencies to protect whole sets of routes, as we saw in *Chapter 5, Dependency Injection in FastAPI*.

This is a very basic example of adding authorization to your API. In this example, we don't have any user management; we are only checking that a token corresponds to a constant value. While it could be useful for private microservices that are not intended to be called by end users, this approach should not be considered very secure.

First, make sure your API is always served using HTTPS to ensure your token is not exposed in the headers. Then, if it's a private microservice, you should also consider not exposing it publicly on the internet and making sure only trusted servers can call it. Since you don't need users to make requests to this service, it's much safer than a simple token key that could be stolen.

Of course, most of the time, you'll want to authenticate real users with their own individual access tokens with which they can access their own data. You have probably already used a service that implements this very typical pattern:

- First, you must register an account on this service, usually by providing your email address and a password.

- Next, you can log in to the service using the same email address and password. The service checks whether the email address exists and that the password is valid.

- In exchange, the service provides you with a session token that can be used on subsequent requests to authenticate yourself. This way, you don't have to provide your email address and password on each request, which would be annoying and dangerous. Usually, such session tokens have a limited lifetime, which means you'll have to log in again after some time. This mitigates any security risks if the session token is stolen.

In the next section, you'll learn how to implement such a system.

Storing a user and their password securely in a database

Storing a user entity in a database is no different from storing any other entity, and you can implement this in the same way as in *Chapter 6, Databases and Asynchronous ORMs*. The only thing you must be extremely cautious about is password storage. You must not store the password as plain text in your database. Why? If, unfortunately, a malicious person manages to get into your database, they'll be able to get the passwords of all your users. Since many people use the same password multiple times, the security of their accounts on other applications and websites would be seriously compromised.

To avoid a disaster like this, we can apply **cryptographic hash functions** to the password. The goal of those functions is to transform the password string into a hash value. This is designed to make it near impossible to retrieve the original data from the hash. Hence, even if your database is compromised, the passwords are still safe.

When users try to log in, we simply compute the hash of the password they input and compare it with the hash we have in our database. If they match, this means it's the right password.

Now, let's learn how to implement such a system with FastAPI and SQLAlchemy ORM.

Creating models

We start by creating the SQLAlchemy ORM model for a user, as shown in the following example:

models.py

```
class User(Base):
    __tablename__ = "users"

    id: Mapped[int] = mapped_column(Integer, primary_key=True,
autoincrement=True)
    email: Mapped[str] = mapped_column(
        String(1024), index=True, unique=True, nullable=False
    )
    hashed_password: Mapped[str] = mapped_column(String(1024),
nullable=False)
```

https://github.com/PacktPublishing/Building-Data-Science-Applica-tions-with-FastAPI-Second-Edition/tree/main/chapter07/authentica-tion/models.py

To keep this example simple, we're only considering the ID, email address, and password in our model. Note that we added a unique constraint to the email column to ensure we can't have duplicate emails in our database.

Next, we can implement the corresponding Pydantic schemas:

schemas.py

```
class UserBase(BaseModel):
    email: EmailStr

    class Config:
        orm_mode = True

class UserCreate(UserBase):
    password: str

class User(UserBase):
    id: int
    hashed_password: str

class UserRead(UserBase):
    id: int
```

https://github.com/PacktPublishing/Building-Data-Science-Applications-with-FastAPI-Second-Edition/tree/main/chapter07/authentication/schemas.py

As you can see, there is a major difference between UserCreate and User: the former accepts the plain text password we'll hash during registration, while the second will only keep the hashed password in the database. We also take care to not include hashed_password in UserRead, so the hash doesn't appear in API responses. Even though hashed data should be indecipherable, it's generally not advised to leak it.

Hashing passwords

Before we look at the registration endpoint, let's implement some important utility functions for hashing passwords. Fortunately, libraries exist that provide the most secure and efficient algorithms for this task. Here, we'll use passlib. You can install it along with argon2_cffi, which is one of the safest hash functions at the time of writing:

```
(venv) $ pip install passlib argon2_cffi
```

Now, we'll just instantiate the `passlib` classes and wrap some of their functions to make our lives easier:

password.py

```
from passlib.context import CryptContext

pwd_context = CryptContext(schemes=["argon2"], deprecated="auto")

def get_password_hash(password: str) -> str:
    return pwd_context.hash(password)
```

https://github.com/PacktPublishing/Building-Data-Science-Applications-with-FastAPI-Second-Edition/tree/main/chapter07/authentication/password.py

`CryptContext` is a very useful class since it allows us to work with different hash algorithms. If, one day, a better algorithm than `argon2` emerges, we can just add it to our allowed schemas. New passwords will be hashed using the new algorithm, but existing passwords will still be recognized (and optionally upgraded to the new algorithm).

Implementing registration routes

Now, we have all the elements to create a proper registration route. Once again, it'll be very similar to what we saw earlier. The only thing we must remember is to hash the password before inserting it into our database.

Let's look at the implementation:

app.py

```
@app.post(
    "/register", status_code=status.HTTP_201_CREATED, response_
model=schemas.UserRead
)
async def register(
    user_create: schemas.UserCreate, session: AsyncSession =
Depends(get_async_session)
) -> User:
    hashed_password = get_password_hash(user_create.password)
    user = User(
        *user_create.dict(exclude={"password"}), hashed_
password=hashed_password
    )

    try:
```

```
        session.add(user)
        await session.commit()
    except exc.IntegrityError:
        raise HTTPException(
            status_code=status.HTTP_400_BAD_REQUEST, detail="Email
    already exists"
        )

    return user
```

https://github.com/PacktPublishing/Building-Data-Science-Applica-
tions-with-FastAPI-Second-Edition/tree/main/chapter07/authentica-
tion/app.py

As you can see, we are calling get_password_hash on the input password before inserting the user into the database. Note that we are catching a possible exc.IntegrityError exception, which means we're trying to insert an email that already exists.

Also, notice that we took care to set response_model to UserRead. By doing this, we're ensuring that hashed_password is not part of the output.

Great! We now have a proper user model and users can create a new account with our API. The next step is to allow them to log in and give them an access token.

Retrieving a user and generating an access token

After successful registration, the next step is being able to log in: the user will send their credentials and receive an authentication token to access the API. In this section, we'll implement the endpoint that allows this. Basically, we'll get the credentials from the request payload, retrieve the user with the given email, and verify their password. If the user exists and their password is valid, we'll generate an access token and return it in the response.

Implementing a database access token

First, let's think about the nature of this access token. It should be a data string that uniquely identifies a user that is impossible to forge by a malicious third party. In this example, we will take a simple but reliable approach: we'll generate a random string and store it in a dedicated table in our database, with a foreign key referring to the user.

This way, when an authenticated request arrives, we simply have to check whether it exists in the database and look for the corresponding user. The advantage of this approach is that tokens are centralized and can easily be invalidated if they are compromised; we only need to delete them from the database.

The first step is to implement the SQLAlchemy ORM model for this new entity:

models.py

```
class AccessToken(Base):
    __tablename__ = "access_tokens"

    access_token: Mapped[str] = mapped_column(
        String(1024), primary_key=True, default=generate_token
    )
    user_id: Mapped[int] = mapped_column(ForeignKey("users.id"),
nullable=False)
    expiration_date: Mapped[datetime] = mapped_column(
        DateTime, nullable=False, default=get_expiration_date
    )

    user: Mapped[User] = relationship("User", lazy="joined")
```

https://github.com/PacktPublishing/Building-Data-Science-Applica-tions-with-FastAPI-Second-Edition/tree/main/chapter07/authentica-tion/models.py

We define three columns:

- `access_token`: This is the string that will be passed in the requests to authenticate them. Notice that we defined the `generate_token` function as the default factory; it's a simple function defined previously that generates a random secure passphrase. Under the hood, it relies on the standard `secrets` module.

- `user_id`: A foreign key referring to the `users` table that identifies the user corresponding to this token.

- `expiration_date`: The date and time when the access token will expire and won't be valid anymore. It's always a good idea to give access tokens an expiry date to mitigate the risk if they are stolen. Here, the `get_expiration_date` factory sets a default validity of 24 hours.

We also don't forget to define the relationship so we can directly access the user entity from an access token object. Notice we set an eager loading strategy by default, so we always retrieve the user when querying for an access token. If you need the rationale behind this, check the *Adding relationships* section of *Chapter 6, Databases and Asynchronous ORMs*.

We won't need Pydantic schemas here, as access tokens will be created and serialized through specific methods.

Implementing a login endpoint

Now, let's think about the login endpoint. Its goal is to take credentials in the request payload, retrieve the corresponding user, check the password, and generate a new access token. Its implementation is quite straightforward, apart from one thing: the model that's used to handle the request. You'll see why thanks to the following example:

app.py

```python
@app.post("/token")
async def create_token(
    form_data: OAuth2PasswordRequestForm =
Depends(OAuth2PasswordRequestForm),
    session: AsyncSession = Depends(get_async_session),
):
    email = form_data.username
    password = form_data.password
    user = await authenticate(email, password, session)

    if not user:
        raise HTTPException(status_code=status.HTTP_401_UNAUTHORIZED)

    token = await create_access_token(user, session)

    return {"access_token": token.access_token, "token_type":
"bearer"}
```

https://github.com/PacktPublishing/Building-Data-Science-Applications-with-FastAPI-Second-Edition/tree/main/chapter07/authentication/app.py

As you can see, we retrieve the request data thanks to the OAuth2PasswordRequestForm module, which is provided by FastAPI in its security module. It expects several fields, especially username and password, in a form encoding rather than JSON.

Why do we use this class? The main benefit of using this class is that it's completely integrated into the OpenAPI schema. This means that the interactive documentation will be able to automatically detect it and present a proper authentication form behind the **Authorize** button, as shown in the following screenshot:

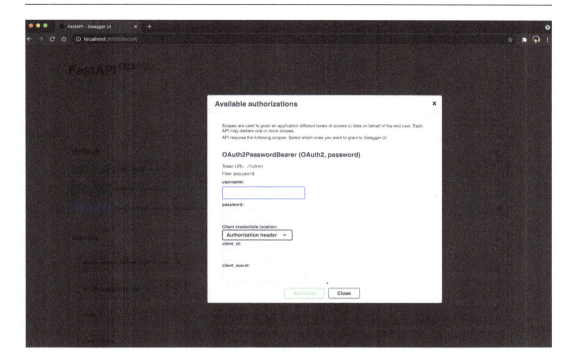

Figure 7.2 – OAuth2 authorization in interactive documentation

But that's not all: it will be able to automatically retrieve the returned access token and set the proper authorization header in subsequent requests. The authentication process is handled transparently by the interactive documentation.

This class follows the OAuth2 protocol, which means you also have fields for the client ID and secret. We won't learn how to implement the complete OAuth2 protocol here, but note that FastAPI provides all the tools needed to do so properly. For our project, we'll just stick with a username and a password. Notice that, following the protocol, the field is named *username*, regardless of whether we are using an email address to identify the user. This isn't a big deal; we just have to remember it while retrieving it.

The rest of the path operation function is quite simple: first, we try to retrieve a user from this email and password. If no corresponding user is found, we raise a 401 error. Otherwise, we generate a new access token before returning it. Notice that the response structure also includes the token_type property. This allows the interactive documentation to automatically set the authorization headers.

In the following example, we'll look at the implementation of the `authenticate` and `create_access_token` functions. We won't go into too much detail here as they are quite simple:

authentication.py

```python
async def authenticate(email: str, password: str, session:
AsyncSession) -> User | None:
    query = select(User).where(User.email == email)
    result = await session.execute(query)
    user: User | None = result.scalar_one_or_none()

    if user is None:
        return None

    if not verify_password(password, user.hashed_password):
        return None

    return user

async def create_access_token(user: User, session: AsyncSession) ->
AccessToken:
    access_token = AccessToken(user=user)
    session.add(access_token)
    await session.commit()
    return access_token
```

https://github.com/PacktPublishing/Building-Data-Science-Applica-tions-with-FastAPI-Second-Edition/tree/main/chapter07/authentica-tion/authentication.py

Notice that we defined a function called `verify_password` to check the validity of the password. Once again, it uses `passlib` under the hood, which takes care of comparing the hashes of the passwords.

> **Password hash upgrade**
>
> To keep this example simple, we implemented a simple password comparison. Usually, it's good practice to implement a mechanism to upgrade the password hash at this stage. Imagine that a new and more robust hash algorithm has been introduced. We can take this opportunity to hash the password with this new algorithm and store it in a database. `passlib` includes a function for verifying and upgrading the hash in one operation. You can learn more about this in the following documentation: https://passlib.readthedocs.io/en/stable/narr/context-tutorial.html#integrating-hash-migration.

We've almost achieved our goal! Users can now log in and get a new access token. All we need to do now is implement a dependency to retrieve the `Authorization` header and verify this token!

Securing endpoints with access tokens

Previously, we learned how to implement a simple dependency to protect an endpoint with a header. Here, we'll also retrieve a token from a request header, but then, we'll have to check the database to see whether it's valid. If it is, we'll return the corresponding user.

Let's see what our dependency looks like:

---

app.py

```python
async def get_current_user(
    token: str = Depends(OAuth2PasswordBearer(tokenUrl="/token")),
    session: AsyncSession = Depends(get_async_session),
) -> User:
    query = select(AccessToken).where(
        AccessToken.access_token == token,
        AccessToken.expiration_date >= datetime.now(tz=timezone.utc),
    )
    result = await session.execute(query)
    access_token: AccessToken | None = result.scalar_one_or_none()

    if access_token is None:
        raise HTTPException(status_code=status.HTTP_401_UNAUTHORIZED)

    return access_token.user
```

https://github.com/PacktPublishing/Building-Data-Science-Applications-with-FastAPI-Second-Edition/tree/main/chapter07/authentication/app.py

---

The first thing to notice is that we used the OAuth2PasswordBearer dependency from FastAPI. It goes hand in hand with OAuth2PasswordRequestForm, which we saw in the previous section. It not only checks for the access token in the Authorization header, but it also informs the OpenAPI schema that the endpoint to get a fresh token is /token. This is the purpose of the tokenUrl argument. This is how the automatic documentation can automatically call the access token endpoint in the login form we saw earlier.

Then we performed a database query with SQLAlchemy. We applied two clauses: one to match the token we got and another to ensure that the expiration date is in the future. If no corresponding record is found in the database, we raise a 401 error. Otherwise, we return the user related to the access token.

And that's it! Our whole authentication system is complete. Now, we can protect our endpoints simply by injecting this dependency. We even have access to the user data so that we can tailor the response according to the current user. You can see this in the following example:

app.py

```
@app.get("/protected-route", response_model=schemas.UserRead)
async def protected_route(user: User = Depends(get_current_user)):
    return user
```

https://github.com/PacktPublishing/Building-Data-Science-Applications-with-FastAPI-Second-Edition/tree/main/chapter07/authentication/app.py

With that, you've learned how to implement a whole registration and authentication system from scratch. We voluntarily kept it simple to focus on the most important points, but it's a good base on which you can expand.

The patterns we showed here are good candidates for a REST API, which is called externally by other client programs. However, you may wish to call your API from a very common piece of software: the browser. In this case, there are some additional security considerations to be taken care of.

Configuring CORS and protecting against CSRF attacks

Nowadays, numerous pieces of software are designed to be used in a browser through an interface built with HTML, CSS, and JavaScript. Traditionally, web servers were responsible for handling browser requests and returning an HTML response to be shown to the user. This is a common use case for frameworks such as Django.

For a few years now, there has been a shift underway in that pattern. With the emergence of JavaScript frameworks such as Angular, React, and Vue, we tend to have a clear separation between the frontend, a highly interactive user interface powered by JavaScript, and the backend. Thus, those backends are now only responsible for data storage and retrieving and executing business logic. This is a task that REST APIs are very good at! From the JavaScript code, the user interface can then just spawn requests to your API and handle the result to present it.

However, we must still handle authentication: we want our user to be able to log in to the frontend application and make authenticated requests to the API. While an Authorization header, as we've seen so far, could work, there is a better way to handle authentication when working in browsers: **cookies**!

Cookies are designed to store user information in browser memory and are sent automatically in every request made to your server. They have been supported for years, and browsers integrate lots of mechanisms to make them safe and reliable.

However, this comes with some security challenges. Websites are very common targets for hackers and lots of attacks have emerged over the years.

One of the most typical is **Cross-Site Request Forgery** (**CSRF**). In this scenario, an attacker on another website tries to trick a user who is currently authenticated with your application to perform a request on your server. Since browsers tend to send cookies with every request, your server wouldn't be able to tell that the request was actually forged. Since it's the users themselves who unintentionally launched the malicious request, these kinds of attacks don't aim to steal data but to execute operations that change the state of the application, such as changing an email address or making a money transfer.

Obviously, we should be prepared for these kinds of risks and have measures in place to mitigate them.

Understanding CORS and configuring it in FastAPI

When you have a clearly separated frontend application and a REST API backend, they are not typically served from the same subdomain. For example, the frontend may be available from `www.myapplication.com`, while the REST API is available from `api.myapplication.com`. As we mentioned in the introduction, we would like to make requests to this API from our frontend application in JavaScript.

However, browsers don't allow **cross-origin resource sharing (CORS) HTTP requests**, meaning domain A can't make requests to domain B. This follows what is called a **same-origin policy**. This is a good thing in general as it's the first barrier to preventing CSRF attacks.

To experience this behavior, we'll run a simple example. In our example repository, the `chapter07/cors` folder contains a FastAPI app called `app_without_cors.py` and a simple HTML file called `index.html` that contains some JavaScript for performing HTTP requests.

First, let's run the FastAPI application using the usual `uvicorn` command:

```
(venv) $ uvicorn chapter07.cors.app_without_cors:app
```

This will launch the FastAPI application on port 8000 by default. On another terminal, we'll serve the HTML file using the built-in Python HTTP server. It's a simple server, but it's ideal for quickly serving static files. We can launch it on port 9000 thanks to the following command:

```
(venv) $ python -m http.server --directory chapter07/cors 9000
```

> **Starting several terminals**
>
> On Linux and macOS, you should be able to simply start a new Terminal by creating a new window or tab. On Windows and WSL, you can also have several tabs if you're using the Windows Terminal application: `https://apps.microsoft.com/store/detail/windows-terminal/9N0DX20HK701`.
>
> Otherwise, you can simply click on the Ubuntu shortcut in your **Start** menu to start another terminal.

We now have two running servers – one on `localhost:8000` and one on `localhost:9000`. Strictly speaking, since they are on different ports, they are of different origins; so, it's a good setup to try out cross-origin HTTP requests.

In your browser, go to `http://localhost:9000`. You'll see the simple application implemented in `index.html`, as shown in the following screenshot:

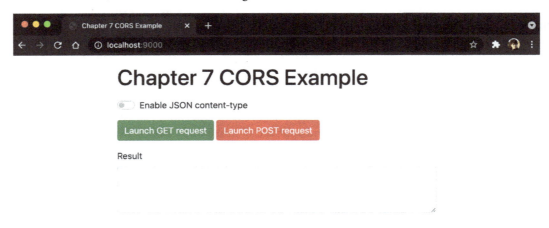

Figure 7.3 – Simple application to try CORS policies

There are two buttons that initiate GET and POST requests to our FastAPI application on port `8000`. If you click on either of those, you'll get a message in the error area stating **Failed to fetch**. If you look at the browser console in the development tools section, you'll see that the request failed because there isn't a CORS policy, as shown in the following screenshot. That's what we wanted – by default, browsers block cross-origin HTTP requests:

Figure 7.4 – CORS error in browser console

However, if you look at the terminal running the FastAPI application, you'll see an output similar to the following:

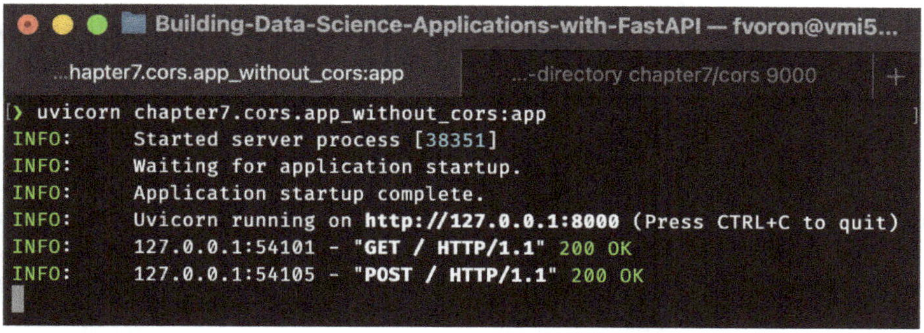

Figure 7.5 – Uvicorn output when performing simple requests

Clearly, both the GET and POST requests have been received and processed: we even returned a 200 status. So, what does this mean? In this case, the browser does send the request to the server. The lack of a CORS policy only forbids it to read the response; the request is still executed.

This is the case for requests that the browser considers **simple requests**. In essence, simple requests are those using the GET, POST, or HEAD methods that don't set custom headers or unusual content types. You can learn more about simple requests and their conditions by going to the following MDN page about CORS: https://developer.mozilla.org/en-US/docs/Web/HTTP/CORS#simple_requests.

This means that, for simple requests, the same-origin policy is not enough to protect us against CSRF attacks.

You may have noticed that our simple web application has a toggle for **Enable JSON content-type**. Enable this and perform the GET and POST requests again. On your FastAPI terminal, you should have an output similar to the following:

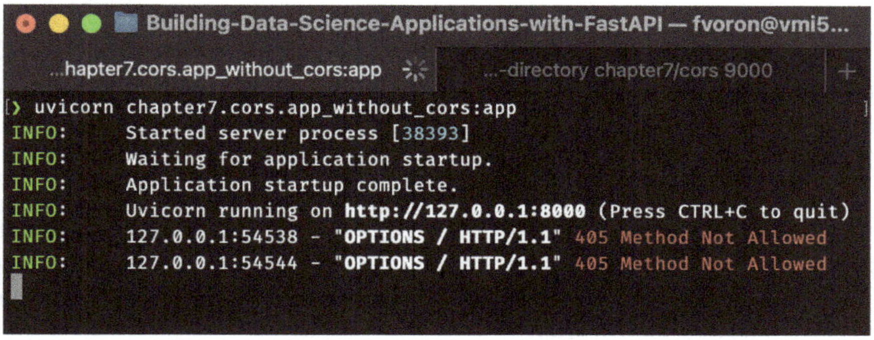

Figure 7.6 – Uvicorn output when receiving preflight requests

As you can see, our server received two strange requests with the OPTIONS method. This is what we call **preflight requests** in the context of CORS policies. Those requests are initiated by the browser before it performs the actual request when it doesn't consider it as a simple request. Here, we added the Content-Type header with a value of application/json, which is against the conditions of simple requests.

By performing this preflight request, the browser expects the server to provide information about what it is and isn't allowed to do in terms of cross-origin HTTP requests. Since we've not implemented anything here, our server can't provide a response to this preflight request. Hence, the browser stops there and doesn't proceed with the actual request.

And that's basically CORS: the server answers preflight queries with a set of HTTP headers that provide information to the browser about whether it's allowed to make the request or not. In that sense, CORS doesn't make your application more secure, it's quite the contrary: it allows the relaxation of some rules so that a frontend application can make requests to a backend residing on another domain. That's why it's crucial to configure CORS properly, so it doesn't expose you to dangerous attacks.

Fortunately, it's fairly easy to do this with FastAPI. All we need to do is import and add the CORSMiddleware class provided by Starlette. You can see what this looks like in the following example:

app_with_cors.py

```
app.add_middleware(
    CORSMiddleware,
    allow_origins=["http://localhost:9000"],
    allow_credentials=True,
    allow_methods=["*"],
    allow_headers=["*"],
    max_age=-1,  # Only for the sake of the example. Remove this in
your own project.
)
```

https://github.com/PacktPublishing/Building-Data-Science-Applications-with-FastAPI-Second-Edition/tree/main/chapter07/cors/app_with_cors.py

A middleware is a special class that adds global logic to an **Asynchronous Server Gateway Interface (ASGI)** application performing things before the request is handled by your path operation functions, and also after to possibly alter the response. FastAPI provides the add_middleware method for wiring such middleware into your application.

Here, CORSMiddleware will catch preflight requests sent by the browser and return the appropriate response with the CORS headers corresponding to your configuration. You can see that there are options to finely tune the CORS policy to your needs.

The most important one is probably `allow_origins`, which is the list of origins allowed to make requests to your API. Since our HTML application is served from `http://localhost:9000`, this is what we put here in this argument. If the browser tries to make requests from any other origin, it will stop as it's not authorized to do so by CORS headers.

The other interesting argument is `allow_credentials`. By default, browsers don't send cookies for cross-origin HTTP requests. If we wish to make authenticated requests to our API, we need to allow this via this option.

We can also finely tune the allowed methods and headers that are sent in the request. You can find a complete list of arguments for this middleware in the official Starlette documentation: `https://www.starlette.io/middleware/#corsmiddleware`.

Let's quickly talk about the `max_age` parameter. This parameter allows you to control the cache duration of the CORS responses. Having to perform a preflight request before the actual one is an expensive operation. To improve performance, browsers can cache the response so that they don't have to do this every time. Here, we are disabling caching with a value of `-1` to make sure you see the behavior of the browser in this example. In your projects, you can remove this argument so that you have a proper cache value.

Now, let's see how our web application behaves with this CORS-enabled application. Stop the previous FastAPI app and run this one using the usual command:

```
(venv) $ uvicorn chapter07.cors.app_with_cors:app
```

Now, if you try to perform the requests from the HTML application, you should see a working response in each case, both with and without a JSON content type. If you look at the FastAPI terminal, you should see an output similar to the following:

```
> uvicorn chapter7.cors.app_with_cors:app
INFO:     Started server process [38408]
INFO:     Waiting for application startup.
INFO:     Application startup complete.
INFO:     Uvicorn running on http://127.0.0.1:8000 (Press CTRL+C to quit)
INFO:     127.0.0.1:54765 - "GET / HTTP/1.1" 200 OK
INFO:     127.0.0.1:54765 - "POST / HTTP/1.1" 200 OK
INFO:     127.0.0.1:54765 - "OPTIONS / HTTP/1.1" 200 OK
INFO:     127.0.0.1:54765 - "GET / HTTP/1.1" 200 OK
INFO:     127.0.0.1:54765 - "OPTIONS / HTTP/1.1" 200 OK
INFO:     127.0.0.1:54765 - "POST / HTTP/1.1" 200 OK
```

Figure 7.7 – Uvicorn output with CORS headers

The two first requests are the "simple requests," which don't need a preflight request according to the browser rules. Then, we can see the requests that were performed with the JSON content type enabled. Before the GET and POST requests, an OPTIONS request was performed: the preflight request!

Thanks to this configuration, you can now make cross-origin HTTP requests between your frontend application and your backend living on another origin. Once again, it's not something that'll improve the security of your application, but it allows you to make this specific scenario work while keeping it secure from the rest of the web.

Even if those policies can be a first layer of defense against CSRF, this doesn't mitigate the risk completely. Indeed, the "simple requests" are still an issue: POST requests are allowed and, even if the response cannot be read, it's actually executed on the server.

Now, let's learn how to implement a pattern so that we're completely safe from such attacks: the **double-submit cookie**.

Implementing double-submit cookies to prevent CSRF attacks

As we mentioned previously, when relying on cookies to store user credentials, we are exposed to CSRF attacks since browsers will automatically send the cookies to your server. This is especially true for what the browser considers "simple requests," which don't enforce the CORS policy before the request is executed. There are also other attack vectors involving traditional HTML form submissions or even the src attribute of the image tag.

For all these reasons, we need to have another layer of security to mitigate this risk. Once again, this is only necessary if you plan to use your API from a browser application and use cookies for authentication.

To help you understand this, we've built a new example application that uses a cookie to store the user access token. It's very similar to the one we saw at the beginning of this chapter; we only modified it so that it looks for the access token in a cookie rather than in a header.

To make this example work, you'll have to install the starlette-csrf library. We'll explain what it does a bit later in this section. For now, just run the following command:

```
(venv) $ pip install starlette-csrf
```

In the following example, you can see the login endpoint that sets a cookie with the access token value:

app.py

```
@app.post("/login")
async def login(
    response: Response,
    email: str = Form(...),
    password: str = Form(...),
    session: AsyncSession = Depends(get_async_session),
```

```
):
    user = await authenticate(email, password, session)

    if not user:
        raise HTTPException(status_code=status.HTTP_401_UNAUTHORIZED)

    token = await create_access_token(user, session)

    response.set_cookie(
        TOKEN_COOKIE_NAME,
        token.access_token,
        max_age=token.max_age(),
        secure=True,
        httponly=True,
        samesite="lax",
    )
```

https://github.com/PacktPublishing/Building-Data-Science-Applica-
tions-with-FastAPI-Second-Edition/tree/main/chapter07/csrf/app.py

Notice that we used the Secure and HttpOnly flags for the resulting cookie. This ensures that it's sent only over HTTPS and that its value can't be read from JavaScript, respectively. While this is not enough to prevent every kind of attack, it's crucial for such sensitive information.

Besides that, we also set the SameSite flag to lax. It's a quite recent flag that allows us to control how the cookie is sent in a cross-origin context. lax is the default value in most browsers and allows the cookie to be sent to subdomains of the cookie domain but prevents it for other sites. In a sense, it's designed to be the standard, built-in protection against CSRF. However, other CSRF mitigation techniques, such as the one we'll implement here, are still needed currently. Indeed, older browsers that are not compatible with the SameSite flag are still vulnerable.

Now, when checking for the authenticated user, we'll just have to retrieve the token from the cookie that was sent in the request. Once again, FastAPI provides a security dependency to help with this, called APIKeyCookie. You can see it in the following example:

app.py

```
async def get_current_user(
    token: str = Depends(APIKeyCookie(name=TOKEN_COOKIE_NAME)),
    session: AsyncSession = Depends(get_async_session),
) -> User:
    query = select(AccessToken).where(
        AccessToken.access_token == token,
        AccessToken.expiration_date >= datetime.now(tz=timezone.utc),
    )
```

```
    result = await session.execute(query)
    access_token: AccessToken | None = result.scalar_one_or_none()

    if access_token is None:
        raise HTTPException(status_code=status.HTTP_401_UNAUTHORIZED)

    return access_token.user
```

https://github.com/PacktPublishing/Building-Data-Science-Applications-with-FastAPI-Second-Edition/tree/main/chapter07/csrf/app.py

And that's basically it! The rest of the code remains the same. Now, let's implement an endpoint that allows us to update the email address of the authenticated user. You can see this in the following example:

app.py

```
@app.post("/me", response_model=schemas.UserRead)
async def update_me(
    user_update: schemas.UserUpdate,
    user: User = Depends(get_current_user),
    session: AsyncSession = Depends(get_async_session),
):
    user_update_dict = user_update.dict(exclude_unset=True)
    for key, value in user_update_dict.items():
        setattr(user, key, value)

    session.add(user)
    await session.commit()

    return user
```

https://github.com/PacktPublishing/Building-Data-Science-Applications-with-FastAPI-Second-Edition/tree/main/chapter07/csrf/app.py

The implementation is not very surprising and follows what we've seen so far. However, it exposes us to a CSRF threat. As you can see, it uses the POST method. If we make a request in the browser to this endpoint without any special header, it will consider it as a simple request and execute it. Therefore, an attacker could change the email of a currently authenticated user, which is a major threat.

This is exactly why we need CSRF protection here. In the context of a REST API, the most straightforward technique is the double-submit cookie pattern. Here is how it works:

1. The user makes a first request with a method that's considered safe. Typically, this is a GET request.

2. In response, it receives a cookie containing a secret random value – that is, the CSRF token.

3. When making an unsafe request, such as POST, the user will read the CSRF token in the cookies and put the exact same value in a header. Since the browser also sends the cookies it has in memory, the request will contain the token both in the cookie and the header. That's why it's called **double submit**.

4. Before processing the request, the server will compare the CSRF token provided in the header with the one present in the cookie. If they match, it will proceed to process the request. Otherwise, it'll throw an error.

This is safe for two reasons:

*   An attacker targeting a third-party website can't read the cookies for a domain they don't own. Thus, they have no way of retrieving the CSRF token value.

*   Adding a custom header is against the conditions of "simple requests." Hence, the browser will have to make a preflight request before sending the request, enforcing the CORS policy.

This is a widely used pattern that works well to prevent such risks. This is why we installed starlette-csrf at the beginning of this section: it provides a piece of middleware for implementing it.

We can use it just like any other middleware, as shown in the following example:

app.py

```
app.add_middleware(
    CSRFMiddleware,
    secret=CSRF_TOKEN_SECRET,
    sensitive_cookies={TOKEN_COOKIE_NAME},
    cookie_domain="localhost",
)
```

https://github.com/PacktPublishing/Building-Data-Science-Applications-with-FastAPI-Second-Edition/tree/main/chapter07/csrf/app.py

We set several important arguments here. First, we have the secret, which should be a strong passphrase that's used to sign the CSRF token. Then, we have sensitive_cookies, which is a set of cookie names that should trigger the CSRF protection. If no cookie is present or if the provided ones are not critical, we can bypass the CSRF check. It's also useful if you have other authentication methods available that don't rely on cookies, such as Authorization headers, which are not vulnerable to CSRF. Finally, setting a cookie domain will allow you to retrieve the cookie containing the CSRF token, even if you are on a different subdomain; this is necessary in a cross-origin situation.

That's all you need to have the necessary protection ready. To ease the process of getting a fresh CSRF token, we implemented a minimal GET endpoint called /csrf. Its sole purpose is to provide us with a simple way to set the CSRF token cookie. We can call it directly when we load our frontend application.

Now, let's try it out in our situation. As we did in the previous section, we'll run the FastAPI application and the simple HTML application on two different ports. To do this, just run the following commands:

```
(venv) $ uvicorn chapter07.csrf.app:app
```

This will run the FastAPI application on port 8000. Now, run the following command:

```
(venv) $ python -m http.server --directory chapter07/csrf 9000
```

The frontend application is now live on http://localhost:9000. Open it in your browser. You should see an interface similar to the following:

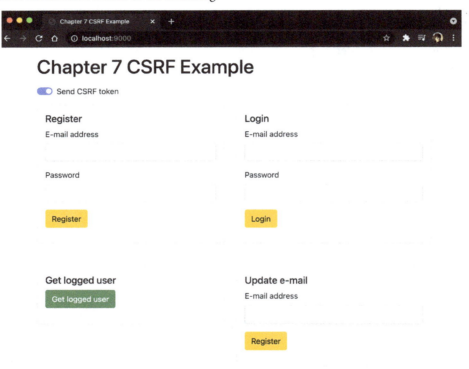

Figure 7.8 – Simple application to try a CSRF-protected API

Here, we've added forms to interact with our API endpoints: register, log in get authenticated user, and update the endpoints. If you try them out, they should work without any issue. If you have a look at the requests that were sent in the **Network** tab of the development tools section, you'll see that the CSRF token is present in the cookies and in a header called x-csrftoken.

At the top, there is a toggle to prevent the application from sending the CSRF token in the header. If you disable it, you'll see that all POST operations will result in an error.

Great! We are now safe from CSRF attacks! Most of the work here is done by the middleware, but it's interesting to understand how it works under the hood and how it protects your application. Bear in mind, however, that it comes with a drawback: it will break the interactive documentation. Indeed, it's not designed to retrieve the CSRF token from the cookie and put it in the headers in each request. Unless you plan on authenticating in another way (through a token in a header, for example), you won't be able to directly call your endpoints in the documentation.

Summary

That's all for this chapter, which covered authentication and security in FastAPI. We saw that implementing a basic authentication system is quite easy thanks to the tools provided by FastAPI. We've shown you one way to do this, but there are plenty of other good patterns out there to tackle this challenge. However, when working on this matter, always keep security in mind and be sure that you don't expose your application and your users' data to dangerous threats. In particular, you've seen that CSRF attacks have to be taken care of when designing a REST API that will be used in a browser application. A good source to understand all the security risks involved in a web application is the OWASP Cheat Sheet Series: `https://cheatsheetseries.owasp.org`.

With that, we've covered most of the important subjects concerning FastAPI application development. In the next chapter, we'll learn how to work with a recent technology that's integrated with FastAPI and that allows real-time, two-way communication between the client and the server: WebSockets.

8

Defining WebSockets for Two-Way Interactive Communication in FastAPI

HTTP is a simple yet powerful technique for sending data to and receiving data from a server. As we've seen, the principles of request and response are at the core of this protocol: when developing our API, our goal is to process the incoming request and build a response for the client. Thus, in order to get data from the server, the client always has to initiate a request first. In some contexts, however, this may not be very convenient. Imagine a typical chat application: when a user receives a new message, we would like them to be notified immediately by the server. Working only with HTTP, we would have to make requests every second to check whether new messages had arrived, which would be a massive waste of resources. This is why a new protocol has emerged: **WebSocket**. The goal of this protocol is to open a communication channel between a client and a server so that they can exchange data in real time, in both directions.

In this chapter, we're going to cover the following main topics:

- Understanding the principles of two-way communication with WebSockets
- Creating a WebSocket with FastAPI
- Handling multiple WebSocket connections and broadcasting messages

Technical requirements

For this chapter, you'll require a Python virtual environment, just as we set up in *Chapter 1*, *Python Development Environment Setup*.

For the *Handling multiple WebSocket connections and broadcasting messages* section, you'll need a running Redis server on your local computer. The easiest way is to run it as a Docker container. If you've never used Docker before, we recommend you read the *Getting started* tutorial in the official documentation at `https://docs.docker.com/get-started/`. Once done, you'll be able to run a Redis server with this simple command:

```
$ docker run -d --name fastapi-redis -p 6379:6379 redis
```

You'll find all the code examples for this chapter in the dedicated GitHub repository at `https://github.com/PacktPublishing/Building-Data-Science-Applications-with-FastAPI-Second-Edition/tree/main/chapter08`.

Understanding the principles of two-way communication with WebSockets

You have probably noticed that the name WebSockets is a direct reference to the traditional concept of **sockets** in Unix systems. While technically unrelated, they achieve the same goal: to open a *communication channel between two applications*. As we said in the introduction, HTTP works only on a request-response principle, which makes the implementation of applications that need real-time communication between the client and the server difficult and inefficient.

WebSockets try to solve that by opening a full-duplex communication channel, meaning that messages can be sent in both directions and possibly at the same time. Once the channel is opened, the server can send messages to the client without having to wait for a request from the client.

Even if HTTP and WebSocket are different protocols, WebSockets have been designed to work with HTTP. Indeed, when opening a WebSocket, the connection is first initiated using an HTTP request and then upgraded to a WebSocket tunnel. This makes it compatible out of the box with the traditional ports `80` and `443`, which is extremely convenient because we can easily add this feature over existing web servers without the need for an extra process.

WebSockets also share another similarity with HTTP: URIs. As with HTTP, WebSockets are identified through classic URIs, with a host, a path, and query parameters. Furthermore, we also have two schemes: `ws` (WebSocket) for insecure connections and `wss` (WebSocket Secure) for SSL-/TLS-encrypted connections.

Finally, this protocol is well supported in browsers nowadays, and opening a connection with a server involves just a few lines of JavaScript, as we'll see in this chapter.

However, handling this two-way communication channel is quite different from handling traditional HTTP requests. Since things happen in real time and in both directions, we'll see that we have to think differently from what we are used to. In FastAPI, the asynchronous nature of the WebSocket implementation will greatly help us in finding our way through that.

Creating a WebSocket with FastAPI

Thanks to Starlette, FastAPI has built-in support for WebSockets. As we'll see, defining a WebSocket endpoint is quick and easy, and we'll be able to get started in minutes. However, things will get more complex as we try to add more features to our endpoint logic. Let's start simple, with a WebSocket that waits for messages and simply echoes them back.

In the following example, you'll see the implementation of such a simple case:

app.py

```python
from fastapi import FastAPI, WebSocket
from starlette.websockets import WebSocketDisconnect


app = FastAPI()


@app.websocket("/ws")
async def websocket_endpoint(websocket: WebSocket):
    await websocket.accept()
    try:
        while True:
            data = await websocket.receive_text()
            await websocket.send_text(f"Message text was: {data}")
    except WebSocketDisconnect:
        pass
```

https://github.com/PacktPublishing/Building-Data-Science-Applica-tions-with-FastAPI-Second-Edition/blob/main/chapter08/echo/app.py

The code is quite understandable by itself, but let's focus on the important parts that differ from classic HTTP endpoints.

First of all, you see that FastAPI provides a special `websocket` decorator to create a WebSocket endpoint. As with regular endpoints, it takes the path at which it'll be available as an argument. However, other arguments that don't make sense in this context, such as the status code or response model, are not available.

Then, in the path operation function, we can inject a `WebSocket` object, which will provide us with all the methods to work with the WebSocket, as we'll see.

The first method we are calling in the implementation is `accept`. This method should be called first as it tells the client that we agree to open the tunnel.

After that, you can see that we start an infinite loop. That's the main difference with an HTTP endpoint: since we are opening a communication channel, it'll remain open until the client or the server decides to close it. While it's open, they can exchange as many messages as they need; hence, the infinite loop is here to remain open and repeat the logic until the tunnel is closed.

Inside the loop, we make the first call to the `receive_text` method. As you may have guessed, this returns the data sent by the client in plain text format. It's important here to understand that *this method will block until data is received from the client*. Until that event, we won't proceed with the rest of the logic.

We can see here the importance of asynchronous input/output, as we presented in *Chapter 2, Python Programming Specificities*. By creating an infinite loop waiting for incoming data, we could have blocked the whole server process in a traditional blocking paradigm. Here, thanks to the event loop, the process is able to answer other requests made by other clients while we are waiting for this one.

When data is received, the method returns the text data and we can proceed with the next line. Here, we simply send back the message to the client thanks to the `send_text` method. Once done, we are going back to the beginning of the loop to wait for another message.

You probably noticed that the whole loop is wrapped inside a `try...except` statement. This is necessary to *handle client disconnection*. Indeed, most of the time, our server will be blocked at the `receive_text` line, waiting for client data. If the client decides to disconnect, the tunnel will be closed and the `receive_text` call will fail, with a `WebSocketDisconnect` exception. That's why it's important to catch it to break the loop and properly finish the function.

Let's try it! You can run the FastAPI application, as usual, thanks to the Uvicorn server. Here's the command you'll need:

```
(venv) $ uvicorn chapter08.echo.app:app
```

Our client will be a simple HTML page with some JavaScript code to interact with the WebSocket. We'll quickly go through this code after the demonstration. To run it, we can simply serve it with the built-in Python server, as follows:

```
(venv) $ python -m http.server --directory chapter08/echo 9000
```

Starting several terminals

On Linux and macOS, you should be able to simply start a new Terminal by creating a new window or tab. On Windows and WSL, you can also have several tabs if you're using the Windows terminal application: `https://apps.microsoft.com/store/detail/windows-terminal/9N0DX20HK701`.

Otherwise, you can simply click on the Ubuntu shortcut in your **Start** menu to start another terminal.

This will serve our HTML page on port 9000 of your local machine. If you open the http://localhost:9000 address, you'll see a simple interface like the one shown here:

Figure 8.1 – Simple application for trying the WebSocket

You have a simple input form, allowing you to send messages to the server through the WebSocket. They appear in green in the list, as seen in the screenshot. The server echoes back your messages, which then appear in yellow in the list.

You can see what's happening under the hood by opening the **Network** tab in the developer tools of your browser. Reload the page to force the WebSocket to reconnect. You should then see a row for the WebSocket connection. If you click on it, you'll see a **Messages** tab where you can see all the messages passing through the WebSocket. You can see this interface in *Figure 8.2*.

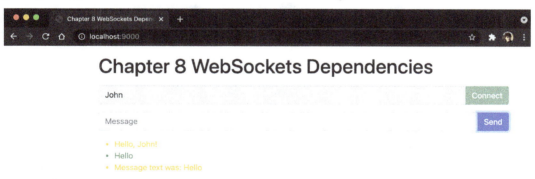

Figure 8.2 – WebSocket messages visualization within the browser developer tools

In the following example, you'll see the JavaScript code used to open the WebSocket connection and to send and receive messages:

script.js

```javascript
const socket = new WebSocket('ws://localhost:8000/ws');

// Connection opened
socket.addEventListener('open', function (event) {

  // Send message on form submission
  document.getElementById('form').addEventListener('submit', (event)
=> {
    event.preventDefault();
    const message = document.getElementById('message').value;

    addMessage(message, 'client');

    socket.send(message);

    event.target.reset();
  });
});

// Listen for messages
socket.addEventListener('message', function (event) {
  addMessage(event.data, 'server');
});
```

https://github.com/PacktPublishing/Building-Data-Science-Applications-with-FastAPI-Second-Edition/blob/main/chapter08/echo/script.js

As you can see, modern browsers provide a very simple API to interact with WebSockets. You just have to instantiate a new `WebSocket` object with the URL of your endpoint and wire some event listeners: `open` when the connection is ready and `message` when data is received from the server. Finally, the `send` method allows you to send data to the server. You can view more details on the WebSocket API in the MDN documentation:

https://developer.mozilla.org/en-US/docs/Web/API/WebSockets_API.

Handling concurrency

In the previous example, we assumed that the client was always sending a message first: we wait for its message before sending it back. Once again, it's the client that takes the initiative in the conversation.

However, in usual scenarios, the server can have data to send to the client without being at the initiative. In a chat application, another user can typically send one or several messages that we want to forward to the first user immediately. In this context, the blocking call to `receive_text` we showed in the previous example is a problem: while we are waiting, the server could have messages to forward to the client.

To solve this, we'll rely on more advanced tools of the `asyncio` module. Indeed, it provides functions that allow us to schedule several coroutines concurrently and wait until one of them is complete. In our context, we can have a coroutine that waits for client messages and another one that sends data to it when it arrives. The first one that is fulfilled wins and we can start again with another loop iteration.

To make this clearer, let's build another example, in which the server will once again echo the message of the client. Besides that, it'll regularly send the current time to the client. You can see the implementation in the following code snippet:

app.py

```python
async def echo_message(websocket: WebSocket):
    data = await websocket.receive_text()
    await websocket.send_text(f"Message text was: {data}")

async def send_time(websocket: WebSocket):
    await asyncio.sleep(10)
    await websocket.send_text(f"It is: {datetime.utcnow().
isoformat()}")

@app.websocket("/ws")
async def websocket_endpoint(websocket: WebSocket):
    await websocket.accept()
    try:
        while True:
            echo_message_task = asyncio.create_task(echo_
message(websocket))
            send_time_task = asyncio.create_task(send_time(websocket))
            done, pending = await asyncio.wait(
                {echo_message_task, send_time_task},
                return_when=asyncio.FIRST_COMPLETED,
            )
            for task in pending:
                task.cancel()
            for task in done:
```

```
                    task.result()
        except WebSocketDisconnect:
            await websocket.close()
```

https://github.com/PacktPublishing/Building-Data-Science-Applications-with-FastAPI-Second-Edition/blob/main/chapter08/concurrency/app.py

As you can see, we defined two coroutines: the first one, echo_message, waits for text messages from the client and sends them back, while the second one, send_time, waits for 10 seconds before sending the current time to the client. Both of them expect a WebSocket instance in the argument.

The most interesting part lives under the infinite loop: as you can see, we call our two functions, wrapped by the create_task function of asyncio. This transforms the coroutine into a task object. Under the hood, a task is how the event loop manages the execution of the coroutine. Put more simply, it gives us full control over the execution of the coroutine – we can retrieve its result or even cancel it.

Those task objects are necessary to work with asyncio.wait. This function is especially useful for running tasks concurrently. It expects a set of tasks to run in the first argument. By default, this function will block until all given tasks are completed. However, we can control that thanks to the return_when argument: in our case, we want it to block until one of the tasks is completed, which corresponds to the FIRST_COMPLETED value. The effect is the following: our server will launch the coroutines concurrently. The first one will block waiting for a client message, while the other one will block for 10 seconds. If the client sends a message before 10 seconds have passed, it'll send the message back and complete. Otherwise, the send_time coroutine will send the current time and complete.

At that point, asyncio.wait will return us two sets: the first one, done, contains a set of completed tasks, while the other one, pending, contains a set of tasks not yet completed.

We want to now go back to the start of the loop to start again. However, we need to first cancel all the tasks that have not been completed; otherwise, they would pile up at each iteration, hence the iteration over the pending set to cancel those tasks.

Finally, we also make an iteration over the done tasks and call the result method on them. This method returns the result of the coroutine but also re-raises an exception that could have been raised inside. This is especially useful for once again handling the disconnection of the client: when waiting for client data, if the tunnel is closed, an exception is raised. Thus, our try...except statement can catch it to properly terminate the function.

If you try this example as we did previously, you'll see that the server will regularly send you the current time but is also able to echo the messages you send.

This `send_time` example shows you how you can implement a process to send data to the client when an event happens on the server: new data is available in the database, an external process has finished a long computation, and so on. In the next section, we'll see how we can properly handle the case of multiple clients sending messages to the server, which then broadcasts them to all the clients.

That's basically how you can handle concurrency with `asyncio`'s tools. So far, everyone is able to connect to those WebSocket endpoints without any restriction. Of course, as with classic HTTP endpoints, you'll likely need to authenticate a user before opening the connection.

Using dependencies

Just as with regular endpoints, you can use dependencies in WebSocket endpoints. They basically work the same way, as FastAPI is able to adapt its behavior to a WebSocket context.

The only drawback is that can't use security dependencies, as we showed in *Chapter 7, Managing Authentication and Security in FastAPI*. Indeed, under the hood, most of them work by injecting the `Request` object, which only works for HTTP requests (we saw that WebSockets are injected in a `WebSocket` object instead). Trying to inject those dependencies in a WebSocket context will result in an error.

However, basic dependencies such as `Query`, `Header`, or `Cookie` work transparently. Let's try them in our next example. In this one, we'll inject two dependencies, as follows:

- A `username` query parameter, which we'll use to greet the user on connection.

- A `token` cookie, which we'll compare with a static value to keep the example simple. Of course, a proper strategy would be to have a proper user lookup, as we implemented in *Chapter 7, Managing Authentication and Security in FastAPI*. If this cookie doesn't have the required value, we'll raise an error.

Let's see the implementation in the following sample:

app.py

```
@app.websocket("/ws")
async def websocket_endpoint(
    websocket: WebSocket, username: str = "Anonymous", token: str =
Cookie(...)
):
    if token != API_TOKEN:
        raise WebSocketException(status.WS_1008_POLICY_VIOLATION)

    await websocket.accept()

    await websocket.send_text(f"Hello, {username}!")
    try:
```

```
        while True:
            data = await websocket.receive_text()
            await websocket.send_text(f"Message text was: {data}")
    except WebSocketDisconnect:
        pass
```

https://github.com/PacktPublishing/Building-Data-Science-Applica-
tions-with-FastAPI-Second-Edition/blob/main/chapter08/dependen-
cies/app.py

As you can see, injecting dependencies is no different from standard HTTP endpoints.

Then, we can have our dummy authentication logic. If it fails, we can raise a `WebSocketException`. It's the WebSocket equivalent of `HTTPException,` which we saw in previous sections. Under the hood, FastAPI will handle this exception by closing the WebSocket with the specified status code. WebSockets have their own set of status codes. You can view a complete list of these on this MDN documentation page: `https://developer.mozilla.org/fr/docs/Web/API/CloseEvent.` The most generic one when an error occurs is `1008`.

If it passes, we can start our classic echo server. Notice that we can use the `username` value as we wish in our logic. Here, we send a first message to greet the user on connection. If you try this with the HTML application, you'll see this message first, as shown in the following screenshot:

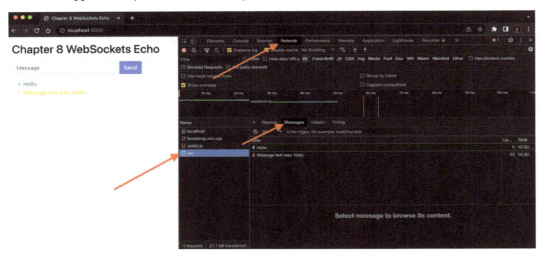

Figure 8.3 – Greeting message on connection

With the browser WebSocket API, query parameters can be passed into the URL and the browser automatically forwards the cookies. However, there is *no way to pass custom headers*. This means that if you rely on headers for authentication, you'll have to either add one using cookies or implement an authentication message mechanism in the WebSocket logic itself. However, if you don't plan to use your WebSocket with a browser, you can still rely on headers since most WebSocket clients support them.

You now have a good overview of how to add WebSockets to your FastAPI application. As we said, they are generally useful when several users are involved in real time and we need to broadcast messages to all of them. We'll see in the next section how to implement this pattern reliably.

Handling multiple WebSocket connections and broadcasting messages

As we said in the introduction to this chapter, a typical use case for WebSockets is to implement real-time communication across multiple clients, such as a chat application. In this configuration, several clients have an open WebSocket tunnel with the server. Thus, the role of the server is to *manage all the client connections and broadcast messages to all of them*: when a user sends a message, the server has to send it to all other clients in their WebSockets. We show you a schema of this principle here:

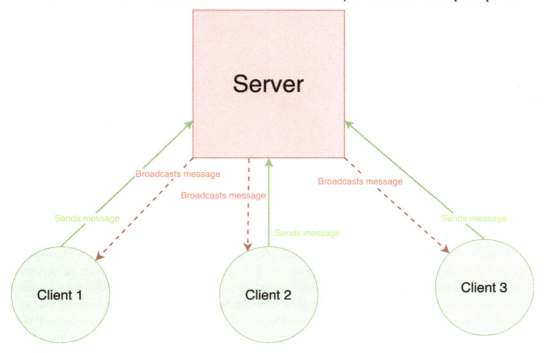

Figure 8.4 – Multiple clients connected through a WebSocket to a server

A first approach could be simply to keep a list of all WebSocket connections and iterate through them to broadcast messages. This would work but would quickly become problematic in a production environment. Indeed, most of the time, server processes run multiple workers when deployed. This means that instead of having only one process serving requests, we can have several ones so that we can answer more requests concurrently. We could also think of deployments on multiple servers spread over several data centers.

Hence, nothing guarantees you that two clients opening a WebSocket are served by the same process. Our simple approach would fail in this configuration: since connections are kept in the process memory, the process receiving the message would not be able to broadcast the message to clients served by another process. We schematize this problem in the following diagram:

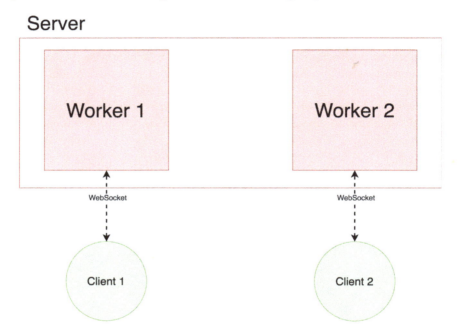

Figure 8.5 – Multiple server workers without a message broker

To solve this, we generally rely on **message brokers**. Message brokers are pieces of software whose role is to receive messages published by a first program and broadcast them to programs that are subscribed to it. Usually, this **publish-subscribe** (**pub-sub**) pattern is organized into different channels so that messages are clearly organized following their topic or usage. Some of the best-known message broker software includes Apache Kafka, RabbitMQ, and cloud-based implementations from **Amazon Web Services** (**AWS**), **Google Cloud Platform** (**GCP**), and Microsoft Azure: Amazon MQ, Cloud Pub/Sub, and Service Bus, respectively.

Hence, our message broker will be unique in our architecture, and several server processes will connect to it to either publish or subscribe to messages. This architecture is schematized in the following diagram:

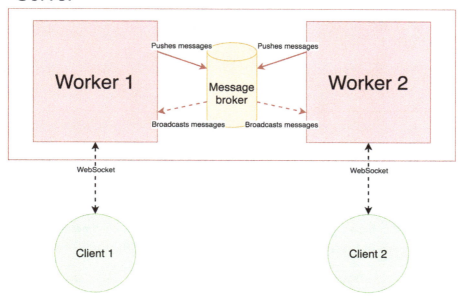

Figure 8.6 – Multiple server workers with a message broker

In this chapter, we'll see how to set up a simple system using the `broadcaster` library from Encode (the creators of Starlette) and *Redis*, which will act as a message broker.

A word on Redis

At its core, Redis is a data store designed to achieve maximum performance. It's widely used in the industry for storing temporary data that we want to access very quickly, such as caches or distributed locks. It also supports a basic pub/sub paradigm, which makes it a good candidate to be used as a message broker. You can learn more about this technology at its official website: `https://redis.io`.

First of all, let's install the library with the following command:

```
(venv) $ pip install "broadcaster[redis]"
```

This library will abstract away all the complexities of publishing and subscribing with Redis for us.

Let's see the details of the implementation. In the following example, you'll see the instantiation of the `Broadcaster` object:

app.py

```
broadcast = Broadcast("redis://localhost:6379")
CHANNEL = "CHAT"
```

https://github.com/PacktPublishing/Building-Data-Science-Applications-with-FastAPI-Second-Edition/blob/main/chapter08/broadcast/app.py

As you can see, it only expects a URL to our Redis server. Notice also that we define a CHANNEL constant. This will be the name of the channel to publish and subscribe to messages. We choose a static value here for the sake of the example, but you could have dynamic channel names in a real-world application—to support several chat rooms, for example.

Then, we define two functions: one to subscribe to new messages and send them to the client and another one to publish messages received in the WebSocket. You can see these functions in the following sample:

app.py

```
class MessageEvent(BaseModel):
    username: str
    message: str

async def receive_message(websocket: WebSocket, username: str):
    async with broadcast.subscribe(channel=CHANNEL) as subscriber:
        async for event in subscriber:
            message_event = MessageEvent.parse_raw(event.message)
            # Discard user's own messages
            if message_event.username != username:
                await websocket.send_json(message_event.dict())

async def send_message(websocket: WebSocket, username: str):
    data = await websocket.receive_text()
    event = MessageEvent(username=username, message=data)
    await broadcast.publish(channel=CHANNEL, message=event.json())
```

https://github.com/PacktPublishing/Building-Data-Science-Applications-with-FastAPI-Second-Edition/blob/main/chapter08/broadcast/app.py

First of all, notice that we defined a Pydantic model, `MessageEvent`, to help us structure the data contained in a message. Instead of just passing raw strings as we've been doing up to now, we have an object bearing both the message and the username.

The first function, `receive_message`, subscribes to the broadcast channel and waits for messages called `event`. The data of the message contains serialized JSON that we deserialize to instantiate a `MessageEvent` object. Notice that we use the `parse_raw` method of the Pydantic model, allowing us to parse the JSON string into an object in one operation.

Then, we check whether the message username is different from the current username. Indeed, since all users are subscribed to the channel, they will also receive the messages they sent themselves. That's why we discard them based on the username to avoid this. Of course, in a real-world application, you'll likely want to rely on a unique user ID rather than a simple username.

Finally, we can send the message through the WebSocket thanks to the `send_json` method, which takes care of serializing the dictionary automatically.

The second function, `send_message`, is there to publish a message to the broker. Quite simply, it waits for new data in the socket, structures it into a `MessageEvent` object, and then publishes it.

That's about it for the `broadcaster` part. We then have the WebSocket implementation in itself, which is very similar to what we saw in the previous sections. You can see it in the following sample:

app.py

```python
@app.websocket("/ws")
async def websocket_endpoint(websocket: WebSocket, username: str =
"Anonymous"):
    await websocket.accept()
    try:
        while True:
            receive_message_task = asyncio.create_task(
                receive_message(websocket, username)
            )
            send_message_task = asyncio.create_task(send_
message(websocket, username))
            done, pending = await asyncio.wait(
                {receive_message_task, send_message_task},
                return_when=asyncio.FIRST_COMPLETED,
            )
            for task in pending:
                task.cancel()
            for task in done:
```

```
            task.result()
    except WebSocketDisconnect:
        pass
```

https://github.com/PacktPublishing/Building-Data-Science-Applications-with-FastAPI-Second-Edition/blob/main/chapter08/broadcast/app.py

Finally, we need to tell FastAPI to open the connection with the broker when it starts the application and to close it when exiting, as you can see in the following extract:

app.py

```
@contextlib.asynccontextmanager
async def lifespan(app: FastAPI):
    await broadcast.connect()
    yield
    await broadcast.disconnect()

app = FastAPI(lifespan=lifespan)
```

https://github.com/PacktPublishing/Building-Data-Science-Applications-with-FastAPI-Second-Edition/blob/main/chapter08/broadcast/app.py

Let's now try this application! First, we'll run the Uvicorn server. Be sure that your Redis container is running before starting, as we explained in the *Technical requirements* section. Here's the command you'll need:

```
(venv) $ uvicorn chapter08.broadcast.app:app
```

We also provided a simple HTML client in the examples. To run it, we can simply serve it with the built-in Python server, as follows:

```
(venv) $ python -m http.server --directory chapter08/broadcast 9000
```

You can now access it through http://localhost:9000. If you open it twice in your browser, in two different windows, you can see whether the broadcasting is working. Input a username in the first window and click on **Connect**. Do the same in the second window with a different username. You can now send messages and see that they are broadcast to the other client, as depicted in the following screenshot:

Figure 8.7 – Multiple WebSockets clients broadcasting messages

That was a very quick overview of how you can implement broadcasting systems involving message brokers. Of course, we only covered the basics here, and much more complex things can be done with those powerful technologies. Once again, we see that FastAPI gives us access to powerful building bricks without locking us inside specific technologies or patterns: it's very easy to include new libraries to expand our possibilities.

Summary

In this chapter, you learned how to work with one of the latest web technologies available: WebSockets. You are now able to open a two-way communication channel between a client and a server, allowing you to implement applications with real-time constraints. As you've seen, FastAPI makes it very easy to add such endpoints. Still, the way of thinking inside WebSockets logic is quite different from traditional HTTP endpoints: managing an infinite loop and handling several tasks at a time are completely new challenges. Fortunately, the asynchronous nature of the framework makes our life easier in this matter and helps us write concurrent code that is easily understandable.

Finally, we also had a quick overview of the challenges to solve when handling multiple clients that share messages between them. You saw that message broker software such as Redis is necessary to make this use case reliable across several server processes.

You are now acquainted with all the features of FastAPI. Up to now, we've shown very simple examples focused on a specific point. In the real world, however, you'll likely develop big applications that can do a lot of things and grow larger over time. To make them reliable and maintainable and keep high-quality code, it's necessary to test them to make sure they behave as intended and that you don't introduce bugs when adding new things.

In the next chapter, you'll see how to set up an efficient test environment for FastAPI.

Testing an API Asynchronously with pytest and HTTPX

In software development, a significant part of the developer's work should be dedicated to writing tests. At first, you may be tempted to manually test your application by running it, making a few requests, and arbitrarily deciding that "everything works." However, this approach is flawed and can't guarantee that your program works in every circumstance and that you didn't break things along the way.

That's why several disciplines have emerged regarding software testing: unit tests, integration tests, end-to-end tests, acceptance tests, and others. These techniques aim to validate the functionality of software from a micro level, where we test single functions (unit tests), to a macro level, where we test a global feature that delivers value to the user (acceptance tests). In this chapter, we'll focus on the first level: unit testing.

Unit tests are short programs designed to verify that our code behaves the way it should in every circumstance. You may think that tests are time-consuming to write and that they don't add value to your software, but this will save you time in the long run: first of all, tests can be run automatically in a few seconds, ensuring that all your software works, without you needing to manually go over every feature. Secondly, when you introduce new features or refactor the code, you're ensuring that you don't introduce bugs to existing parts of the software. In conclusion, tests are just as important as the program itself, and they help you deliver reliable and high-quality software.

In this chapter, you'll learn how to write tests for your FastAPI application, both for HTTP endpoints and WebSockets. To help with this, you'll learn how to configure pytest, a well-known Python test framework, and HTTPX, an asynchronous HTTP client for Python.

In this chapter, we're going to cover the following main topics:

- An introduction to unit testing with pytest
- Setting up the testing tools for FastAPI with HTTPX
- Writing tests for REST API endpoints
- Writing tests for WebSocket endpoints

Technical requirements

For this chapter, you'll require a Python virtual environment, just as we set up in *Chapter 1, Python Development Environment Setup.*

For the *Communicating with a MongoDB database using Motor* section, you'll need a running MongoDB server on your local computer. The easiest way to do this is to run it as a Docker container. If you've never used Docker before, we recommend that you refer to the *Getting started* tutorial in the official documentation at `https://docs.docker.com/get-started/`. Once you have done this, you'll be able to run a MongoDB server using this simple command:

```
$ docker run -d --name fastapi-mongo -p 27017:27017 mongo:6.0
```

The MongoDB server instance will then be available on your local computer at port `27017`.

You'll find all the code examples of this chapter in the dedicated GitHub repository at `https://github.com/PacktPublishing/Building-Data-Science-Applications-with-FastAPI-Second-Edition/tree/main/chapter09`.

An introduction to unit testing with pytest

As we mentioned in the introduction, writing unit tests is an essential task in software development to deliver high-quality software. To help us be productive and efficient, a lot of libraries exist that provide tools and shortcuts dedicated to testing. In the Python standard library, a module exists for unit testing called `unittest`. Even though it's quite common in Python code bases, many Python developers tend to prefer pytest, which provides a more lightweight syntax and powerful tools for advanced use cases.

In the following examples, we'll write a unit test for a function called `add`, both with `unittest` and pytest, so that you can see how they compare on a basic use case. First, we'll install pytest:

```
(venv) $ pip install pytest
```

Now, let's see our simple `add` function, which simply performs an addition:

chapter09_introduction.py

```
def add(a: int, b: int) -> int:
    return a + b
```

`https://github.com/PacktPublishing/Building-Data-Science-Applications-with-FastAPI-Second-Edition/tree/main/chapter09/chapter09_introduction.py`

Now, let's implement a test that checks that *2 + 3* is indeed equal to *5* with `unittest`:

chapter09_introduction_unittest.py

```
import unittest

from chapter09.chapter09_introduction import add

class TestChapter09Introduction(unittest.TestCase):
    def test_add(self):
        self.assertEqual(add(2, 3), 5)
```

https://github.com/PacktPublishing/Building-Data-Science-Applications-with-FastAPI-Second-Edition/tree/main/chapter09/chapter09_introduction_unittest.py

As you can see, `unittest` expects us to define a class inheriting from `TestCase`. Then, each test lives in its own method. To assert that two values are equal, we must use the `assertEqual` method.

To run this test, we can call the `unittest` module from the command line and pass it through the dotted path to our test module:

```
(venv) $ python -m unittest chapter09.chapter09_introduction_unittest
.
----------------------------------------------------------------------
Ran 1 test in 0.000s

OK
```

In the output, each successful test is represented by a dot. If one or several tests are not successful, you will get a detailed error report for each, highlighting the failing assertion. You can try it by changing the assertion in the test.

Now, let's write the same test with pytest:

chapter09_introduction_pytest.py

```
from chapter09.chapter09_introduction import add

def test_add():
    assert add(2, 3) == 5
```

https://github.com/PacktPublishing/Building-Data-Science-Applications-with-FastAPI-Second-Edition/tree/main/chapter09/chapter09_introduction_pytest.py

As you can see, it's much shorter! Indeed, with pytest, you don't necessarily have to define a class: a simple function is enough. The only constraint to making it work is that the function name has to start with `test_`. This way, pytest can automatically discover the test functions. Secondly, it relies on the built-in `assert` statement instead of specific methods, allowing you to write comparisons more naturally.

To run this test, we must simply call the `pytest` executable with the path to our test file:

```
(venv) $ pytest chapter09/chapter09_introduction_pytest.py
================ test session starts ================
platform darwin -- Python 3.10.8, pytest-7.2.0, pluggy-1.0.0
rootdir: /Users/fvoron/Development/Building-Data-Science-Applications-with-FastAPI-Second-Edition, configfile: pyproject.toml
plugins: asyncio-0.20.2, cov-4.0.0, anyio-3.6.2
asyncio: mode=strict
collected 1 item

chapter09/chapter09_introduction_pytest.py
.                              [100%]

================ 1 passed in 0.01s ================
```

Once again, the output represents each successful test with a dot. Of course, if you change the test to make it fail, you'll get a detailed error for the failing assertion.

It's worth noting that if you run pytest without any arguments, it'll automatically discover all the tests living in your project, as long as their name starts with `test_`.

Here, we made a small comparison between `unittest` and pytest. For the rest of this chapter, we'll stick with pytest, which should give you a more productive experience while writing tests.

Before focusing on FastAPI testing, let's review two of the most powerful features of pytest: `parametrize` and fixtures.

Generating tests with parametrize

In our previous example, with the `add` function, we only tested one addition test, *2 + 3*. Most of the time, we'll want to check for more cases to ensure our function works in every circumstance. Our first approach could be to add more assertions to our test, like so:

```python
def test_add():
    assert add(2, 3) == 5
    assert add(0, 0) == 0
    assert add(100, 0) == 100
    assert add(1, 1) == 2
```

While working, this method has two drawbacks: first, it may be a bit cumbersome to write the same assertion several times with only some parameters changing. In this example, it's not too bad, but tests can be way more complex, as we'll see with FastAPI. Second, we still only have one test: the first failing assertion will stop the test and the following ones won't be executed. Thus, we'll only know the result if we fix the failing assertion first and run the test again.

To help with this specific task, pytest provides the parametrize marker. In pytest, a **marker** is a special decorator that's used to easily pass metadata to the test. Special behaviors can then be implemented, depending on the markers used by the test.

Here, parametrize allows us to define several sets of variables that will be passed as arguments to the test function. At runtime, each set will generate a new and independent test. To understand this better, let's look at how to use this marker to generate several tests for our add function:

chapter09_introduction_pytest_parametrize.py

```python
import pytest

from chapter09.chapter09_introduction import add

@pytest.mark.parametrize("a,b,result", [(2, 3, 5), (0, 0, 0), (100, 0,
100), (1, 1, 2)])
def test_add(a, b, result):
    assert add(a, b) == result
```

https://github.com/PacktPublishing/Building-Data-Science-Applications-with-FastAPI-Second-Edition/tree/main/chapter09/chapter09_introduction_pytest_parametrize.py

Here, you can see that we simply decorated our test function with the parametrize marker. The basic usage is as follows: the first argument is a string with the name of each parameter separated by a comma. Then, the second argument is a list of tuples. Each tuple contains the values of the parameters in order.

Our test function receives those parameters in arguments, each one named the way you specified previously. Thus, you can use them at will in the test logic. As you can see, the great benefit here is that we only have to write the assert statement once. Besides, it's very quick to add a new test case: we just have to add another tuple to the parametrize marker.

Now, let's run this test to see what happens by using the following command:

```
(venv) $ pytest chapter09/chapter09_introduction_pytest_parametrize.py
================ test session starts =================
platform darwin -- Python 3.10.8, pytest-7.2.0, pluggy-1.0.0
rootdir: /Users/fvoron/Development/Building-Data-Science-Applications-
with-FastAPI-Second-Edition, configfile: pyproject.toml
```

```
plugins: asyncio-0.20.2, cov-4.0.0, anyio-3.6.2
asyncio: mode=strict
collected 4 items

chapter09/chapter09_introduction_pytest_parametrize.py ....    [100%]

================ 4 passed in 0.01s ================
```

As you can see, pytest executed *four tests instead of one*! This means that it generated four independent tests, along with their own sets of parameters. If several tests fail, we'll be informed, and the output will tell us which set of parameters caused the error.

To conclude, `parametrize` is a very convenient way to test different outcomes when it's given a different set of parameters.

While writing unit tests, you'll often need variables and objects several times across your tests, such as app instances, fake data, and so on. To avoid having to repeat the same things over and over across your tests, pytest proposes an interesting feature: fixtures.

Reusing test logic by creating fixtures

When testing a large application, tests tend to become quite repetitive: lots of them will share the same boilerplate code before their actual assertion. Consider the following Pydantic models representing a person and their postal address:

chapter09_introduction_fixtures.py

```python
from datetime import date
from enum import Enum

from pydantic import BaseModel

class Gender(str, Enum):
    MALE = "MALE"
    FEMALE = "FEMALE"
    NON_BINARY = "NON_BINARY"

class Address(BaseModel):
    street_address: str
    postal_code: str
    city: str
    country: str

class Person(BaseModel):
    first_name: str
```

```
        last_name: str
        gender: Gender
        birthdate: date
        interests: list[str]
        address: Address
```

https://github.com/PacktPublishing/Building-Data-Science-Applications-with-FastAPI-Second-Edition/tree/main/chapter09/chapter09_introduction_fixtures.py

This example may look familiar: it was taken from *Chapter 4*, *Managing Pydantic Data Models in FastAPI*. Now, let's say that we want to write tests with some instances of those models. Obviously, it would be a bit annoying to instantiate them in each test, filling them with fake data.

Fortunately, fixtures allow us to write them once and for all. The following example shows how to use them:

chapter09_introduction_fixtures_test.py

```python
import pytest

from chapter09.chapter09_introduction_fixtures import Address, Gender, Person

@pytest.fixture
def address():
    return Address(
        street_address="12 Squirell Street",
        postal_code="424242",
        city="Woodtown",
        country="US",
    )

@pytest.fixture
def person(address):
    return Person(
        first_name="John",
        last_name="Doe",
        gender=Gender.MALE,
        birthdate="1991-01-01",
        interests=["travel", "sports"],
        address=address,
    )

def test_address_country(address):
```

```
        assert address.country == "US"

    def test_person_first_name(person):
        assert person.first_name == "John"

    def test_person_address_city(person):
        assert person.address.city == "Woodtown"
```

https://github.com/PacktPublishing/Building-Data-Science-Applica-tions-with-FastAPI-Second-Edition/tree/main/chapter09/chapter09_introduction_fixtures_test.py

Once again, pytest makes it very straightforward: fixtures are *simple functions* decorated *with the fixture decorator*. Inside, you can write any logic and return the object you'll need in your tests. Here, in address, we instantiate an Address object with fake data and return it.

Now, how can we use this fixture? If you look at the test_address_country test, you'll see some magic happening: by setting an address argument on the test function, pytest automatically detects that it corresponds to the address fixture, executes it, and passes its return value. Inside the test, we have our Address object ready to use. pytest calls this *requesting a fixture*.

You may have noticed that we also defined another fixture, person. Once again, we instantiate a Person model with dummy data. The interesting thing to note, however, is that we actually requested the address fixture to use it inside! That's what makes this system so powerful: fixtures can depend on other fixtures, which can also depend on others, and so on. In some way, it's quite similar to dependency injection, as we discussed in *Chapter 5, Dependency Injection in FastAPI*.

With that, our quick introduction to pytest has come to an end. Of course, there are so many more things to say, but this will be enough for you to get started. If you want to explore this topic further, you can read the official pytest documentation, which includes tons of examples showing you how you can benefit from all its features: https://docs.pytest.org/en/latest/.

Now, let's focus on FastAPI. We'll start by setting up the tools for testing our applications.

Setting up testing tools for FastAPI with HTTPX

If you look at the FastAPI documentation regarding testing, you'll see that it recommends that you use TestClient provided by Starlette. In this book, we'll show you a different approach involving an HTTP client called HTTPX.

Why? The default `TestClient` is implemented in a way that makes it completely synchronous, meaning you can write tests without worrying about `async` and `await`. This might sound nice, but we found that it causes some problems in practice: since your FastAPI app is designed to work asynchronously, you'll likely have lots of services working asynchronously, such as the database drivers we saw in *Chapter 6, Databases and Asynchronous ORMs*. Thus, in your tests, you'll probably need to perform some actions on those asynchronous services, such as filling a database with dummy data, which will make your tests asynchronous anyway. Melding the two approaches often leads to strange errors that are hard to debug.

Fortunately, HTTPX, an HTTP client created by the same team as Starlette, allows us to have a pure asynchronous HTTP client able to make requests to our FastAPI app. To make this approach work, we'll need three libraries:

- `HTTPX`, the client that will perform HTTP requests
- `asgi-lifespan`, a library for managing the lifespan events of your FastAPI app programmatically
- `pytest-asyncio`, an extension for pytest that allows us to write asynchronous tests

Let's install those libraries using the following command:

```
(venv) $ pip install httpx asgi-lifespan pytest-asyncio
```

Great! Now, let's write some fixtures so that we can easily get an HTTP test client for a FastAPI application. This way, when writing a test, we'll only have to request the fixture and we'll be able to make a request right away.

In the following example, we are considering a simple FastAPI application that we want to test:

---

chapter09_app.py

```python
import contextlib

from fastapi import FastAPI

@contextlib.asynccontextmanager
async def lifespan(app: FastAPI):
    print("Startup")
    yield
    print("Shutdown")

app = FastAPI(lifespan=lifespan)

@app.get("/")
```

```
async def hello_world():
    return {"hello": "world"}
```

https://github.com/PacktPublishing/Building-Data-Science-Applica-
tions-with-FastAPI-Second-Edition/tree/main/chapter09/chapter09_
app.py

In a separate test file, we'll implement two fixtures.

The first one, `event_loop`, will ensure that we always work with the same event loop instance. It's automatically requested by `pytest-asyncio` before executing asynchronous tests. You can see its implementation in the following example:

chapter09_app_test.py

```
@pytest.fixture(scope="session")
def event_loop():
    loop = asyncio.new_event_loop()
    yield loop
    loop.close()
```

https://github.com/PacktPublishing/Building-Data-Science-Applica-
tions-with-FastAPI-Second-Edition/tree/main/chapter09/chapter09_
app_test.py

Here, you can see that we simply create a new event loop before *yielding* it. As we discussed in *Chapter 2, Python Programming Specificities*, using a generator allows us to "pause" the function's execution and get back to the execution of its caller. This way, when the caller is done, we can execute cleanup operations, such as closing the loop. pytest is smart enough to handle this correctly in fixtures, so this is a very common pattern for setting up test data, using it, and destroying it after. We also use the same approach for lifespan functions in FastAPI.

Of course, this function is decorated with the `fixture` decorator to make it a fixture for pytest. You may have noticed that we set an argument called `scope` with the `session` value. This argument controls at which level the fixture should be instantiated. By default, it's recreated *at the beginning of each single test function*. The `session` value is the highest level, meaning that the fixture is only created once at the beginning of the whole test run, which is relevant for our event loop. You can find out more about this more advanced feature in the official documentation: https://docs.
pytest.org/en/latest/how-to/fixtures.html#scope-sharing-fixtures-
across-classes-modules-packages-or-session.

Next, we'll implement our `test_client` fixture, which will create an instance of HTTPX for our FastAPI application. We must also remember to trigger the app events with `asgi-lifespan`. You can see what it looks like in the following example:

chapter09_app_test.py

```
@pytest_asyncio.fixture
async def test_client():
    async with LifespanManager(app):
        async with httpx.AsyncClient(app=app, base_url="http://app.
io") as test_client:
            yield test_client
```

https://github.com/PacktPublishing/Building-Data-Science-Applica-tions-with-FastAPI-Second-Edition/tree/main/chapter09/chapter09_app_test.py

Only three lines are needed. The first difference with fixtures we've seen so far is that this is an async function. In this case, notice that we used the `@pytest_asyncio.fixture` decorator instead of `@pytest.fixture`. It's the async counterpart of this decorator provided by `pytest-asyncio` so async fixtures are correctly handled. In previous versions, using the standard decorator used to work but it's now discouraged.

Then, we have two context managers: `LifespanManager` and `httpx.AsyncClient`. The first one ensures startup and shutdown events are executed, while the second one ensures that an HTTP session is ready. On both of them, we set the `app` variable: this is our FastAPI application instance we imported from its module, `chapter09.chapter09_app import app`.

Notice that we once again used a generator here, with `yield`. This is important because, even if we don't have any more code after, *we need to close the context managers after we use our client*. If we used `return`, Python would have immediately closed them and we would end up with an unusable client.

Organizing tests and global fixtures in projects

In larger projects, you'll likely have several test files to keep your tests organized. Usually, those files are placed in a `tests` folder at the root of your project. If your test files are prefixed with `test_`, they will be automatically discovered by pytest. *Figure 9.1* shows an example of this.

Besides this, you'll need the fixtures we defined in this section for all your tests. Rather than repeating them again and again in all your test files, pytest allows you to write global fixtures in a file named `conftest.py`. After putting it in your `tests` folder, it will automatically be imported, allowing you to request all the fixtures you define inside it. You can read more about this in the official documentation at `https://docs.pytest.org/en/latest/reference/fixtures.html#conftest-py-sharing-fixtures-across-multiple-files`.

As mentioned previously, *Figure 9.1* shows the test files in the `tests` folder:

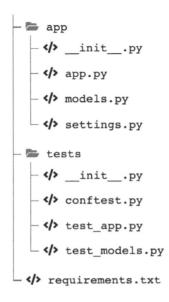

Figure 9.1 – Structure of a project with tests

That's it! We now have all the fixtures ready to write tests for our REST API endpoints. That's what we'll do in the next section.

Writing tests for REST API endpoints

All the tools we need to test our FastAPI application are now ready. All these tests boil down to performing an HTTP request and checking the response to see whether it corresponds to what we expect.

Let's start simply with a test for our `hello_world` path operation function. You can see it in the following code:

chapter09_app_test.py

```python
@pytest.mark.asyncio
async def test_hello_world(test_client: httpx.AsyncClient):
    response = await test_client.get("/")

    assert response.status_code == status.HTTP_200_OK
```

```
    json = response.json()
    assert json == {"hello": "world"}
```

https://github.com/PacktPublishing/Building-Data-Science-Applications-with-FastAPI-Second-Edition/tree/main/chapter09/chapter09_app_test.py

First of all, notice that the test function is defined as async. As we mentioned previously, to make it work with pytest, we had to install pytest-asyncio. This extension provides the asyncio marker: each asynchronous test should be decorated with this marker to make it work properly.

Next, we request our test_client fixture, which we defined earlier. It gives us an HTTPX client instance ready to make requests to our FastAPI app. Note that we manually type hinted the fixture. While not strictly required, it'll greatly help you if you use an IDE such as Visual Studio Code, which uses type hints to provide you with convenient auto-completion features.

Then, in the body of our test, we perform the request. Here, it's a simple GET request to the / path. It returns an HTTPX Response object (which is *different* from the Response class of FastAPI) containing all the data of the HTTP response: the status code, the headers, and the body.

Finally, we make assertions based on this data. As you can see, we verify that the status code is indeed 200. We also check the content of the body, which is a simple JSON object. Notice that the Response object has a convenient method called json for automatically parsing JSON content.

Great! We wrote our first FastAPI test! Of course, you'll likely have more complex tests, typically ones for POST endpoints.

Writing tests for POST endpoints

Testing a POST endpoint is not very different from what we've seen earlier. The difference is that we'll likely have more cases to check whether data validation is working. In the following example, we are implementing a POST endpoint that accepts a Person model in the body:

chapter09_app_post.py

```
class Person(BaseModel):
    first_name: str
    last_name: str
    age: int


@app.post("/persons", status_code=status.HTTP_201_CREATED)
async def create_person(person: Person):
    return person
```

https://github.com/PacktPublishing/Building-Data-Science-Applications-with-FastAPI-Second-Edition/tree/main/chapter09/chapter09_app_post.py

An interesting test could be to ensure that an error is raised if some fields are missing in the request payload. In the following extract, we wrote two tests – one with an invalid payload and another with a valid one:

chapter09_app_post_test.py

```
@pytest.mark.asyncio
class TestCreatePerson:
    async def test_invalid(self, test_client: httpx.AsyncClient):
        payload = {"first_name": "John", "last_name": "Doe"}
        response = await test_client.post("/persons", json=payload)

        assert response.status_code == status.HTTP_422_UNPROCESSABLE_
ENTITY

    async def test_valid(self, test_client: httpx.AsyncClient):
        payload = {"first_name": "John", "last_name": "Doe", "age":
30}
        response = await test_client.post("/persons", json=payload)

        assert response.status_code == status.HTTP_201_CREATED

        json = response.json()
        assert json == payload
```

```
https://github.com/PacktPublishing/Building-Data-Science-Appli-
cations-with-FastAPI-Second-Edition/tree/main/chapter09/chap-
ter09_app_post_test.py
```

The first thing you may have noticed is that we wrapped our two tests inside a class. While not required in pytest, it could help you organize your tests – for example, to regroup tests that concern a single endpoint. Notice that, in this case, we only have to decorate the class with the `asyncio` marker; it will be automatically applied on single tests. Also, ensure that you add the `self` argument to each test: since we are now inside a class, they become methods.

These tests are not very different from our first example. As you can see, the HTTPX client makes it very easy to perform POST requests with a JSON payload: you just have to pass a dictionary to the `json` argument.

Of course, HTTPX helps you build all kinds of HTTP requests with headers, query parameters, and so on. Be sure to check its official documentation to learn more about its usage: `https://www.python-httpx.org/quickstart/`.

Testing with a database

Your application will likely have a database connection to read and store data. In this context, you'll need to work with a fresh test database in each run to have a clean and predictable set of data to write your tests.

For this, we'll use two things. The first one, `dependency_overrides`, is a FastAPI feature that allows us to replace some dependencies at runtime. For example, we can replace the dependency that returns the database instance with another one that returns a test database instance. The second one is, once again, fixtures, which will help us create fake data in the test database before we run the tests.

To show you a working example, we'll consider the same example we built in the *Communicating with a MongoDB database with Motor* section of *Chapter 6, Databases and Asynchronous ORMs*. In that example, we built REST endpoints to manage blog posts. As you may recall, we had a `get_database` dependency that returned the database instance. As a reminder, we show it again here:

database.py

```
from motor.motor_asyncio import AsyncIOMotorClient,
AsyncIOMotorDatabase

# Connection to the whole server
motor_client = AsyncIOMotorClient("mongodb://localhost:27017")
# Single database instance
database = motor_client["chapter6_mongo"]

def get_database() -> AsyncIOMotorDatabase:
    return database
```

https://github.com/PacktPublishing/Building-Data-Science-Applications-with-FastAPI-Second-Edition/tree/main/chapter6/mongodb/database.py

Path operation functions and other dependencies would then use this dependency to retrieve the database instance.

For our tests, we'll create a new instance of `AsyncIOMotorDatabase` that points to another database. Then, we'll create a new dependency, directly in our test file, that returns this instance. You can see this in the following example:

chapter09_db_test.py

```
motor_client = AsyncIOMotorClient(
    os.getenv("MONGODB_CONNECTION_STRING", "mongodb://
localhost:27017")
)
```

```
    database_test = motor_client["chapter09_db_test"]

def get_test_database():
    return database_test
```

https://github.com/PacktPublishing/Building-Data-Science-Applications-with-FastAPI-Second-Edition/tree/main/chapter09/chapter09_db_test.py

Then, in our test_client fixture, we'll override the default get_database dependency by using our current get_test_database dependency. The following example shows how this is done:

chapter09_db_test.py

```
@pytest_asyncio.fixture
async def test_client():
    app.dependency_overrides[get_database] = get_test_database
    async with LifespanManager(app):
        async with httpx.AsyncClient(app=app, base_url="http://app.
io") as test_client:
            yield test_client
```

https://github.com/PacktPublishing/Building-Data-Science-Applications-with-FastAPI-Second-Edition/tree/main/chapter09/chapter09_db_test.py

FastAPI provides a property called dependency_overrides, which is a dictionary that maps original dependency functions with substitutes. Here, we directly used the get_database function as a key. The rest of the fixture doesn't have to change. Now, whenever the get_database dependency is injected into the application code, FastAPI will automatically replace it with get_test_database. As a result, our endpoints will now work with the test database instance.

> **app and dependency_overrides are global**
>
> Since we are directly importing app from its module, it's instantiated only once for the whole test run. It means that dependency_overrides is common for every test. Keep this in mind if someday you want to override a dependency for a single test: once you've set it, it'll be set for the rest of the execution. In this case, you can reset dependency_overrides by using app.dependency_overrides = {}.

To test some behaviors, such as retrieving a single post, it's usually convenient to have some base data in our test database. To allow this, we'll create a new fixture that will instantiate dummy `PostDB` objects and insert them into the test database. You can see this in the following example:

chapter09_db_test.py

```python
@pytest_asyncio.fixture(autouse=True, scope="module")
async def initial_posts():
    initial_posts = [
        Post(title="Post 1", content="Content 1"),
        Post(title="Post 2", content="Content 2"),
        Post(title="Post 3", content="Content 3"),
    ]
    await database_test["posts"].insert_many(
        [post.dict(by_alias=True) for post in initial_posts]
    )

    yield initial_posts

    await motor_client.drop_database("chapter09_db_test")
```

https://github.com/PacktPublishing/Building-Data-Science-Applications-with-FastAPI-Second-Edition/tree/main/chapter09/chapter09_db_test.py

Here, you can see that we just had to make an `insert_many` request to the MongoDB database to create the posts.

Notice that we used the `autouse` and `scope` arguments of the `fixture` decorator. The first one tells pytest to automatically call this fixture *even if it's not requested in any test*. In this case, it's convenient because we'll always ensure that the data has been created in the database, without the risk of forgetting to request it in the tests. The other one, `scope`, allows us, as we mentioned previously, to not run this fixture at the beginning of each test. With the `module` value, the fixture will create the objects only once, at the beginning of this particular test file. It helps make the test fast because, in this case, it doesn't make sense to recreate the posts before each test.

Once again, we *yield* the posts instead of returning them. This pattern allows us to delete the test database after the tests run. By doing this, we're making sure that we always start with a fresh database when we've run the tests.

And we are done! We can now write tests while knowing exactly what we have in the database. In the following example, you can see tests that are used to verify the behavior of the endpoint retrieving a single post:

chapter09_db_test.py

```python
@pytest.mark.asyncio
class TestGetPost:
    async def test_not_existing(self, test_client: httpx.AsyncClient):
        response = await test_client.get("/posts/abc")

        assert response.status_code == status.HTTP_404_NOT_FOUND

    async def test_existing(
        self, test_client: httpx.AsyncClient, initial_posts:
list[Post]
    ):
        response = await test_client.get(f"/posts/{initial_posts[0].
id}")

        assert response.status_code == status.HTTP_200_OK

        json = response.json()
        assert json["_id"] == str(initial_posts[0].id)
```

```
https://github.com/PacktPublishing/Building-Data-Science-Applica-
tions-with-FastAPI-Second-Edition/tree/main/chapter09/chapter09_
db_test.py
```

Notice that we requested the `initial_posts` fixture in the second test to retrieve the identifier of the post that truly exists in our database.

Of course, we can also test our endpoints by creating data and checking whether it was correctly inserted into the database. You can see this in the following example:

chapter09_db_test.py

```python
@pytest.mark.asyncio
class TestCreatePost:
    async def test_invalid_payload(self, test_client: httpx.
AsyncClient):
        payload = {"title": "New post"}
        response = await test_client.post("/posts", json=payload)

        assert response.status_code == status.HTTP_422_UNPROCESSABLE_
ENTITY
```

```
    async def test_valid_payload(self, test_client: httpx.
AsyncClient):
        payload = {"title": "New post", "content": "New post content"}
        response = await test_client.post("/posts", json=payload)

        assert response.status_code == status.HTTP_201_CREATED

        json = response.json()
        post_id = ObjectId(json["_id"])
        post_db = await database_test["posts"].find_one({"_id": post_
id})

        assert post_db is not None
```

https://github.com/PacktPublishing/Building-Data-Science-Applica-
tions-with-FastAPI-Second-Edition/tree/main/chapter09/chapter09_
db_test.py

In the second test, we used the `database_test` instance to perform a request and check that the object was inserted correctly. This shows the benefit of using asynchronous tests: we can use the same libraries and tools inside our tests.

That's all you need to know about `dependency_overrides`. This feature is also very helpful when you need to write tests for logic involving external services, such as external APIs. Instead of making real requests to those external services during your tests, which could cause issues or incur costs, you'll be able to replace them with another dependency that fakes the requests. To understand this, we've built another example application with an endpoint for retrieving data from an external API:

chapter09_app_external_api.py

```
class ExternalAPI:
    def __init__(self) -> None:
        self.client = httpx.AsyncClient(base_url="https://dummyjson.
com")

    async def __call__(self) -> dict[str, Any]:
        async with self.client as client:
            response = await client.get("/products")
            return response.json()

external_api = ExternalAPI()

@app.get("/products")
```

```
async def external_products(products: dict[str, Any] =
Depends(external_api)):
    return products
```

https://github.com/PacktPublishing/Building-Data-Science-Applica-
tions-with-FastAPI-Second-Edition/tree/main/chapter09/chapter09_
app_external_api.py

To call our external API, we've built a class dependency, as we saw in the *Creating and using a parameterized dependency with a class* section of *Chapter 5, Dependency Injection in FastAPI*. We use HTTPX as an HTTP client to make a request to the external API and retrieve the data. This external API is a dummy API containing fake data – very useful for experiments like this: https://dummyjson.com.

The /products endpoint is simply injected with this dependency and directly returns the data provided by the external API.

Of course, to test this endpoint, we don't want to make real requests to the external API: it may take time and could be subject to rate limiting. Besides, you may want to test behavior that is not easy to reproduce in the real API, such as errors.

Thanks to dependency_overrides, it's very easy to replace our ExternalAPI dependency class with another one that returns static data. In the following example, you can see how we implemented such a test:

chapter09_app_external_api_test.py

```
class MockExternalAPI:
    mock_data = {
        "products": [
            {
                "id": 1,
                "title": "iPhone 9",
                "description": "An apple mobile which is nothing like
apple",
                "thumbnail": "https://i.dummyjson.com/data/products/1/
thumbnail.jpg",
            },
        ],
        "total": 1,
        "skip": 0,
        "limit": 30,
    }

    async def __call__(self) -> dict[str, Any]:
        return MockExternalAPI.mock_data
```

```
@pytest_asyncio.fixture
async def test_client():
    app.dependency_overrides[external_api] = MockExternalAPI()
    async with LifespanManager(app):
        async with httpx.AsyncClient(app=app, base_url="http://app.
io") as test_client:
            yield test_client
```

https://github.com/PacktPublishing/Building-Data-Science-Applications-with-FastAPI-Second-Edition/tree/main/chapter09/chapter09_app_external_api_test.py

Here, you can see that we wrote a simple class called `MockExternalAPI` that returns hardcoded data. All we have to do then is override the original dependency with this one. During the tests, the external API won't be called; we'll only work with the static data.

With the guidelines we've seen so far, you can now write tests for any HTTP endpoints in your FastAPI app. However, there is another kind of endpoint that behaves differently: WebSockets. As we'll see in the next section, unit testing WebSockets is also quite different from what we described for REST endpoints.

Writing tests for WebSocket endpoints

In *Chapter 8, Defining WebSockets for Two-Way Interactive Communication in FastAPI*, we explained how WebSockets work and how you can implement such endpoints in FastAPI. As you may have guessed, writing unit tests for WebSockets endpoints is quite different from what we've seen so far.

For this task, we'll need to tweak our `test_client` fixture a little bit. Indeed, HTTPX doesn't have built-in support to communicate with WebSockets. Hence, we'll need to use a plugin, HTTPX WS. Let's install it with the following command:

```
(venv) $ pip install httpx-ws
```

To enable support for WebSockets on our test client, we'll change it like this:

chapter09_websocket_test.py

```
from httpx_ws.transport import ASGIWebSocketTransport


@pytest_asyncio.fixture
async def test_client():
    async with LifespanManager(app):
        async with httpx.AsyncClient(
            transport=ASGIWebSocketTransport(app), base_url="http://
app.io"
        ) as test_client:
```

```
        yield test_client
```

https://github.com/PacktPublishing/Building-Data-Science-Applica-
tions-with-FastAPI-Second-Edition/tree/main/chapter09/chapter09_
websocket_test.py

You can see that, instead of directly setting the app argument, we set `transport` with a class provided by HTTPX WS. This class provides support to test apps with WebSockets endpoints. Other than that, nothing changes. It's worth noting that testing standard HTTP endpoints will still work correctly, so you can use this test client for all your tests.

Now, let's consider a simple WebSocket endpoint example:

chapter09_websocket.py

```python
@app.websocket("/ws")
async def websocket_endpoint(websocket: WebSocket):
    await websocket.accept()
    try:
        while True:
            data = await websocket.receive_text()
            await websocket.send_text(f"Message text was: {data}")
    except WebSocketDisconnect:
        await websocket.close()
```

https://github.com/PacktPublishing/Building-Data-Science-Applica-
tions-with-FastAPI-Second-Edition/tree/main/chapter09/chapter09_
websocket.py

You may have recognized the "echo" example from *Chapter 8, Defining WebSockets for Two-Way Interactive Communication in FastAPI.*

Now, let's write a test for our WebSocket using our test client:

Chapter09_websocket_test.py

```python
from httpx_ws import aconnect_ws

@pytest.mark.asyncio
async def test_websocket_echo(test_client: httpx.AsyncClient):
    async with aconnect_ws("/ws", test_client) as websocket:
        await websocket.send_text("Hello")

        message = await websocket.receive_text()
        assert message == "Message text was: Hello"
```

```
https://github.com/PacktPublishing/Building-Data-Science-Applica-
tions-with-FastAPI-Second-Edition/tree/main/chapter09/chapter09_
websocket_test.py
```

As you can see, HTTPX WS provides the `aconnect_ws` function to open a connection to a WebSocket endpoint. It expects the path of your WebSocket endpoint and a valid HTTPX client in an argument. By using `test_client`, we'll make requests directly against our FastAPI application.

It opens a context manager, giving you the `websocket` variable. It's an object that exposes several methods to either send or receive data. Each of those methods will block until a message has been sent or received.

Here, to test our "echo" server, we send a message thanks to the `send_text` method. Then, we retrieve a message with `receive_text` and assert that it corresponds to what we expect. Equivalent methods also exist for sending and receiving JSON data directly: `send_json` and `receive_json`.

This is what makes WebSocket testing a bit special: you have to think about the sequence of sent and received messages and implement them programmatically to test the behavior of your WebSocket.

Other than that, all the things we've seen so far regarding testing are applicable, especially `dependency_overrides`, when you need to use a test database.

Summary

Congratulations! You are now ready to build high-quality FastAPI applications that have been well tested. In this chapter, you learned how to use pytest, a powerful and efficient testing framework for Python. Thanks to pytest fixtures, you saw how to create a reusable test client for your FastAPI application that can work asynchronously. Using this client, you learned how to make HTTP requests to assert the behavior of your REST API. Finally, we reviewed how to test WebSocket endpoints, which involves a fairly different way of thinking.

Now that you can build a reliable and efficient FastAPI application, it's time to bring it to the whole world! In the next chapter, we'll review the best practices and patterns for preparing a FastAPI application for the world before studying several deployment methods.

10

Deploying a FastAPI Project

Building a good application is great, but it's even better if customers can enjoy it. In this chapter, you'll look at different techniques and the best practices for deploying your FastAPI application to make it available on the web. First, you'll learn how to structure your project to make it ready for deployment by using environment variables to set the configuration options you need, as well as by managing your dependencies properly with `pip`. Once that's done, we'll show you three ways to deploy your application: with a serverless cloud platform, with a Docker container, and with a traditional Linux server.

In this chapter, we're going to cover the following main topics:

- Setting and using environment variables

- Managing Python dependencies

- Deploying a FastAPI application on a serverless platform

- Deploying a FastAPI application with Docker

- Deploying a FastAPI application on a traditional server

Technical requirements

For this chapter, you'll require a Python virtual environment, just as we set up in *Chapter 1, Python Development Environment Setup*.

You'll find all the code examples for this chapter in the dedicated GitHub repository at `https://github.com/PacktPublishing/Building-Data-Science-Applications-with-FastAPI-Second-Edition/tree/main/chapter10`.

Setting and using environment variables

Before deep-diving into the different deployment techniques, we need to structure our application to enable reliable, fast, and secure deployments. One of the key things in this process is handling configuration variables: a database URL, an external API token, a debug flag, and so on. When handling those variables, it's necessary to handle them dynamically instead of hardcoding them into your source code. Why?

First of all, those variables will likely be different in your local environment and in production. Typically, your database URL will point to a local database on your computer while developing but will point to a proper production database in production. This is even more pertinent if you want to have other environments such as a staging or pre-production environment. Furthermore, if we need to change one of the values, we'll have to change the code, commit it, and deploy it again. Thus, we need a convenient mechanism to set those values.

Secondly, it's unsafe to write those values in your code. Values such as database connection strings or API tokens are extremely sensitive. If they appear in your code, they'll likely be committed to your repository: they can be read by anyone who has access to your repository, which causes obvious security issues.

To solve this, we usually use **environment variables**. Environment variables are values that aren't set in the program itself but in the whole operating system. Most programming languages have the required functions to read those variables from the system. You can try this very easily in a Unix command line:

```
$ export MY_ENVIRONMENT_VARIABLE="Hello" # Set a temporary variable on
the system
$ python
>>> import os
>>> os.getenv("MY_ENVIRONMENT_VARIABLE")  # Get it in Python
'Hello'
```

In the Python source code, we can get the value dynamically from the system. During deployment, we'll only have to make sure that we set the correct environment variables on the server. This way, we can easily change a value without redeploying the code and have several deployments of our application containing different configurations sharing the same source code. However, bear in mind that sensitive values that have been set in environment variables can still leak if you don't pay attention – for example, in log files or error stack traces.

To help us with this task, we'll use a very convenient feature of Pydantic: settings management. This allows us to structure and use our configuration variables as we do for any other data model. It even takes care of automatically retrieving the values from environment variables!

For the rest of this chapter, we'll work with an application that you can find in `chapter10/project` within our example repository. It's a simple FastAPI application that uses SQLAlchemy, very similar to the one we reviewed in the *Communicating with a SQL database with the SQLAlchemy ORM* section of *Chapter 6, Databases and Asynchronous ORMs*.

> **Running the commands from the project directory**
>
> If you cloned the example repository, be sure to run the commands shown in this chapter from the `project` directory. On the command line, simply type `cd chapter10/project`.

To structure a settings model, all you need to do is create a class that inherits from `pydantic.BaseSettings`. The following example shows a configuration class with a debug flag, an environment name, and a database URL:

settings.py

```python
from pydantic import BaseSettings

class Settings(BaseSettings):
    debug: bool = False
    environment: str
    database_url: str

    class Config:
        env_file = ".env"

settings = Settings()
```

https://github.com/PacktPublishing/Building-Data-Science-Applications-with-FastAPI-Second-Edition/tree/main/chapter10/project/project/settings.py

As you can see, creating this class is very similar to creating a standard Pydantic model. We can even define default values, as we did for `debug` here.

To use it, we only have to create an instance of this class. We can then import it wherever we need it in our project. For example, here is how to retrieve the database URL to create our SQLAlchemy engine:

database.py

```python
from project.settings import settings

engine = create_async_engine(settings.database_url)
```

https://github.com/PacktPublishing/Building-Data-Science-Applications-with-FastAPI-Second-Edition/tree/main/chapter10/project/project/database.py

We also use the debug flag to print all the settings in the lifespan event at startup:

app.py

```
@contextlib.asynccontextmanager
async def lifespan(app: FastAPI):
    if settings.debug:
        print(settings)
    yield
```

https://github.com/PacktPublishing/Building-Data-Science-Appli-
cations-with-FastAPI-Second-Edition/tree/main/chapter10/project/
project/app.py

Since our application is designed to work with SQLAlchemy, we also took care of initializing a database migration environment with Alembic, as we showed in *Chapter 6, Databases and Asynchronous ORMs*. The difference here is that we use our settings object to dynamically configure the database URL; instead of hardcoding it in alembic.ini, we can set it from our settings in env.py, as you can see here:

env.py

```
config.set_main_option(
    "sqlalchemy.url", settings.database_url.replace("+aiosqlite", "")
)
```

https://github.com/PacktPublishing/Building-Data-Science-Appli-
cations-with-FastAPI-Second-Edition/tree/main/chapter10/project/
alembic/env.py

Notice that we take care of manually removing the aiosqlite driver part of the URL. Indeed, as we mentioned previously, Alembic is designed to work synchronously, so we need to pass it a standard URL. Now, we can generate migrations from our development database and apply them in production without changing anything in our Alembic configuration!

The good thing with this Settings model is that it works just like any other Pydantic model: it automatically parses the values it finds in environment variables and raises an error if one value is missing in your environment. This way, you can ensure you don't forget any values directly when the app starts. You can test this behavior by running the application:

```
(venv) $ uvicorn project.app:app
pydantic.error_wrappers.ValidationError: 2 validation errors for
Settings
environment
  field required (type=value_error.missing)
```

```
database_url
  field required (type=value_error.missing)
```

We have a clear list of the missing variables. Let's set those variables in our environment and try again:

```
(venv) $ export DEBUG="true" ENVIRONMENT="development" DATABASE_
URL="sqlite+aiosqlite:///chapter10_project.db"
(venv) $ uvicorn project.app:app
INFO:     Started server process [34880]
INFO:     Waiting for application startup.
debug=True environment='development' database_
url='sqlite+aiosqlite:///chapter10_project.db'
INFO:     Application startup complete.
INFO:     Uvicorn running on http://127.0.0.1:8000 (Press CTRL+C to
quit)
```

The application started! You can even see that our lifespan handler printed our settings values. Notice that Pydantic is case-insensitive (by default) when retrieving environment variables. By convention, environment variables are usually set in all caps on the system.

Using a .env file

In local development, it's a bit annoying to set environment variables by hand, especially if you're working on several projects at the same time on your machine. To solve this, Pydantic allows you to read the values from a .env file. This file contains a simple list of environment variables and their associated values. It's usually easier to edit and manipulate during development.

To make this work, we'll need a new library, python-dotenv, whose task is to parse those .env files. You can install it as usual with the following command:

```
(venv) $ pip install python-dotenv
```

To enable this feature, notice how we added the Config subclass with the env_file property:

settings.py

```
class Settings(BaseSettings):
    debug: bool = False
    environment: str
    database_url: str

    class Config:
        env_file = ".env"
```

```
https://github.com/PacktPublishing/Building-Data-Science-Appli-
cations-with-FastAPI-Second-Edition/tree/main/chapter10/project/
project/settings.py
```

By doing this, we simply tell Pydantic to look for environment variables set in a file named .env, if it's available.

Finally, you can create your .env file at the root of the project with the following content:

```
DEBUG=true
ENVIRONMENT=development
DATABASE_URL=sqlite+aiosqlite:///chapter10_project.db
```

And that's it! The values will now be read from this .env file. If the file is missing, Settings will try to read them from the environment variables as usual. Of course, this is only for convenience while developing: this file *shouldn't be committed* and you should rely on *properly set environment variables in production*. To ensure you don't commit this file by accident, it's usually recommended that you add it to your .gitignore file.

> **Creating hidden files such as .env files**
>
> In Unix systems, files starting with a dot, such as .env, are considered hidden files. If you try to create them from the operating system's file explorer, it might show you warnings or even prevent you from doing so. Thus, it's usually more convenient to create them from your IDE, such as Visual Studio Code, or from the command line by executing the following command: touch .env.

Great! Our application now supports dynamic configuration variables, which are now easy to set and change on our deployment platforms. Another important thing to take care of is dependencies: we've installed quite a lot of them at this point, but we must make sure they are installed properly during deployments!

Managing Python dependencies

Throughout this book, we've installed libraries using pip to add some useful features to our application: FastAPI, of course, but also SQLAlchemy, pytest, and so on. When deploying a project to a new environment, such as a production server, we have to make sure all those dependencies are installed for our application to work properly. This is also true if you have colleagues that also need to work on the project: they need to know the dependencies they must install on their machines.

Fortunately, pip comes with a solution for this so that we don't have to remember all this in our heads. Indeed, most Python projects define a requirements.txt file, which contains a list of all Python dependencies. It usually lives at the root of your project. pip has a special option for reading this file and installing all the needed dependencies.

When you already have a working environment, such as the one we've used since the beginning of this book, people usually recommend that you run the following command:

```
(venv) $ pip freeze
aiosqlite==0.17.0
alembic==1.8.1
anyio==3.6.2
argon2-cffi==21.3.0
argon2-cffi-bindings==21.2.0
asgi-lifespan==2.0.0
asyncio-redis==0.16.0
attrs==22.1.0
...
```

The result of pip freeze is a list of *every Python package currently installed in your environment*, along with their corresponding versions. This list can be directly used in the requirements.txt file.

The problem with this approach is that it lists every package, including the sub-dependencies of the libraries you install. Said another way, in this list, you'll see packages that you don't directly use but that are needed by the ones you installed. If, for some reason, you decide to not use a library anymore, you'll be able to remove it, but it'll be very hard to guess which sub-dependencies it has installed. In the long term, your requirements.txt file will grow larger and larger, with lots of dependencies that are useless in your project.

To solve this, some people recommend that you *manually maintain your* requirements.txt *file*. With this approach, you have to list yourself all the libraries you use, along with their respective versions. During installation, pip will take care of installing the sub-dependencies, but they'll never appear in requirements.txt. This way, when you remove one of your dependencies, you make sure any useless packages are not kept.

In the following example, you can see the requirements.txt file for the project we are working on in this chapter:

requirements.txt

```
aiosqlite==0.17.0
alembic==1.8.1
fastapi==0.88.0
sqlalchemy[asyncio]==1.4.44
uvicorn[standard]==0.20.0
gunicorn==20.1.0
```

https://github.com/PacktPublishing/Building-Data-Science-Applications-with-FastAPI-Second-Edition/tree/main/chapter10/project/requirements.txt

As you can see, the list is much shorter! Now, whenever we install a new dependency, our responsibility is to add it manually to `requirements.txt`.

> **A word on alternate package managers such as Poetry, Pipenv, and Conda**
>
> While exploring the Python community, you may hear about alternate package managers such as Poetry, Pipenv, and Conda. These managers were created to solve some issues posed by `pip`, especially related to sub-dependency management. While they are very good tools, lots of cloud platforms expect a traditional `requirements.txt` file to specify the dependencies, rather than those more modern tools. Therefore, they may not be the best choice for a FastAPI application.

The `requirements.txt` file should be committed along with your source code. When you need to install the dependencies on a new computer or server, you'll simply need to run this command:

```
(venv) $ pip install -r requirements.txt
```

Of course, make sure that you're working on proper virtual environments when doing this, as we described in *Chapter 1, Python Development Environment Setup*.

You have probably noticed the `gunicorn` dependency in `requirements.txt`. Let's look at what it is and why it's needed.

Adding Gunicorn as a server process for deployment

In *Chapter 2, Python Programming Specificities*, we briefly introduced the WSGI and ASGI protocols. They define the norm and data structure for building web servers in Python. Traditional Python web frameworks, such as Django and Flask, rely on the WSGI protocol. ASGI appeared recently and is presented as the "spiritual successor" of WSGI, providing a protocol for developing web servers running asynchronously. This protocol is at the heart of FastAPI and Starlette.

As we mentioned in *Chapter 3, Developing RESTful APIs with FastAPI*, we use *Uvicorn* to run our FastAPI applications: its role is to accept HTTP requests, transform them according to the ASGI protocol, and pass them to the FastAPI application, which returns an ASGI-compliant response object. Then, Uvicorn can form a proper HTTP response from this object.

In the WSGI world, the most widely used server is *Gunicorn*. It has the same role in the context of a Django or Flask application. Why are we talking about it, then? Gunicorn has lots of refinements and features that make it more robust and reliable in production than Uvicorn. However, Gunicorn is designed to work for WSGI applications. So, what can we do?

Actually, we can use both: Gunicorn will be used as a robust process manager for our production server. However, we'll specify a special worker class provided by Uvicorn, which will allow us to run ASGI applications such as FastAPI. This is the recommended way of doing deployments in the official Uvicorn documentation: `https://www.uvicorn.org/deployment/#using-a-process-manager`.

So, let's install Gunicorn to our dependencies by using the following command (remember to add it to your `requirements.txt` file):

```
(venv) $ pip install gunicorn
```

If you wish, you can try to run our FastAPI project using Gunicorn by using the following command:

```
(venv) $ gunicorn -w 4 -k uvicorn.workers.UvicornWorker project.
app:app
```

Its usage is quite similar to Uvicorn, except that we tell it to use a Uvicorn worker. Once again, this is necessary to make it work with an ASGI application. Also, notice the `-w` option. This allows us to set the number of workers to launch for our server. Here, we launch four instances of our application. Then, Gunicorn takes care of load-balancing the incoming requests between each worker. This is what makes Gunicorn more robust: if, for any reason, your application blocks the event loop with a synchronous operation, other workers will be able to process other requests while this is happening.

Now, we are ready to deploy our FastAPI application! In the next section, you'll learn how to deploy one on a serverless platform.

Deploying a FastAPI application on a serverless platform

In recent years, serverless platforms have gained a lot of popularity and have become a very common way to deploy web applications. Those platforms completely hide the complexity of setting up and managing a server, giving you the tools to automatically build and deploy your application in minutes. Google App Engine, Heroku, and Azure App Service are among the most popular. Even though they have their own specificities, all these serverless platforms work on the same principles. This is why, in this section, we'll outline the common steps you should follow.

Usually, serverless platforms expect you to provide the source code in the form of a GitHub repository, which you push directly to their servers or which they pull automatically from GitHub. Here, we'll assume that you have a GitHub repository with the source code structured like so:

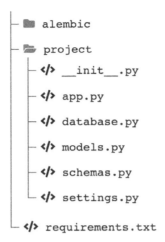

Figure 10.1 – Project structure for serverless deployment

Here are the general steps you should follow to deploy your projects on this kind of platform:

1. Create an account on a cloud platform of your choice. You must do this before you can start any work. It's worth noting that most cloud platforms offer free credits when you are getting started so that you can try their services for free.

2. Install the necessary command-line tools. Most cloud providers supply a complete CLI for managing their services. Typically, this is required for deploying your application. Here are the relevant documentation pages for the most popular cloud providers:

    *   Google Cloud: `https://cloud.google.com/sdk/gcloud`

    *   Microsoft Azure: `https://docs.microsoft.com/en-us/cli/azure/install-azure-cli`

    *   Heroku: `https://devcenter.heroku.com/articles/heroku-cli`

3. Set up the application configuration. Depending on the platform, you'll either have to create a configuration file or use the CLI or the web interface to do this. Here are the relevant documentation pages for the most popular cloud providers:

    *   Google App Engine (configuration file): `https://cloud.google.com/appengine/docs/standard/python3/configuring-your-app-with-app-yaml`

    *   Azure App Service (web interface and CLI): `https://docs.microsoft.com/en-us/azure/app-service/quickstart-python` and `https://docs.microsoft.com/en-us/azure/app-service/configure-language-python`

    *   Heroku (configuration file): `https://devcenter.heroku.com/articles/getting-started-with-python#define-a-procfile`

The key point in this step is to correctly *set the startup command*. As we saw in the previous section, it's essential to set the Uvicorn worker class using the `gunicorn` command, as well as set the correct path to your application.

4. Set the environment variables. Depending on the cloud provider, you should be able to do so during configuration or deployment. Remember that they are key for your application to work. Here are the relevant documentation pages for the most popular cloud providers:

    *   Google App Engine (configuration file): `https://cloud.google.com/appengine/docs/standard/python/config/appref`

    *   Azure App Service (web interface): `https://docs.microsoft.com/en-us/azure/app-service/configure-common#configure-app-settings`

    *   Heroku (CLI or web interface): `https://devcenter.heroku.com/articles/config-vars`

5. Deploy the application. Some platforms can automatically deploy when they detect changes on a hosted repository, such as GitHub. Others require that you start deployment from the command-line tools. Here are the relevant documentation pages for the most popular cloud providers:

    *   Google App Engine (CLI): `https://cloud.google.com/appengine/docs/standard/python3/testing-and-deploying-your-app#deploying_your_application`

    *   Azure App Service (continuous deployment or manual Git deployment): `https://docs.microsoft.com/en-us/azure/app-service/deploy-continuous-deployment?tabs=github` and `https://docs.microsoft.com/en-us/azure/app-service/deploy-local-git?tabs=cli`

    *   Heroku (CLI): `https://devcenter.heroku.com/articles/getting-started-with-python#deploy-the-app`

Your application should now be live on the platform. Under the hood, most cloud platforms actually automatically build and deploy Docker containers while following the configuration you provide.

They will make your application available on a generic subdomain such as `myapplication.herokuapp.com`. Of course, they also provide mechanisms for binding it to your own domain or subdomain. Here are the relevant documentation pages for the most popular cloud providers:

*   Google App Engine: `https://cloud.google.com/appengine/docs/standard/python3/mapping-custom-domains`

*   Azure App Service: `https://docs.microsoft.com/en-us/azure/app-service/manage-custom-dns-migrate-domain`

*   Heroku: `https://devcenter.heroku.com/articles/custom-domains`

Adding database servers

Most of the time, your application will be backed by a database engine, such as PostgreSQL. Fortunately, cloud providers propose fully managed databases, billed according to the computing power, memory, and storage you need. Once created, you'll have access to a connection string to connect to the database instance. All you have to do then is set it in the environment variables of your application. Here are the relevant documentation pages for getting started with managed databases with the most popular cloud providers:

- Google Cloud SQL: `https://cloud.google.com/sql/docs/postgres/create-instance`

- Azure Database for PostgreSQL: `https://docs.microsoft.com/en-us/azure/postgresql/quickstart-create-server-database-portal`

- Amazon RDS: `https://docs.aws.amazon.com/AmazonRDS/latest/UserGuide/CHAP_GettingStarted.html`

- Heroku Postgres: `https://devcenter.heroku.com/articles/heroku-postgresql`

As we've seen, serverless platforms are the quickest and easiest way to deploy a FastAPI application. However, in some situations, you may wish to have more control of how things are deployed, or you may need system packages that are not available on serverless platforms. In those cases, it may be worthwhile to use a Docker container.

Deploying a FastAPI application with Docker

Docker is a widely used technology for containerization. **Containers** are small, self-contained systems running on a computer. Each container contains all the files and configurations necessary for running a single application: a web server, a database engine, a data processing application, and so on. The main goal is to be able to run those applications without worrying about the dependency and version conflicts that often happen when trying to install and configure them on the system.

Besides, Docker containers are designed to be *portable and reproducible*: to create a Docker container, you simply have to write a **Dockerfile** containing all the necessary instructions to build the small system, along with all the files and configuration you need. Those instructions are executed during a **build**, which results in a Docker **image**. This image is a package containing your small system, ready to use, which you can easily share on the internet through **registries**. Any developer who has a working Docker installation can then download this image and run it on their system in a container.

Docker has been quickly adopted by developers as it greatly eases the setup of complex development environments, allowing them to have several projects with different system package versions, all without worrying about their installation on their local machine.

However, Docker is not only for local development: it's also widely used for deploying applications to production. Since the builds are reproducible, we can ensure that the local and production environments remain the same, which limits any issues when moving to production.

In this section, we'll learn how to write a Dockerfile for a FastAPI application, how to build an image, and how to deploy it on a cloud platform.

Writing a Dockerfile

As we mentioned in the introduction to this section, a Dockerfile is a set of instructions for building your Docker image, a self-contained system containing all the required components to run your applications. To begin with, all Dockerfiles derive from a base image; usually, this is a standard Linux installation, such as Debian or Ubuntu. From this base, we can copy files from our local machine into the image (usually, the source code of our application) and execute Unix commands – for example, to install packages or execute scripts.

In our case, the creator of FastAPI has created a base Docker image that contains all the necessary tools to run a FastAPI app! All we have to do is start from this image, copy our source files, and install our dependencies! Let's learn how to do that!

First of all, you'll need a working Docker installation on your machine. Follow the official *Getting Started* tutorial, which should guide you in this process: https://docs.docker.com/get-started/.

To create a Docker image, we simply have to create a file named Dockerfile at the root of our project. The following example shows the content of this file for our current project:

Dockerfile

```
FROM tiangolo/uvicorn-gunicorn-fastapi:python3.10

ENV APP_MODULE project.app:app

COPY requirements.txt /app

RUN pip install --upgrade pip && \
    pip install -r /app/requirements.txt

COPY ./ /app
```

```
https://github.com/PacktPublishing/Building-Data-Science-Appli-
cations-with-FastAPI-Second-Edition/tree/main/chapter10/project/
Dockerfile
```

Let's go through each instruction. The first instruction, FROM, is the base image we derive from. Here, we took the uvicorn-gunicorn-fastapi image, which was created by the creator of FastAPI. Docker images have tags, which can be used to pick a specific version of the image. Here, we chose Python version 3.10. Lots of variations exist for this image, including ones with other versions of Python. You can check them out in the official README file: https://github.com/tiangolo/uvicorn-gunicorn-fastapi-docker.

Then, we set the APP_MODULE environment variable thanks to the ENV instruction. In a Docker image, environment variables can be set at build time, as we did here, or at runtime. APP_MODULE is an environment variable defined by the base image. It should point to the path of your FastAPI application: it's the same argument that we set at the end of Uvicorn and Gunicorn commands to launch the application. You can find the list of all the accepted environment variables for the base image in the official README file.

Next, we have our first COPY statement. As you may have guessed, this instruction will copy a file from your local system to the image. Here, we only copied our requirements.txt file. We'll explain why shortly. Notice that we copied the file into the /app directory of the image; it's the main working directory defined by the base image.

We then have a RUN statement. This instruction is used to execute Unix commands. In our case, we ran pip to install our dependencies, following the requirements.txt file we just copied. This is essential to make sure all our Python dependencies are present.

Finally, we copied the rest of our source code files into the /app directory. Now, let's explain why we separately copied requirements.txt. The important thing to understand is that Docker images are built using layers: each instruction will create a new layer in the build system. To improve performance, Docker does its best to reuse layers it has already built. Therefore, if it detects no changes from the previous build, it'll reuse the ones it has in memory without rebuilding them.

By copying the requirements.txt file alone and installing the Python dependencies before the rest of the source code, we allow Docker to reuse the layer where the dependencies have been installed. If we edit our source code but not requirements.txt, the Docker build will only execute the last COPY instruction, reusing all the previous layers. Thus, the image is built in a few seconds instead of minutes.

Most of the time, Dockerfiles end with a CMD instruction, which should be the command to execute when the container is started. In our case, we would have used the Gunicorn command we saw in the *Adding Gunicorn as a server* section. However, in our case, the base image already handles this for us.

Adding a prestart script

When deploying an application, it's quite common to run several commands before the application starts. The most typical case is to execute database migrations so that our production database has the correct set of tables and columns. To help us with this, our base Docker image allows us to create a bash script named prestart.sh. If this file is present, it'll be automatically run before the FastAPI application is started.

In our case, we just run the Alembic command to execute migrations:

prestart.sh

```
#! /usr/bin/env bash

# Let the DB start
sleep 10;
# Run migrations
alembic upgrade head
```

https://github.com/PacktPublishing/Building-Data-Science-Appli-cations-with-FastAPI-Second-Edition/tree/main/chapter10/project/prestart.sh

Bear in mind that this is a mechanism provided only for convenience by the tiangolo/uvicorn-gunicorn-fastapi image. If you start from a more basic image, you'll have to come up with your own solution to run a prestart script.

Building a Docker image

We can now build our Docker image! From the root of your project, just run the following command:

```
$ docker build -t fastapi-app  .
```

The dot (.) denotes the path of the root context to build your image – in this case, the current directory. The -t option is here to tag the image and give it a practical name.

Docker will then perform the build. You'll see that it'll download the base image and sequentially run your instructions. This should take a few minutes. If you run the command again, you'll experience what we explained earlier about layers: if there is no change, layers are reused and the build takes only a few seconds.

Running a Docker image locally

Before deploying it to production, you can try to run your image locally. To do this, run the following command:

```
$ docker run -p 8000:80 -e ENVIRONMENT=production -e DATABASE_
URL=sqlite+aiosqlite:///app.db fastapi-app
```

Here, we used the `run` command with the name of the image we just built. There are, of course, a few options here:

- `-p` allows you to publish ports on your local machine. By default, Docker containers are not accessible on your local machine. If you publish ports, they will be available through `localhost`. On the container side, the FastAPI application is executed on port `80`. We publish it on port `8000` on our local machine – that is, `8000:80`.

- `-e` is used to set environment variables. As we mentioned in the *Setting and using environment variables* section, we need those variables to configure our application. Docker allows us to set them easily and dynamically at runtime. Notice that we set a simple SQLite database for testing purposes. However, in production, it should point to a proper database.

- You can review the numerous options of this command in the official Docker documentation: `https://docs.docker.com/engine/reference/commandline/run/#options`.

This command will run your application, which will be accessible through `http://localhost:8000`. Docker will show you the logs in the terminal.

Deploying a Docker image

Now that you have a working Docker image, you can deploy it on virtually any machine that runs Docker. This can be your own server or a dedicated platform. Lots of serverless platforms have emerged to help you deploy container images automatically: Google Cloud Run, Amazon Elastic Container Service, and Microsoft Azure Container Instances are just a few.

Usually, what you have to do is upload (**push**, in Docker jargon) your image to a registry. By default, Docker pulls and pushes images from Docker Hub, the official Docker registry, but lots of services and platforms propose their own registries. Usually, using the private cloud registry proposed by the cloud platform is necessary to deploy it on this platform. Here are the relevant documentation pages for getting started with private registries with the most popular cloud providers:

- Google Artifact Registry: `https://cloud.google.com/artifact-registry/docs/docker/quickstart`

- Amazon ECR: `https://docs.aws.amazon.com/AmazonECR/latest/userguide/getting-started-console.html`

- Microsoft Azure Container Registry: `https://docs.microsoft.com/en-us/azure/container-registry/container-registry-get-started-docker-cli?tabs=azure-cli`

If you followed the relevant instructions, you should have a private registry for storing Docker images. The instructions probably showed you how to authenticate your local Docker command line with it and how to push your first image. Basically, all you have to do is tag the image you built with the path to your private registry:

```
$ docker tag fastapi-app aws_account_id.dkr.ecr.region.amazonaws.com/
fastapi-app
```

Then, you need to push it to the registry:

```
$ docker push fastapi-app aws_account_id.dkr.ecr.region.amazonaws.com/
fastapi-app
```

Your image is now safely stored in the cloud platform registry. You can now use a serverless container platform to deploy it automatically. Here are the relevant documentation pages for getting started with private registries with the most popular cloud providers:

- Google Cloud Run: `https://cloud.google.com/run/docs/quickstarts/build-and-deploy/python`

- Amazon Elastic Container Service: `https://docs.aws.amazon.com/AmazonECS/latest/developerguide/getting-started-ecs-ec2.html`

- Microsoft Azure Container Instances: `https://docs.microsoft.com/en-us/azure/container-instances/container-instances-tutorial-deploy-app`

Of course, you'll be able to set the environment variables just like you can for fully managed apps. Those environments also provide lots of options for tuning the scalability of your containers, both vertically (using more powerful instances) and horizontally (spawning more instances).

Once done, your application should be live on the web! The great thing about deploying Docker images compared to automated serverless platforms is that you are not limited to the features supported by the platform: you can deploy anything, even complex applications that require a lot of exotic packages, without worrying about compatibility.

At this point, we've seen the easiest and most efficient ways to deploy a FastAPI application. However, you may wish to deploy one the old-fashioned way and manually set up your server. In the next section, we'll provide some guidelines for doing so.

Deploying a FastAPI application on a traditional server

In some situations, you may not have the chance to use a serverless platform to deploy your application. Some security or regulatory policies may force you to deploy on physical servers with specific configurations. In this case, it's worth knowing some basic things so that you can deploy your application on traditional servers.

In this section, we'll consider you are working on a Linux server:

1. First of all, make sure a *recent version of Python has been installed* on your server, ideally with the version matching the one you used in development. The easiest way to do this is to set up `pyenv`, as we saw in *Chapter 1, Python Development Environment Setup*.

2. To retrieve your source code and keep it in sync with your latest developments, you can *clone your Git repository* on your server. This way, you only have to pull the changes and restart the server process to deploy a new version.

3. Set up a *Python virtual environment*, as we explained in *Chapter 1, Python Development Environment Setup*. You can install the dependencies with `pip` thanks to your `requirements.txt` file.

4. At that point, you should be able to run Gunicorn and start serving your FastAPI application. However, some improvements are strongly recommended.

5. *Use a process manager* to ensure your Gunicorn process is always running and restarted when the server is restarted. A good option for this is *Supervisor*. The Gunicorn documentation provides good guidelines for this: `https://docs.gunicorn.org/en/stable/deploy.html#supervisor`.

6. It's also recommended to *put Gunicorn behind an HTTP proxy* instead of directly putting it on the front line. Its role is to handle SSL connections, perform load balancing, and serve static files such as images or documents. The Gunicorn documentation recommends using nginx for this task and provides a basic configuration: `https://docs.gunicorn.org/en/stable/deploy.html#nginx-configuration`.

As you can see, in this context, there are quite a lot of configurations and decisions to make regarding your server configuration. Of course, you should also pay attention to security and make sure your server is well protected against the usual attacks. In the following DigitalOcean tutorial, you'll find some guidelines for securing your server: `https://www.digitalocean.com/community/tutorials/recommended-security-measures-to-protect-your-servers`.

If you're not an experienced system administrator, we recommend that you favor serverless platforms; professional teams handle security, system updates, and server scalability for you, letting you focus on what matters most to you: developing a great application!

Summary

Your application is now live on the web! In this chapter, we covered the best practices to apply before deploying your application to production: use environment variables to set configuration options, such as database URLs, and manage your Python dependencies with a `requirements.txt` file. Then, we showed you how to deploy your application to a serverless platform, which handles everything for you by retrieving your source code, packaging it with its dependencies, and serving it on the web. Next, you learned how to build a Docker image for FastAPI using the base image created by the creator of FastAPI. As you saw, it allows you to be flexible while configuring the system, but you can still deploy it in a few minutes with a serverless platform that's compatible with containers. Finally, we provided you with some guidelines for manual deployment on a traditional Linux server.

This marks the end of the second part of this book. You should now be confident in writing efficient, reliable FastAPI applications and be able to deploy them on the web.

In the next chapter, we will begin some data science tasks and integrate them efficiently into a FastAPI project.

Part 3:
Building Resilient and Distributed Data Science Systems with FastAPI

This part will introduce you to the basic concepts of data science and machine learning, as well as the most popular Python tools and libraries for those tasks. We'll see how to integrate those tools into a FastAPI backend and how to build a distributed system to perform resource-intensive tasks in a scalable way.

This section comprises the following chapters:

- *Chapter 11, Introduction to Data Science in Python*
- *Chapter 12,, Creating an Efficient Prediction API Endpoint with FastAPI*
- *Chapter 13,, Implementing a Real-Time Object Detection System Using WebSockets with FastAPI*
- *Chapter 14, Creating a Distributed Text-to-Image AI System Using the Stable Diffusion Model*
- *Chapter 15, Monitoring the Health and Performance of a Data Science System*

11

Introduction to Data Science in Python

In recent years, Python has gained a lot of popularity in the data science field. Its very efficient and readable syntax makes the language a very good choice for scientific research, while still being suitable for production workloads; it's very easy to deploy research projects into real applications that will bring value to users. Thanks to this growing interest, a lot of specialized Python libraries have emerged and are now standards in the industry. In this chapter, we'll introduce the fundamental concepts of machine learning before diving into the Python libraries used daily by data scientists.

In this chapter, we're going to cover the following main topics:

- Understanding the basic concepts of machine learning
- Creating and manipulating NumPy arrays and pandas datasets
- Training and evaluating machine learning models with scikit-learn

Technical requirements

For this chapter, you'll require a Python virtual environment, just as we set up in *Chapter 1*, *Python Development Environment Setup*.

You'll find all the code examples for this chapter in the dedicated GitHub repository at `https://github.com/PacktPublishing/Building-Data-Science-Applications-with-FastAPI-Second-Edition/tree/main/chapter11`.

What is machine learning?

Machine learning (**ML**) is often seen as a subfield of artificial intelligence. While this categorization is the subject of debate, ML has had a lot of exposure in recent years due to its vast and visible field of applications, such as spam filters, natural language processing, and image generation.

ML is a field where we build mathematical models from existing data so that the machine can understand this data by itself. The machine is "learning" in the sense that the developer doesn't have to program a step-by-step algorithm to solve the problem, which would be impossible for complex tasks. Once a model has been "trained" on existing data, it can be used to predict new data or understand new observations.

Consider the spam filter example: if we have a sufficiently large collection of emails manually labeled "spam" or "not spam," we can use ML techniques to build a model that can tell us whether a new incoming email is spam or not.

In this section, we'll review the most fundamental concepts of ML.

Supervised versus unsupervised learning

ML techniques can be divided into two main categories: **supervised learning** and **unsupervised learning**.

With supervised learning, the existing dataset is already labeled, which means we have both the input (the characteristics of an observation), known as **features**, and the output. If we consider the spam filter example here, the features could be the frequencies of each word and the **label** could be the category – that is, "spam" or "not spam." Supervised learning is subdivided into two groups:

- **Classification problems**, to classify data with a finite set of categories – for example, the spam filter
- **Regression problems**, to predict continuous numerical values – for example, the number of rented electric scooters, given the day of the week, the weather, and the location

Unsupervised learning, on the other hand, operates on data without any reference to a label. The goal here is to discover interesting patterns from the features themselves. The two main problems that unsupervised learning tries to solve are as follows:

- **Clustering**, where we want to find groups of similar data points – for example, a recommender system to suggest products that you might like, given what other people similar to you like.
- **Dimensionality reduction**, where the goal is to find a more compact representation of datasets that contain a lot of different features. Doing this will allow us to keep only the most meaningful and discriminant features while working with smaller dataset dimensions.

Model validation

One of the key aspects of ML is evaluating whether your model is performing well or not. How can you say that your model will perform well on newly observed data? When building your model, how can you tell whether one algorithm performs better than another? All of these questions can and should be answered with model validation techniques.

As we mentioned previously, ML methods start with an existing set of data that we'll use to train a model.

Intuitively, we may want to use all the data we have to train our model. Once done, what can we do to test it? We could apply our model to the same data and see whether the output was correct... and we would get a surprisingly good result! Here, we are testing the model with the same data we used to train it. Obviously, the model will overperform on this data because it has already seen it. As you may have guessed, this is not a reliable way to measure the accuracy of our model.

The right way to validate a model is to split the data into two: we keep one part for training the data and another for testing it. This is known as the **holdout set**. This way, we'll test the model on data that it has never seen before and compare the result that's predicted by the model with the real value. Hence, the accuracy we are measuring is much more sensible.

This technique works well; however, it poses a problem: by retaining some data, we are losing precious information that could have helped us build a better model. This is especially true if our initial dataset is small. To solve this, we can use **cross-validation**. With this method, we once again split the data into two sets. This time, we are training the model twice, using each set as training and testing sets. You can see a schematic representation of this operation in the following diagram:

Figure 11.1 – Two-fold cross-validation

At the end of the operation, we obtain two accuracies, which will give us a better overview of how our model performs on the whole dataset. This technique can be applied to help us perform more trials with a smaller testing set, as shown in the following diagram:

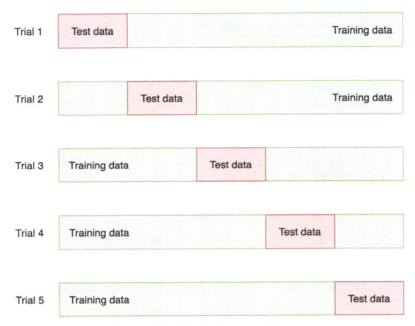

Figure 11.2 – Five-fold cross-validation

We'll stop here regarding this very quick introduction to ML. We've barely scratched the surface: ML is a vast and complex field, and there are lots of books dedicated to this subject. Still, this information should be sufficient to help you understand the basic concepts we'll show throughout the rest of this chapter.

Manipulating arrays with NumPy and pandas

As we said in the introduction, numerous Python libraries have been developed to help with common data science tasks. The most fundamental ones are probably NumPy and pandas. Their goal is to provide a set of tools to manipulate a big set of data in an efficient way, much more than what we could actually achieve with standard Python, and we'll show how and why in this section. NumPy and pandas are at the heart of most data science applications in Python; knowing about them is therefore the first step on your journey into Python for data science.

Before starting to use them, let's explain why such libraries are needed. In *Chapter 2, Python Programming Specificities*, we stated that Python is a dynamically typed language. This means that the interpreter automatically detects the type of a variable at runtime, and this type can even change throughout the program. For example, you can do something like this in Python:

```
$ python
>>> x = 1
>>> type(x)
```

```
<class 'int'>
>>> x = "hello"
>>> type(x)
<class 'str'>
```

The interpreter was able to determine the type of x at each assignation.

Under the hood, the standard implementation of Python, CPython, is written in C. The C language is a compiled and statically typed language. This means that the nature of the variables is fixed at compile time, and they can't change during execution. Thus, in the Python implementation, a variable doesn't only consist of its value: it's actually a structure containing information about the variable, including its type and size, in addition to its value.

Thanks to this, we can manipulate variables very dynamically in Python. However, it comes at a cost: each variable has a significantly higher memory footprint to store all its metadata than just the plain value.

This is particularly true for data structures. Say we consider a simple list like this:

```
$ python
>>> l = [1, 2, 3, 4, 5]
```

Each item in the list is a Python integer, with all the metadata associated. In a statically typed language such as C, the same list would only be a suite of values in memory sharing the same type.

Let's now imagine a big set of data, like the kind we usually encounter in data science: the cost of storing it in memory would be huge. That's exactly the purpose of NumPy: to provide a powerful and efficient array structure for manipulating a big set of data. Under the hood, it uses a fixed-type array, meaning all elements of the structure are of the same type, which allows NumPy to get rid of the costly metadata of every single element. Moreover, common arithmetic operations, such as additions or multiplications, are much faster. In the *Manipulating arrays with NumPy – computation, aggregations, and comparisons* section, we'll make a speed comparison to show you the difference with standard Python lists.

Getting started with NumPy

Let's see how NumPy works! The first thing is to install it using the following command:

```
(venv) $ pip install numpy
```

In a Python interpreter, we can now import the library:

```
(venv) $ python
>>> import numpy as np
```

Notice that, by convention, *NumPy is generally imported with the alias* np. Let's now discover its basic features!

Creating arrays

To create an array with NumPy, we can simply use the `array` function and pass it a Python list:

```
>>> np.array([1, 2, 3, 4, 5])
array([1, 2, 3, 4, 5])
```

NumPy will detect the nature of the Python list. However, we can force the resulting type by using the `dtype` argument:

```
>>> np.array([1, 2, 3, 4, 5], dtype=np.float64)
array([1., 2., 3., 4., 5.])
```

All elements were upcasted to the specified type. It is key to remember that a *NumPy array is of a fixed type*. This means that every element will have the same type and NumPy will silently cast a value to the `array` type. For example, let's consider an integer list into which we want to insert a floating-point value:

```
>>> l = np.array([1, 2, 3, 4, 5])
>>> l[0] = 13.37
>>> l
array([13, 2, 3, 4, 5])
```

The `13.37` value has been truncated to fit into an integer.

If the value cannot be cast to the type of array, an error is raised. For example, let's try to change the first element with a string:

```
>>> l[0] = "a"
Traceback (most recent call last):
  File "<stdin>", line 1, in <module>
ValueError: invalid literal for int() with base 10: 'a'
```

As we said in the introduction to this section, Python lists are not very efficient for large datasets. This is why it's generally more efficient to use NumPy functions to create arrays. The most commonly used ones are generally the following:

- `np.zeros`, to create an array filled with zeros
- `np.ones`, to create an array filled with ones
- `np.empty`, to create an empty array of the desired size in memory, without initializing the values
- `np.arange`, to create an array with a range of elements

Let's see them in action:

```
>>> np.zeros(5)
array([0., 0., 0., 0., 0.])
>>> np.ones(5)
array([1., 1., 1., 1., 1.])
>>> np.empty(5)
array([1., 1., 1., 1., 1.])
>>> np.arange(5)
array([0, 1, 2, 3, 4])
```

Notice that the result of np.empty can vary: since the values in the array are not initialized, *they take whatever value there is currently in this memory block*. The main motivation behind this function is speed, allowing you to quickly allocate memory, but don't forget to fill every element after.

By default, NumPy creates arrays with a floating-point type (float64). Once again, by using the dtype argument, you can force another type to be used:

```
>>> np.ones(5, dtype=np.int32)
array([1, 1, 1, 1, 1], dtype=int32)
```

NumPy provides a wide range of types, allowing you to finely optimize the memory consumption of your program by selecting the right type for your data. You can find the whole list of types supported by NumPy in the official documentation: https://numpy.org/doc/stable/reference/arrays.scalars.html#sized-aliases.

NumPy also proposes a function to create an array with random values:

```
>>> np.random.seed(0)   # Set the random seed to make examples
reproducible
>>> np.random.randint(10, size=5)
array([5, 0, 3, 3, 7])
```

The first argument is the maximum range of the random value, and the size argument sets the number of values to generate.

Until now, we showed how to create one-dimensional arrays. However, the great strength of NumPy is that it natively handles multi-dimensional arrays! For example, let's create a *3 x 4* matrix:

```
>>> m = np.ones((3,4))
>>> m
array([[1., 1., 1., 1.],
       [1., 1., 1., 1.],
       [1., 1., 1., 1.]])
```

NumPy did create an array with three rows and four columns! All we had to do was to pass a tuple to the NumPy function to specify our dimensions. When having such an array, NumPy gives us access to properties for knowing the number of dimensions, as well as the shape and size of it:

```
>>> m.ndim
2
>>> m.shape
(3, 4)
>>> m.size
12
```

Accessing elements and sub-arrays

NumPy arrays closely follow the standard Python syntax to manipulate lists. Therefore, to access an element in a one-dimensional array, just do the following:

```
>>> l = np.arange(5)
>>> l[2]
2
```

For multi-dimensional arrays, we just have to add another index:

```
>>> np.random.seed(0)
>>> m = np.random.randint(10, size=(3,4))
>>> m
array([[5, 0, 3, 3],
       [7, 9, 3, 5],
       [2, 4, 7, 6]])
>>> m[1][2]
3
```

Of course, this can be used to re-assign elements:

```
>>> m[1][2] = 42
>>> m
array([[ 5,  0,  3,  3],
       [ 7,  9, 42,  5],
       [ 2,  4,  7,  6]])
```

But that's not all. Thanks to the slicing syntax, we can access sub-arrays with a start index, an end index, and even a step. For example, on a one-dimensional array, we can do the following:

```
>>> l = np.arange(5)
>>> l
array([0, 1, 2, 3, 4])
>>> l[1:4]  # From index 1 (inclusive) to 4 (exclusive)
array([1, 2, 3])
```

```
>>> l[::2]   # Every second element
array([0, 2, 4])
```

This is exactly what we saw for standard Python lists in *Chapter 2, Python Programming Specificities*. Of course, it also works for multi-dimensional arrays, with one slice for each dimension:

```
>>> np.random.seed(0)
>>> m = np.random.randint(10, size=(3,4))
>>> m
array([[5, 0, 3, 3],
       [7, 9, 3, 5],
       [2, 4, 7, 6]])
>>> m[1:, 0:2]   # From row 1 to end and column 0 to 2
array([[7, 9],
       [2, 4]])
>>> m[::, 3:]   # Every row, only last column
array([[3],
       [5],
       [6]])
```

You can assign those sub-arrays to variables. However, for performance reasons, NumPy doesn't copy the values by default: it's only a **view** (or shallow copy), a representation of the existing data. This is important to bear in mind because if you change a value in the view, it will also change the value in the original array:

```
>>> v = m[::, 3:]
>>> v[0][0] = 42
>>> v
array([[42],
       [ 5],
       [ 6]])
>>> m
array([[ 5,  0,  3, 42],
       [ 7,  9,  3,  5],
       [ 2,  4,  7,  6]])
```

If you need to really **copy** the values in memory, you just have to use the copy method on the array:

```
>>> m2 = m[::, 3:].copy()
```

m2 is now a separate copy of m, and changes in its values won't change the values in m.

You now have the basics for handling arrays with NumPy. As we've seen, the syntax is very similar to standard Python. The key points to remember when working with NumPy are the following:

- NumPy arrays are of fixed types, meaning all items in the array are of the same type
- NumPy natively handles multi-dimensional arrays and allows us to subset them using the standard slicing notation

Of course, NumPy can do much more than that: actually, it can apply common computations to those arrays in a very performant way.

Manipulating arrays with NumPy – computation, aggregations, and comparisons

As we said, NumPy is all about manipulating large arrays with great performance and controlled memory consumption. Let's say, for example, that we want to compute the double of each element in a large array. In the following example, you can see an implementation of such a function with a standard Python loop:

chapter11_compare_operations.py

```
import numpy as np
np.random.seed(0)  # Set the random seed to make examples reproducible
m = np.random.randint(10, size=1000000)  # An array with a million of
elements
def standard_double(array):
    output = np.empty(array.size)
    for i in range(array.size):
        output[i] = array[i] * 2
    return output
```

https://github.com/PacktPublishing/Building-Data-Science-Applications-with-FastAPI-Second-Edition/tree/main/chapter11/chapter11_compare_operations.py

We instantiate an array with a million random integers. Then, we have our function building an array with the double of each element. Basically, we first instantiate an empty array of the same size before looping over each element to set the double.

Let's measure the performance of this function. In Python, there is a standard module, `timeit`, dedicated to this purpose. We can use it directly from the command line and pass valid Python statements we want to measure performance for. The following command will measure the performance of `standard_double` with our big array:

```
python -m timeit "from chapter11.chapter11_compare_operations import
m, standard_double; standard_double(m)"
1 loop, best of 5: 146 msec per loop
```

The results will vary depending on your machine, but the magnitude should be equivalent. What `timeit` does is repeat your code a certain number of times and measure its execution time. Here, our function took around 150 milliseconds to compute the double of each element in our array. For such simple computations on a modern computer, that's not very impressive.

Let's compare this with the equivalent operation using NumPy syntax. You can see it in the next sample:

chapter11_compare_operations.py

```
def numpy_double(array):
    return array * 2
```

https://github.com/PacktPublishing/Building-Data-Science-Applications-with-FastAPI-Second-Edition/tree/main/chapter11/chapter11_compare_operations.py

The code is much shorter! NumPy implements the basic arithmetic operations and can apply them to each element of the array. By multiplying the array by a value directly, we implicitly tell NumPy to multiply each element by this value. Let's measure the performance with `timeit`:

```
python -m timeit "from chapter11.chapter11_compare_operations import
m, numpy_double; numpy_double(m)"
500 loops, best of 5: 611 usec per loop
```

Here, the best loop achieved the computation in 600 microseconds! That's 250 times faster than the previous function! How can we explain such a variation? In a standard loop, Python (because of its dynamic nature) has to check for the type of value at each iteration to apply the right function for this type, which adds significant overhead. With NumPy, the operation is deferred to an optimized and compiled loop where types are known ahead of time, which saves a lot of useless checks.

We once again see here the benefits of NumPy arrays over standard lists when working on a large dataset: it implements operations natively to help you make computations very fast.

Adding and multiplying arrays

As you saw in the previous example, NumPy supports the arithmetic operators to make operations over arrays.

This means that you can operate directly over two arrays of the same dimensions:

```
>>> np.array([1, 2, 3]) + np.array([4, 5, 6])
array([5, 7, 9])
```

In this case, NumPy applies the operation element-wise. But it also works in certain situations if one of the operands is not of the same shape:

```
>>> np.array([1, 2, 3]) * 2
array([2, 4, 6])
```

NumPy automatically understands that it should multiply each element by two. This is called **broadcasting**: NumPy "expands" the smaller array to match the shape of the larger array. The previous example is equivalent to this one:

```
>>> np.array([1, 2, 3]) * np.array([2, 2, 2])
array([2, 4, 6])
```

Note that even if those two examples are conceptually equivalent, the first one is more memory-efficient and computationally efficient: NumPy is smart enough to use only one 2 value, without having to create a full array of 2.

More generally, broadcasting works if the rightmost dimensions of the arrays are of the same size or if one of them is 1. For example, we can add an array of dimensions *4 x 3* to an array of dimensions *1 x 3*:

```
>>> a1 = np.ones((4, 3))
>>> a1
array([[1., 1., 1.],
       [1., 1., 1.],
       [1., 1., 1.],
       [1., 1., 1.]])
>>> a2 = np.ones((1, 3))
>>> a2
array([[1., 1., 1.]])
>>> a1 + a2
array([[2., 2., 2.],
       [2., 2., 2.],
       [2., 2., 2.],
       [2., 2., 2.]])
```

However, adding an array of dimensions *4 x 3* to an array of dimensions *1 x 4* is not possible:

```
>>> a3 = np.ones((1, 4))
>>> a3
array([[1., 1., 1., 1.]])
>>> a1 + a3
Traceback (most recent call last):
```

```
  File "<stdin>", line 1, in <module>
ValueError: operands could not be broadcast together with shapes (4,3)
(1,4)
```

If this sounds complicated or confusing, that's normal; it takes time to understand it conceptually, especially in three or more dimensions. For a more detailed explanation of the concept, take time to read the related article in the official documentation: `https://numpy.org/doc/stable/user/basics.broadcasting.html`.

Aggregating arrays – sum, min, max, mean, and so on

When working with arrays, we often need to summarize the data to extract some meaningful statistics: the mean, the minimum, the maximum, and so on. Fortunately, NumPy also provides those operations natively. Quite simply, they are provided as methods that you can call directly from an array:

```
>>> np.arange(10).mean()
4.5
>>> np.ones((4,4)).sum()
16.0
```

You can find the whole list of aggregating operations in the official documentation: `https://numpy.org/doc/stable/reference/arrays.ndarray.html#calculation`.

Comparing arrays

NumPy also implements the standard comparison operators to compare arrays. As with arithmetic operators, which we saw in the *Adding and multiplying arrays* section, broadcasting rules apply. This means that you can compare an array with a single value:

```
>>> l = np.array([1, 2, 3, 4])
>>> l < 3
array([ True,  True, False, False])
```

And you can also compare arrays with arrays, given that they are compatible on the basis of the broadcasting rules:

```
>>> m = np.array(
    [[1., 5., 9., 13.],
     [2., 6., 10., 14.],
     [3., 7., 11., 15.],
     [4., 8., 12., 16.]]
)
>>> m <= np.array([1, 5, 9, 13])
array([[ True,  True,  True,  True],
       [False, False, False, False],
       [False, False, False, False],
```

```
[False, False, False, False]])
```

The resulting array is filled with the Boolean result of the comparison for each element.

That's it for this very quick introduction to NumPy. There is a lot more to know and discover with this library, so we strongly encourage you to read the official user guide: https://numpy.org/doc/stable/user/index.html.

For the rest of this book, this should be enough for you to understand future examples. Let's now have a look at a library often cited and used alongside NumPy: pandas.

Getting started with pandas

In the previous section, we introduced NumPy and its ability to efficiently store and work with a large array of data. We'll now introduce another widely used library in data science: pandas. This library is built on top of NumPy to provide convenient data structures able to efficiently store large datasets with *labeled rows and columns*. This is, of course, especially handy when working with most datasets representing real-world data that we want to analyze and use in data science projects.

To get started, we will, of course, install the library with the usual command:

```
(venv) $ pip install pandas
```

Once done, we can start to use it in a Python interpreter:

```
(venv) $ python
>>> import pandas as pd
```

Just like we alias numpy as np, the convention is to alias pandas as pd when importing it.

Using pandas Series for one-dimensional data

The first pandas data structure we'll introduce is Series. This data structure behaves very similarly to a one-dimensional array in NumPy. To create one, we can simply initialize it with a list of values:

```
>>> s = pd.Series([1, 2, 3, 4, 5])
>>> s
0    1
1    2
2    3
3    4
4    5
dtype: int64
```

Under the hood, pandas creates a NumPy array. As such, it uses the same data types to store the data. You can verify this by accessing the `values` property of the `Series` object and checking its type:

```
>>> type(s.values)
<class 'numpy.ndarray'>
```

Indexing and slicing work exactly the same way as in NumPy:

```
>>> s[0]
1
>>> s[1:3]
1    2
2    3
dtype: int64
```

So far, this is not very different from a regular NumPy array. As we said, the main purpose of pandas is to *label the data*. To allow this, pandas data structures maintain an index to allow this data labeling. It is accessible through the `index` property:

```
>>> s.index
RangeIndex(start=0, stop=5, step=1)
```

Here, we have a simple range integer index, but we can actually have any arbitrary index. In the next example, we create the same series, labeling each value with a letter:

```
>>> s = pd.Series([1, 2, 3, 4, 5], index=["a", "b", "c", "d", "e"])
>>> s
a    1
b    2
c    3
d    4
e    5
```

The `index` argument on the `Series` initializer allows us to set the list of labels. We can now access values with those labels instead:

```
>>> s["c"]
3
```

Surprisingly, even slicing notation works with those kinds of labels:

```
>>> s["b":"d"]
b    2
c    3
d    4
dtype: int64
```

Under the hood, pandas keep the order of the index to allow such useful notations. Notice, however, that with this notation, the *last index is inclusive* (d is included in the result), unlike standard index notation, where the last index is exclusive:

```
>>> s[1:3]
b    2
c    3
dtype: int64
```

To avoid confusion between those two styles, pandas exposes two special notations to explicitly indicate which indexing style you wish to use: `loc` (label notation with the last index being inclusive) and `iloc` (standard index notation). You can read more about this in the official documentation: https://pandas.pydata.org/docs/user_guide/indexing.html#different-choices-for-indexing.

`Series` can also be instantiated directly from dictionaries:

```
>>> s = pd.Series({"a": 1, "b": 2, "c": 3, "d": 4, "e": 5})
>>> s
a    1
b    2
c    3
d    4
e    5
dtype: int64
```

In this case, the keys of the dictionaries are used as labels.

Of course, in the real world, you'll more likely have to work with two-dimensional (or more!) datasets. This is exactly what DataFrames are for!

Using pandas DataFrames for multi-dimensional data

Most of the time, datasets consist of two-dimensional data, where you have several columns for each row, as in a classic spreadsheet application. In Pandas, DataFrames are designed to work with this kind of data. As for `Series`, it can work with a large set of data that is labeled both by rows and columns.

The following examples will use a tiny dataset representing the number of tickets (paid and free) delivered in French museums in 2018. Let's consider we have this data in the form of two dictionaries:

```
>>> paid = {"Louvre Museum": 5988065, "Orsay Museum": 1850092,
"Pompidou Centre": 2620481, "National Natural History Museum": 404497}
>>> free = {"Louvre Museum": 4117897, "Orsay Museum": 1436132,
"Pompidou Centre": 1070337, "National Natural History Museum": 344572}
```

Each key in those dictionaries is a label for a row. We can build a DataFrame directly from those two dictionaries like this:

```
>>> museums = pd.DataFrame({"paid": paid, "free": free})
>>> museums
                                   paid     free
Louvre Museum                    5988065  4117897
Orsay Museum                     1850092  1436132
Pompidou Centre                  2620481  1070337
National Natural History Museum   404497   344572
```

The `DataFrame` initializer accepts a dictionary of dictionaries, where keys represent the label for the columns.

We can have a look at the `index` property, storing the rows index, and the `columns` property, storing the columns index:

```
>>> museums.index
Index(['Louvre Museum', 'Orsay Museum', 'Pompidou Centre',
       'National Natural History Museum'],
     dtype='object')
>>> museums.columns
Index(['paid', 'free'], dtype='object')
```

Once again, we can now use indexing and slicing notation to get subsets of columns or rows:

```
>>> museums["free"]
Louvre Museum                      4117897
Orsay Museum                       1436132
Pompidou Centre                    1070337
National Natural History Museum     344572
Name: free, dtype: int64
>>> museums["Louvre Museum":"Orsay Museum"]
                  paid     free
Louvre Museum  5988065  4117897
Orsay Museum   1850092  1436132
>>> museums["Louvre Museum":"Orsay Museum"]["paid"]
Louvre Museum    5988065
Orsay Museum     1850092
Name: paid, dtype: int64
```

Something that is even more powerful: you can write a Boolean condition inside the brackets to match some data. This operation is called **masking**:

```
>>> museums[museums["paid"] > 2000000]
                  paid      free
Louvre Museum     5988065   4117897
Pompidou Centre   2620481   1070337
```

Finally, you can easily set new columns with this very same indexing notation:

```
>>> museums["total"] = museums["paid"] + museums["free"]
>>> museums
                                  paid      free       total
Louvre Museum                     5988065   4117897    10105962
Orsay Museum                      1850092   1436132    3286224
Pompidou Centre                   2620481   1070337    3690818
National Natural History Museum   404497    344572     749069
```

As you can see, just like NumPy arrays, pandas fully supports arithmetic operations over two DataFrames.

Of course, all the basic aggregation operations are supported, including `mean` and `sum`:

```
>>> museums["total"].sum()
17832073
>>> museums["total"].mean()
4458018.25
```

You can find the whole list of operations available in the official documentation: `https://pandas.pydata.org/pandas-docs/stable/user_guide/basics.html#descriptive-statistics`.

Importing and exporting CSV data

One very common way of sharing datasets is through CSV files. This format is very convenient because it only consists of a simple text file, each line representing a row of data, with each column separated by a comma. Our simple *museums* dataset is available in the examples repository as a CSV file, which you can see in the next sample:

museums.csv

```
name,paid,free
Louvre Museum,5988065,4117897
Orsay Museum,1850092,1436132
Pompidou Centre,2620481,1070337
National Natural History Museum,404497,344572
```

```
https://github.com/PacktPublishing/Building-Data-Science-Applica-
tions-with-FastAPI-Second-Edition/tree/main/chapter11/museums.csv
```

Importing CSV files is so common that pandas provides a function to load a CSV file into a DataFrame directly:

```
>>> museums = pd.read_csv("./chapter11/museums.csv", index_col=0)
>>> museums
                                      paid      free
name
Louvre Museum                      5988065   4117897
Orsay Museum                       1850092   1436132
Pompidou Centre                    2620481   1070337
National Natural History Museum     404497    344572
```

The function simply expects the path to the CSV file. Several arguments are available to finely control the operation: here, we used `index_col` to specify the index of the column that should be used as row labels. You can find the whole list of arguments in the official documentation: `https://pandas.pydata.org/pandas-docs/stable/reference/api/pandas.read_csv.html`.

Of course, the opposite operation exists to export a DataFrame to a CSV file:

```
>>> museums["total"] = museums["paid"] + museums["free"]
>>> museums.to_csv("museums_with_total.csv")
```

We will conclude this very quick introduction to pandas here. Of course, we've only covered the tip of the iceberg, and we recommend that you go through the official user guide to know more: `https://pandas.pydata.org/pandas-docs/stable/user_guide/index.html`.

Still, you should now be able to perform basic operations and operate efficiently on large datasets. In the next section, we'll introduce scikit-learn, one of the fundamental Python toolkits for data science, and you'll see that it relies a lot on NumPy and pandas.

Training models with scikit-learn

scikit-learn is one of the most widely used Python libraries for data science. It implements dozens of classic ML models, but also numerous tools to help you while training them, such as preprocessing methods and cross-validation. Nowadays, you'll probably hear about more modern approaches, such as PyTorch, but scikit-learn is still a solid tool for a lot of use cases.

The first thing you must do to get started is to install it in your Python environment:

```
(venv) $ pip install scikit-learn
```

We can now start our scikit-learn journey!

Training models and predicting

In scikit-learn, ML models and algorithms are called **estimators**. Each is a Python class that implements the same methods. In particular, we have fit, which is used to train a model, and predict, which is used to run the trained model on new data.

To try this, we'll load a sample dataset. scikit-learn comes with a few toy datasets that are very useful for performing experiments. You can find out more about them in the official documentation: https://scikit-learn.org/stable/datasets.html.

Here, we'll use the *digits* dataset, a collection of pixel matrices representing handwritten digits. As you may have guessed, the goal of this dataset is to train a model to automatically recognize handwritten digits. The following example shows how to load this dataset:

chapter11_load_digits.py

```
from sklearn.datasets import load_digits

digits = load_digits()

data = digits.data
targets = digits.target

print(data[0].reshape((8, 8)))  # First handwritten digit 8 x 8 matrix
print(targets[0])  # Label of first handwritten digit
```

https://github.com/PacktPublishing/Building-Data-Science-Applications-with-FastAPI-Second-Edition/tree/main/chapter11/chapter11_load_digits.py

Notice that the toy dataset's functions are imported from the datasets package of scikit-learn. The load_digits function returns an object that contains the data and some metadata.

The most interesting parts of this object are data, which contains the handwritten digit pixels matrices, and targets, which contains the corresponding label for those digits. Both are NumPy arrays.

To get a grasp of what this looks like, we will take the first digit in the data and reshape it into an 8 x 8 matrix; this is the size of the source images. Each value represents a pixel on a grayscale, from 0 to 16.

Then, we print the label of this first digit, which is 0. If you run this code, you'll get the following output:

```
[[ 0.  0.  5. 13.  9.  1.  0.  0.]
 [ 0.  0. 13. 15. 10. 15.  5.  0.]
 [ 0.  3. 15.  2.  0. 11.  8.  0.]
 [ 0.  4. 12.  0.  0.  8.  8.  0.]
 [ 0.  5.  8.  0.  0.  9.  8.  0.]
```

```
[ 0.  4. 11.  0.  1. 12.  7.  0.]
[ 0.  2. 14.  5. 10. 12.  0.  0.]
[ 0.  0.  6. 13. 10.  0.  0.  0.]]
0
```

Somehow, we can guess the shape of the zero from the matrix.

Now, let's try to build a model that recognizes handwritten digits. To start simple, we'll use a Gaussian Naive Bayes model, a classic and easy-to-use algorithm that can quickly yield good results. The following example shows the entire process:

chapter11_fit_predict.py

```python
from sklearn.datasets import load_digits
from sklearn.metrics import accuracy_score
from sklearn.model_selection import train_test_split
from sklearn.naive_bayes import GaussianNB

digits = load_digits()

data = digits.data
targets = digits.target

# Split into training and testing sets
training_data, testing_data, training_targets, testing_targets =
train_test_split(
    data, targets, random_state=0
)

# Train the model
model = GaussianNB()
model.fit(training_data, training_targets)

# Run prediction with the testing set
predicted_targets = model.predict(testing_data)

# Compute the accuracy
accuracy = accuracy_score(testing_targets, predicted_targets)
print(accuracy)
```

https://github.com/PacktPublishing/Building-Data-Science-Applications-with-FastAPI-Second-Edition/tree/main/chapter11/chapter11_fit_predict.py

Now that we've loaded the dataset, you can see that we take care of splitting it into a training and a testing set. As we mentioned in the *Model validation* section, this is essential for computing meaningful accuracy scores to check how our model performs.

To do this, we can rely on the `train_test_split` function, which is provided in the `model_selection` package. It selects random instances from our dataset to form the two sets. By default, it keeps 25% of the data to create a testing set, but this can be customized. The `random_state` argument allows us to set the random seed to make the example reproducible. You can find out more about this function in the official documentation: `https://scikit-learn.org/stable/modules/generated/sklearn.model_selection.train_test_split.html#sklearn-model-selection-train-test-split`.

Then, we must instantiate the `GaussianNB` class. This class is one of the numerous ML estimators that's implemented in scikit-learn. Each has its own set of parameters, to finely tune the behavior of the algorithm. However, scikit-learn is designed to provide sensible defaults for all the estimators, so it's usually good to start with the defaults before tinkering with them.

After that, we must call the `fit` method to train our model. It expects an argument and two arrays: the first one is the actual data, with all its features, while the second one is the corresponding labels. And that's it! You've trained your first ML model!

Now, let's see how it behaves: we'll call `predict` on our model with the testing set so that it automatically classifies the digits of the testing set. The result of this is a new array with the predicted labels.

All we have to do now is compare it with the actual labels of our testing set. Once again, scikit-learn helps by providing the `accuracy_score` function in the `metrics` package. The first argument is the true labels, while the second is the predicted labels.

If you run this code, you'll get an accuracy score of around 83%. That isn't too bad for a first approach! As you have seen, training and running prediction on an ML model is straightforward with scikit-learn.

In practice, we often need to perform preprocessing steps on the data before feeding it to an estimator. Rather than doing this sequentially by hand, scikit-learn proposes a convenient feature that can automate this process: **pipelines**.

Chaining preprocessors and estimators with pipelines

Quite often, you'll need to preprocess your data so that it can be used by the estimator you wish to use. Typically, you'll want to transform an image into an array of pixel values or, as we'll see in the following example, transform raw text into numerical values so that we can apply some math to them.

Rather than writing those steps by hand, scikit-learn proposes a feature that can automatically chain preprocessors and estimators: pipelines. Once created, they expose the very same interface as any other estimator, allowing you to run training and prediction in one operation.

To show you what this looks like, we'll look at an example of another classic dataset, the *20 newsgroups* text dataset. It consists of 18,000 newsgroup articles categorized into 20 topics. The goal of this dataset is to build a model that will automatically categorize an article in one of those topics.

The following example shows how we can load this data thanks to the `fetch_20newsgroups` function:

chapter11_pipelines.py

```python
import pandas as pd
from sklearn.datasets import fetch_20newsgroups
from sklearn.feature_extraction.text import TfidfVectorizer
from sklearn.metrics import accuracy_score, confusion_matrix
from sklearn.naive_bayes import MultinomialNB
from sklearn.pipeline import make_pipeline

# Load some categories of newsgroups dataset
categories = [
    "soc.religion.christian",
    "talk.religion.misc",
    "comp.sys.mac.hardware",
    "sci.crypt",
]
newsgroups_training = fetch_20newsgroups(
    subset="train", categories=categories, random_state=0
)
newsgroups_testing = fetch_20newsgroups(
    subset="test", categories=categories, random_state=0
)
```

https://github.com/PacktPublishing/Building-Data-Science-Applications-with-FastAPI-Second-Edition/tree/main/chapter11/chapter11_pipelines.py

Since the dataset is rather large, we'll only load a subset of the categories. Also, notice that it's already been split into training and testing sets, so we only have to load them with the corresponding argument. You can find out more about the functionality of this dataset in the official documentation: https://scikit-learn.org/stable/datasets/real_world.html#the-20-newsgroups-text-dataset.

Before moving on, it's important to understand what the underlying data is. Actually, this is the raw text of an article. You can check this by printing one of the samples in the data:

```
>>> newsgroups_training.data[0]
"From: sandvik@newton.apple.com (Kent Sandvik)\nSubject: Re: Ignorance
is BLISS, was Is it good that Jesus died?\nOrganization: Cookamunga
Tourist Bureau\nLines: 17\n\nIn article <f1682Ap@quack.kfu.com>,
```

```
pharvey@quack.kfu.com (Paul Harvey)\nwrote:\n> In article <sandvik-
170493104859@sandvik-kent.apple.com> \n> sandvik@newton.apple.com
(Kent Sandvik) writes:\n> >Ignorance is not bliss!\n \n> Ignorance is
STRENGTH!\n> Help spread the TRUTH of IGNORANCE!\n\nHuh, if ignorance
is strength, then I won't distribute this piece\nof information if I
want to follow your advice (contradiction above).\n\n\nCheers,\nKent\
n---\nsandvik@newton.apple.com. ALink: KSAND -- Private activities on
the net.\n"
```

So, we need to extract some features from this text before feeding it to an estimator. A common approach for this when working with textual data is to use the **Term Frequency-Inverse Document Frequency (TF-IDF)**. Without going into too much detail, this technique will count the occurrences of each word in all the documents (term frequency), weighted by the importance of this word in every document (inverse document frequency). The idea is to give more weight to rarer words, which should convey more sense than frequent words such as "the." You can find out more about this in the scikit-learn documentation: https://scikit-learn.org/dev/modules/feature_extraction.html#tfidf-term-weighting.

This operation consists of splitting each word in the text samples and counting them. Usually, we apply a lot of techniques to refine this, such as removing **stop words** (common words such as "and" or "is" that don't bring much information). Fortunately, scikit-learn provides an all-in-one tool for this: TfidfVectorizer.

This preprocessor can take an array of text, tokenize each word, and compute the TF-IDF for each of them. A lot of options are available for finely tuning its behavior, but the defaults are a good start for English text. The following example shows how to use it with an estimator in a pipeline:

chapter11_pipelines.py

```
# Make the pipeline
model = make_pipeline(
    TfidfVectorizer(),
    MultinomialNB(),
)
```

https://github.com/PacktPublishing/Building-Data-Science-Applications-with-FastAPI-Second-Edition/tree/main/chapter11/chapter11_pipelines.py

The make_pipeline function accepts any number of preprocessors and an estimator in its argument. Here, we're using the Multinomial Naive Bayes classifier, which is suitable for features representing frequency.

Then, we can simply train our model and run prediction to check its accuracy, as we did previously. You can see this in the following example:

chapter11_pipelines.py

```
# Train the model
model.fit(newsgroups_training.data, newsgroups_training.target)

# Run prediction with the testing set
predicted_targets = model.predict(newsgroups_testing.data)

# Compute the accuracy
accuracy = accuracy_score(newsgroups_testing.target, predicted_
targets)
print(accuracy)

# Show the confusion matrix
confusion = confusion_matrix(newsgroups_testing.target, predicted_
targets)
confusion_df = pd.DataFrame(
    confusion,
    index=pd.Index(newsgroups_testing.target_names, name="True"),
    columns=pd.Index(newsgroups_testing.target_names,
name="Predicted"),
)
print(confusion_df)
```

```
https://github.com/PacktPublishing/Building-Data-Science-Applica-
tions-with-FastAPI-Second-Edition/tree/main/chapter11/chapter11_
pipelines.py
```

Notice that we also printed a confusion matrix, which is a very convenient representation of the global results. Scikit-learn has a dedicated function for this called confusion_matrix. Then, we wrap the result in a pandas DataFrame so that we can set the axis labels to improve readability. If you run this example, you'll get an output similar to what's shown in the following screenshot. Depending on your machine and system, it could take a couple of minutes to run:

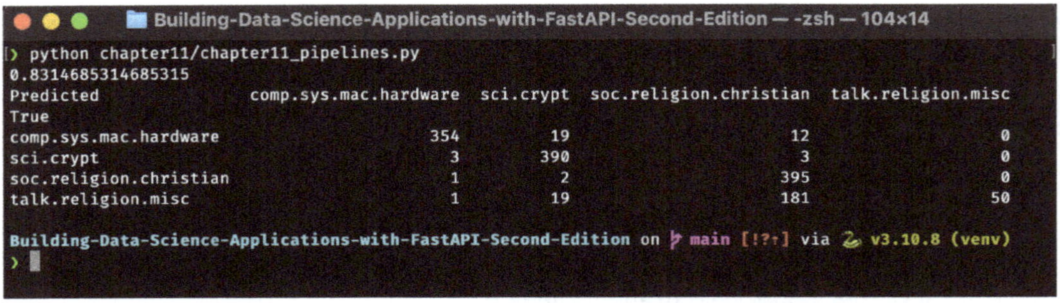

```
> python chapter11/chapter11_pipelines.py
0.8314685314685315
Predicted               comp.sys.mac.hardware  sci.crypt  soc.religion.christian  talk.religion.misc
True
comp.sys.mac.hardware                     354         19                      12                   0
sci.crypt                                   3        390                       3                   0
soc.religion.christian                      1          2                     395                   0
talk.religion.misc                          1         19                     181                  50
```

Figure 11.3 – Confusion matrix on the 20 newsgroups dataset

Here, you can see that our results weren't too bad for our first try. Notice that there is one big area of confusion between the soc.religion.christian and talk.religion.misc categories, which is not very surprising, given their similarity.

As you've seen, building a pipeline with a preprocessor is very straightforward. The nice thing about this is that it automatically applies it to the training data, but also when you're predicting the results.

Before moving on, let's look at one more important feature of scikit-learn: cross-validation.

Validating the model with cross-validation

In the *Model validation* section, we introduced the cross-validation technique, which allows us to use data in training or testing sets. As you may have guessed, this technique is so common that it's implemented natively in scikit-learn!

Let's take another look at the handwritten digit example and apply cross-validation:

chapter11_cross_validation.py

```python
from sklearn.datasets import load_digits
from sklearn.model_selection import cross_val_score
from sklearn.naive_bayes import GaussianNB

digits = load_digits()

data = digits.data
targets = digits.target

# Create the model
model = GaussianNB()

# Run cross-validation
score = cross_val_score(model, data, targets)
```

```
print(score)
print(score.mean())
```

This time, we don't have to split the data ourselves: the `cross_val_score` function performs the folds automatically. In argument, it expects the estimator, `data`, which contains the handwritten digits' pixels matrices, and `targets`, which contains the corresponding label for those digits. By default, it performs five folds.

The result of this operation is an array that provides the accuracy score of the five folds. To get a global overview of this result, we can take, for example, the mean. If you run this example, you'll get the following output:

```
python chapter11/chapter11_cross_validation.py
[0.78055556 0.78333333 0.79387187 0.8718663  0.80501393]
0.8069281956050759
```

As you can see, our mean accuracy is around 80%, which is a bit lower than the 83% we obtained with single training and testing sets. That's the main benefit of cross-validation: we obtain a more statistically accurate metric regarding the performance of our model.

With that, you have learned the basics of working with scikit-learn. It's obviously a very quick introduction to this vast framework, but it'll give you the keys to train and evaluate your first ML models.

Summary

Congratulations! You've discovered the basic concepts of ML and made your first experiments with the fundamental toolkits of the data scientist. Now, you should be able to explore your first data science problems in Python. Of course, this was by no means a complete lesson on ML: the field is vast and there are tons of algorithms and techniques to explore. However, I hope that this has sparked your curiosity and that you'll deepen your knowledge of this subject.

Now, it's time to get back to FastAPI! With our new ML tools at hand, we'll be able to leverage the power of FastAPI to serve our estimators and propose a reliable and efficient prediction API to our users.

12

Creating an Efficient Prediction API Endpoint with FastAPI

In the previous chapter, we introduced the most common data science techniques and libraries largely used in the Python community. Thanks to those tools, we can now build machine learning models that can make efficient predictions and classify data. Of course, we now have to think about a convenient interface so that we can take advantage of their intelligence. This way, microservices or frontend applications can ask our model to make predictions to improve the user experience or business operations. In this chapter, we'll learn how to do that with FastAPI.

As we've seen throughout this book, FastAPI allows us to implement very efficient REST APIs with a clear and lightweight syntax. In this chapter, you'll learn how to use them as efficiently as possible in order to serve thousands of prediction requests. To help us with this task, we'll introduce another library, Joblib, which provides tools to help us serialize a trained model and cache predicted results.

In this chapter, we're going to cover the following main topics:

- Persisting a trained model with Joblib
- Implementing an efficient prediction endpoint
- Caching results with Joblib

Technical requirements

For this chapter, you'll require a Python virtual environment, just as we set up in *Chapter 1*, *Python Development Environment Setup*.

You'll find all the code examples for this chapter in the dedicated GitHub repository at `https://github.com/PacktPublishing/Building-Data-Science-Applications-with-FastAPI-Second-Edition/tree/main/chapter12`.

Persisting a trained model with Joblib

In the previous chapter, you learned how to train an estimator with scikit-learn. When building such models, you'll likely obtain a rather complex Python script to load your training data, pre-process it, and train your model with the best set of parameters. However, when deploying your model in a web application such as FastAPI, you don't want to repeat this script and run all those operations when the server is starting. Instead, you need a ready-to-use representation of your trained model that you can just load and use.

This is what Joblib does. This library aims to provide tools for efficiently saving Python objects to disk, such as large arrays of data or function results: this operation is generally called **dumping**. Joblib is already a dependency of scikit-learn, so we don't even need to install it. Actually, scikit-learn itself uses it internally to load the bundled toy datasets.

As we'll see, dumping a trained model involves just one line of code with Joblib.

Dumping a trained model

In this example, we're using the newsgroups example we saw in the *Chaining preprocessors and estimators with pipelines* section of *Chapter 11, Introduction to Data Science in Python*. As a reminder, we load 4 of the 20 categories in the newsgroups dataset and build a model to automatically categorize news articles into those categories. Once we've done this, we dump the model into a file called newsgroups_model.joblib:

---

chapter12_dump_joblib.py

```python
# Make the pipeline
model = make_pipeline(
        TfidfVectorizer(),
        MultinomialNB(),
)

# Train the model
model.fit(newsgroups_training.data, newsgroups_training.target)

# Serialize the model and the target names
model_file = "newsgroups_model.joblib"
model_targets_tuple = (model, newsgroups_training.target_names)
joblib.dump(model_targets_tuple, model_file)
```

https://github.com/PacktPublishing/Building-Data-Science-Applications-with-FastAPI-Second-Edition/tree/main/chapter12/chapter12_dump_joblib.py

---

As you can see, Joblib exposes a function called `dump`, which simply expects two arguments: the Python object to save and the path of the file.

Notice that we don't dump the `model` variable alone: instead, we wrap it in a tuple, along with the name of the categories, `target_names`. This allows us to retrieve the actual name of the category after the prediction has been made without us having to reload the training dataset.

If you run this script, you'll see that the `newsgroups_model.joblib` file was created:

```
(venv) $ python chapter12/chapter12_dump_joblib.py
$ ls -lh *.joblib
-rw-r--r--    1 fvoron      staff       3,0M 10 jan 08:27 newsgroups_
model.joblib
```

Notice that this file is rather large: it's more than 3 MB! It stores all the probabilities of each word in each category, as computed by the multinomial Naive Bayes model.

That's all we need to do. This file now contains a static representation of our Python model, which will be easy to store, share, and load. Now, let's learn how to load it and check that we can run predictions on it.

Loading a dumped model

Now that we have our dumped model file, let's learn how to load it again using Joblib and check that everything is working. In the following example, we're loading the Joblib dump present in the `chapter12` directory of the examples repository and running a prediction:

chapter12_load_joblib.py

```python
import os

import joblib
from sklearn.pipeline import Pipeline

# Load the model
model_file = os.path.join(os.path.dirname(__file__), "newsgroups_
model.joblib")
loaded_model: tuple[Pipeline, list[str]] = joblib.load(model_file)
model, targets = loaded_model

# Run a prediction
p = model.predict(["computer cpu memory ram"])
print(targets[p[0]])
```

https://github.com/PacktPublishing/Building-Data-Science-Applications-with-FastAPI-Second-Edition/tree/main/chapter12/chapter12_load_joblib.py

All we need to do here is call the `load` function from Joblib and pass it as a valid path to a dump file. The result of this function is the very same Python object we dumped. Here, it's a tuple composed of the scikit-learn estimator and a list of categories.

Notice that we added some type hints: while not necessary, it helps mypy or whichever IDE you use identify the nature of the objects you loaded and benefit from type-checking and auto-completion.

Finally, we run a prediction on the model: it's a true scikit-learn estimator, with all the necessary training parameters.

That's it! As you've seen, Joblib is straightforward to use. Nevertheless, it's an essential tool for exporting your scikit-learn models and being able to use them in external services without repeating the training phase. Now, we can use those dump files in FastAPI projects.

Implementing an efficient prediction endpoint

Now that we have a way to save and load our machine learning models, it's time to use them in a FastAPI project. As you'll see, the implementation shouldn't be too much of a surprise if you've followed this book. The main part of the implementation is the class dependency, which will take care of loading the model and making predictions. If you need a refresher on class dependencies, check out *Chapter 5, Dependency Injection in FastAPI*.

Let's go! Our example will be based on the `newgroups` model we dumped in the previous section. We'll start by showing you how to implement the class dependency, which will take care of loading the model and making predictions:

---

chapter12_prediction_endpoint.py

```
class PredictionInput(BaseModel):
        text: str

class PredictionOutput(BaseModel):
        category: str

class NewsgroupsModel:
        model: Pipeline | None = None
        targets: list[str] | None = None

        def load_model(self) -> None:
                """Loads the model"""
                model_file = os.path.join(os.path.dirname(__
file__), "newsgroups_model.joblib")
                loaded_model: tuple[Pipeline, list[str]] =
joblib.load(model_file)
                model, targets = loaded_model
```

```
                                 self.model = model
                                 self.targets = targets

            async def predict(self, input: PredictionInput) ->
    PredictionOutput:
                                 """Runs a prediction"""
                                 if not self.model or not self:targets:
                                             raise RuntimeError("Model is
    not loaded")

                                 prediction = self.model.predict([input.text])
                                 category = self.targets[prediction[0]]
                                 return PredictionOutput(category=category)
```

https://github.com/PacktPublishing/Building-Data-Science-Applica-tions-with-FastAPI-Second-Edition/tree/main/chapter12/chapter12_prediction_endpoint.py

First, we start by defining two Pydantic models: `PredictionInput` and `PredictionOutput`. In a pure FastAPI philosophy, they will help us validate the request payload and return a structured JSON response. Here, as input, we simply expect a `text` property containing the text we want to classify. As output, we expect a `category` property containing the predicted category.

The most interesting part of this extract is the `NewsgroupsModel` class. It implements two methods: `load_model` and `predict`.

The `load_model` method loads the model using Joblib, as we saw in the previous section, and stores the model and targets in class properties. Hence, they will be available to use in the `predict` method.

On the other hand, the `predict` method will be injected into the path operation function. As you can see, it directly accepts `PredictionInput`, which will be injected by FastAPI. Inside this method, we are making a prediction, as we usually do with scikit-learn. We return a `PredictionOutput` object with the category we predicted.

You may have noticed that, first, we check whether the model and its targets have been assigned in the class properties before performing the prediction. Of course, we need to ensure `load_model` was called at some point before making a prediction. You may be wondering why we are not putting this logic in an initializer, `__init__`, so that we can ensure the model is loaded at class instantiation. This would work perfectly fine; however, it would cause some issues. As we'll see, we are instantiating a `NewsgroupsModel` instance right after FastAPI so that we can use it in our routes. If the loading logic was in `__init__`, the model would be loaded whenever we imported some variables (such as the `app` instance) from this file, such as in unit tests. In most cases, this would incur unnecessary I/O operations and memory consumption. As we'll see, it's better to use the lifespan handler of FastAPI to load the model when the app is run.

The following extract shows the rest of the implementation, along with the actual FastAPI route for handling predictions:

chapter12_prediction_endpoint.py

```
newgroups_model = NewsgroupsModel()

@contextlib.asynccontextmanager
async def lifespan(app: FastAPI):
        newgroups_model.load_model()
        yield

app = FastAPI(lifespan=lifespan)

@app.post("/prediction")
async def prediction(
        output: PredictionOutput = Depends(newgroups_model.
predict),
) -> PredictionOutput:
        return output
```

```
https://github.com/PacktPublishing/Building-Data-Science-Applica-
tions-with-FastAPI-Second-Edition/tree/main/chapter12/chapter12_
prediction_endpoint.py
```

As we mentioned previously, we are creating an instance of `NewsgroupsModel` so that we can inject it into our path operation function. Moreover, we are implementing a lifespan handler to call `load_model`. This way, we are making sure that the model is loaded during application startup and is ready to use.

The prediction endpoint is quite straightforward: as you can see, we directly depend on the `predict` method, which will take care of injecting the payload and validating it. We only have to return the output.

That's it! Once again, FastAPI makes our life very easy by allowing us to write very simple and readable code, even for complex tasks. We can run this application using Uvicorn, as usual:

```
(venv) $ uvicorn chapter12.chapter12_prediction_endpoint:app
```

Now, we can try to run some predictions with HTTPie:

```
$ http POST http://localhost:8000/prediction text="computer cpu memory
ram"
HTTP/1.1 200 OK
content-length: 36
content-type: application/json
date: Tue, 10 Jan 2023 07:37:22 GMT
```

```
server: uvicorn

{
        "category": "comp.sys.mac.hardware"
}
```

Our machine learning classifier is alive! To push this further, let's see how we can implement a simple caching mechanism using Joblib.

Caching results with Joblib

If your model takes time to make predictions, it may be interesting to cache the results: if the prediction for a particular input has already been done, it makes sense to return the same result we saved on disk rather than running the computations again. In this section, we'll learn how to do this with the help of Joblib.

Joblib provides us with a very convenient and easy-to-use tool to do this, so the implementation is quite straightforward. The main concern will be about whether we should choose standard or async functions to implement the endpoints and dependencies. This will allow us to explain some of the technical details of FastAPI in more detail.

We'll build upon the example we provided in the previous section. The first thing we must do is initialize a Joblib `Memory` class, which is the helper for caching function results. Then, we can add a decorator to the functions we want to cache. You can see this in the following example:

chapter12_caching.py
```python
memory = joblib.Memory(location="cache.joblib")

@memory.cache(ignore=["model"])
def predict(model: Pipeline, text: str) -> int:
        prediction = model.predict([text])
        return prediction[0]
```

```
https://github.com/PacktPublishing/Building-Data-Science-Applica-
tions-with-FastAPI-Second-Edition/tree/main/chapter12/chapter12_
caching.py
```

When initializing `memory`, the main argument is `location`, which is the directory path where Joblib will store the results. Joblib automatically saves cached results on the hard disk.

Then, you can see that we implemented a `predict` function, which accepts our scikit-learn model and some text input and then returns the predicted category index. This is the same prediction operation we've seen so far. Here, we extracted it from the `NewsgroupsModel` dependency class because Joblib caching is primarily designed to work with regular functions. Caching class methods is not recommended. As you can see, we simply have to add a `@memory.cache` decorator on top of this function to enable Joblib caching.

Whenever this function is called, Joblib will check whether it has the result on disk for the same arguments. If it does, it returns it directly. Otherwise, it proceeds with the regular function call.

As you can see, we added an `ignore` argument to the decorator, which allows us to tell Joblib to not take into account some arguments in the caching mechanism. Here, we excluded the `model` argument. Joblib cannot dump complex objects, such as scikit-learn estimators. This isn't a problem, though: the model doesn't change between several predictions, so we don't care about having it cached. If we make improvements to our model and deploy a new one, all we have to do is clear the whole cache so that older predictions are made again with the new model.

Now, we can tweak the `NewsgroupsModel` dependency class so that it works with this new `predict` function. You can see this in the following example:

chapter12_caching.py

```
class NewsgroupsModel:
        model: Pipeline | None = None
        targets: list[str] | None = None

        def load_model(self) -> None:
                """Loads the model"""
                model_file = os.path.join(os.path.dirname(__
file__), "newsgroups_model.joblib")
                loaded_model: tuple[Pipeline, list[str]] =
joblib.load(model_file)
                model, targets = loaded_model
                self.model = model
                self.targets = targets

        def predict(self, input: PredictionInput) ->
PredictionOutput:
                """Runs a prediction"""
                if not self.model or not self.targets:
                        raise RuntimeError("Model is
not loaded")
                prediction = predict(self.model, input.text)
```

```
            category = self.targets[prediction]
            return PredictionOutput(category=category)
```

https://github.com/PacktPublishing/Building-Data-Science-Applications-with-FastAPI-Second-Edition/tree/main/chapter12/chapter12_caching.py

In the `predict` method, we are calling the external `predict` function instead of doing so directly inside the method, taking care to pass the model and the input text as arguments. All we have to do after that is retrieve the corresponding category name and build a `PredictionOutput` object.

Finally, we have the REST API endpoints. Here, we added a `delete/cache` route so that we can clear the whole Joblib cache with an HTTP request. This can be seen in the following example:

chapter12_caching.py

```
@app.post("/prediction")
def prediction(
            output: PredictionOutput = Depends(newgroups_model.
predict),
) -> PredictionOutput:
            return output

@app.delete("/cache", status_code=status.HTTP_204_NO_CONTENT)
def delete_cache():
            memory.clear()
```

https://github.com/PacktPublishing/Building-Data-Science-Applications-with-FastAPI-Second-Edition/tree/main/chapter12/chapter12_caching.py

The `clear` method on the `memory` object removes all the Joblib cache files on the disk.

Our FastAPI application is now caching prediction results. If you make a request with the same input twice, the second response will show you the cached result. In this example, our model is fast, so you won't notice a difference in terms of execution time; however, this could be interesting with more complex models.

Choosing between standard or async functions

You may have noticed that we changed the `predict` method and the `prediction` and `delete_cache` path operation functions so that they're *standard, non-async* functions.

Since the beginning of this book, we've shown you how FastAPI completely embraces asynchronous I/O and why it's good for the performance of your applications. We've also recommended libraries that work asynchronously, such as database drivers, to leverage that power.

In some cases, however, that's not always possible. In this case, Joblib is implemented to work synchronously. Nevertheless, it's performing long I/O operations: it reads and writes cache files on the hard disk. Hence, it will block the process and won't be able to answer other requests while this is happening, as we explained in the *Asynchronous I/O* section of *Chapter 2, Python Programming Specificities*.

To solve this, FastAPI implements a neat mechanism: *if you define a path operation function or a dependency as a standard, non-async function, it'll run it in a separate thread*. This means that blocking operations, such as synchronous file reading, won't block the main process. In a sense, we could say that it mimics an asynchronous operation.

To understand this, we'll perform a simple experiment. In the following example, we are building a dummy FastAPI application with three endpoints:

- /fast, which directly returns a response
- /slow-async, a path operation defined as async, which creates a synchronous blocking operation that takes 10 seconds to run
- /slow-sync, a path operation that's defined as a standard method, which creates a synchronous blocking operation that takes 10 seconds to run

You can read the corresponding code here:

chapter12_async_not_async.py

```python
import time

from fastapi import FastAPI

app = FastAPI()

@app.get("/fast")
async def fast():
        return {"endpoint": "fast"}

@app.get("/slow-async")
async def slow_async():
        """Runs in the main process"""
        time.sleep(10)    # Blocking sync operation
        return {"endpoint": "slow-async"}

@app.get("/slow-sync")
```

```
def slow_sync():
        """Runs in a thread"""
        time.sleep(10)     # Blocking sync operation
        return {"endpoint": "slow-sync"}
```

https://github.com/PacktPublishing/Building-Data-Science-Applica-tions-with-FastAPI-Second-Edition/tree/main/chapter12/chapter12_async_not_async.py

With this simple application, the goal is to see how those blocking operations block the main process. Let's run this application with Uvicorn:

```
(venv) $ uvicorn chapter12.chapter12_async_not_async:app
```

Next, open two new terminals. In the first one, make a request to the /slow-async endpoint:

```
$ http GET http://localhost:8000/slow-async
```

Without waiting for the response, in the second terminal, make a request to the /fast endpoint:

```
$ http GET http://localhost:8000/fast
```

You'll see that you have to wait 10 seconds before you get the response for the /fast endpoint. This means that /slow-async blocked the process and prevented the server from answering the other request while this was happening.

Now, let's perform the same experiment with the /slow-sync endpoint:

```
$ http GET http://localhost:8000/slow-sync
```

And again, run the following command:

```
$ http GET http://localhost:8000/fast
```

You'll immediately get the response of /fast without having to wait for /slow-sync to finish. Since it's defined as a standard, non-async function, FastAPI will run it in a thread to prevent blocking. However, bear in mind that sending the task to a separate thread implies a small overhead, so it's important to think about the best approach to your current problem.

So, when developing with FastAPI, how can you choose between standard or async functions for path operations and dependencies? The rules of thumb for this are as follows:

- If the functions don't involve long I/O operations (file reading, network requests, and so on), define them as async.
- If they involve I/O operations, see the following:

- Try to choose libraries that are compatible with asynchronous I/O, as we saw for databases or HTTP clients. In this case, your functions will be `async`.

- If it's not possible, which is the case for Joblib caching, define them as standard functions. FastAPI will run them in a separate thread.

Since Joblib is completely synchronous at making I/O operations, we switched the path operations and the dependency method so that they were synchronous, standard methods.

In this example, the difference is not very noticeable because the I/O operations are small and fast. However, it's good to keep this in mind if you have to implement slower operations, such as for performing file uploads to cloud storage.

Summary

Congratulations! You're now able to build a fast and efficient REST API to serve your machine learning models. Thanks to Joblib, you learned how to dump a trained scikit-learn estimator into a file that's easy to load and use inside your application. We also saw an approach to caching prediction results using Joblib. Finally, we discussed how FastAPI handles synchronous operations by sending them to a separate thread to prevent blocking. While this was a bit technical, it's important to bear this aspect in mind when dealing with blocking I/O operations.

We're near the end of our FastAPI journey. Before letting you build awesome data science applications by yourself, we will provide three more chapters to push this a bit further and study more complex use cases. We'll start with an application that can perform real-time object detection, thanks to WebSockets and a computer vision model.

13

Implementing a Real-Time Object Detection System Using WebSockets with FastAPI

In the previous chapter, you learned how to create efficient REST API endpoints to make predictions with trained machine learning models. This approach covers a lot of use cases, given that we have a single observation we want to work on. In some cases, however, we may need to continuously perform predictions on a stream of input – for instance, an object detection system that works in real time with video input. This is exactly what we'll build in this chapter. How? If you remember, besides HTTP endpoints, FastAPI also has the ability to handle WebSockets endpoints, which allow us to send and receive streams of data. In this case, the browser will send into the WebSocket a stream of images from the webcam, and our application will run an object detection algorithm and send back the coordinates and label of each detected object in the image. For this task, we'll rely on **Hugging Face**, which is both a set of tools and a library of pretrained AI models.

In this chapter, we're going to cover the following main topics:

- Using a computer vision model with Hugging Face libraries
- Implementing an HTTP endpoint to perform object detection on a single image
- Sending a stream of images from the browser in a WebSocket
- Showing the object detection results in a browser

Technical requirements

For this chapter, you'll require a Python virtual environment, just as we set up in *Chapter 1, Python Development Environment Setup*.

You'll find all the code examples for this chapter in the dedicated GitHub repository at `https://github.com/PacktPublishing/Building-Data-Science-Applications-with-FastAPI-Second-Edition/tree/main/chapter13`.

Using a computer vision model with Hugging Face

Computer vision is a field of study and technology that focuses on enabling computers to extract meaningful information from digital images or videos, simulating human vision capabilities. It involves developing algorithms based on statistical methods or machine learning that allow machines to understand, analyze, and interpret visual data. A typical example of computer vision's application is object detection: a system able to detect and recognize objects in an image. This is the kind of system we'll build in this chapter.

To help us in this task, we'll use a set of tools provided by Hugging Face. Hugging Face is a company whose goal is to allow developers to use the most recent and powerful AI models quickly and easily. For this, it has built two things:

- A set of open source Python tools built on top of machine learning libraries such as PyTorch and TensorFlow. We'll use some of them in this chapter.
- An online library to share and download pretrained models for various machine learning tasks, such as computer vision or image generation.

You can read more about what it's doing on its official website: `https://huggingface.co/`.

You'll see that it'll greatly help us build a powerful and accurate object detection system in no time! To begin with, we'll install all the libraries we need for this project:

```
(venv) $ pip install "transformers[torch]" Pillow
```

The `transformers` library from Hugging Face will allow us to download and run pretrained machine learning models. Notice that we install it with the optional `torch` dependency. Hugging Face tools can be used either with PyTorch or TensorFlow, which are both very powerful ML frameworks. Here, we chose to use PyTorch. Pillow is a widely used Python library for working with images. We'll see why we need it soon.

Before starting to work with FastAPI, let's implement a simple script to run an object detection algorithm. It consists of four main steps:

1. Load an image from the disk using Pillow.
2. Load a pretrained object detection model.
3. Run the model on our image.
4. Display the results by drawing rectangles around the detected objects.

We'll go step by step through the implementation:

chapter13_object_detection.py

```
from pathlib import Path

import torch
from PIL import Image, ImageDraw, ImageFont
from transformers import YolosForObjectDetection, YolosImageProcessor

root_directory = Path(__file__).parent.parent
picture_path = root_directory / "assets" / "coffee-shop.jpg"
image = Image.open(picture_path)
```

https://github.com/PacktPublishing/Building-Data-Science-Applica-tions-with-FastAPI-Second-Edition/tree/main/chapter13/chapter13_object_detection.py

As you can see, the first step is to load our image from the disk. For this example, we use the image named coffee-shop.jpg, which is available in our examples repository at https://github.com/PacktPublishing/Building-Data-Science-Applications-with-FastAPI-Second-Edition/blob/main/assets/coffee-shop.jpg:

chapter13_object_detection.py

```
image_processor = YolosImageProcessor.from_pretrained("hustvl/yolos-tiny")
model = YolosForObjectDetection.from_pretrained("hustvl/yolos-tiny")
```

https://github.com/PacktPublishing/Building-Data-Science-Applica-tions-with-FastAPI-Second-Edition/tree/main/chapter13/chapter13_object_detection.py

Next, we load a model from Hugging Face. For this example, we chose the YOLOS model. It's a cutting-edge approach to object detection that has been trained on 118K annotated images. You can read more about the technical approach in the following Hugging Face article: https://huggingface.co/docs/transformers/model_doc/yolos. To limit the download size and preserve your computer disk space, we chose here to use the tiny version, which is a lighter version of the original model that can be run on an average machine while maintaining good accuracy. This particular version is described here on Hugging Face: https://huggingface.co/hustvl/yolos-tiny.

Notice that we instantiate two things: an **image processor** and a **model**. If you remember what we said in *Chapter 11, Introduction to Data Science in Python*, you know that we need to have a set of features that will feed our ML algorithm. Hence, the role of the image processor is to transform a raw image into a set of characteristics that are meaningful to the model.

And that's exactly what we're doing in the following lines: we create an `inputs` variable by calling `image_processor` on our image. Notice that the `return_tensors` argument is set to `pt` for PyTorch since we chose to go with PyTorch as our underlying ML framework. Then, we can feed this `inputs` variable to our model to get `outputs`:

chapter13_object_detection.py

```
inputs = image_processor(images=image, return_tensors="pt")
outputs = model(**inputs)
```

https://github.com/PacktPublishing/Building-Data-Science-Applications-with-FastAPI-Second-Edition/tree/main/chapter13/chapter13_object_detection.py

You might think that this is it for the prediction phase and that we could now display the results. However, that's not the case. The result of such algorithms is a set of multi-dimensional matrices, the famous **tensors**, which don't really make sense to us as humans. That's why we need to revert those tensors into something that makes sense for the input image. That's the purpose of the `post_process_object_detection` operation provided by `image_processor`:

chapter13_object_detection.py

```
target_sizes = torch.tensor([image.size[::-1]])
results = image_processor.post_process_object_detection(
    outputs, target_sizes=target_sizes
)[0]
```

https://github.com/PacktPublishing/Building-Data-Science-Applications-with-FastAPI-Second-Edition/tree/main/chapter13/chapter13_object_detection.py

The result of this operation is a dictionary with the following:

- `labels`: The list of labels of each detected object

- `boxes`: The coordinates of the bounding box of each detected object

- `scores`: The confidence score of the algorithm for each detected object

All we need to do then is to iterate over them so we can draw the rectangle and the corresponding label thanks to Pillow. We just show the resulting image at the end. Notice that we only consider objects with a score greater than 0.7 to limit the number of false positives:

chapter13_object_detection.py

```
draw = ImageDraw.Draw(image)
font_path = root_directory / "assets" / "OpenSans-ExtraBold.ttf"
font = ImageFont.truetype(str(font_path), 24)
for score, label, box in zip(results["scores"], results["labels"],
results["boxes"]):
    if score > 0.7:
        box_values = box.tolist()
        label = model.config.id2label[label.item()]
        draw.rectangle(box_values, outline="red", width=5)
        draw.text(box_values[0:2], label, fill="red", font=font)
image.show()
```

https://github.com/PacktPublishing/Building-Data-Science-Applica-tions-with-FastAPI-Second-Edition/tree/main/chapter13/chapter13_object_detection.py

Thanks to Pillow, we're able to draw rectangles and add a label above the detected objects. Notice that we loaded a custom font, Open Sans, which is an open font available on the web: https://fonts.google.com/specimen/Open+Sans. Let's try to run this script and see the result:

```
(venv) $ python chapter13/chapter13_object_detection.py
```

The first time it'll run, you'll see the model being downloaded. The prediction can then take a few seconds to run depending on your computer. When it's done, the resulting image should automatically open, as shown in *Figure 13.1*.

Figure 13.1 – Object detection result on a sample image

You can see that the model detected several persons in the image, along with various objects such as the couch and a chair. And that's it! Less than 30 lines of code to have a working object detection script! Hugging Face lets us harness all the power of the latest AI advances very efficiently.

Of course, our goal in this chapter is to put all this intelligence on a remote server so that we can serve this experience to thousands of users. Once again, FastAPI will be our ally here.

Implementing a REST endpoint to perform object detection on a single image

Before working with WebSockets, we'll start simple and implement, using FastAPI, a classic HTTP endpoint to accept image uploads and perform object detection on them. As you'll see, the main difference from the previous example is in how we acquire the image: instead of reading it from the disk, we get it from a file upload that we have to convert into a Pillow image object.

Besides, we'll also use the exact same pattern we saw in *Chapter 12, Creating an Efficient Prediction API Endpoint with FastAPI* – that is, having a dedicated class for our prediction model, which will be loaded during the lifespan handler.

The first thing we do in this implementation is to define Pydantic models in order to properly structure the output of our prediction model. You can see this as follows:

chapter13_api.py

```
class Object(BaseModel):
    box: tuple[float, float, float, float]
    label: str

class Objects(BaseModel):
    objects: list[Object]
```

https://github.com/PacktPublishing/Building-Data-Science-Applications-with-FastAPI-Second-Edition/tree/main/chapter13/chapter13_api.py

We have a model for a single detected object, which consists of box, a tuple of four numbers describing the coordinates of the bounding box, and label, which corresponds to the type of detected object. The Objects model is a simple structure bearing a list of objects.

We won't go through the model prediction class, as it's very similar to what we saw in the previous chapter and section. Instead, let's directly focus on the FastAPI endpoint implementation:

chapter13_api.py

```
object_detection = ObjectDetection()

@contextlib.asynccontextmanager
async def lifespan(app: FastAPI):
    object_detection.load_model()
    yield

app = FastAPI(lifespan=lifespan)

@app.post("/object-detection", response_model=Objects)
async def post_object_detection(image: UploadFile = File(...)) ->
Objects:
    image_object = Image.open(image.file)
    return object_detection.predict(image_object)
```

https://github.com/PacktPublishing/Building-Data-Science-Applications-with-FastAPI-Second-Edition/tree/main/chapter13/chapter13_api.py

Nothing very surprising here! The main point of attention is to correctly use the `UploadFile` and `File` dependencies so we get the uploaded file. If you need a refresher on this, you can check the *Form data and file uploads* section from *Chapter 3, Developing a RESTful API with FastAPI*. All we need to do then is to instantiate it as a proper Pillow image object and call our prediction model.

As we said, we don't forget to load the model inside the lifespan handler.

You can run this example using the usual Uvicorn command:

```
(venv) $ uvicorn chapter13.chapter13_api:app
```

We'll use the same coffee shop picture we already saw in the previous section. Let's upload it on our endpoint with HTTPie:

```
$ http --form POST http://localhost:8000/object-detection image@./
assets/coffee-shop.jpg
{
    "objects": [
        {
            "box": [659.8709716796875, 592.8882446289062,
792.0460815429688, 840.2132568359375],
            "label": "person"
        },
        {
            "box": [873.5499267578125, 875.7918090820312,
1649.1378173828125, 1296.362548828125],
            "label": "couch"
        }
    ]
}
```

We correctly get the list of detected objects, each one with its bounding box and label. Great! Our object detection system is now available as a web server. However, our goal is still to make a real-time system: thanks to WebSockets, we'll be able to handle a stream of images.

Implementing a WebSocket to perform object detection on a stream of images

One of the main benefits of WebSockets, as we saw in *Chapter 8, Defining WebSockets for Two-Way Interactive Communication in FastAPI*, is that it opens a full-duplex communication channel between the client and the server. Once the connection is established, messages can be passed quickly without having to go through all the steps of the HTTP protocol. Therefore, it's much more suited to sending a lot of data in real time.

The point here will be to implement a WebSocket endpoint that is able to both accept image data and run object detection on it. The main challenge here will be to handle a phenomenon known as **backpressure**. Put simply, we'll receive more images from the browser than the server is able to handle because of the time needed to run the detection algorithm. Thus, we'll have to work with a queue (or buffer) of limited size and drop some images along the way to handle the stream in near real time.

We'll go step by step through the implementation:

app.py

```python
async def receive(websocket: WebSocket, queue: asyncio.Queue):
    while True:
        bytes = await websocket.receive_bytes()
        try:
            queue.put_nowait(bytes)
        except asyncio.QueueFull:
            pass

async def detect(websocket: WebSocket, queue: asyncio.Queue):
    while True:
        bytes = await queue.get()
        image = Image.open(io.BytesIO(bytes))
        objects = object_detection.predict(image)
        await websocket.send_json(objects.dict())
```

https://github.com/PacktPublishing/Building-Data-Science-Applications-with-FastAPI-Second-Edition/tree/main/chapter13/websocket_object_detection/app.py

We defined two tasks: `receive` and `detect`. The first one is waiting for raw bytes from the WebSocket, while the second one is performing the detection and sending the result, exactly as we saw in the last section.

The key here is to use the `asyncio.Queue` object. This is a convenient structure allowing us to queue some data in memory and retrieve it in a **first in, first out** (**FIFO**) strategy. We are able to set a limit on the number of elements we store in the queue: this is how we'll be able to limit the number of images we handle.

The `receive` function receives data and puts it at the end of the queue. When working with `asyncio.Queue`, we have two methods to put a new element in the queue: `put` and `put_nowait`. If the queue is full, the first one will wait until there is room in the queue. This is not what we want here: we want to drop images that we won't be able to handle in time. With `put_nowait`, the `QueueFull` exception is raised if the queue is full. In this case, we just pass and drop the data.

On the other hand, the `detect` function pulls the first message from the queue and runs its detection before sending the result. Notice that since we get raw image bytes directly, we have to wrap them with `io.BytesIO` to make it acceptable for Pillow.

The WebSocket implementation in itself is similar to what we saw in *Chapter 8, Defining WebSockets for Two-Way Interactive Communication in FastAPI*. We are scheduling both tasks and waiting until one of them has stopped. Since they both run an infinite loop, this will happen when the WebSocket is disconnected:

app.py

```
@app.websocket("/object-detection")
async def ws_object_detection(websocket: WebSocket):
    await websocket.accept()
    queue: asyncio.Queue = asyncio.Queue(maxsize=1)
    receive_task = asyncio.create_task(receive(websocket, queue))
    detect_task = asyncio.create_task(detect(websocket, queue))
    try:
        done, pending = await asyncio.wait(
            {receive_task, detect_task},
            return_when=asyncio.FIRST_COMPLETED,
        )
        for task in pending:
            task.cancel()
        for task in done:
            task.result()
    except WebSocketDisconnect:
        pass
```

https://github.com/PacktPublishing/Building-Data-Science-Applications-with-FastAPI-Second-Edition/tree/main/chapter13/websocket_object_detection/app.py

> **Serving static files**
>
> If you look at the full implementation of the preceding example, you'll notice that we defined two more things in our server: an `index` endpoint, which just returns the `index.html` file, and a `StaticFiles` app, which is mounted under the `/assets` path. Both of them are here to allow our FastAPI application to directly serve our HTML and JavaScript code. This way, browsers will be able to query those files on the same server.
>
> The key takeaway of this is that even though FastAPI was designed to build REST APIs, it's also perfectly able to serve HTML and static files.

Our backend is now ready! Let's now see how to use its power from a browser.

Sending a stream of images from the browser in a WebSocket

In this section, we'll see how you can capture images from the webcam in the browser and send them through a WebSocket. Since it mainly involves JavaScript code, it's admittedly a bit beyond the scope of this book, but it's necessary to make the application work fully.

The first step is to enable a camera input in the browser, open the WebSocket connection, pick a camera image, and send it through the WebSocket. Basically, it'll work like this: thanks to the `MediaDevices` browser API, we'll be able to list all the camera inputs available on the device. With this, we'll build a selection form so the user can select the camera they want to use. You can see the concrete JavaScript implementation in the following code:

script.js

```js
window.addEventListener('DOMContentLoaded', (event) => {
  const video = document.getElementById('video');
  const canvas = document.getElementById('canvas');
  const cameraSelect = document.getElementById('camera-select');
  let socket;

  // List available cameras and fill select
  navigator.mediaDevices.getUserMedia({ audio: true, video: true
}).then(() => {
    navigator.mediaDevices.enumerateDevices().then((devices) => {
      for (const device of devices) {
        if (device.kind === 'videoinput' && device.deviceId) {
          const deviceOption = document.createElement('option');
          deviceOption.value = device.deviceId;
          deviceOption.innerText = device.label;
          cameraSelect.appendChild(deviceOption);
        }
      }
    });
  });
});
```

https://github.com/PacktPublishing/Building-Data-Science-Applications-with-FastAPI-Second-Edition/tree/main/chapter13/websocket_object_detection/assets/script.js

Once the user submits the form, we call a `startObjectDetection` function with the selected camera. Most of the actual detection logic is implemented in this function:

script.js

```
// Start object detection on the selected camera on submit
document.getElementById('form-connect').addEventListener('submit',
(event) => {
  event.preventDefault();

  // Close previous socket is there is one
  if (socket) {
    socket.close();
  }

  const deviceId = cameraSelect.selectedOptions[0].value;
  socket = startObjectDetection(video, canvas, deviceId);
});
});
```

https://github.com/PacktPublishing/Building-Data-Science-Applications-with-FastAPI-Second-Edition/tree/main/chapter13/websocket_object_detection/assets/script.js

Let's have a look at the `startObjectDetection` function in the following code block. First, we establish a connection with the WebSocket. Once it's opened, we can start to get an image stream from the selected camera. For this, we use the `MediaDevices` API to start capturing video and display the output in an HTML `<video>` element. You can read all the details about the `MediaDevices` API in the MDN documentation: https://developer.mozilla.org/en-US/docs/Web/API/MediaDevices:

script.js

```
const startObjectDetection = (video, canvas, deviceId) => {
  const socket = new WebSocket(`ws://${location.host}/object-detection`);
  let intervalId;

  // Connection opened
  socket.addEventListener('open', function () {

    // Start reading video from device
    navigator.mediaDevices.getUserMedia({
      audio: false,
      video: {
```

```
            deviceId,
            width: { max: 640 },
            height: { max: 480 },
        },
    }).then(function (stream) {
        video.srcObject = stream;
        video.play().then(() => {
            // Adapt overlay canvas size to the video size
            canvas.width = video.videoWidth;
            canvas.height = video.videoHeight;
```

https://github.com/PacktPublishing/Building-Data-Science-Appli-
cations-with-FastAPI-Second-Edition/tree/main/chapter13/websock-
et_object_detection/assets/script.js

Then, as shown in the next code block, we launch a repetitive task that captures an image from the video input and sends it to the server. To do this, we have to use a <canvas> element, an HTML tag dedicated to graphics drawing. It comes with a complete JavaScript API so that we can programmatically draw images in it. There, we'll be able to draw the current video image and convert it into valid JPEG bytes. If you want to know more about this, MDN gives a very detailed tutorial on <canvas>: https://developer.mozilla.org/en-US/docs/Web/API/Canvas_API/Tutorial:

script.js

```
        // Send an image in the WebSocket every 42 ms
        intervalId = setInterval(() => {

            // Create a virtual canvas to draw current video image
            const canvas = document.createElement('canvas');
            const ctx = canvas.getContext('2d');
            canvas.width = video.videoWidth;
            canvas.height = video.videoHeight;
            ctx.drawImage(video, 0, 0);

            // Convert it to JPEG and send it to the WebSocket
            canvas.toBlob((blob) => socket.send(blob), 'image/jpeg');
        }, IMAGE_INTERVAL_MS);
    });
```

```
    });
  });
```

https://github.com/PacktPublishing/Building-Data-Science-Appli-
cations-with-FastAPI-Second-Edition/tree/main/chapter13/websock-
et_object_detection/assets/script.js

Notice that we limit the size of the video input to 640 by 480 pixels, so that we don't blow up the server with images that are too big. Besides, we set the interval to run every 42 milliseconds (the value is set in the IMAGE_INTERVAL_MS constant), which is roughly equivalent to 24 images per second.

Finally, we wire the event listener to handle the messages received from the WebSocket. It calls the drawObjects function, which we'll detail in the next section:

script.js

```
  // Listen for messages
  socket.addEventListener('message', function (event) {
    drawObjects(video, canvas, JSON.parse(event.data));
  });

  // Stop the interval and video reading on close
  socket.addEventListener('close', function () {
    window.clearInterval(intervalId);
    video.pause();
  });

  return socket;
};
```

https://github.com/PacktPublishing/Building-Data-Science-Appli-
cations-with-FastAPI-Second-Edition/tree/main/chapter13/websock-
et_object_detection/assets/script.js

Showing the object detection results in the browser

Now that we are able to send input images to the server, we have to show the result of the detection in the browser. In a similar way to what we showed in the *Using a computer vision model with Hugging Face* section, we'll draw a green rectangle around the detected objects, along with their label. Thus, we have to find a way to take the rectangle coordinates sent by the server and draw them in the browser.

To do this, we'll once again use a `<canvas>` element. This time, it'll be visible to the user and we'll draw the rectangles using it. The trick here is to use CSS so that this element overlays the video: this way, the rectangles will be shown right on top of the video and the corresponding objects. You can see the HTML code here:

index.html

```
<body>
  <div class="container">
    <h1 class="my-3">Chapter 13 - Real time object detection</h1>
    <form id="form-connect">
      <div class="input-group mb-3">
        <select id="camera-select"></select>
        <button class="btn btn-success" type="submit" id="button-
start">Start</button>
      </div>
    </form>
    <div class="position-relative" style="width: 640px; height:
480px;">
      <video id="video"></video>
      <canvas id="canvas" class="position-absolute top-0 start-0"></
canvas>
    </div>
  </div>

  <script src="/assets/script.js"></script>
</body>
```

```
https://github.com/PacktPublishing/Building-Data-Science-Appli-
cations-with-FastAPI-Second-Edition/tree/main/chapter13/websock-
et_object_detection/index.html
```

We are using CSS classes from Bootstrap, a very common CSS library with a lot of helpers like this. Basically, we set the canvas with absolute positioning and put it at the top left so that it covers the video element.

The key now is to use the Canvas API to draw the rectangles according to the received coordinates. This is the purpose of the `drawObjects` function, which is shown in the next sample code block:

script.js

```
const drawObjects = (video, canvas, objects) => {
  const ctx = canvas.getContext('2d');

  ctx.width = video.videoWidth;
  ctx.height = video.videoHeight;
```

```
ctx.beginPath();
ctx.clearRect(0, 0, ctx.width, ctx.height);
for (const object of objects.objects) {
  const [x1, y1, x2, y2] = object.box;
  const label = object.label;
  ctx.strokeStyle = '#49fb35';
  ctx.beginPath();
  ctx.rect(x1, y1, x2 - x1, y2 - y1);
  ctx.stroke();

  ctx.font = 'bold 16px sans-serif';
  ctx.fillStyle = '#ff0000';
  ctx.fillText(label, x1 - 5 , y1 - 5);
}
};
```

https://github.com/PacktPublishing/Building-Data-Science-Appli-
cations-with-FastAPI-Second-Edition/tree/main/chapter13/websock-
et_object_detection/assets/script.js

With the <canvas> element, we can use a 2D context to draw things in the object. Notice that we first clean everything to remove the rectangles from the previous detection. Then, we loop through all the detected objects and draw a rectangle with the given coordinates: x1, y1, x2, and y2. Finally, we take care of drawing the label slightly above the rectangle.

Our system is now complete! *Figure 13.2* gives you an overview of the file structure we've implemented.

Figure 13.2 – Object detection application structure

It's time to give it a try! We can start it using the usual Uvicorn command:

```
(venv) $ uvicorn chapter13.websocket_object_detection.app:app
```

You can access the application in your browser with the address `http://localhost:8000`. As we said in the previous section, the `index` endpoint will be called and will return our `index.html` file.

You'll see an interface inviting you to choose the camera you want to use, as shown in *Figure 13.3*:

Figure 13.3 – Webcam selection for the object detection web application

Select the webcam you wish to use and click on **Start**. The video output will show up, object detection will start via the WebSocket, and green rectangles will be drawn around the detected objects. We show this in *Figure 13.4*:

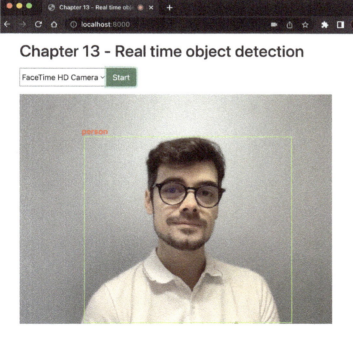

Figure 13.4 – Running the object detection web application

It works! We brought the intelligence of our Python system right to the user's web browser. This is just an example of what you could achieve using WebSockets and ML algorithms, but this definitely enables you to create near real-time experiences for your users.

Summary

In this chapter, we showed how WebSockets can help us bring a more interactive experience to users. Thanks to the pretrained models provided by the Hugging Face community, we were able to quickly implement an object detection system. Then, we integrated it into a WebSocket endpoint with the help of FastAPI. Finally, by using a modern JavaScript API, we sent video input and displayed algorithm results directly in the browser. All in all, a project like this might sound complex to make at first, but we saw that powerful tools such as FastAPI enable us to get results in a very short time and with very comprehensible source code.

Until now, in our different examples and projects, we assumed the ML model we used was fast enough to be run directly in an API endpoint or a WebSocket task. However, that's not always the case. In some cases, the algorithm is so complex it takes a couple of minutes to run. If we run this kind of algorithm directly inside an API endpoint, the user would have to wait a long time before getting a response. Not only would this be strange for them but this would also quickly block the whole server, preventing other users from using the API. To solve this, we'll need a companion for our API server: a worker.

In the next chapter, we'll study a concrete example of this challenge: we'll build our very own AI system to generate images from a text prompt!

14

Creating a Distributed Text-to-Image AI System Using the Stable Diffusion Model

Until now, in this book, we've built APIs where all the operations were computed inside the request handling. Said another way, before they could get their response, the user had to wait for the server to do everything we had defined: request validation, database queries, ML predictions, and so on. However, this behavior is not always desired or possible.

A typical example is email notifications. It happens quite often in a web application that we need to send an email to the user because they just registered or they performed a specific action. To do this, the server needs to send a request to an email server so the email can be sent. This operation could take a few milliseconds. If we do this inside the request handling, the response will be delayed until we send the email. This is not a very good experience since the user doesn't really care how and when the email is sent. This example is typical of what we usually call **background operations**: things that need to be done in our application but don't require direct user interaction.

Another case is when the user requests an expensive operation that can't be done in a reasonable time. It's usually the case for complex data exports or heavy AI models. In this context, the user would like to get the result directly, but doing this in the request handler would block the server process until it's done. If lots of users were requesting this kind of operation, it would quickly make our server unresponsive. Besides, some network infrastructure such as proxy or web clients, like browsers, have quite strict timeout settings, meaning they will usually cancel an operation if it takes too much time to respond.

To solve this, we'll introduce a typical architecture for web applications: **web-queue-worker**. As we'll see in this chapter, we'll defer the most expensive, long operations to a background process, a **worker**. To show you this architecture in action, we'll build our very own AI system to generate images from text prompts using the **Stable Diffusion** model.

In this chapter, we're going to cover the following main topics:

- Using the Stable Diffusion model with Hugging Face Diffusers to generate images from text prompts
- Implementing a worker process using Dramatiq and an image-generation task
- Storing and serving files in object storage

Technical requirements

For this chapter, you'll require a Python virtual environment, just as we set up in *Chapter 1, Python Development Environment Setup.*

To run the Stable Diffusion model correctly, we recommend you have a recent computer equipped with at least 16 GB of RAM and, ideally, a dedicated GPU with 8 GB of VRAM. For Mac users, recent models equipped with the M1 Pro or M2 Pro chips are also a good fit. If you don't have that kind of machine, don't worry: we'll show you ways to run the system anyway – the only drawback is that image generation will be slow and show poor results.

For running the worker, you'll need a running **Redis server** on your local computer. The easiest way is to run it as a Docker container. If you've never used Docker before, we recommend you read the *Getting started* tutorial in the official documentation at https://docs.docker.com/get-started/. Once done, you'll be able to run a Redis server with this simple command:

```
$ docker run -d --name worker-redis -p 6379:6379 redis
```

You'll find all the code examples of this chapter in the dedicated GitHub repository at https://github.com/PacktPublishing/Building-Data-Science-Applications-with-FastAPI-Second-Edition/tree/main/chapter14.

Generating images from text prompts with Stable Diffusion

Recently, a new generation of AI tools has emerged and fascinated the whole world: image-generation models, such as DALL-E or Midjourney. Those models are trained on huge amounts of image data and are able to generate completely new images from a simple text prompt. These AI models are very good use cases for background workers: they take seconds or even minutes to process, and they need lots of resources in the CPU, RAM, and even the GPU.

To build our system, we'll rely on Stable Diffusion, a very popular image-generation model that was released in 2022. This model is available publicly and can be run on a modern gaming computer. As we did in the previous chapter, we'll rely on Hugging Face tools for both downloading the model and running it.

Let's first install the required tools:

```
(venv) $ pip install accelerate diffusers
```

We're now ready to use diffuser models thanks to Hugging Face.

Implementing the model in a Python script

In the following example, we'll show you the implementation of a class able to instantiate the model and run an image generation. Once again, we'll apply our lazy loading pattern with separate load_model and generate methods. Let's first focus on load_model:

text_to_image.py

```python
class TextToImage:
    pipe: StableDiffusionPipeline | None = None

    def load_model(self) -> None:
        # Enable CUDA GPU
        if torch.cuda.is_available():
            device = "cuda"
        # Enable Apple Silicon (M1) GPU
        elif torch.backends.mps.is_available():
            device = "mps"
        # Fallback to CPU
        else:
            device = "cpu"

        pipe = StableDiffusionPipeline.from_pretrained("runwayml/
stable-diffusion-v1-5")
        pipe.to(device)
        self.pipe = pipe
```

https://github.com/PacktPublishing/Building-Data-Science-Applications-with-FastAPI-Second-Edition/tree/main/chapter14/basic/text_to_image.py

The first part of this method aims to find the most efficient way to run the model given your computer. These diffusion models are faster when run on the GPU – that's why we check first if there are CUDA (NVIDIA GPU) or MPS (Apple Silicon) devices available. If there are none, we fall back to the CPU.

Then, we simply have to create a StableDiffusionPipeline pipeline, as provided by Hugging Face. We simply have to set the model we want to download from the hub. For this example, we chose runwayml/stable-diffusion-v1-5. You can find its details on Hugging Face: https://huggingface.co/runwayml/stable-diffusion-v1-5.

We can now focus on the `generate` method:

text_to_image.py

```python
    def generate(
        self,
        prompt: str,
        *,
        negative_prompt: str | None = None,
        num_steps: int = 50,
        callback: Callable[[int, int, torch.FloatTensor], None] | None
    = None,
    )    Image.Image:
        if not self.pipe:
            raise RuntimeError("Pipeline is not loaded")
        return self.pipe(
            prompt,
            negative_prompt=negative_prompt,
            num_inference_steps=num_steps,
            guidance_scale=9.0,
            callback=callback,
        ).images[0]
```

https://github.com/PacktPublishing/Building-Data-Science-Appli-
cations-with-FastAPI-Second-Edition/tree/main/chapter14/basic/
text_to_image.py

You can see it accepts four parameters:

- `prompt`, which is, of course, the text prompt describing the image we want to generate.

- `negative_prompt`, which is an optional prompt to tell the model what we absolutely don't want.

- `num_steps`, which is the number of inference steps the model should run. More steps lead to a better image, but each iteration delays the inference. The default, `50`, should provide a good balance between speed and quality.

- `callback`, which is an optional function that will be called at each iteration step. This is helpful to be informed about the progress of the generation and possibly execute more logic, such as saving the progress in a database.

> **What does the asterisk (*) in the method signature mean?**
>
> You may have noticed the asterisk, *, in the method signature. It tells Python that the arguments coming after this symbol should only be treated as keyword-only arguments. Said another way, you can only call them like this: `.generate("PROMPT", negative_prompt="NEGATIVE", num_steps=10)`.
>
> While not necessary, it's a way to keep your functions clear and self-explanatory. It's especially true if you develop classes or functions that are meant to be used by other developers.
>
> Another syntax also exists to force arguments to be positional-only, using a slash (`/`) symbol. You can read more about it here: `https://docs.python.org/3/whatsnew/3.8.html#positional-only-parameters`.

All we have to do then is to pass those parameters to `pipe`. There are a lot more parameters for you to tune if needed, but the default ones should give you quite good results. You can find the whole list of them in the Hugging Face documentation: `https://huggingface.co/docs/diffusers/api/pipelines/stable_diffusion/text2img#diffusers.StableDiffusionPipeline.__call__`. This `pipe` object is able to generate several images per prompt, that's why the result of this operation is a list of Pillow images. The default here is to generate only one image, so we directly return the first one.

And that's about it! Once again, Hugging Face makes our lives really easy by allowing us to run cutting-edge models in dozens of lines!

Executing the Python script

We bet that you're eager to try it yourself – that's why we added a small `main` script at the bottom of our example:

---

text_to_image.py

```python
if __name__ == "__main__":
    text_to_image = TextToImage()
    text_to_image.load_model()

    def callback(step: int, _timestep, _tensor):
        print(f"🪄 Step {step}")

    image = text_to_image.generate(
        "A Renaissance castle in the Loire Valley",
        negative_prompt="low quality, ugly",
        callback=callback,
```

```
    )
    image.save("output.png")
```

```
https://github.com/PacktPublishing/Building-Data-Science-Appli-
cations-with-FastAPI-Second-Edition/tree/main/chapter14/basic/
text_to_image.py
```

This small script instantiates our `TextToImage` class, loads the model, and generates an image before saving it to disk. We also define a dummy callback function so you can see how it works.

When you run this script for the first time, you'll notice that Hugging Face downloads files of several gigabytes to your computer: that's the Stable Diffusion model, and it's indeed quite big!

Then, the inference will start. You'll see a progress bar showing you how many inference steps are left, along with the `print` statement from our callback, as shown in *Figure 14.1*.

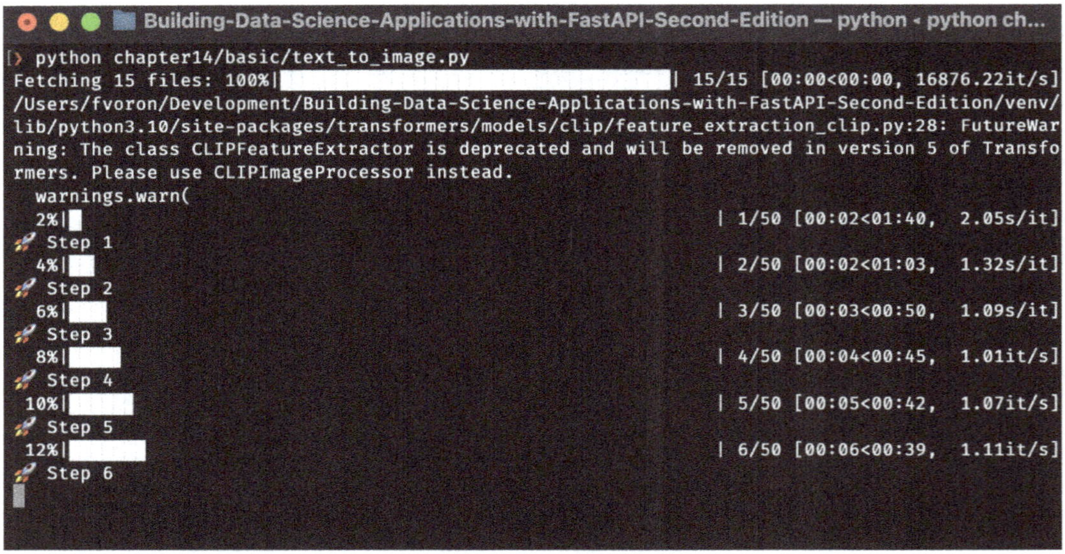

Figure 14.1 – Stable Diffusion generating an image

How much time does it take to generate a single image?

We've run several tests on different types of computers. With a modern NVIDIA GPU with 8 GB of RAM or a Mac with an M1 Pro chip, the model is able to generate an image with 50 inference steps in *around a minute*, with reasonable RAM usage. When run on a CPU, it takes around *5 to 10 minutes* and eats up to 16 GB of RAM.

If the inference is really too slow on your computer, you can try to reduce the `num_steps` parameter.

When the inference is done, you'll find your generated image on the disk along with your script. *Figure 14.2* shows an example of such a result. Nice, isn't it?

Figure 14.2 – Result of a Stable Diffusion image generation

We now have the fundamental brick of our AI system. Now, we need to build an API so users can generate their own images. As we've just seen, generating a single image takes some time. As we said in the introduction, we'll need to introduce a web-queue-worker architecture to make this system reliable and scalable.

Creating a Dramatiq worker and defining an image-generation task

As we mentioned in the introduction of this chapter, it's not conceivable to run our image-generation model directly on our REST API server. As we saw in the previous section, the operation can take several minutes and consumes a massive amount of memory. To solve this, we'll define another process, apart from the server process, that'll take care of this image-generation task: the **worker**. In essence, a worker can be any program whose role is to compute a task in the background.

In web development, this concept usually implies a bit more than this. A worker is a process running continuously in the background, waiting for incoming tasks. The tasks are usually sent by the web server, which asks for specific operations given the user actions.

Therefore, we see that we need a communication channel between the web server and the worker. That's the role of the **queue**. It'll accept and stack messages coming from the web server and make them available to read for the worker. That's the web-queue-worker architecture. To better understand it, *Figure 14.4* shows you the schema of such an architecture.

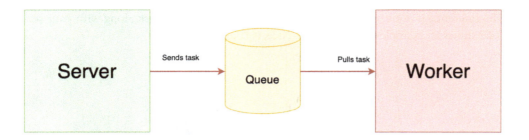

Figure 14.3 – Schema of web-queue-worker architecture

Does it ring a bell? Yes, it's very similar to what we saw in *Chapter 8*, in the *Handling multiple WebSocket connections and broadcasting messages* section. Actually, this is the same principle: we solve the problem of having separate processes by having a single central data source.

The great feature of this architecture is that it scales very easily. Imagine your application is a huge success and thousands of users want to generate images: a single worker wouldn't be able to meet the demand. Actually, all we need to do is to start more worker processes. Since there is a single message broker in the architecture, each worker will pull messages as they come, allowing tasks to be processed in parallel. They don't even need to be on the same physical machine. This is shown in *Figure 14.4*.

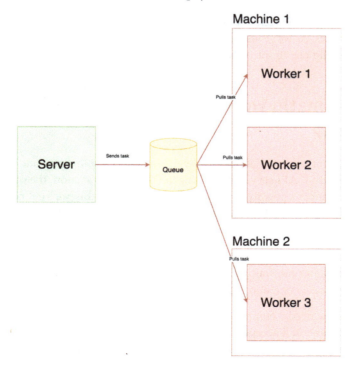

Figure 14.4 – Web-queue-worker architecture with multiple workers

In Python, there are several libraries to help implement a worker. They provide the required tools to define tasks, schedule them in the queue, and run a process, pulling them and executing them. In this book, we'll use Dramatiq, a lightweight but powerful and modern background task-processing library. As we did in *Chapter 8*, we'll use Redis as a message broker.

Implementing a worker

As usual, we'll start by installing the required dependency. Run the following command:

```
(venv) $ pip install "dramatiq[redis]"
```

This will install Dramatiq with the required dependencies to talk with a Redis broker.

In a minimal example, setting up a Dramatiq worker involves two things:

1. Setting the broker type and URL.

2. Defining tasks by wrapping functions with the @dramatiq.actor decorator.

It works very well for the vast majority of tasks, such as sending emails or generating exports.

In our case, however, we need to load the heavy Stable Diffusion model. As we usually do in the FastAPI server with the startup event, we want to do this only when the process is actually started. To do this with Dramatiq, we implement a *middleware*. They allow us to plug custom logic at several key events in the lifetime of the worker, including when it's started.

You can see the implementation of our custom middleware in the following sample:

worker.py

```
class TextToImageMiddleware(Middleware):
    def __init__(self) -> None:
        super().__init__()
        self.text_to_image = TextToImage()

    def after_process_boot(self, broker):
        self.text_to_image.load_model()
        return super().after_process_boot(broker)


text_to_image_middleware = TextToImageMiddleware()
redis_broker = RedisBroker(host="localhost")
redis_broker.add_middleware(text_to_image_middleware)
dramatiq.set_broker(redis_broker)
```

https://github.com/PacktPublishing/Building-Data-Science-Applications-with-FastAPI-Second-Edition/tree/main/chapter14/basic/worker.py

We define a `TextToImageMiddleware` class whose role is to bear an instance of `TextToImage`, the image generation service we defined in the previous section. It inherits from the `Middleware` class of Dramatiq. The key thing here is the `after_process_boot` method. It's one of the event hooks exposed by Dramatiq, allowing us to plug our own logic. Here, we tell it to load the Stable Diffusion model when the worker process has booted up. You can see the full list of supported hooks in the official documentation: `https://dramatiq.io/reference.html#middleware`.

The next lines allow us to configure our worker. We first instantiate an instance of our custom middleware. Then, we create a broker class corresponding to the technology we chose; in our case, Redis. We take care of adding our middleware to this broker before telling Dramatiq to use it. Our worker is now completely configured to connect to a Redis broker and load our model at startup.

Now, let's see how we can define a task to generate images:

worker.py

```python
@dramatiq.actor()
def text_to_image_task(
    prompt: str, *, negative_prompt: str | None = None, num_steps: int
= 50
):
    image = text_to_image_middleware.text_to_image.generate(
        prompt, negative_prompt=negative_prompt, num_steps=num_steps
    )
    image.save(f"{uuid.uuid4()}.png")
```

`https://github.com/PacktPublishing/Building-Data-Science-Applications-with-FastAPI-Second-Edition/tree/main/chapter14/basic/worker.py`

The implementation is straightforward: Dramatiq tasks are actually plain functions that we decorated with `@dramatiq.actor`. We can define arguments as we would for any other function. However, there is an important pitfall to avoid here: when we schedule tasks from our server, the arguments will have to be stored in the queue storage. Thus, *Dramatiq will internally serialize the arguments to JSON*. It means your task arguments must be serializable data – you can't have arbitrary Python objects, such as class instances or functions.

The function body calls our `TextToImage` instance loaded in `text_to_image_middleware`, before saving the image to the disk. To avoid file overrides, we choose here to generate a **UUID**, a **Universally Unique IDentifier**. It's a big random string that's guaranteed to be unique in each generation. Thanks to this, we can safely use it as a filename and be sure it won't already exist on our disk.

That's it for the worker implementation.

Starting the worker

We don't have the web server code to call it yet, but we can already try it manually. First, make sure you have a Redis server started, as explained in the *Technical requirements* section. Then, we can start the Dramatiq worker using the following command:

```
(venv) $ dramatiq -p 1 -t 1 chapter14.basic.worker
```

Dramatiq comes with command-line tools to take care of starting the worker processes. The main positional argument is the dotted path of your worker module. It's similar to what we do with Uvicorn. We also set two optional parameters, -p and -t. They control the number of processes and threads Dramatiq will start. By default, it starts 10 processes, each one with 8 threads. This means there will be 80 workers able to pull and execute tasks. While this default is good for common needs, it doesn't work with our Stable Diffusion model for two reasons:

- Each thread in a process shares the same memory space. This means that if two (or more) threads try to generate an image, they will read and write on the same objects in memory. For our model here, this causes concurrency problems. We say that it's *not thread-safe*. Hence, each process should start only one thread: that's the point of the -t 1 option.

- Each process should load the model in memory. This means that if we start 8 processes, we'll load the model 8 times. As we saw earlier, it takes quite a huge amount of memory, so doing this would probably blow up your computer's memory. To be safe here, we start only one process thanks to the -p 1 option. If you want to try parallelization and see that our worker is able to generate two images in parallel, you can try -p 2 to spawn two processes. Make sure your computer can handle it though!

If you run the preceding command, you should see an output like this:

```
[2023-02-02 08:52:11,479] [PID 44348] [MainThread] [dramatiq.
MainProcess] [INFO] Dramatiq '1.13.0' is booting up.
Fetching 19 files:    0%|            | 0/19 [00:00<?, ?it/s]
Fetching 19 files: 100%|███████████| 19/19 [00:00<00:00, 13990.83it/s]
[2023-02-02 08:52:11,477] [PID 44350] [MainThread] [dramatiq.
WorkerProcess(0)] [INFO] Worker process is ready for action.
[2023-02-02 08:52:11,578] [PID 44355] [MainThread] [dramatiq.
ForkProcess(0)] [INFO] Fork process 'dramatiq.middleware.prometheus:_
run_exposition_server' is ready for action.
```

You can see the output of the Stable Diffusion pipeline checking whether the model files are downloaded before the worker is fully started. This means that it has been correctly loaded.

Scheduling tasks in the worker

We can now try to schedule tasks in our worker. For this, we can start a Python interactive shell and import the `task` function. Open a new command line and run the following commands (make sure you enabled your Python virtual environment):

```
(venv) $ python
>>> from chapter14.basic.worker import text_to_image_task
>>> text_to_image_task.send("A Renaissance castle in the Loire
Valley")
Message(queue_name='default', actor_name='text_to_image_task',
args=('A Renaissance castle in the Loire Valley',), kwargs={},
options={'redis_message_id': '663df44a-cfc1-4f13-8457-05d8181290c1'},
message_id='bf57d112-6c20-49bc-a926-682ca43ea7ea', message_
timestamp=1675324585644)
```

That's it – we scheduled a task in the worker! Notice how we used the `send` method on our `task` function instead of calling it directly: this is how you tell Dramatiq to send it in the queue.

If you go back to your worker terminal, you'll see the Stable Diffusion output generating the image. After a moment, you'll have your image saved on disk. You can also try to send two tasks in a row in a short time. You'll find that Dramatiq processes them one after the other.

Great job! We have our background process ready and are even able to schedule tasks in it. The next step now is to implement a REST API so the users can ask for image generation themselves.

Implementing the REST API

To schedule tasks in our worker, we need a safe interface users can interact with. A REST API is a good choice for this, since it can be easily integrated into any software, such as a website or a mobile app. In this section, we'll very quickly review a simple API endpoint we implemented to send image-generation tasks into our queue. Here's the implementation:

api.py

```
class ImageGenerationInput(BaseModel):
    prompt: str
    negative_prompt: str | None
    num_steps: int = Field(50, gt=0, le=50)


class ImageGenerationOutput(BaseModel):
    task_id: UUID4


app = FastAPI()
```

```
@app.post(
    "/image-generation",
    response_model=ImageGenerationOutput,
    status_code=status.HTTP_202_ACCEPTED,
)
async def post_image_generation(input: ImageGenerationInput) ->
ImageGenerationOutput:
    task: Message = text_to_image_task.send(
        input.prompt, negative_prompt=input.negative_prompt, num_
steps=input.num_steps
    )
    return ImageGenerationOutput(task_id=task.message_id)
```

https://github.com/PacktPublishing/Building-Data-Science-Applica-
tions-with-FastAPI-Second-Edition/tree/main/chapter14/basic/api.
py

If you have followed along since the beginning of this book, this shouldn't surprise you. We took care of defining proper Pydantic models to structure and validate the endpoint payload. This data is then directly used to send a task to Dramatiq, as we saw in the previous section.

In this simple implementation, the output consists only of the message ID, which is automatically assigned to each task by Dramatiq. Notice that we set the HTTP status code to 202, which means *Accepted*. Semantically, it means the server understood and accepted the request, but the processing has not yet finished or even started. It's specifically designed for cases where the processing is done in the background, which is exactly our case here.

If you start both the worker and this API, you'll be able to trigger image generations with an HTTP call.

You're probably wondering here: *That's nice… But how will the users retrieve the result? How will they know whether the task is done?*. You're right – we didn't talk at all about this problem! Actually, there are two aspects to solve here: how do we keep track of the pending tasks and their execution? How do we store and serve the resulting images? That's the subject of the next section.

Storing results in a database and object storage

In the previous section, we showed how to implement a background worker to do the heavy computation and an API to schedule tasks on this worker. However, we are still missing two important aspects: the user doesn't have any way to know the progress of the task nor to retrieve the final result. Let's fix this!

Sharing data between the worker and the API

As we've seen, the worker is a program running in the background executing the computations the API has asked it to do. However, the worker doesn't have any way to talk with the API server. That's expected: since there could be any number of server processes, and since they could even run on different physical servers, processes cannot communicate directly. It's always the same problem of having a central data source on which processes can write and read data.

Actually, the first approach to solve the lack of communication between the API and the worker could be to use the same broker we use to schedule tasks: the worker could write results in the broker, and the API could read from it. This is something possible with most background task libraries, including Dramatiq. However, this solution has some limitations, the principal one being the limited time we can retain the data. Brokers, such as Redis, are not really suited to storing data reliably for a long period. At some point, we'll need to erase the most ancient data to limit memory usage.

Yet, we already know of something able to store structured data efficiently: a database, of course! That's the approach we'll show here. By having a central database where we'll store our image generation requests and results, we'll be able to share information between the worker and the API. For this, we'll reuse a lot of techniques we showed in the *Communicating with a SQL database with SQLAlchemy ORM* section of *Chapter 6*. Let's go!

Defining an SQLAlchemy model

The first step is defining an SQLAlchemy model to store a single image-generation task. You can see it as follows:

models.py

```
class GeneratedImage(Base):
    __tablename__ = "generated_images"

    id: Mapped[int] = mapped_column(Integer, primary_key=True,
autoincrement=True)
    created_at: Mapped[datetime] = mapped_column(
        DateTime, nullable=False, default=datetime.now
    )
    progress: Mapped[int] = mapped_column(Integer, nullable=False,
default=0)

    prompt: Mapped[str] = mapped_column(Text, nullable=False)
    negative_prompt: Mapped[str | None] = mapped_column(Text,
nullable=True)
    num_steps: Mapped[int] = mapped_column(Integer, nullable=False)
```

```
    file_name: Mapped[str | None] = mapped_column(String(255),
nullable=True)
```

https://github.com/PacktPublishing/Building-Data-Science-Applica-
tions-with-FastAPI-Second-Edition/tree/main/chapter14/complete/
models.py

As usual, we define an auto-incremented ID as the primary key. We also add `prompt`, `negative_prompt`, and `num_steps` columns, which correspond to the arguments we give to the worker task. This way, we'll be able to directly give the ID to the worker, and it'll take the parameter directly from the object. Besides, it'll allow us to store and remember the parameters we used for a specific generation.

The `progress` column is an integer where we'll store the current progress of the generation task.

Finally, `file_name` will store the actual filename we'll store on our system. We'll see how we use it in the next section, about object storage.

Adapting the API to save image-generation tasks in a database

With this model at hand, our approach to scheduling image generation in the API changes a bit. Instead of directly sending the task to the worker, we first create a row in our database and use the ID of this object as input for the worker task. The endpoint implementation is shown here:

api.py

```
@app.post(
    "/generated-images",
    response_model=schemas.GeneratedImageRead,
    status_code=status.HTTP_201_CREATED,
)
async def create_generated_image(
    generated_image_create: schemas.GeneratedImageCreate,
    session: AsyncSession = Depends(get_async_session),
)   GeneratedImage:
    image = GeneratedImage(**generated_image_create.dict())
    session.add(image)
    await session.commit()

    text_to_image_task.send(image.id)

    return image
```

https://github.com/PacktPublishing/Building-Data-Science-Applica-
tions-with-FastAPI-Second-Edition/tree/main/chapter14/complete/
api.py

We won't go into the details about how to create an object in a database with SQLAlchemy ORM. If you need a refresher, you can refer to the *Communicating with a SQL database with SQLAlchemy ORM* section of *Chapter 6*.

The main thing to notice in this snippet is that we pass the ID of the newly created object as an argument of `text_to_image_task`. As we'll see right after, the worker will read it again from the database to retrieve the generation parameters.

The response of this endpoint is simply a representation of our `GeneratedImage` model, using the Pydantic schema `GeneratedImageRead`. Thus, the user will get a response like this to their request:

```
{
    "created_at": "2023-02-07T10:17:50.992822",
    "file_name": null,
    "id": 6,
    "negative_prompt": null,
    "num_steps": 50,
    "progress": 0,
    "prompt": "a sunset over a beach"
}
```

It shows the prompt we gave in our request and, most importantly, *it gives it an ID*. This means that the user will be able to query for this specific request again to retrieve the data and see whether it's done. That's the purpose of the `get_generated_image` endpoint defined below the previous snippet. We won't show it here, but you can read it in the examples repository.

Adapting the worker to read and update image-generation tasks from a database

You probably have guessed that we need to change the implementation of our task so it can retrieve objects from the database instead of reading the parameters directly. Let's go through this step by step.

The first thing we do is retrieve a `GeneratedImage` from the database using the ID we got in the task argument.

worker.py

```
@dramatiq.actor()
def text_to_image_task(image_id: int):
    image = get_image(image_id)
```

https://github.com/PacktPublishing/Building-Data-Science-Applications-with-FastAPI-Second-Edition/tree/main/chapter14/complete/worker.py

To achieve this, you see that we use a helper function called `get_image`. It's defined right above the task. Let's review it:

worker.py

```
def get_image(id: int) -> GeneratedImage:
    async def _get_image(id: int) -> GeneratedImage:
        async with async_session_maker() as session:
            select_query = select(GeneratedImage).
where(GeneratedImage.id == id)
            result = await session.execute(select_query)
            image = result.scalar_one_or_none()

            if image is None:
                raise Exception("Image does not exist")

            return image

    return asyncio.run(_get_image(id))
```

https://github.com/PacktPublishing/Building-Data-Science-Applica-
tions-with-FastAPI-Second-Edition/tree/main/chapter14/complete/
worker.py

It may look quite strange, but actually, you are already familiar with most of its logic. If you look closely, you'll see that it defines a nested and private function where we define the actual logic to retrieve and save the object using SQLAlchemy ORM. Notice that it's *async*, and that we make great use of async I/O patterns, as we've seen throughout this book.

That's the exact reason why we need a helper function like this. Indeed, Dramatiq is not designed to run async functions natively, so we need to manually schedule their execution using `asyncio.run`. We already saw this function in *Chapter 2*, where we presented async I/O. Its role is to run an async function and return its result. That's how we can call the wrapping function synchronously in our task without any issues.

> **Other approaches could work to tackle the async I/O problem**
>
> The approach we show here is the most straightforward and robust one to tackle the problem of asynchronous workers.
>
> Another approach could be to set up a decorator or middleware for Dramatiq so it could natively run async functions, but this is complex and subject to bugs.
>
> We could also consider having another SQLAlchemy engine and session maker that works synchronously. However, this would require us to have a lot of duplicated things in our code. Besides, this wouldn't help if we had async functions other than SQLAlchemy.

Now, let's get back to the implementation of `text_to_image_task`:

worker.py

```python
@dramatiq.actor()
def text_to_image_task(image_id: int):
    image = get_image(image_id)

    def callback(step: int, _timestep, _tensor):
        update_progress(image, step)
```

https://github.com/PacktPublishing/Building-Data-Science-Applications-with-FastAPI-Second-Edition/tree/main/chapter14/complete/worker.py

We define a `callback` function for the Stable Diffusion pipeline. Its role is to save the current progress in a database for the current `GeneratedImage`. For this, we once again use a helper function, `update_progress`:

worker.py

```python
def update_progress(image: GeneratedImage, step: int):
    async def _update_progress(image: GeneratedImage, step: int):
        async with async_session_maker() as session:
            image.progress = int((step / image.num_steps) * 100)
            session.add(image)
            await session.commit()

    asyncio.run(_update_progress(image, step))
```

https://github.com/PacktPublishing/Building-Data-Science-Applications-with-FastAPI-Second-Edition/tree/main/chapter14/complete/worker.py

We use the same approach we explained for `get_image`, so we can wrap the async function.

Going back to `text_to_image_task`, we can now call our `TextToImage` model to generate an image. It's exactly the same call we showed in the previous section. The only difference is that we take the parameters from the `image` object. We also generate a random filename using a UUID:

worker.py

```python
image_output = text_to_image_middleware.text_to_image.generate(
    image.prompt,
    negative_prompt=image.negative_prompt,
```

```
        num_steps=image.num_steps,
        callback=callback,
    )

    file_name = f"{uuid.uuid4()}.png"
```

https://github.com/PacktPublishing/Building-Data-Science-Applica-
tions-with-FastAPI-Second-Edition/tree/main/chapter14/complete/
worker.py

The following part is designed to upload the image to object storage. We'll explain this in more detail in the next section:

worker.py

```
    storage = Storage()
    storage.upload_image(image_output, file_name, settings.storage_
  bucket)
```

https://github.com/PacktPublishing/Building-Data-Science-Applica-
tions-with-FastAPI-Second-Edition/tree/main/chapter14/complete/
worker.py

Finally, we call another helper function, update_file_name, to save the random filename in the database. It'll allow us to retrieve the file for the user:

worker.py

```
    update_file_name(image, file_name)
```

https://github.com/PacktPublishing/Building-Data-Science-Applica-
tions-with-FastAPI-Second-Edition/tree/main/chapter14/complete/
worker.py

As you can see, the main point of attention throughout this implementation is that we read and write information about GeneratedImage from and to the database. This is how we can *synchronize* between the API server and the worker. That's it for the worker! With this logic, we are able to schedule an image-generation task from the API, and the worker is able to regularly update the task progress before setting the resulting filename. Thus, from the API, a simple GET request allows us to see the status of our task.

Storing and serving files in object storage

The last challenge we have to tackle concerns the storage of our resulting images. We need a way to store them reliably while letting users retrieve them easily from the internet.

Traditionally, web applications handled this quite simply. They stored the files directly on the server hard disk, in a defined directory, and configured their web server to serve those files when accessed under a certain URL. This is actually what we did in *Chapter 13*, in the WebSocket example: we used the `StaticFiles` middleware to statically serve the JavaScript script we had on disk.

While this works well for static files, such as JavaScript or CSS files, for which each server has its own copy, it is not suitable for dynamic files uploaded by the user or generated by the backend, in particular for complex architectures where several processes are run on different physical machines. Once again, this is the problem of having a central source of data that the different processes read from. In the previous sections, we saw that message brokers and databases could solve this issue in several contexts. In the case of arbitrary binary files, whether they are images, videos, or simple text files, we need something else. Let's introduce **object storage**.

Object storage is a bit different from the standard file storage we use daily in computers, where the disk is organized in a hierarchy of directories and files. Instead, object storage will store each file as an object, which includes the actual data and all its metadata, such as its name, size, type, and a unique ID. The main benefit of such conceptualization is that it's easier to spread those files across multiple physical machines: *we can store billions of files on the same object storage*. From the user's point of view, we just ask for a specific file, and the storage will take care of loading the file from the actual physical disk.

In the cloud era, this approach has obviously gained a lot of popularity. In 2006, **Amazon Web Services (AWS)** launched Amazon S3, its own implementation of object storage. It gave developers access to virtually unlimited disk space to store files using a simple API, all at a very cheap price. Amazon S3 gained so much popularity its API became the de facto standard in the industry. Nowadays, most cloud object storage, including storage from competitors such as Microsoft Azure or Google Cloud, is compatible with the S3 API. Open source implementations have also emerged, such as MinIO. The main benefit of this common S3 API is that you can use the same code and libraries in your project to talk with any object storage provider and easily switch if needed.

To sum up, object storage is a very convenient way to store and serve files at scale, no matter the number of processes that need to access this data. At the end of this section, the global architecture of our project will look like the one shown in *Figure 14.5*.

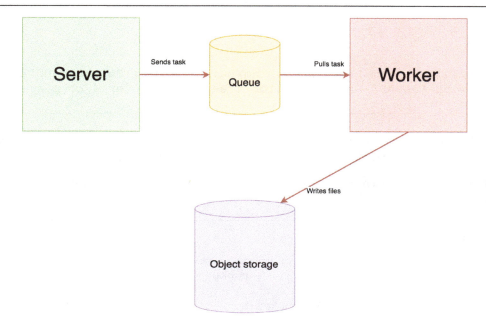

Figure 14.5 – Web-queue-worker architecture and object storage

It's worth noting that the *object storage will serve the file directly to the user*. There won't be an endpoint where the server would act as a proxy by downloading the file from the object storage before sending it to the user. There isn't much benefit in doing it that way, even in terms of authentication. We'll see that S3-compatible storage has built-in mechanisms to protect files from unauthorized access.

Implementing an object storage helper

Let's get to the code then! We'll use the MinIO client for Python, a library to interact with any S3-compatible storage. Let's install it:

```
(venv) $ pip install minio
```

We can now implement a class to have all the operations we need at hand. Let's first go with the initializer:

storage.py

```
class Storage:
    def __init__(self) -> None:
        self.client = Minio(
            settings.storage_endpoint,
            access_key=settings.storage_access_key,
```

```
            secret_key=settings.storage_secret_key,
        )
```

https://github.com/PacktPublishing/Building-Data-Science-Applications-with-FastAPI-Second-Edition/tree/main/chapter14/complete/storage.py

In the initializer of this class, we create a `Minio` client instance. You'll see that we use a `settings` object to pull the storage URL and credentials. Thus, it's very easy to switch them by using environment variables.

We'll then implement several methods that'll help us work with object storage. The first one is `ensure_bucket`:

storage.py

```
    def ensure_bucket(self, bucket_name: str):
        bucket_exists = self.client.bucket_exists(bucket_name)
        if not bucket_exists:
            self.client.make_bucket(bucket_name)
```

https://github.com/PacktPublishing/Building-Data-Science-Applications-with-FastAPI-Second-Edition/tree/main/chapter14/complete/storage.py

The role of this method is to make sure the right bucket is created in our object storage. In S3 implementations, a **bucket** is like a folder that you own and in which you can store your files. Each file you upload has to be put into an existing bucket.

Then, we define `upload_image`:

storage.py

```
    def upload_image(self, image: Image, object_name: str, bucket_
name: str):
        self.ensure_bucket(bucket_name)

        image_data = io.BytesIO()
        image.save(image_data, format="PNG")
        image_data.seek(0)
        image_data_length = len(image_data.getvalue())

        self.client.put_object(
            bucket_name,
            object_name,
            image_data,
```

```
        length=image_data_length,
        content_type="image/png",
    )
```

https://github.com/PacktPublishing/Building-Data-Science-Applications-with-FastAPI-Second-Edition/tree/main/chapter14/complete/storage.py

This is for uploading an image to the storage. To simplify things, this method accepts a Pillow `Image`, as it's the result we get at the end of the Stable Diffusion pipeline. We implemented some logic to convert this `Image` object into a raw stream of bytes suitable for the S3 upload. This method also expects `object_name`, which will be the actual name of the file in the storage, along with `bucket_name`. Notice that we first ensure the bucket is correctly created before trying to upload the file.

Finally, we add the `get_presigned_url` method:

storage.py

```
def get_presigned_url(
    self,
    object_name: str,
    bucket_name: str,
    *,
    expires: timedelta = timedelta(days=7)
)    str:
    return self.client.presigned_get_object(
        bucket_name, object_name, expires=expires
    )
```

https://github.com/PacktPublishing/Building-Data-Science-Applications-with-FastAPI-Second-Edition/tree/main/chapter14/complete/storage.py

This method will help us to serve the file securely to the user. By default, for security reasons, files in S3 storage are not accessible by any user on the internet. To give access to a file, we can do either of the following:

- Set the file as public so anybody with the URL can access it. This is suitable for public files but certainly not for private user files.

- Generate a URL with a temporary access key. Thus, we can give access to the file to the user, knowing that even if the URL is stolen, the access will be revoked after a certain time. The huge benefit of this is that this URL generation happens on our API server using the S3 client. Therefore, we could check whether the user is correctly authenticated and has the rights to this specific file following our own logic before generating the file URL. This is the approach we adopt here, and this method generates the pre-signed URL on a specific file in a specific bucket for a certain amount of time.

As you can see, our class is just a thin wrapper around the MinIO client. All we have to do now is to use it to upload the images and get a pre-signed URL from the API.

Using the object storage helper in the worker

In the previous section, we showed the following lines in our task implementation:

worker.py

```
storage = Storage()
storage.upload_image(image_output, file_name, settings.storage_
bucket)
```

https://github.com/PacktPublishing/Building-Data-Science-Applica-
tions-with-FastAPI-Second-Edition/tree/main/chapter14/complete/
worker.py

Now that we've talked about the Storage class, you should guess what we're doing here: we take the generated image and its random name and upload it to a bucket defined in settings. And… That's it!

Generating a pre-signed URL on the server

On the API's side, we implement a new endpoint whose role is to return a pre-signed URL for a given GeneratedImage:

server.py

```
@app.get("/generated-images/{id}/url")
async def get_generated_image_url(
    image: GeneratedImage = Depends(get_generated_image_or_404),
    storage: Storage = Depends(get_storage),
)   schemas.GeneratedImageURL:
    if image.file_name is None:
        raise HTTPException(
            status_code=status.HTTP_400_BAD_REQUEST,
            detail="Image is not available yet. Please try again
later.",
```

```
    )

    url = storage.get_presigned_url(image.file_name, settings.storage_
bucket)
    return schemas.GeneratedImageURL(url=url)
```

https://github.com/PacktPublishing/Building-Data-Science-Applica-
tions-with-FastAPI-Second-Edition/tree/main/chapter14/complete/
server.py

Before generating the URL, we first check whether the `file_name` property is set on the `GeneratedImage` object. If it's not, it means the worker has not completed the task yet. If it is, we can proceed with the call to the `get_presigned_url` method of our `Storage` class.

Notice that we took care of defining a dependency injection to get our `Storage` instance. As we've seen throughout this book, using dependencies in FastAPI is a very good practice when dealing with external services.

Well, it seems that we're all set! Let's see it in action.

Running the image-generation system

First of all, we need to populate the environment variables for our project with, in particular, a database URL and S3 credentials. To keep things simple, we'll use a simple SQLite database and the MinIO playground for the S3 storage. It's a free and open instance of MinIO object storage that's perfect for examples and toy projects. When going into production, you'll be able to easily switch to any S3-compatible provider. Let's create a `.env` file at the root of the project:

```
DATABASE_URL=sqlite+aiosqlite:///chapter14.db
STORAGE_ENDPOINT=play.min.io
STORAGE_ACCESS_KEY=Q3AM3UQ867SPQQA43P2F
STORAGE_SECRET_KEY=zuf+tfteSlswRu7BJ86wekitnifILbZam1KYY3TG
STORAGE_BUCKET=fastapi-book-text-to-image
```

The storage endpoint, access key, and secret key are the parameters for the MinIO playground. Make sure to check their official documentation to see whether they have changed since we wrote this book: https://min.io/docs/minio/linux/developers/python/minio-py.html#id5.

Our `Settings` class will automatically load this file to populate the settings we use throughout the code. Make sure to check the *Setting and using environment variables* section of *Chapter 10* if you need a refresher on this concept.

We can now run our system. Make sure your Redis server is still running, as explained in the *Technical requirements* section. First of all, let's run the FastAPI server:

```
(venv) $ uvicorn chapter14.complete.api:app
```

Then, start the worker:

```
(venv) $ dramatiq -p 1 -t 1 chapter14.complete.worker
```

The stack is now ready to generate images. Let's make a request with HTTPie to start a new task:

```
$ http POST http://localhost:8000/generated-images prompt="a sunset
over a beach"
HTTP/1.1 201 Created
content-length: 151
content-type: application/json
date: Mon, 13 Feb 2023 07:24:44 GMT
server: uvicorn

{
    "created_at": "2023-02-13T08:24:45.954240",
    "file_name": null,
    "id": 1,
    "negative_prompt": null,
    "num_steps": 50,
    "progress": 0,
    "prompt": "a sunset over a beach"
}
```

A new GeneratedImage has been created in the database with the assigned ID 1. The progress is at *0%*; the processing has not started yet. Let's try to query it with our API:

```
http GET http://localhost:8000/generated-images/1
HTTP/1.1 200 OK
content-length: 152
content-type: application/json
date: Mon, 13 Feb 2023 07:25:04 GMT
server: uvicorn

{
    "created_at": "2023-02-13T08:24:45.954240",
    "file_name": null,
    "id": 1,
    "negative_prompt": null,
    "num_steps": 50,
```

```
    "progress": 36,
    "prompt": "a sunset over a beach"
}
```

The API returns the same object with all its properties. Notice that the progress has been updated and that it's now at *36%*. After a while, we can try the same request again:

```
$ http GET http://localhost:8000/generated-images/1
HTTP/1.1 200 OK
content-length: 191
content-type: application/json
date: Mon, 13 Feb 2023 07:25:34 GMT
server: uvicorn

{
    "created_at": "2023-02-13T08:24:45.954240",
    "file_name": "affeec65-5d9b-480e-ac08-000c74e22dc9.png",
    "id": 1,
    "negative_prompt": null,
    "num_steps": 50,
    "progress": 100,
    "prompt": "a sunset over a beach"
}
```

This time, the progress is at *100%* and the filename has been filled. The image is ready! We can now ask our API to generate a pre-signed URL for this image:

```
$ http GET http://localhost:8000/generated-images/1/url
HTTP/1.1 200 OK
content-length: 366
content-type: application/json
date: Mon, 13 Feb 2023 07:29:53 GMT
server: uvicorn

{
    "url": "https://play.min.io/fastapi-book-text-to-image/
affeec65-5d9b-480e-ac08-000c74e22dc9.png?X-Amz-Algorithm=AWS4-
HMAC-SHA256&X-Amz-Credential=Q3AM3UQ867SPQQA43P2F%2F20230213%2
Fus-east-1%2Fs3%2Faws4_request&X-Amz-Date=20230213T072954Z&X-Amz-
Expires=604800&X-Amz-SignedHeaders=host&X-Amz-Signature=6ffddb81702bed
6aac50786578eb75af3c1f6a3db28e4990467c973cb3b457a9"
}
```

We get a very long URL on the MinIO server. If you open it in your browser, you'll see the image that has just been generated by our system, as you can see in *Figure 14.6*.

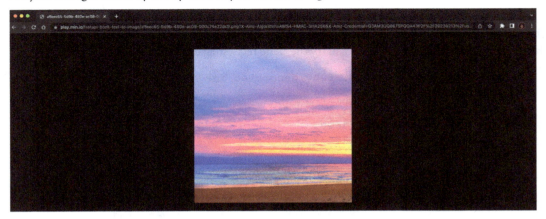

Figure 14.6 – Generated image hosted on object storage

Quite nice, isn't it? We now have a fully featured system where the user is able to do the following:

- Request to generate images following their own prompt and parameters
- Get information about the progress of the request
- Get the resulting image from reliable storage

The architecture we see here is already deployable in a cloud environment with multiple machines. Typically, we may have a standard, cheap server to serve the API and a more expensive one with a dedicated GPU and a good amount of RAM to run the worker. The code doesn't have to change to handle this kind of deployment since the communication between processes is handled by the central elements – the message broker, the database, and the object storage.

Summary

Awesome! You may not have realized it yet, but in this chapter, you learned how to architect and implement a very complex machine learning system that could rival existing image-generation services you see out there. The concepts we showed here are essential and are at the heart of all the distributed systems you could imagine, whether they are designed to run machine learning models, extraction pipelines, or math computations. By using modern tools such as FastAPI and Dramatiq, you'll be able to implement this kind of architecture in a short time with a minimum amount of code, leading to a very quick and robust result.

We're near the end of our journey. Before letting you live your own adventures with FastAPI, we'll study one last important aspect when building data science applications: logging and monitoring.

15

Monitoring the Health and Performance of a Data Science System

In this chapter, we will cover the extra mile so you are able to build robust, production-ready systems. One of the most important aspects to achieve this is to have all the data we need to ensure the system is operating correctly and detect as soon as possible when something goes wrong so we can take corrective actions. In this chapter, we'll see how to set up a proper logging facility and how we can monitor the performance and health of our software in real time.

We're near the end of our journey into FastAPI for data science. Until now, we've mainly focused on the functionality of the programs we implemented. However, there is another aspect that is often overlooked by developers but is actually very important: *assessing whether the system is functioning correctly and reliably in production* and being warned as soon as possible when that's not the case.

For this, lot of tools and techniques exist so we can gather the maximum amount of data about how our program is performing. That's what we'll review in this chapter.

We're going to cover the following main topics:

- Configuring and using a logging facility with Loguru
- Configuring Prometheus metrics and monitoring them in Grafana
- Configuring Sentry for reporting errors

Technical requirements

For this chapter, you'll require a Python virtual environment, just as we set up in *Chapter 1, Python Development Environment Setup*.

To run a Dramatiq worker, you'll need a running Redis server on your local computer. The easiest way is to run it as a Docker container. If you've never used Docker before, we recommend you read the *Getting started* tutorial in the official documentation at `https://docs.docker.com/get-started/`. Once done, you'll be able to run a Redis server with this simple command:

```
$ docker run -d --name worker-redis -p 6379:6379 redis
```

You'll find all the code examples of this chapter in the dedicated GitHub repository at `https://github.com/PacktPublishing/Building-Data-Science-Applications-with-FastAPI-Second-Edition/tree/main/chapter15`.

> **A note about the screenshots**
>
> In the course of this chapter, we'll present several screenshots, in particular of the Grafana interface. Their goal is to show you the general layout of the UI to help you identify its different parts. Don't worry if you struggle to read the actual content: the explanations around them will explain where to look at and what to interact with.

Configuring and using a logging facility with Loguru

In software development, logs are probably the simplest but most powerful way to control the behavior of a system. They usually consist of lines of plain text that are printed at specific points of a program. By reading them chronologically, we are able to trace the behavior of the program and check that everything goes well. Actually, we've already seen log lines in this book. When you run a FastAPI app with Uvicorn and make some requests, you'll see these lines in the console output:

```
INFO:      Started server process [94918]
INFO:      Waiting for application startup.
INFO:      Application startup complete.
INFO:      Uvicorn running on http://127.0.0.1:8000 (Press CTRL+C to
quit)
INFO:      127.0.0.1:60736 - "POST /generated-images HTTP/1.1" 201
Created
```

Those are the logs generated by Uvicorn, which tell us when it has started and when it has handled a request. As you can see, logs can help us to know what happened in our program and what actions it performed. They can also tell us when something goes wrong, which could be a bug that needs to be solved.

Understanding log levels

Notice that before each log line, we have the INFO keyword. This is what we call the **log level**. It's a way to classify the importance of this log. In general, the following levels are defined:

- DEBUG

- INFO

- WARNING

- ERROR

You can consider this the *level of importance*: DEBUG is really specific information about what the program does, which could help you to debug the code, while ERROR means that something bad happened in your program, which probably requires action on your part. The good thing about those levels is that we can *configure the minimum level* that should be output by the logger. The actual call to the log function is still there in the code, but it's ignored by the logger if it doesn't match the minimum level.

Typically, we can set the DEBUG level in local development so we have all the information to help us develop and fix our program. On the other hand, we can set the level to INFO or WARNING in production so we have only the most important messages.

Adding logs with Loguru

Adding your own logs to a Python program can be fairly easy using the logging module available in the standard library. You could do something like this:

```
>>> import logging
>>> logging.warning("This is my log")
WARNING:root:This is my log
```

As you can see, it's just a function call with a string in the argument. Typically, logging modules expose the different levels as methods, as you see here with warning.

The standard logging module is really powerful and allows you to finely customize how your logs are handled, printed, and formatted. If you go through the logging tutorials in the official documentation, https://docs.python.org/3/howto/logging.html, you'll see it can quickly become really complex, even for simple cases.

That's why Python developers usually use libraries wrapping the logging module and exposing much more friendly functions and interfaces. In this chapter, we'll review how to use and configure **Loguru**, a modern yet simple approach to logging.

As always, the first thing to do is to install it in our Python environment:

```
(venv) $ pip install loguru
```

We can try it right away in a Python shell:

```
>>> from loguru import logger
>>> logger.debug("This is my log!")
2023-02-21 08:44:00.168 | DEBUG    | __main__:<module>:1 - This is my
log!
```

You may think that's not very different from what we did with the standard `logging` module. However, notice the resulting log already includes the timestamp, the level, and the position of the function call in the code. That's one of the main benefits of Loguru: it comes with sensible defaults working out of the box.

Let's see it in action in a more complete script. We'll define a simple function to check whether an integer, n, is odd or not. We'll add a debug line to let us know the function starts its logic. Then, before computing the result, we'll first check whether n truly is an integer and log an error if not. The implementation of this function looks like this:

chapter15_logs_01.py

```python
from loguru import logger


def is_even(n) -> bool:
    logger.debug("Check if {n} is even", n=n)
    if not isinstance(n, int):
        logger.error("{n} is not an integer", n=n)
        raise TypeError()
    return n % 2 == 0


if __name__ == "__main__":
    is_even(2)
    is_even("hello")
```

https://github.com/PacktPublishing/Building-Data-Science-Applications-with-FastAPI-Second-Edition/tree/main/chapter15/chapter15_logs_01.py

As you can see, it's really simple to use: we just have to import `logger` and call it wherever we need to log something. Notice also how we can add variables to format our string: we just need to add a placeholder around curly braces inside the string and then map each placeholder to its value with keyword arguments. This syntax is actually similar to the standard `str.format` method. You can read more about it in the official Python documentation: `https://docs.python.org/fr/3/library/stdtypes.html#str.format`.

If we run this simple script, we'll see our log lines in the console output:

```
(venv) $ python chapter15/chapter15_logs_01.py
2023-03-03 08:16:40.145 | DEBUG     | __main__:is_even:5 - Check if 2
is even
2023-03-03 08:16:40.145 | DEBUG     | __main__:is_even:5 - Check if
hello is even
2023-03-03 08:16:40.145 | ERROR     | __main__:is_even:7 - hello is not
an integer
Traceback (most recent call last):
  File "/Users/fvoron/Development/Building-Data-Science-Applications-
with-FastAPI-Second-Edition/chapter15/chapter15_logs_01.py", line 14,
in <module>
    is_even("hello")
  File "/Users/fvoron/Development/Building-Data-Science-Applications-
with-FastAPI-Second-Edition/chapter15/chapter15_logs_01.py", line 8,
in is_even
    raise TypeError()
TypeError
```

Our log lines are correctly added to the output before the actual exception is raised. Notice how Loguru is able to precisely tell us where the log call comes from in the code: we have the function's name and line.

Understanding and configuring sinks

We've seen that, by default, logs are added to the console output. By default, Loguru defines a **sink** targeted at a standard error. A sink is a concept introduced by Loguru to define how log lines should be handled by the logger. We're not limited to console output: we can also save them to a file, or a database, or even send them to a web service!

The good thing is that you're not limited to only one sink; you can have as many as you need! Then, each log call will be processed through each sink accordingly. You can see a schematic representation of this approach in *Figure 15.1*.

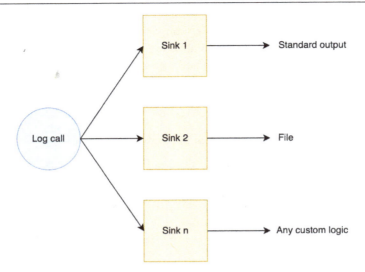

Figure 15.1 – Schema of Loguru sinks

Each *sink is associated with a log level*. This means that we could have different log levels depending on the sink. For example, we could choose to output all logs to a file and keep only the most important warning and error logs in the console. Let's again take our previous example and configure Loguru with this approach:

chapter15_logs_02.py

```
logger.remove()
logger.add(sys.stdout, level="WARNING")
logger.add("file.log", level="DEBUG", rotation="1 day")
```

https://github.com/PacktPublishing/Building-Data-Science-Applica-
tions-with-FastAPI-Second-Edition/tree/main/chapter15/chapter15_
logs_02.py

The remove method of logger is helpful for removing a previously defined sink. When calling it like this with no parameter, all the defined sinks are removed. By doing this, we start fresh without the default sink.

Then, we call add to define new sinks. The first parameter, like sys.stdout or file.log here, defines how the log calls should be handled. This parameter can be many things, such as a callable function, but Loguru allows us, for convenience, to directly pass file-like objects, such as sys.stdout, or strings, which will be interpreted as filenames. Several arguments are accepted to customize all the aspects of the sink and, in particular, the level.

As we said, the standard output sink will only log messages with at least a WARNING level, while the file sink will log all messages.

Notice also that we added a `rotation` parameter for the file sink. Since logs will continuously be appended to a file, it can quickly grow in size during the lifetime of your application. That's why we have access to a couple of options:

- **"Rotate" the file**: This means that the current file will be renamed, and new logs will be added to a new file. This operation can be configured so it happens after a certain amount of time (for example, every day, as in our example) or when it reaches a certain size.

- **Remove older files**: After a certain amount of time, it's probably not very useful to keep older logs that take up unnecessary space on your disk.

You can read all the details about these features in the official documentation for Loguru: `https://loguru.readthedocs.io/en/stable/api/logger.html#file`.

Now, if we run this example, we'll see this in the console output:

```
(venv) $ python chapter15/chapter15_logs_02.py
2023-03-03 08:15:16.804 | ERROR    | __main__:is_even:12 - hello is
not an integer
Traceback (most recent call last):
  File "/Users/fvoron/Development/Building-Data-Science-Applications-
with-FastAPI-Second-Edition/chapter15/chapter15_logs_02.py", line 19,
in <module>
    is_even("hello")
  File "/Users/fvoron/Development/Building-Data-Science-Applications-
with-FastAPI-Second-Edition/chapter15/chapter15_logs_02.py", line 13,
in is_even
    raise TypeError()
TypeError
```

The `DEBUG` logs don't appear anymore. However, if we read the `file.log` file, we'll have both:

```
$ cat file.log
2023-03-03 08:15:16.803 | DEBUG    | __main__:is_even:10 - Check if 2
is even
2023-03-03 08:15:16.804 | DEBUG    | __main__:is_even:10 - Check if
hello is even
2023-03-03 08:15:16.804 | ERROR    | __main__:is_even:12 - hello is
not an integer
```

That's it! Sinks are really useful for routing our logs to different places depending on their nature or importance.

Structuring logs and adding context

In their simplest form, logs consist of free-form text. While convenient, we've seen that we usually need to log variable values to better understand what's going on. With only strings, this usually ends up in a messy string consisting of multiple concatenated values.

A better approach to handle this is to adopt **structured logging**. The goal is to have a clear and proper structure for each log line, so we can embed all the information we need without sacrificing readability. Loguru supports this approach natively, thanks to contexts. The next example shows you how to use it:

chapter15_logs_03.py

```python
def is_even(n) -> bool:
    logger_context = logger.bind(n=n)
    logger_context.debug("Check if even")
    if not isinstance(n, int):
        logger_context.error("Not an integer")
        raise TypeError()
    return n % 2 == 0
```

https://github.com/PacktPublishing/Building-Data-Science-Applications-with-FastAPI-Second-Edition/tree/main/chapter15/chapter15_logs_03.py

We once again took the same example as before. As you can see, we use the bind method of logger to retain extra information. Here, we set the n variable. This method returns a new instance of our logger with those attributes attached. Then, we can use this instance normally to log things. We don't need to add n in the formatted string anymore.

However, if you try this example directly, you won't see the value of n in the logs. That's normal: by default, Loguru doesn't add context information to the formatted log line. We need to customize it! Let's see how:

chapter15_logs_04.py

```python
logger.add(
    sys.stdout,
    level="DEBUG",
    format="<green>{time:YYYY-MM-DD HH:mm:ss.SSS}</green> | "
    "<level>{level: <8}</level> | "
    "<cyan>{name}</cyan>:<cyan>{function}</cyan>:<cyan>{line}</cyan> - <level>{message}</level>"
    " - {extra}",
)
```

https://github.com/PacktPublishing/Building-Data-Science-Applications-with-FastAPI-Second-Edition/tree/main/chapter15/chapter15_logs_04.py

To format log output, we have to use the `format` parameter when configuring a sink. It expects a template string. Here, we copied and pasted the default Loguru format and added a part with the `extra` variable. `extra` is a dictionary where Loguru stores all the values you added in context. Here, we just output it directly so we can see all variables.

Format syntax and available variables

You can find all the available variables you can output in the format string, such as `extra` or `level`, in the Loguru documentation: `https://loguru.readthedocs.io/en/stable/api/logger.html#record`.

The format string supports standard formatting directives, which are useful for retrieving values, format numbers, pad strings, and so on. You can read more about it in the Python documentation: `https://docs.python.org/3/library/string.html#format-string-syntax`.

Also, Loguru adds special markup so you can color the output. You can read more about it here: `https://loguru.readthedocs.io/en/stable/api/logger.html#color`.

This time, if you run this example, you'll see the extra context added to the log lines:

```
(venv) $ python chapter15/chapter15_logs_04.py
2023-03-03 08:30:10.905 | DEBUG    | __main__:is_even:18 - Check if
even - {'n': 2}
2023-03-03 08:30:10.905 | DEBUG    | __main__:is_even:18 - Check if
even - {'n': 'hello'}
2023-03-03 08:30:10.905 | ERROR    | __main__:is_even:20 - Not an
integer - {'n': 'hello'}
```

This approach is very convenient and powerful: if you want to keep track of a value you care about across logs, you just have to add it once.

Logs as JSON objects

Another approach to structured logging is to serialize all the data of a log into a JSON object. This can be enabled easily with Loguru by setting `serialize=True` when configuring the sink. This approach can be interesting if you plan to use a log ingestion service such as Logstash or Datadog: they will be able to parse the JSON data and make it available for querying.

You now have the basics of adding and configuring logs with Loguru. Let's now see how we can leverage them in a FastAPI application.

Configuring Loguru as the central logger

Adding logs to your FastAPI application can be really useful to know what's happening in your different routes and dependencies.

Let's take an example from *Chapter 5*, where we added a global dependency to check for a secret value that should be set in the header. In this new version, we'll add a debug log to trace when the `secret_header` dependency is called and a warning log to inform us when this secret is missing or invalid:

chapter15_logs_05.py

```
from loguru import logger

def secret_header(secret_header: str | None = Header(None)) -> None:
    logger.debug("Check secret header")
    if not secret_header or secret_header != "SECRET_VALUE":
        logger.warning("Invalid or missing secret header")
        raise HTTPException(status.HTTP_403_FORBIDDEN)
```

https://github.com/PacktPublishing/Building-Data-Science-Applications-with-FastAPI-Second-Edition/tree/main/chapter15/chapter15_logs_05.py

That's nothing really surprising if you have followed us so far! Now, let's run this application with Uvicorn and make a request with an invalid header:

```
INFO:      Started server process [47073]
INFO:      Waiting for application startup.
INFO:      Application startup complete.
INFO:      Uvicorn running on http://127.0.0.1:8000 (Press CTRL+C to
quit)
2023-03-03 09:00:47.324 | DEBUG    | chapter15.chapter15_
logs_05:secret_header:6 - Check secret header
2023-03-03 09:00:47.324 | WARNING  | chapter15.chapter15_
logs_05:secret_header:8 - Invalid or missing secret header
INFO:      127.0.0.1:58190 - "GET /route1 HTTP/1.1" 403 Forbidden
```

Our own logs are here, but there is a problem: Uvicorn also adds its own logs, but it doesn't follow our format! Actually, that's expected: other libraries, such as Uvicorn, may have their own logs with their own settings. As such, they won't follow what we defined with Loguru. It's a bit annoying because if we have a complex, well-thought-out setup, we would like every log to follow it. Fortunately, there are ways to configure this.

First of all, we'll create a module named `logger.py`, where we'll put all our logger configurations. It's a good practice in your project to have this module so your configuration is centralized in one place. The first thing we do in this file is to configure Loguru:

logger.py

```
LOG_LEVEL = "DEBUG"

logger.remove()
logger.add(
    sys.stdout,
    level=LOG_LEVEL,
    format="<green>{time:YYYY-MM-DD HH:mm:ss.SSS}</green> | "
    "<level>{level: <8}</level> | "
    "<cyan>{name}</cyan>:<cyan>{function}</cyan>:<cyan>{line}</cyan> -
<level>{message}</level>"
    " - {extra}",
)
```

https://github.com/PacktPublishing/Building-Data-Science-Applica-tions-with-FastAPI-Second-Edition/tree/main/chapter15/logger.py

As we did in the previous section, we removed the default handler and defined our own. Notice that we set the level thanks to a constant named LOG_LEVEL. We hardcoded it here, but a better way would be to take the value from a `Settings` object, as we showed in *Chapter 10*. This way, we could directly set the level from environment variables!

After that, we have a quite complex piece of code in the class named `InterceptHandler`. It's a custom handler for the standard logging module that will forward every standard log call to Loguru. This code is directly taken from the Loguru documentation. We won't go into much detail about its functioning but just know that it'll retrieve the log level and go through the call stack to retrieve the original caller and forward this information to Loguru.

The most important part, however, is how we use this class. Let's see this here:

logger.py

```
logging.basicConfig(handlers=[InterceptHandler()], level=0,
force=True)

for uvicorn_logger_name in ["uvicorn.error", "uvicorn.access"]:
    uvicorn_logger = logging.getLogger(uvicorn_logger_name)
```

```
uvicorn_logger.propagate = False
uvicorn_logger.handlers = [InterceptHandler()]
```

https://github.com/PacktPublishing/Building-Data-Science-Applica-tions-with-FastAPI-Second-Edition/tree/main/chapter15/logger.py

The trick here is to call the `basicConfig` method from the standard logging module to set our custom interception handler. This way, every log call made with the root logger, even ones from external libraries, will go through it and be handled by Loguru.

In some cases, however, this configuration is not sufficient. Some libraries define their own loggers with their own handlers, so they won't use the root configuration. That's the case for Uvicorn, which defines two main loggers: `uvicorn.error` and `uvicorn.access`. By retrieving those loggers and changing their handler, we force them to go through Loguru as well.

If you use other libraries that define their own loggers like Uvicorn does, you'll probably need to apply the same technique. All you need to determine is the name of their logger, which should be quite easy to find in the library's source code.

> **It works out of the box with Dramatiq**
>
> If you implement a worker with Dramatiq, as we showed in *Chapter 14*, you'll see that, if you use the `logger` module, the default logs of Dramatiq will be correctly handled by Loguru.

Finally, we take care of setting the __all__ variable at the end of the module:

logger.py

```
__all__ = ["logger"]
```

https://github.com/PacktPublishing/Building-Data-Science-Applica-tions-with-FastAPI-Second-Edition/tree/main/chapter15/logger.py

__all__ is a special variable telling Python which variables should be made publicly available when importing this module. Here, we'll expose `logger` from Loguru, so we can easily import it everywhere we need in our project.

Bear in mind that it's not strictly necessary to use __all__: we could very well import `logger` without it, but it's a clean way to hide other things we want to keep private, such as `InterceptHandler`, for example.

Finally, we can use it as we saw previously in our code:

logger.py

```
from chapter15.logger import logger

def secret_header(secret_header: str | None = Header(None))      None:
    logger.debug("Check secret header")
    if not secret_header or secret_header != "SECRET_VALUE":
        logger.warning("Invalid or missing secret header")
        raise HTTPException(status.HTTP_403_FORBIDDEN)
```

https://github.com/PacktPublishing/Building-Data-Science-Applications-with-FastAPI-Second-Edition/tree/main/chapter15/logger.py

If we run it with Uvicorn, you'll now see that all our logs are formatted the same way:

```
2023-03-03 09:06:16.196 | INFO      | uvicorn.server:serve:75 - Started
server process [47534] - {}
2023-03-03 09:06:16.196 | INFO      | uvicorn.lifespan.on:startup:47 -
Waiting for application startup. - {}
2023-03-03 09:06:16.196 | INFO      | uvicorn.lifespan.on:startup:61 -
Application startup complete. - {}
2023-03-03 09:06:16.196 | INFO      | uvicorn.server:_log_started_
message:209 - Uvicorn running on http://127.0.0.1:8000 (Press CTRL+C
to quit) - {}
2023-03-03 09:06:18.500 | DEBUG     | chapter15.chapter15_
logs_06:secret_header:7 - Check secret header - {}
2023-03-03 09:06:18.500 | WARNING   | chapter15.chapter15_
logs_06:secret_header:9 - Invalid or missing secret header - {}
2023-03-03 09:06:18.500 | INFO      | uvicorn.protocols.http.httptools_
impl:send:489 - 127.0.0.1:59542 - "GET /route1 HTTP/1.1" 403 - {}
```

Great! Now, whenever you need to add logs in your app, all you need to do is to import `logger` from your `logger` module.

You now have the basics to add logs to your application, with plenty of options to fine-tune how and where you output them. Logs are very useful for monitoring what your application is doing at a micro-level, operation per operation. Another important aspect of monitoring is to have information at a more general level in order to have big figures and quickly detect if something goes wrong. That's what we'll see now with metrics.

Adding Prometheus metrics

In the previous section, we saw how logs can help us understand what our program is doing by finely tracing the operations it does over time. However, most of the time, you can't afford to keep an eye on the logs all day: they are useful for understanding and debugging a particular situation but way less useful for getting global insights to alert you when something goes wrong.

To solve this, we'll see in this section how to add **metrics** to our application. Their role is to measure things that matter in the execution of our program: the number of requests made, the time taken to give a response, the number of pending tasks in the worker queue, the accuracy of our ML predictions… Anything that we could easily monitor over time – usually, with charts and graphs – so we can easily monitor the health of our system. We say that we **instrument** our application.

To achieve this task, we'll use two widely used technologies in the industry: Prometheus and Grafana.

Understanding Prometheus and the different metrics

Prometheus is a technology to help you instrument your application. It consists of three things:

- Libraries for a wide range of programming languages, including Python, to add metrics to an application
- A server to aggregate and store those metrics over time
- A query language, PromQL, so we can pull data from those metrics into visualization tools

Prometheus has very precise guidelines and conventions about how to define metrics. Actually, it defines four different types of metrics.

The counter metric

The counter metric is a way to measure a *value that goes up over time*. For example, this could be the number of requests answered or the number of predictions done. This will not be used for values that can go down. For that, there is the gauge metric.

Figure 15.2 – Possible representation of a counter

The gauge metric

The gauge metric is a way to measure a *value that can go up or down over time*. For example, this could be the current memory usage or the number of pending tasks in a worker queue.

Figure 15.3 – Possible representation of a gauge

The histogram metric

Contrary to counters and gauges, a histogram will *measure values and count them in buckets*. Typically, if we want to measure the response time of our API, we can count the number of requests that have been processed in less than 10 milliseconds, less than 100 milliseconds, and less than 1 second. Doing this is much more insightful than getting a simple average or median, for example.

When using a histogram, it's our responsibility to define the buckets we want with their value threshold.

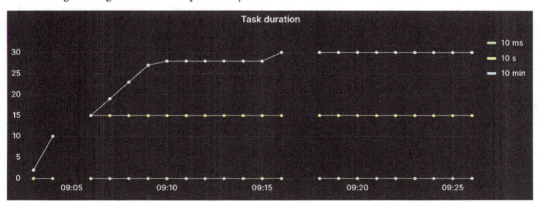

Figure 15.4 – Possible representation of a histogram

Prometheus defines a fourth type of metric, a summary. It's quite similar to the histogram metric, but it works with sliding quantiles instead of defined buckets. We won't go through it since it has quite limited support in Python. Besides, we'll see in the Grafana section of this chapter that we'll be able to compute quantiles with the histogram metric.

You can read more details about those metrics in the official Prometheus documentation:

```
https://prometheus.io/docs/concepts/metric_types/
```

Measuring and exposing metrics

Once the metrics have been defined, we can start to measure things during the lifetime of our program. Similar to what we do with logs, metrics expose methods so we can store values during the execution of the application. Prometheus will then retain those values in memory to build the metrics.

But then, how can we access those metrics so we can actually analyze and monitor them? Quite simply, apps using Prometheus usually expose an HTTP endpoint called /metrics, which will return the current values of all metrics in a specific format. You can see what it looks like in *Figure 15.5*.

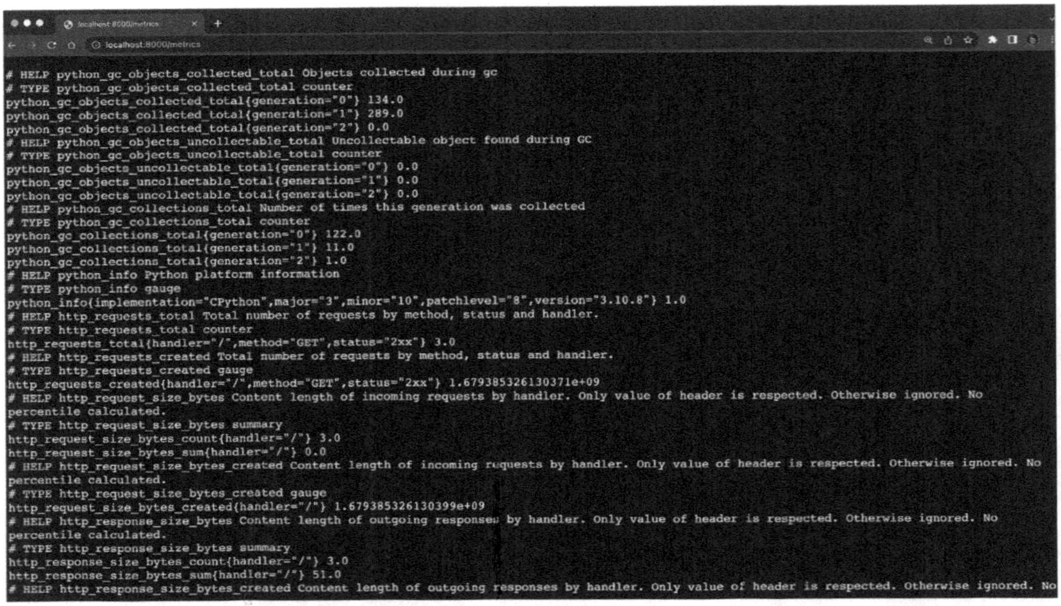

Figure 15.5 – Output of a Prometheus metrics endpoint

This endpoint can then be polled at regular intervals by a Prometheus server, which will store those metrics over time and make them available through PromQL.

> **Metrics are reset when your application restarts**
>
> It's worth noting that every time you restart your application, like your FastAPI server, metric values are lost, and you start from zero. It may be a bit surprising, but it's key to understand that metric values are only stored in memory in your app. The responsibility for properly storing them permanently belongs to the Prometheus server.

Now that we have a good idea of how they work, let's see how to add metrics to FastAPI and Dramatiq applications.

Adding Prometheus metrics to FastAPI

As we said, Prometheus maintains official libraries for various languages, including Python.

We could very well use it on its own and manually define various metrics to monitor our FastAPI app. We would also need to come up with some logic to hook into a FastAPI request handler so we could measure things such as the requests count, response time, payload size, and so on.

While definitely doable, we'll take a shortcut and rely once again on the open source community, which proposes a ready-to-use library for integrating Prometheus into a FastAPI project: **Prometheus FastAPI Instrumentator**. It comes with useful metrics by default, such as the total number of requests or the response size in bytes. It also takes care of exposing the /metrics endpoint.

The first thing is, of course, to install it with pip. Run the following command:

```
(venv) $ pip install prometheus_fastapi_instrumentator
```

In the following example, we've implemented a very simple FastAPI app and enabled the instrumentator:

chapter15_metrics_01.py

```
from fastapi import FastAPI
from prometheus_fastapi_instrumentator import Instrumentator, metrics


app = FastAPI()


@app.get("/")
async def hello():
    return {"hello": "world"}


instrumentator = Instrumentator()
instrumentator.add(metrics.default())
instrumentator.instrument(app).expose(app)
```

https://github.com/PacktPublishing/Building-Data-Science-Applications-with-FastAPI-Second-Edition/tree/main/chapter15/chapter15_metrics_01.py

Enabling the instrumentator consists of three lines:

1. Instantiate the `Instrumentator` class.

2. Enable the default metrics proposed by the library.

3. Wire it to our FastAPI app and expose the `/metrics` endpoint.

That's it! FastAPI is instrumented with Prometheus!

Let's run this app with Uvicorn and access the `hello` endpoint. Internally, Prometheus will measure things about this request. Let's now access `/metrics` to see the result. If you scroll down this big list of metrics, you should come across these lines:

```
# HELP http_requests_total Total number of requests by method, status
and handler.
# TYPE http_requests_total counter
http_requests_total{handler="/",method="GET",status="2xx"} 1.0
```

This is the metrics counting the number of requests. We see that we have one request in total, which corresponds to our call to `hello`. Notice that the instrumentator is smart enough to label the metrics by path, method, and even status code. This is very convenient, as it'll enable us to pull interesting figures depending on the characteristics of the request.

Adding custom metrics

The built-in metrics are a good start, but we'll likely need to come up with our own to measure things specific to our application.

Let's say we want to implement a function that rolls a dice with six faces and exposes it via a REST API. We want to define a metric allowing us to count the number of times each face has appeared. For this task, a counter is a good match. Let's see how to declare it in the code:

chapter15_metrics_02.py

```
DICE_COUNTER = Counter(
    "app_dice_rolls_total",
    "Total number of dice rolls labelled per face",
    labelnames=["face"],
)
```

https://github.com/PacktPublishing/Building-Data-Science-Applica-tions-with-FastAPI-Second-Edition/tree/main/chapter15/chapter15_metrics_02.py

We have to instantiate a Counter object. The two first arguments are, respectively, the name and description of the metric. The name will be used by Prometheus to uniquely identify this metric. Since we want to count the rolls per face, we also add a single label named face. Every time we count a roll of the dice, we'll have to set this label to the corresponding result face.

> **Conventions for metric names**
>
> Prometheus defines very precise conventions for naming your metrics. In particular, it should start with the domain the metrics belong to, such as http_ or app_, and should end with the unit, such as _seconds, _bytes, or _total if this is just a value count. We strongly recommend you read the Prometheus guidelines: https://prometheus.io/docs/practices/naming/.

We can now use this metric in our code. In the following snippet, you'll see the implementation of the roll_dice function:

chapter15_metrics_02.py

```python
def roll_dice() -> int:
    result = random.randint(1, 6)
    DICE_COUNTER.labels(result).inc()
    return result
```

https://github.com/PacktPublishing/Building-Data-Science-Applications-with-FastAPI-Second-Edition/tree/main/chapter15/chapter15_metrics_02.py

You can see that we directly use the metrics instance, DICE_COUNTER, and first call the labels method to set the face, and then inc to actually increment the counter.

That's all we need to do: our metric is automatically registered in the Prometheus client and will start to be exposed by the /metrics endpoint. In *Figure 15.6*, you can see a possible visualization of this metric in Grafana.

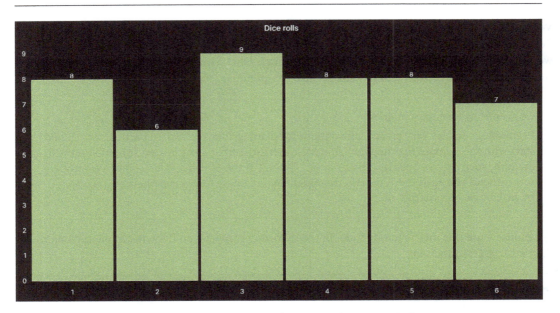

Figure 15.6 – Representation of the dice roll metric in Grafana

As you can see, declaring and using a new metric is quite straightforward: we can just call it directly in the code we want to monitor.

Handling multiple processes

In *Chapter 10*, we mentioned in the *Adding Gunicorn as a server process for deployment* section that, in a production deployment, FastAPI apps are usually run with several workers. Basically, it spawns several processes of the same application and balances the incoming requests between them. This allows us to serve more requests concurrently and avoid blocks if one of the operations is blocking the process.

> **Do not confuse Gunicorn workers and Dramatiq workers**
>
> When we talk about workers in the context of a Gunicorn deployment for FastAPI, we are referring to the fact that we are spawning multiple processes that'll be able to serve our API requests concurrently. We are not talking about workers in the context of Dramatiq that are processing tasks in the background.

Having multiple processes for the same application is a bit problematic for Prometheus metrics. Indeed, as we mentioned before, those metrics are only stored in memory and exposed through a / metrics endpoint.

If we have several processes answering requests, each one will have its own set of metrics values. Then, when the Prometheus server asks for /metrics, we'll get the values of the process that answered our request but not the ones of the others. And it may change in the next poll! Obviously, this will totally defeat our initial goal.

To circumvent this, the Prometheus client has a special multiprocess mode. Basically, instead of storing the values in memory, it'll store them in files in a dedicated folder. When calling /metrics, it'll take care of loading all the files and reconciling the values of all processes together.

Enabling this mode requires us to set the environment variable called PROMETHEUS_MULTIPROC_DIR. It should point to a valid folder in your filesystem where the metrics files will be stored. Here is a command example of how to set this variable and start Gunicorn with four workers:

```
(venv) $ PROMETHEUS_MULTIPROC_DIR=./prometheus-tmp gunicorn -w 4 -k
uvicorn.workers.UvicornWorker chapter15.chapter15_metrics_01:app
```

Of course, in a production deployment, you would set the environment variable globally on your platform, as we explained in *Chapter 10*.

If you try this command, you'll see that Prometheus will start to store some .db files inside the folder, each one corresponding to a metric and a process. The side effect is that *metrics won't be cleared when restarting the process*. It can lead to unexpected behaviors if you change your metrics definition or if you run a completely different application. Make sure to choose a dedicated folder for each of your apps and clean it up when you run a new version.

We are now able to precisely instrument a FastAPI app. However, we saw in the previous chapter that data science applications can be constituted of a separate worker process, where a lot of logic and intelligence is run. Thus, it's also crucial to instrument this part of the application.

Adding Prometheus metrics to Dramatiq

In *Chapter 14*, we implemented a complex application with a distinct worker process that was in charge of loading and executing the Stable Diffusion model to generate images. Hence, this part of the architecture is critical and needs to be monitored to be sure everything is going well.

In this section, we'll see how to add Prometheus metrics to a Dramatiq worker. The good news is that Dramatiq already comes with built-in metrics and exposes the /metrics endpoint by default. Really, there is nothing much to do!

Let's take a very basic example of a Dramatiq worker with a dummy task:

chapter15_metrics_03.py

```
import time

import dramatiq
```

```
from dramatiq.brokers.redis import RedisBroker

redis_broker = RedisBroker(host="localhost")
dramatiq.set_broker(redis_broker)

@dramatiq.actor()
def addition_task(a: int, b: int):
    time.sleep(2)
    print(a + b)
```

https://github.com/PacktPublishing/Building-Data-Science-Applications-with-FastAPI-Second-Edition/tree/main/chapter15/chapter15_metrics_03.py

As you probably understand by now, Dramatiq is by nature a multiprocessing program: it spawns several workers to handle tasks concurrently. As such, we need to make sure Prometheus is in multiprocessing mode, as we mentioned in the *Handling multiple processes* section. Thus, we'll need to set the PROMETHEUS_MULTIPROC_DIR environment variable, as we explained earlier, but also dramatiq_prom_db. Indeed, Dramatiq implements its own mechanism to enable Prometheus's multiprocessing mode, which should work out of the box, but it turns out, in our experience, that it's better to be explicit about it.

The following command shows you how to start our worker with PROMETHEUS_MULTIPROC_DIR and dramatiq_prom_db set:

```
(venv) $ PROMETHEUS_MULTIPROC_DIR=./prometheus-tmp-dramatiq dramatiq_
prom_db=./prometheus-tmp-dramatiq dramatiq chapter15.chapter15_
metrics_03
```

To allow you to schedule a task easily in this worker, we've added a small __name__ == "__main__" instruction. In another terminal, run the following command:

```
(venv) $ python -m chapter15.chapter15_metrics_03
```

It'll schedule a task in the worker. You'll probably see it being executed in the worker logs.

Now, try to open the following URL in your browser: http://localhost:9191/metrics. You'll see a result similar to what we show in *Figure 15.7*.

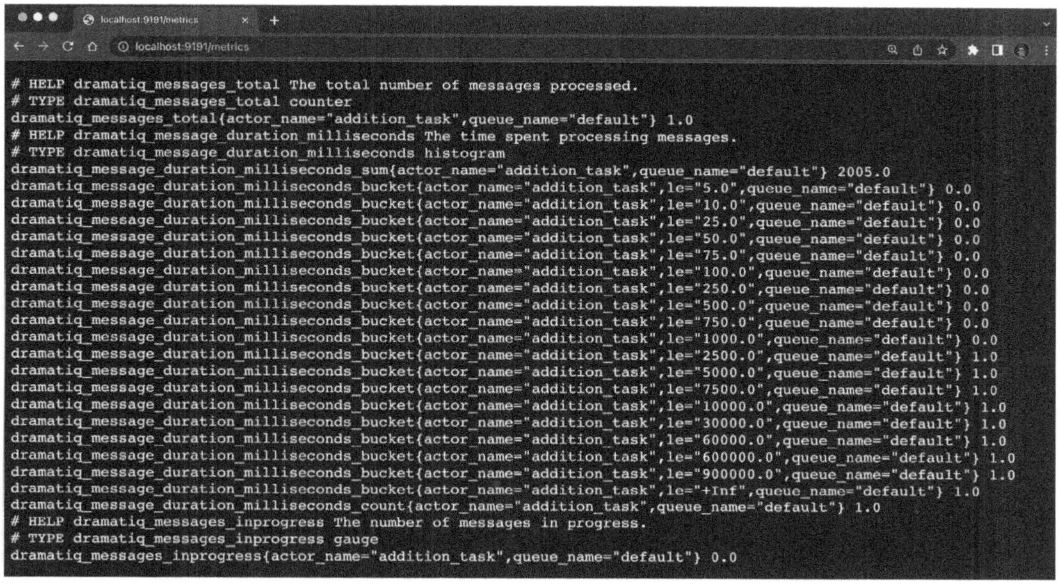

Figure 15.7 – Output of a Dramatiq Prometheus metrics endpoint

We already see several metrics, including a counter for the total number of messages processed by Dramatiq, a histogram to measure the execution time of our tasks, and a gauge to measure the number of tasks currently in progress. You can review the complete list of metrics included by Dramatiq in its official documentation: `https://dramatiq.io/advanced.html#prometheus-metrics`.

Adding custom metrics

Of course, as for FastAPI, we would probably like to add our own metrics to the Dramatiq worker. Actually, this is very similar to what we saw in the previous section. Let's again take the dice roll example:

---

chapter15_metrics_04.py

```python
DICE_COUNTER = Counter(
    "worker_dice_rolls_total",
    "Total number of dice rolls labelled per face",
    labelnames=["face"],
)

@dramatiq.actor()
def roll_dice_task():
    result = random.randint(1, 6)
    time.sleep(2)
```

```
DICE_COUNTER.labels(result).inc()
print(result)
```

https://github.com/PacktPublishing/Building-Data-Science-Applica-
tions-with-FastAPI-Second-Edition/tree/main/chapter15/chapter15_
metrics_04.py

All we needed to do was to create our `Counter` object, as we did before, and use it in our task. If you try to run the worker and request the `/metrics` endpoint, you'll see this new metric appear.

We are now able to instrument our FastAPI and Dramatiq apps. As we have already mentioned several times, we now need to aggregate those metrics in a Prometheus server and visualize them in Grafana. That's what we'll look at in the next section.

Monitoring metrics in Grafana

Having metrics is nice, but being able to visualize them is better! In this section, we'll see how we can collect Prometheus metrics, send them to Grafana, and create dashboards to monitor them.

Grafana is an open source web application for data visualization and analytics. It's able to connect to various data sources, such as timeseries databases and, of course, Prometheus. Its powerful query and graph builder allows us to create detailed dashboards where we can monitor our data in real time.

Configuring Grafana to collect metrics

Since it's open source, you can run it from your own machine or server. Detailed instructions are available in the official documentation: `https://grafana.com/docs/grafana/latest/setup-grafana/installation/`. However, to speed things up and get you started quickly, we'll rely here on Grafana Cloud, an official hosting platform. It offers a free plan, which should be enough for you to get started. You can create your account here: `https://grafana.com/auth/sign-up/create-user`. Once done, you'll be asked to create your own instance, a "Grafana Stack," by choosing a subdomain and a data center region, as you can see in *Figure 15.8*. Choose a region close to your geographic location.

Figure 15.8 – Instance creation on Grafana Cloud

You'll then be presented with a set of common actions to get started with Grafana. The first thing we'll do is add Prometheus metrics. Click on **Scale and centralize existing data**, then **Hosted Prometheus metrics**. You'll be taken to a page to configure a Prometheus metrics collection. Click on the tab named **Configuration Details** at the top. The page will look like the one shown in *Figure 15.9*.

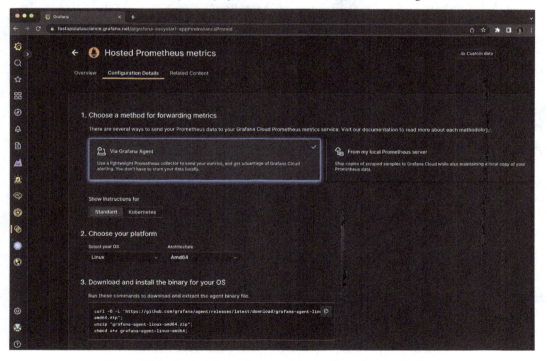

Figure 15.9 – Hosted Prometheus metrics configuration on Grafana

You see that we have two ways to forward metrics: via Grafana Agent or via a Prometheus server.

As we mentioned earlier, a Prometheus server is responsible for collecting metrics for all our apps and storing the data in a database. It's the standard way to do it. You can find instructions on how to install it in the official documentation: `https://prometheus.io/docs/prometheus/latest/installation/`. Bear in mind, though, that it's a dedicated application server that'll need proper backups, as it'll store all your metrics data.

The most straightforward way is to use Grafana Agent. It consists of a small command-line program with a single configuration file. When it runs, it'll poll the metrics of each of your apps and send the data to Grafana Cloud. All the data is stored on Grafana Cloud, so nothing is lost, even if you stop or delete the agent. This is what we'll use here.

Grafana shows you commands on the page to download, unzip, and execute the Grafana Agent program. Execute those commands so you have it at the root of your project.

Then, in the last step, you'll have to create an API token so Grafana Agent can send data to your instance. Give it a name and click on **Create API Token**. A new text area will appear with a new command to create the agent's configuration file, as you can see in *Figure 15.10*.

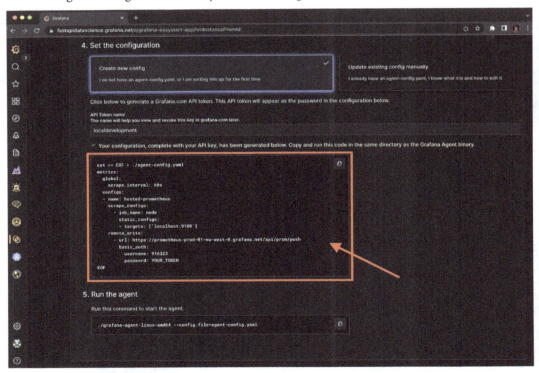

Figure 15.10 – Command to create Grafana Agent configuration

Execute the `./grafana-agent-linux-amd64 -config.file=agent-config.yaml` command. A file named `agent-config.yaml` will be created in your project. We now have to edit it so we can configure our actual FastAPI and Dramatiq applications. You can see the result in the following snippet:

agent-config.yaml

```
metrics:
  global:
    scrape_interval: 60s
  configs:
  - name: hosted-prometheus
    scrape_configs:
      - job_name: app
        static_configs:
        - targets: ['localhost:8000']
      - job_name: worker
        static_configs:
        - targets: ['localhost:9191']
    remote_write:
      - url: https://prometheus-prod-01-eu-west-0.grafana.net/api/
prom/push
        basic_auth:
          username: 811873
          password: __YOUR_API_TOKEN__
```

```
https://github.com/PacktPublishing/Building-Data-Science-Applica-
tions-with-FastAPI-Second-Edition/tree/main/chapter15/agent-con-
fig.yaml
```

It's a YAML configuration file where we can set the various options for Grafana Agent. The most important part is the `scrape_configs` key. As you can see, we can define the list of all the apps we want to gather the metrics for and specify their hostname, the "target": `localhost:8000` for the FastAPI app and `localhost:9191` for the Dramatiq worker. Of course, this configuration is valid for local development, but you'll have to adapt it with the proper hostnames of your apps in a production deployment.

We are now ready to start Grafana Agent and collect the metrics! Make sure your FastAPI and Dramatiq apps are running, and then run Grafana Agent. Depending on your system, the name of the executable will vary, but it'll look similar to this:

```
$ ./grafana-agent-linux-amd64 --config.file=agent-config.yaml
```

Grafana Agent will start and will collect the metrics at regular intervals before sending them to Grafana. We're now ready to plot some data!

Visualizing metrics in Grafana

Our metrics data is now sent to Grafana. We're ready to query it and build some graphs. The first step is to create a new **dashboard**, a place where you'll be able to create and organize multiple graphs. Click on the plus button at the top right and then **New dashboard**.

A new blank dashboard will appear, as you can see in *Figure 15.11*.

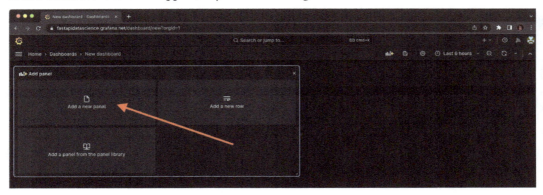

Figure 15.11 – Create a new dashboard in Grafana

Click on **Add a new panel**. The interface to build a new graph will appear. There are three main parts:

- The graph preview at the top left. When starting, it's empty.

- The query builder at the bottom left. This is where we'll query the metrics data.

- The graph settings on the right. This is where we'll choose the type of graph and finely configure its look and feel, similar to what we have in spreadsheet software.

Let's try to create a graph for the duration of HTTP requests in our FastAPI app. In the select menu called **Metric**, you'll have access to all the Prometheus metrics that have been reported by our apps. Select **http_request_duration_seconds_bucket**. This is the histogram metric defined by default by Prometheus FastAPI Instrumentator to measure the response time of our endpoints.

Then, click on **Run queries**. Under the hood, Grafana will build and execute PromQL queries to retrieve the data.

At the top right of the graph, let's select a shorter time span, such as **Last 15 minutes**. Since we do not have much data yet, we'll have a clearer view if we look at only a few minutes of data instead of hours. You should see a graph similar to the one in *Figure 15.12*.

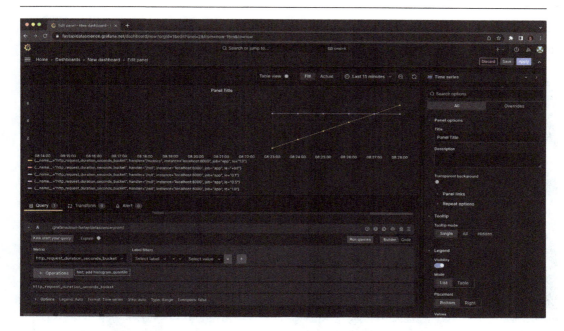

Figure 15.12 – Basic plot of a histogram metric in Grafana

Grafana has plotted several series: for each `handler` (which corresponds to the endpoint pattern), we have several buckets, `le`. Each line roughly represents *the number of times we answered "handler" in less than "le" seconds.*

This is the raw representation of the metric. However, you probably see that it's not very convenient to read and analyze. It would be better if we could look at this data another way, in terms of response time, arranged by quantiles.

Fortunately, PromQL includes some math operations so we can arrange the raw data. The part below the **Metric** menu allows us to add those operations. We can even see that Grafana suggests we use **add histogram_quantile**. If you click on this blue button, Grafana will automatically add three operations: a *Rate*, a *Sum by le*, and finally, a *Histogram quantile*, set by default to *0.95*.

By doing this, we'll now have a view of the evolution of our response time: 95% of the time, we answer in less than *x* seconds.

The default y axis unit is not very convenient. Since we know we work with seconds, let's select this unit in the graph options. On the right, look for the **Standard options** part and, in the **Unit** menu, look for **seconds (s)** under the **Time** group. Your graph will now look like *Figure 15.13*.

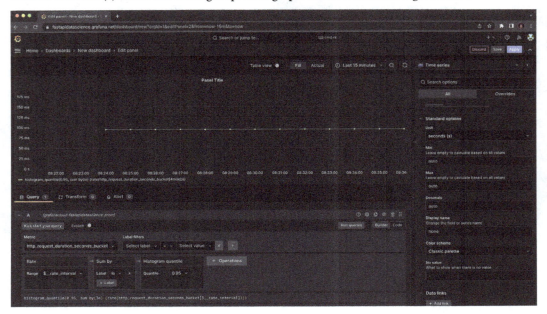

Figure 15.13 – Quantile representation of a histogram metric in Grafana

Now it's much more insightful: we can see that we answer nearly all our requests (95%) in under 100 milliseconds. If our server starts to slow down, we'll immediately see an increase in our graph, which could alert us that something has gone wrong.

If we want to have other quantiles on the same graph, we can duplicate this query by clicking on the **Duplicate** button right above **Run queries**. Then, all we have to do is to select another quantile. We show the result with quantiles *0.95*, *0.90*, and *0.50* in *Figure 15.14*.

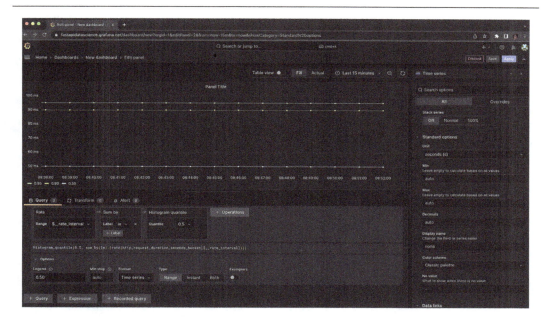

Figure 15.14 – Several quantiles on the same graph in Grafana

The legend can be customized

Notice that the name of the series in the legend can be customized. Under the **Options** part of each query, you can customize it at will. You can even include dynamic values coming from the query, such as metrics labels.

Finally, we can give a name to our graph by setting **Panel title**, in the right column. Now that we're happy with our graph, we can click on **Apply** at the top right to add it to our dashboard, as we see in *Figure 15.15*.

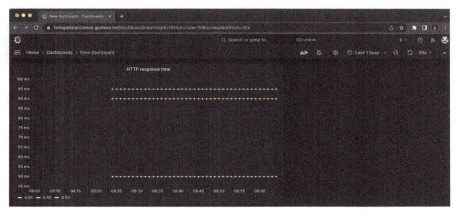

Figure 15.15 – Grafana dashboard

That's it! We can start to monitor our application. You can resize and position each panel at will. You can set the query time span you want to look at and even enable auto-refresh so the data gets updated in real time! Don't forget to click on the **Save** button to save your dashboard.

We can build a similar graph with the exact same configuration to monitor the time needed to execute tasks in Dramatiq, thanks to the metric named `dramatiq_message_duration_milliseconds_bucket`. Notice that this one is expressed in milliseconds instead of seconds, so you should be careful when selecting the unit of your graph. We see here one of the benefits of the Prometheus naming convention for metrics!

Adding a bar chart graph

There are a lot of different types of graphs available in Grafana. For example, we could plot our dice roll metric in the form of a bar chart, where each bar represents the number of times a face has been seen. Let's try it: add a new panel and select the `app_dice_rolls_total` metric. You'll see something similar to what is shown in *Figure 15.6*.

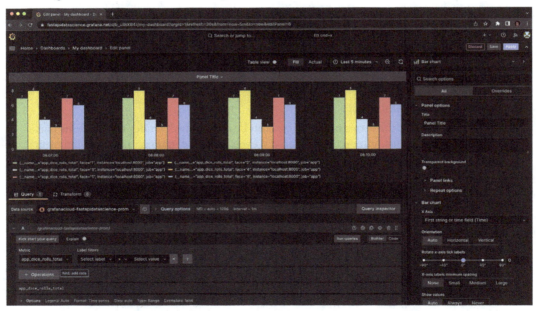

Figure 15.16 – Default representation of a counter metric with a bar chart in Grafana

We do have a bar for each face, but there is something strange: there are bars for each point in time. That's a key thing to understand with Prometheus metrics and PromQL: all metrics are stored as *time series*. This allows us to go back in time and see the evolution of the metrics over time.

However, for some representations, like the one shown here, it's not really insightful. For this case, it would be better to show us the latest values for the time span we selected. We can do this by setting **Type** to **Instant** under the **Options** part of the metric panel. We'll see that we now have a single graph with a single point in time, as you can see in *Figure 15.17*.

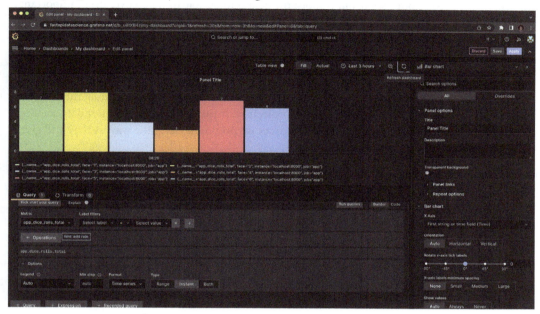

Figure 15.17 – Counter metric configured as Instant in Grafana

It's better, but we can go further. Typically, we would like the *x* axis to show the face labels instead of the point in time. First, let's customize the legend with a **Custom** label and type {{face}}. The legend will now only show the face label.

Now, we'll transform the data so the *x* axis is the face label. Click on the **Transform** tab. You'll see a list of functions that can be applied by Grafana to your data before visualizing it. For our case here, we'll choose **Reduce**. The effect of this function is to take each series, take a specific value from it, and plot it on the *x* axis. By default, Grafana will take the maximum value, **Max**, but there are other choices, such as **Last**, **Mean**, or **StdDev**. In this context, they won't make a difference since we already queried the instant value.

That's it! Our graph now shows the number of times we've seen a face. This is the one we showed in *Figure 15.6* earlier in the chapter.

Summary

Congratulations! You are now able to report metrics and build your own dashboards in Grafana to monitor your data science applications. Over time, don't hesitate to add new metrics or complete your dashboards if you notice some blind spots: the goal is to be able to watch over every important part at a glance so you can quickly take corrective actions. Those metrics can also be used to drive the evolution of your work: by monitoring the performance and accuracy of your ML models, you can track the effects of your changes and see whether you are going in the right direction.

This is the end of this book and our FastAPI journey. We sincerely hope that you liked it and that you learned a lot along the way. We've covered many subjects, sometimes just by scratching the surface, but you should now be ready to build your own projects with FastAPI and serve smart data science algorithms. Be sure to check all the external resources we proposed along the way, as they will give you all the insights you need to master them.

In recent years, Python has gained a lot of popularity, especially in data science communities, and the FastAPI framework, even though still very young, is already a game-changer and has seen an unprecedented adoption rate. It'll likely be at the heart of many data science systems in the coming years... And as you read this book, you'll probably be one of the developers behind them. Cheers!

Index

Symbols

*args syntax
 using 27, 28
**kwargs syntax
 using 27, 28
== None 22

A

access token
 endpoints, securing with 189
 generating 184
aggregating operations, NumPy
 reference link 279
Amazon ECR
 reference link 260
Amazon Elastic Container Service
 reference link 261
Amazon RDS
 reference link 256
Amazon Web Services (AWS) 214, 344
Any annotation
 using 49
apt 4

arrays
 adding 278
 aggregating 279
 comparing 279
 creating, with NumPy 272-274
 manipulating 270, 271
 manipulating, with NumPy 276, 277
 multiplying 278
asynchronous generator 170
asynchronous I/O
 working with 51-54
**Asynchronous Server Gateway
  Interface (ASGI) 52, 57**
automatic interactive documentation 57
Azure Database for PostgreSQL
 reference link 256

B

background operations 325
backpressure 315
Boolean logic
 membership operators, reviewing 22, 23
 performing 21
 variable similarity, checking 22
brew 4

broadcasting 278
  reference link 279
bucket 346
built-in types, Python 16, 17
  reference link 21

C

caching
  implementing, with Joblib 301-303
  standard or async functions,
      selecting between 304-306
Callable class
  type signature, using with 48, 49
camel case 35
cast function
  using 50
central logger
  Loguru, configuring as 362-365
classification problems 268
class inheritance
  used, for creating model variations 110-112
class methods
  using, as dependencies 131, 132
class properties 35
cloud providers, documentation pages
  references 254, 255
clustering 268
collections 144
collections.abc module 48
columns 142
computer vision 308
computer vision model
  using, with Hugging Face 308-312
concurrency
  handling, in WebSocket 209, 210
Conda 8

conditional statements
  elif statement 23, 24
  else statement 23, 24
  for loop statement 24, 25
  if statement 23, 24
  while loop statement 25, 26
containers 256
context
  adding, to logs 361
context manager 151
cookies 76, 78, 178, 190
coroutines 52
CORS
  configuring 190
  configuring, in FastAPI 191-196
counter metric 366
cross-origin HTTP requests 191
Cross-Site Request Forgery (CSRF) 191
cross-validation 269
  models, validating with 292, 293
cryptographic hash functions 181
CSRF attacks
  preventing, with double-submit
      cookies 196-200
  protecting against 190
CSV data
  exporting 285
  importing 284, 285
cURL 9
custom data validation with Pydantic
  validation, applying at field level 112, 113
  validation, applying at object level 113, 114
  validation, applying before
      Pydantic parsing 114, 115
custom response 94, 95
  building 90
  file, serving 93, 94

redirection, making 92
response_class argument, using 91, 92

D

DALL-E 326
dashboard 380
database access token
    implementing 184, 185
databases
    selecting, factors 144, 145
    testing with 235-241
dataset loading utilities, scikit-learn
    reference link 286
data, sharing between worker and API 338
    API, adapting to save image-generation
        tasks in database 339, 340
    SQLAlchemy model, defining 338, 339
    worker, adapting to read and update image-
        generation tasks in database 340-343
data structures, Python
    dictionary 20
    lists 17, 18
    sets 20, 21
    tuples 18-20
decorator 56
default values 105, 106
dependencies 125
    404 error, raising 129
    class methods, using as 131, 132
    object, obtaining 128
    using, in WebSocket 211-213
    using, on path decorator 133, 134
    using, on whole application 136
    using, on whole router 134, 135
dependency injection 50, 123-125
dictionaries 20
    Pydantic objects, converting into 115-117

dimensionality reduction 268
Docker 256
    FastAPI application, deploying with 256
Dockerfile 256
    writing 257, 258
Docker image
    building 259
    deploying 260
    running, locally 259
document 143
document-oriented databases 143-145
double-submit cookies
    implementing, to prevent CSRF
        attacks 196-200
Dramatiq worker
    creating 333, 334
    starting 335
    tasks, scheduling 336
dumped model
    loading 297, 298
dumping 296
dynamic default values 107

E

eager loading 161
efficient prediction endpoint
    implementing 298-301
ellipsis syntax 63
email addresses
    validating, with Pydantic types 108-110
email notifications 325
endpoint
    creating 56
    running, locally 56
    securing, with access tokens 189

environment variables

setting 246-249

setting, with .env file 249, 250

using 246-249

estimators 286

chaining, with pipelines 288-292

event loop 51

F

FastAPI 9, 55, 56

CORS, configuring 191-196

security dependencies 178-180

WebSockets, creating with 205-208

FastAPI application

database servers, adding 256

deploying, on serverless platform 253-255

deploying, on traditional server 261, 262

**FastAPI application, deploying
    with Docker** 256

Dockerfile, writing 257, 258

Docker image, building 259

Docker image, deploying 260

Docker image, running locally 259, 260

prestart script, writing 258, 259

FastAPI, with HTTPX

testing tools, setting up 228-232

features 268

Field customization, Pydantic

reference link 107

file-like interface 74

**files, storing and serving in object
    storage** 344, 345

image-generation system, running 349-352

object storage helper, implementing 345-348

object storage helper, using in worker 348

pre-signed URL, generating
    on server 348, 349

file uploads

handling 73-76

first in, first out (FIFO) strategy 315

five-fold cross-validation 269

fixtures

creating, for reusing test logic 226-228

foreign key 143

for loop statement 24

form data 72, 73

forward reference 158

f-strings 15

function dependency

creating 125

using 126, 127

functions

defining 26, 27

defining, with *args and **kwargs 27, 28

G

gauge metric 367

generator functions 33

generators 33, 34

generic CamelCase types

reference link 147

generics 45

Google Artifact Registry

reference link 260

Google Cloud Platform (GCP) 214

Google Cloud Run

reference link 261

Google Cloud SQL

reference link 256

Grafana 376

bar chart graph, adding 384, 385

configuring, to collect metrics 376-379

metrics, monitoring in 376

metrics, visualizing in 380-384

Gunicorn
  adding, as server process for
    deployment 252, 253

H

hashing passwords 182, 183
headers 76, 77
Heroku Postgres
  reference link 256
histogram metric 367
holdout set 269
Homebrew package
  URL 3
HTTP authentication 178
HTTP errors
  raising 88-90
HTTPie command-line utility
  installing 9-12
Hugging Face 307
  computer vision model, using with 308-312
  URL 308

I

idiomatic constructions
  generators 33, 34
  list comprehensions 31, 32
image-generation system
  running 349-352
image-generation task
  REST API, implementing 336, 337
image processor 310
indexing, pandas
  reference link 282
inheritance
  used, for avoiding repetition 40, 41

**integrated development
  environment (IDE)** 7
is None 22
iterator 24

J

Joblib 296
  results, caching with 301-303
  trained model, persisting with 296
join query 143

K

keyword arguments 27

L

label 268
lazy loading 161
list comprehensions 31, 32
lists 17
  immutable 18
  mutable 18
logging module 355
  reference link 355
login endpoint
  implementing 186-188
logs 354, 359
  adding, with Loguru 355-357
  as JSON objects 361
  context, adding to 361
  levels 355
Loguru 355
  configuring, as central logger 362-365
  logs, adding with 355-357
  reference link 359

M

machine learning (ML) 267, 268
  model validation 268, 269
  supervised learning 268
  unsupervised learning 268
magic methods
  __call__ method 39, 40
  __eq__ method 38, 39
  __gt__ method 38, 39
  implementing 36
  __lt__ method 38, 39
  operators 39
  __repr__ method 37
  __str__ method 37
mapped_column arguments
  reference link 147
marker 225
masking 284
message brokers 214
Method Resolution Order (MRO) 43
metric names
  conventions 371
metrics 366
  exposing 368
  measuring 368
  monitoring, in Grafana 376
  visualizing, in Grafana 380-384
metrics, Prometheus
  counter metric 366
  gauge metric 367
  histogram metric 367
  reference link 368
Microsoft Azure Container Instances
  reference link 261
Microsoft Azure Container Registry
  reference link 260
Midjourney 326

mixins 42
models 310
  creating 181, 182
  training, with scikit-learn 285-288
  validating, with cross-validation 292, 293
model validation 268, 269
model variations
  creating, with class inheritance 110-112
modules
  using 28, 29
MongoDB
  reference link 173
Motor, used for communication with
    MongoDB database 166
  database connection 167, 168
  documents, deleting 172, 173
  documents, inserting 168, 169
  documents, nesting 173, 174
  documents, obtaining 169-172
  documents, updating 172, 173
  models compatible with MongoDB,
    creating 166, 167
multi-dimensional data
  pandas DataFrames, using for 282-284
multiple WebSocket connections
  handling 213-219
  messages, broadcasting 213-219
mypy
  reference link 45
  used, for type checking 45
  used, for type hinting 43, 45

N

namespace package
  reference link 30
negative indexing 17
NoSQL databases 142-144

NumPy
  arrays, manipulating with 276, 277
  working 271
NumPy arrays
  adding 278
  creating 272-274
  elements, accessing 274-276
  multiplying 278
  sub-arrays 274-276
NumPy user guide
  reference link 280

O

object detection results
  displaying, in browser 320-324
object-oriented programming 35
  class, defining 35, 36
  inheritance, used for avoiding
      repetition 40, 41
  magic methods, implementing 36
  multiple inheritance 42, 43
object storage 344
one-dimensional data
  pandas Series, using for 280-282
operations, pandas
  reference link 284
optional fields 105, 106

P

package managers 4
packages
  using 28-30
pandas 280
pandas DataFrames
  using, for multi-dimensional data 282-284

pandas Series
  using, for one-dimensional data 280-282
parameterized dependency
  creating 129
  using 130, 131
parametrize
  tests, generating with 224-226
pass statement 41
path 56
path operation function 56
path operation parameters 79
  response model 81-83
  status code 79-81
path parameters 59-61
  advanced validation 63-65
  allowed values, limiting 62, 63
pip
  Python packages, installing with 8
pipelines 288
  estimators, chaining with 288-292
  preprocessors, chaining with 288-292
Pipenv 8
Poetry 8
POST endpoints
  tests, writing for 233, 234
Postman 9
preflight requests 194
preprocessors
  chaining, with pipelines 288-292
primary key 143
private methods 36
Prometheus 366
Prometheus FastAPI Instrumentator 369
Prometheus metrics 366
**Prometheus metrics, adding to
      Dramatiq 373-375**
  custom metrics, adding 375, 376

Prometheus metrics, adding to FastAPI 369, 370
    custom metrics, adding 370, 371
    multiple processes, handling 372, 373
publish-subscribe (pub-sub) pattern 214
Pydantic 99
    URL 59
    used, for adding custom data validation 112
Pydantic models 68, 217
Pydantic objects
    converting, into dictionary 115-117
    instance, creating from sub-class object 117-119
    instance, updating partially 119, 120
    working with 115
Pydantic types
    reference link 109
    used, for validating email addresses 108-110
    used, for validating URLs 108-110
pyenv
    reference link 4
    used, for installing Python distribution 4-6
pytest
    used, for unit testing 222
Python 3.10 6
Python 3.11 6
Python dependencies
    managing 250-252
Python distribution
    installing, with pyenv 4, 5, 6
Python Package Index (PyPi)
    URL 7
Python programming
    Boolean logic, performing 21
    built-in types 16, 17
    data structures 17
    flow, controlling 23
    functions, defining 26, 27

    indentation 15, 16
    key aspects 14
    modules, using 29
    packages, structuring 29, 30
    packages, using 28
    scripts, running 14
Python scripts
    running 14, 15
Python virtual environment
    creating 7, 8

Q

query parameters 65-67
queue 331

R

Redis 215
    URL 215
registration routes
    implementing 183, 184
regression problems 268
relational databases 142-144
relationships 142
representational state transfer (REST) API 9, 59, 336
request body 67-69
    multiple objects 69, 70
request object 78, 79
Request object from Starlette
    reference link 79
request parameters
    handling 59
    path parameters 59-61
    query parameters 65-67
response
    customizing 79

response parameter 84
cookies, setting 85, 86
headers, setting 84, 85
status code, setting dynamically 87, 88
REST API endpoints
tests, writing for 232, 233
REST endpoint
implementing, to perform object
    detection on single image 312-314
routers 95
project, structuring 95-97

S

same-origin policy 191
schemas 148
scikit-learn 285
models, training with 285-288
security dependencies, FastAPI 178-180
serverless platform
FastAPI application, deploying on 253-255
sessions 150
sets 20, 21
shell 5
singular body values 70
sinks
configuring 357-359
sized aliases, NumPy
reference link 273
snake case 27
sockets 204
SQLAlchemy Core 145
SQLAlchemy ORM model
creating 181
**SQLAlchemy ORM, used for
    communication with SQL database**
database connection 149-152

**database migration system, setting
    up with Alembic 161-165**
objects, deleting 155, 156
objects, filtering 153-155
objects, gathering 153-155
objects, inserting into database 152, 153
objects, updating 155, 156
ORM models, defining 146-148
Pydantic models, defining 148, 149
relationships, adding 157-161
square brackets 17
Stable Diffusion 325, 326
**Stable Diffusion, used for generating
    images from text prompts**
model implementation, in
    Python script 327-329
Python script, executing 329-331
standard field types 100-104
Starlette
URL 59
startup event 152
static type checkers 43
status code 79, 80
stop words 290
structured logging 360
supervised learning 268
Swagger
URL 58

T

tables 142
tensors 310
**Term Frequency-Inverse Document
    Frequency (TF-IDF) 290**
reference link 290

tests
  and global fixtures, organizing 231
  generating, with parametrize 224-226
  logic, reusing by creating fixtures 226-228
  writing, for POST endpoints 233, 234
  writing, for REST API endpoints 232, 233
  writing, for WebSocket endpoints 241-243
tokens 178
traditional server
  FastAPI application, deploying on 261, 262
trained model
  dumping 296, 297
  persisting, with Joblib 296
transformers library 308
tuples 18-20
two-fold cross-validation 269
two-way communication principles
  with WebSockets 204
type annotations 43
  working 44, 45
type checking
  with mypy 45
type data structures 45-47
type hinting
  with mypy 43-45
type signature
  using, with Callable 48, 49

U

unit testing, with pytest 222-224
  test logic, reusing by creating
    fixtures 226-228
  tests, generating with parametrize 224-226
Universally Unique IDentifier (UUID) 334
unpacking syntax 20
unsupervised learning 268

URLs
  validating, with Pydantic types 108-110
user
  retrieving 184
user agent 78
user and password
  storing, securely in database 181
Uvicorn 57
Uvicorn, as process manager
  reference link 253

V

virtual environments 7

W

web-queue-worker
    architecture 325, 331, 332
Web Server Gateway Interface (WSGI) 51
WebSocket endpoints
  tests, writing for 241-243
WebSockets
  concurrency, handling 209, 210
  creating, with FastAPI 205-208
  dependencies, using 211-213
  implementing, to perform object detection
    on stream of images 314-317
  multiple WebSocket connections,
    handling 213-219
  stream of images, sending from
    browser 317-320
  two-way communication principles 204
whitespace indentation 15
Windows Subsystem for Linux (WSL)
  reference link 3
worker 325, 331

Packtpub.com

Subscribe to our online digital library for full access to over 7,000 books and videos, as well as industry leading tools to help you plan your personal development and advance your career. For more information, please visit our website.

Why subscribe?

- Spend less time learning and more time coding with practical eBooks and Videos from over 4,000 industry professionals

- Improve your learning with Skill Plans built especially for you

- Get a free eBook or video every month

- Fully searchable for easy access to vital information

- Copy and paste, print, and bookmark content

Did you know that Packt offers eBook versions of every book published, with PDF and ePub files available? You can upgrade to the eBook version at packtpub.com and as a print book customer, you are entitled to a discount on the eBook copy. Get in touch with us at customercare@packtpub.com for more details.

At www.packtpub.com, you can also read a collection of free technical articles, sign up for a range of free newsletters, and receive exclusive discounts and offers on Packt books and eBooks.

Other Books You May Enjoy

If you enjoyed this book, you may be interested in these other books by Packt:

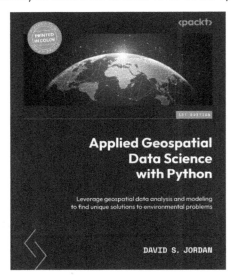

Applied Geospatial Data Science with Python

David S. Jordan

ISBN: 978-1-80323-812-8

- Understand the fundamentals needed to work with geospatial data
- Transition from tabular to geo-enabled data in your workflows
- Develop an introductory portfolio of spatial data science work using Python
- Gain hands-on skills with case studies relevant to different industries
- Discover best practices focusing on geospatial data to bring a positive change in your environment
- Explore solving use cases, such as traveling salesperson and vehicle routing problems

Building Data Science Solutions with Anaconda

Dan Meador

ISBN: 978-1-80056-878-5

- Install packages and create virtual environments using conda
- Understand the landscape of open source software and assess new tools
- Use scikit-learn to train and evaluate model approaches
- Detect bias types in your data and what you can do to prevent it
- Grow your skillset with tools such as NumPy, pandas, and Jupyter Notebooks
- Solve common dataset issues, such as imbalanced and missing data
- Use LIME and SHAP to interpret and explain black-box models

Packt is searching for authors like you

If you're interested in becoming an author for Packt, please visit authors.packtpub.com and apply today. We have worked with thousands of developers and tech professionals, just like you, to help them share their insight with the global tech community. You can make a general application, apply for a specific hot topic that we are recruiting an author for, or submit your own idea.

Share Your Thoughts

Now you've finished *Building Data Science Applications with FastAPI, Second Edition*, we'd love to hear your thoughts! Scan the QR code below to go straight to the Amazon review page for this book and share your feedback or leave a review on the site that you purchased it from.

https://packt.link/r/1-837-63274-X

Your review is important to us and the tech community and will help us make sure we're delivering excellent quality content.

Download a free PDF copy of this book

Thanks for purchasing this book!

Do you like to read on the go but are unable to carry your print books everywhere?

Is your eBook purchase not compatible with the device of your choice?

Don't worry, now with every Packt book you get a DRM-free PDF version of that book at no cost.

Read anywhere, any place, on any device. Search, copy, and paste code from your favorite technical books directly into your application.

The perks don't stop there, you can get exclusive access to discounts, newsletters, and great free content in your inbox daily

Follow these simple steps to get the benefits:

1. Scan the QR code or visit the link below

https://packt.link/free-ebook/9781837632749

2. Submit your proof of purchase
3. That's it! We'll send your free PDF and other benefits to your email directly

www.ingramcontent.com/pod-product-compliance
Lightning Source LLC
Chambersburg PA
CBHW081502050326
40690CB00015B/2896